ADVANCE PRAISE FOR *A Radiant Life*

"Merle Massie is an excellent storyteller, and what a story this is—of Sylvia Fedoruk—academic, physicist, inventor, athlete, chancellor, lieutenant-governor, role model and a friend to many. This biography is a page-turner, and I didn't want the story to end! Merle has captured the true essence of the full life of Sylvia, covering both the public and private life of a Saskatchewan leader with humour, insight, and sensitivity." —THE HONOURABLE GORDON BARNHART, OC SOM, 20th Lieutenant-Governor of Saskatchewan

"Merle Massie has given us a remarkable biography of a remarkable woman. Sylvia Fedoruk's outstanding, and in many respects trailblazing, career in medical science, sports, and public service deserved the best. She got it." —JOHN COURTNEY, Senior Policy Fellow, Johnson-Shoyama Graduate School of Public Policy

"*A Radiant Life* is an important, well-researched story of the fascinating, well-lived journey of one of Saskatchewan's most accomplished citizens." —VERA PEZER, former Chancellor of the University of Saskatchewan, inductee in the Canadian Curling Hall of Fame, Saskatchewan Centennial Medal recipient

"A very important history about a very important Canadian" —THE HONOURABLE ROY ROMANOW, PC OC SOM QC, 12th Premier of Saskatchewan

A RADIANT LIFE

THE HONOURABLE
SYLVIA FEDORUK
Scientist, Sports Icon, and Stateswoman

MERLE MASSIE

© 2020 University of Regina Press

All rights reserved. No part of this work covered by the copyrights hereon may be reproduced or used in any form or by any means—graphic, electronic, or mechanical—without the prior written permission of the publisher. Any request for photocopying, recording, taping or placement in information storage and retrieval systems of any sort shall be directed in writing to Access Copyright.

COVER ART: Sylvia Fedoruk fonds, University of Saskatchewan Archives.
   Attempts were made to locate original photograph copyright holders.
   Copyright information will be updated in subsequent editions.
COVER AND TEXT DESIGN: Duncan Campbell, University of Regina Press
COPY EDITOR: Dallas Harrison
PROOFREADER: Rachel Taylor
INDEXER: Patricia Furdek

Library and Archives Canada Cataloguing in Publication

TITLE: A radiant life : the honourable Sylvia Fedoruk, scientist, sports icon, and statewoman / Merle Massie.

OTHER TITLES: Sylvia Fedoruk, scientist, sports icon, and statewoman

NAMES: Massie, Merle, 1971- author.

DESCRIPTION: Includes index.

IDENTIFIERS: Canadiana (print) 20200256424 | Canadiana (ebook) 20200256769 | ISBN 9780889777330 (softcover) | ISBN 9780889777392 (hardcover) | ISBN 9780889777354 (PDF) | ISBN 9780889777378 (EPUB)

SUBJECTS: LCSH: Fedoruk, Sylvia, 1927-2012. | LCSH: Physicists—Biography. | LCSH: Lieutenant governors—Saskatchewan—Biography. | LCGFT: Biographies.

CLASSIFICATION: LCC QC16.F43 M37 2020 | DDC 530.092—dc23

10 9 8 7 6 5 4 3 2 1

University of Regina Press, University of Regina
Regina, Saskatchewan, Canada, S4S 0A2
TEL: (306) 585-4758 FAX: (306) 585-4699
       WEB: www.uofrpress.ca

We acknowledge the support of the Canada Council for the Arts for our publishing program. We acknowledge the financial support of the Government of Canada. / Nous reconnaissons l'appui financier du gouvernement du Canada. This publication was made possible with support from Creative Saskatchewan's Book Publishing Production Grant Program and the Saskatchewan Arts Board Independent Artist Program.

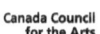   

*This book is dedicated to the memory
of Mary Kirychuk McGowan,
whose wisdom offered a path to bravery.*

CONTENTS

Preface—1

    1. Blizzards and Fireworks—9
    2. Walkerville Wonder—23
    3. Rampaging Amazon—33
    4. Cobalt Bomb—59
    5. The Friendly Atom—83
    6. Pinpricks of Light—101
    7. We Call This Meeting to Order—133
    8. Madame Chancellor—165
    9. The Honourable Left-Handed Governor—181
    10. Hurricane—235
    11. Sunset—255

Afterword—279
Photo Credits—281
Notes—283
Index—313

PREFACE

Searching for Sylvia—that's a description of the path that led to this book. The traditional Saskatchewan media iconography of Sylvia Olga Fedoruk has painted an astonishing portrait of a woman whose excellence in science, sport, and public service became nothing short of a touchstone, a story of leadership, Saskatchewan grit, and the power of possibility. With Ukrainian roots in east-central Saskatchewan and an education in one-room schools, Sylvia represents the essence of Saskatchewan, of building a life with world impact in a place well used to being forgotten. It has been a privilege to dive deep and follow her legendary accomplishments, from smashing sports stories in school athletics, ball, curling, and golf; to her international reputation as a cancer physicist; to excellence in leadership, culminating in the capstone as the first female lieutenant-governor of Saskatchewan.

I came to this biography by way of friendship. C. Stuart Houston, Saskatchewan's famed radiologist–ornithologist–medical historian, was looking for help. A long-time friend and colleague of Sylvia, he had co-taught* with her for years as the "Stuart and Sylvia Show," otherwise known as first-year radiation physics for medical students at the University of Saskatchewan. The two had also co-authored several works on Saskatchewan's early role in radiation history, particularly regarding the betatron and the cobalt bomb. Sylvia had written the foreword for Stuart's original *Steps on the Road to Medicare*, published in 2002.

PREFACE

Stuart and I began working together on short essays and longer manuscripts in about 2007, including a revised and expanded version of Saskatchewan's medical history, published as *36 Steps on the Road to Medicare: How Saskatchewan Led the Way*, which included Sylvia's original foreword. Soon after her death in 2012, Stuart began contemplating and outlining a biography of Sylvia and invited me to be his co-author. Amassing and curating from his own files and via correspondence with Sylvia's other colleagues, Stuart built the paper bones of her life. Enumerating her many firsts, those biographical outlines of accomplishments and accolades were long but needed flesh on the bones. My role was to dive deep into the research and understand Sylvia's rich life beyond her accolades and scientific accomplishments.

Following Sylvia's death in 2012, her friends and relations had to find a balance between clearing out her house and memorializing her life. What should be kept, and who should keep it? Sylvia had been her own archivist and museum curator, cataloguing with meticulous detail. In some cases, she had already gifted specific items to museums or archives. The majority remained. The house had papers, photographs, videos, and artifacts crammed into every corner. Sylvia's executor, Myrna Berwick, dispersed the contents of the house with the help and support of Sylvia's cousin Garry Vann. The University of Saskatchewan was one of the first callers. Archivists Cheryl Avery and Patrick Hayes brought a crew to see and understand the scope of Sylvia's potential archival collection. The team moved through the house, expert eyes and minds in assessment mode, finding that balance between artifacts (which take up so much space) and archival documentation. Photographs, videos, and of course textual records were efficiently identified and hauled back to the university by truck to the third-floor Archives and Special Collections division. There they sat.[1]

When I finally arrived at the archives in the summer of 2016 to let staff know about the potential biography project, they asked me "Are you sure you're ready for this? You need to see it for yourself." I was then taken through the archival labyrinth to the Sylvia aisle. My eyes flew open in shock, my head tipping up and down, left and right, to try to take it all in. Trophies peeked out of boxes. Photograph albums and oddly shaped artifacts pushed lids upward. Some of the boxes had yellow Post-it Notes stating the origins of their contents: "black filing cabinet" or "TV console" or "basement shelf." The archivists had not had the opportunity or the time to go through and create a detailed accession record of the fonds, but we created a research agreement based on the facts that I had lots of archival experience as a historian and would use best practices. Setting up a desk near the collection, I worked to find my way into Sylvia's life.

There is so much more to Sylvia Fedoruk than a list of accomplishments and achievements. I met a deeply interesting character bursting with audacity, overflowing with generosity, unable to contain a raging energy for life. Sylvia burned with a need to prove herself, always to be at her best. Her personal archive showcases pride in her life and accomplishments, yet she was her own toughest critic. Sylvia self-curated to highlight excellence and downplay disaster. As an example, her curling scrapbooks from 1959 to 1962 focus on the two successful runs for national championships but nearly eliminate the run for the third championship, when the team came up short. I realized that wins brought happy memories and that losses or other stumbles caused Sylvia real pain, not for the losses or mistakes or missteps but because she blamed herself for them.

In part because she was hardest on herself, Sylvia worked to put others at ease. A natural grace and self-deprecating sense of humour gave her an approachable, open countenance, laughing direct eyes, and a zest for the funny side of any situation. She loved practical jokes, delighted in dressing up for skits, sang lustily, laughed uproariously and often, and believed that life was for living. The candid shots in her archive—playfully sticking out her tongue for the camera, saluting with a drink, smoking a stogie, rolling up money to shove in her ears—showcase a playful woman of confidence. If a reporter talked about her sports exploits, Sylvia was more than willing to share less-than-stellar klutzy stories to provide some balance. Great at basketball and baseball? Sure, but I can't swim, she would point out, deflecting and demurring. Sylvia was also practical and helpful. At an official function in Canora as the lieutenant-governor, she ended the event in the kitchen with her aunts, cousins, extended family members, friends, and old neighbours, an apron tied around her middle, helping with dishes.

Even so, for all her public roles and athletic exploits, Sylvia was an intensely private person. She needed solitude, and lots of it, to recharge and refresh. That privacy included her closest friends, with whom she was simply *Syl*. Although Sylvia made friends with great ease and came from a large extended family, her private circle was built of close, long-term connections. These connections spill across her archival holdings, which adroitly connect her public and private lives via letters, photographs and slides, notes, home videos, and day-planners. The intensity and importance of these private connections stand in marked contrast to the public persona of a single, busy, no-nonsense professional physicist, leader, athlete, and political figurehead. The two halves of her life are inextricable, though the one was virtually invisible to the public during her lifetime. Sylvia rarely articulated the importance of her private support system in giving her the freedom and time to build her public life, but during times of stress or celebration she reached out to her closest friends and confidantes. Their presence was a constant.

Research is not a straight path, and some decisions are not easy. With about six chapters written, from Sylvia's earliest days to her summer ball exploits and national curling championships, I paused in the research for and writing of this biography. I struggled to reconcile the well-known public story with archival evidence that revealed a somewhat different reality behind the public persona. I needed to work through how to tell Sylvia's story, the whole story. The hints and abrupt comments in her files forced me to conduct research elsewhere. Her files are extensive, but even so they are incomplete and a bit truncated. I had holes to fill.

One area in particular required deeper investigation: University of Saskatchewan graduate student Christopher Lefler, whose impact is clearly found in the pages of Sylvia's archives. I had to understand the extent of that story, which led to an investigation of the larger Saskatchewan community, including the university, the provincial government, and the media. It was not a small, short, or easy task.

As that story took shape, I had to think clearly through a choice between two possible biographies. The first would be a traditional view of Sylvia's life. Curated and repeated by Sylvia via countless media interviews through a career that spanned more than sixty years in the Canadian spotlight, her life was well known, its shape and tenor defined. My original co-researcher, Stuart Houston, championed the traditional view. In that story, Christopher Lefler rated no more than a couple of sentences, a paragraph at most. He did not deserve more. Others might agree. But I could not share the perspective that Lefler's artistic practices had no place in Sylvia's biography. His impact was clear in her files, in high contrast to her public statements during the period in question. I had to address that dissonance. Life is messy, life has dark moments, and life has pain. I could not produce a biography without including that chapter of her life, out of respect for my training as a historian. I moved forward as a single author, following the Lefler story to build my understanding of its scope. I remain grateful to Stuart for his insight, compassion, original energy, and support, and I'm thankful for his grace as I built a picture of Sylvia that includes stories less well known to the larger public.

By 2018, I had developed the chapter in question, and still I fretted. Sitting by the hospital bed as my mother succumbed to cancer in the spring of 2018, I laid out the Lefler story and its permutations across Saskatchewan history. Mom listened to my struggles with the morality of the piece. Would it overshadow Sylvia's story? Would that be the only piece that the media asked about? Would Sylvia want it told? The last was the toughest question, and it hurt to face it. Sylvia would not, I knew, want it told. But the wisdom of my mom was stark and fierce. Even though she felt great affinity with Sylvia, who had a similar Ukrainian background, and had great admiration for her life, my mother insisted that there is a critical difference between an autobiography and a biography. We do not always see what impacts we have, and perhaps we should not be the ones to try to articulate what our own lives mean. Assessment should be left for others. Mom insisted that an investigation of the Lefler story belongs and that Sylvia's story would be incomplete without it. It is in telling the darkest parts, in revealing the shadows, Mom said, that Sylvia's light truly shines. I agreed.

Looking to build some much-needed writing time into my schedule and to return to the archives and move forward, I applied for and won a Saskatchewan Arts Board Independent Artist grant in the fall of 2018. I am grateful for the support of the board. I've also had the great fortune throughout the project to conduct interviews with friends, family members, and both professional and political colleagues of Sylvia. Their insights helped me to develop a sense of Sylvia's life beyond a mere list of accomplishments—however lengthy—into a living and laughing person, a complex woman full of mischief and laughter, sternness and fierceness. I conducted most of those interviews after I'd spent time getting to know Sylvia through her archive. It was important to have solid and detailed pictures of events and places and people. Then oral stories and interviews filled in the personality and pugnaciousness and *presence* of Sylvia the woman. Their stories added much to my understanding of a woman given to pranks and fun, competitive in sports but giving in friendship, a traveller and fisher and dog lover and excellent cook. I am grateful.

The interviews also reminded me of complexity and how people are people, warts and all. Sylvia's self-drive toward excellence would spill over, on occasion, and become something less than charitable, less than perfect. Demanding high standards for herself, Sylvia wanted the same high standards from others. As a result, on occasion she could be short. With a strong personality and physical presence, Sylvia had a way of commanding a room. She was not afraid to direct people or tell them what she thought they should be doing. Sylvia did not suffer fools lightly, nor did she waste time. If the conversation was done, or she thought your visit to her house had been long enough, she would say that it was time for you to leave or abruptly hang up the phone. In a way, it reminded me that I, too, needed to learn that trick: I'd simply have to stop researching and writing and "hang up the phone," otherwise Sylvia's story would go on and on and on. I thank those who gave interviews or met me for lunch or received phone calls, including Vera Pezer, Irene Bell, Myrna Berwick, Doreen Fairburn, Joan Borsa, Garry Vann and his partner Carol, Michael Vann, Trevor Cradduck, Peggy McKercher, Pat Lawson, Mona Finlayson, Jim Russell, Peter Dickof, Pat Langston, Rock Mackie, Roy Romanow, and Gordon Barnhart. My own family members and friends chimed in with their connections and memories when they heard I was working on the biography, and friends on social media contributed more. I value your insight and support and your stories of Sylvia.

One interviewee sent a shiver down my spine. "Syl would have hated it," she casually remarked. "Hated what?" I asked. "Oh, she was tired of having things written about her. She thought it was time they found some new people to talk about." As I drove away, I thought *I disagree.* One of the secrets of Sylvia Fedoruk is that she understood the art and necessity of self-promotion—with a generous underscoring of modesty. Throughout her life and exploits, only once did she shy away from the media. If she had an accomplishment that deserved recognition, she would make sure that the right people knew about it, quietly sending a copy of a newspaper clipping or letter of appointment or invitation to her professional or academic superiors or the media. The Sylvia Fedoruk collection itself is a testament to her belief that her life had worth and that someone would come along to tell her story. A guest appearance on the Canadian television show *Front Page Challenge* in 1989 foreshadowed this belief:

PREFACE

BETTY KENNEDY: Are you intending to do any writing?

SYLVIA FEDORUK: Not really.

BETTY KENNEDY: Because it seems to me that your whole life is something that, that is a very interesting story.

SYLVIA FEDORUK: Well, I'm keeping good notes.

Sylvia wasn't going to write an autobiography. Crowing about her own successes and exploits wouldn't fit her sense of modesty. But someone would likely come along to delve into her notes and build from them a story of her life. And she did her best to make sure that she kept all the notes that a biographer might find interesting. She was right. Her archive is a fascinating collection with great breadth and intensity, even with its holes.

I am also grateful to a number of people who read through an earlier draft of this biography to provide feedback and direction. University of Saskatchewan colleague Tim Jardine gave me part of his sabbatical time to read the manuscript as a scientist; historians Bill Waiser and Jennie Hansen gave sharp-eyed critiques and suggestions for direction; Vera Pezer was a generous support as an interviewee, a sounding board, and a sharp fellow author-critic, and she helped me to identify people in pictures; Roy Romanow gave an important interview and then reviewed the political portion of Sylvia's time as lieutenant-governor; Trevor Cradduck sifted the manuscript for physics errors and gave some of the best work-related anecdotes; and both Stuart and Mary Houston read the manuscript, each with a different-coloured pen for comments. I treasure the notations made by Mary on that draft, for she passed away before the manuscript moved into the final stage of editing.

Despite its length, this biography of Sylvia Fedoruk is incomplete from a theoretical or classical academic perspective. Her life should be read within the context of numerous critical events and movements. They include the postwar nuclear era, feminism's push for equal pay and equal rights, the rise of women in sport, the promotion of women in science, the changing role and perspective of Ukrainians in Saskatchewan and Canada, the role of women in politics, changes within academia and academic publishing, technological advances during the twentieth century and twenty-first century, advances in cancer diagnostics and treatments, the changing perception of the monarchy, and the role and importance of achievement, merit, and hall of fame accolades. I was unable to travel to Ottawa to view the files of the Atomic Energy Control Board, which might have added a whole chapter. The Saskatchewan rumour mill posits that Sylvia can be credited with scientific inventions that helped Canadian nuclear plants to solve some thorny technological issues. Her role within the AECB is ripe for in-depth research. The problem, simply, is that of scope: her life can be read in so many different directions and discussed in so many different ways that pursuing all of them to the fullest possible extent would drag me as author and you as reader into an endless quagmire of words. I chose a simpler path.

Because Sylvia moved through Saskatchewan both geographically and across so many lines of academia, science, cancer treatment and research, sports, politics, and social consciousness, thousands of Saskatchewan people have their own stories and memories of Sylvia Fedoruk. I hope that you share those stories with others. The oral counterhistory that accompanies any history book has its own value and becomes part of why we write history: together the written and the oral stories go forward to a new generation, reflecting and growing and building new meanings of the past.

Sylvia loved this province and drew on her sense of place to build both a personal life and a professional life dedicated to achieving excellence, to travelling its backroads and fishing its northern waters, and to having fun. She was a proud Saskatchewan citizen born of its *terroir*, the environmental and social factors of place that coalesced into her unique qualities and character. Her brilliant essence, palpable and strong, made firm the path to becoming the province's foremost cheerleader, an ambassador of sport, science, and social volunteerism focused on making the province a better place. It is with immense pleasure and pride that I give you this story of Saskatchewan's own "rampaging Amazon."

1. BLIZZARDS AND FIREWORKS

On Sunday, June 22, 1924, there was a wedding in the bustling Ukrainian village of Donwell in east-central Saskatchewan. With spring seeding done and gardens planted, late June was a time of celebration, a deep breath of green growing grass and fields surging with new life. Haying season was around the corner. It was a time to create newlyweds and give them the summer to have a honeymoon, set up housekeeping, and get used to each other before winter closed in again. The groom and bride were the centre of attention: Theodore Fedoruk, a dashing, bespectacled schoolteacher, and Annie Romaniuk, a slim young farmer's daughter whose intelligence and wit needed someone with education to keep up with her. We should imagine that this was a large and happy affair like all Ukrainian weddings in the tightly knit community. The Romaniuk-Fedoruk wedding vows took place at the Ukrainian Greek Orthodox Church of Transfiguration west and south of Donwell, to which the Romaniuks belonged.[1]

The wedding vows happily made, it was time for feasting and dancing, with women bustling and carrying pots and pans and baskets and bowls filled with the makings of a true Ukrainian wedding feast. Fresh bread and buns, farm-churned butter, pickles, varenyky (perogies), kolbassa, and holubtsi (cabbage rolls). No doubt ham or some roast beef, potatoes, and sauerkraut. And dessert—*khrustyky* or sweet nothings—was always a favourite. The band would perhaps be oiling their elbows and voices with a cold beer or a sip of something stronger. The groom, Ted Fedoruk, was a fiddler, too, but he would be too busy to join in. As guests entered, the band would greet each one at the front of the hall. Traditionally, guests would pay the band by stuffing coins and bills into their instruments. For a large wedding dance, those playing stringed instruments such as guitars and fiddles would have to take quick breaks to shake the money out of them. If they were too full of money, it would deaden their sounds.

The Romaniuk family were among the first settlers in the Donwell-Hamton region. Annie Romaniuk's grandparents, Dmetro and Oksana Romaniuk, immigrated to Canada in 1897 from Borschivski Povit near Lviv, Halychyna, part of the Austro-Hungarian Empire. They sailed from Hamburg, Germany, and it took three weeks to arrive in Halifax at Pier 21, then another long train ride from Halifax across Canada to Yorkton, North-West Territories. They brought their four children, one girl and three boys; another girl was born to the family in Canada. The eldest son, Ivan, took the Canadianized name of John. He was fifteen when the family immigrated and went to work in Yorkton for a prosperous businessman, earning cash to buy cattle and horses and taking classes in English. There he met Anastasia Tarnowetzki, working in a hotel and restaurant. Anastasia had emigrated with her family from Bukovina in 1901. Married in 1902, the couple took their own homestead next door to his parents. John and Anastasia had six children, four boys and two girls. Annie was the third child and eldest daughter, born in 1907.

She grew up on her parents' half-section farm three miles south of Donwell, west of the village of Hamton and east of Gorlitz. Well situated near freshwater streams and sloughs, it was also kitty-corner from the local schoolyard of Mennofeldt. But it had been a few years since Annie Romaniuk, even at seventeen, had been a student. Family lore suggests that Annie, a keen student with an astonishing mind, wanted to go to high school in Saskatoon—and some family members suggest that she actually made the trip and was starting to settle in, possibly even at the newly built Ukrainian Orthodox Mohyla residence. But circumstances intervened. Ill health at home meant that Annie was needed at the farm. Her chalk-fingered days were exchanged for bread baking and milking, butter churning and gardening, staying home to help her mother with farm chores after finishing grade eight. Her truncated school career haunted Annie throughout her life. Marrying

1. BLIZZARDS AND FIREWORKS

a schoolteacher brought a new, sharp edge to the old pain.

The groom, Theodore (Ted) Fedoruk, was born in 1898 in the Bukovina region of Austria, known for its large Ukrainian population. Ted was the third son of Alexander Fedoruk and Martha Boychuk, farm citizens of the village of Hawrylowtsi. Alex and Martha, with one-year-old Ted in tow along with older brothers Stephen and Michael, made the long trip from Bukovina to Canada in 1899. Ted was as ambitious and adventurous as his parents but scholastic. Farming was a pastime, not a passion, for him. He pursued high school at Yorkton Collegiate, working for room and board. He returned home and began teaching in small, one-room schools in the Rhein-Hamton-Donwell

Theodore (Ted) and Annie Fedoruk on their wedding day, 1924.

district in 1919, but he soon decided to take his teaching to a professional level. By 1922, Ted was in Saskatoon, staying at the Mohyla residence and graduating from Normal School with a provincial teaching diploma. By 1924, he was a fully fledged schoolteacher, earning a decent salary, free to woo and win his bride. As the dancing finished and the stars came out that June night in 1924, the newlyweds slipped away.

Throughout his teaching career, Ted led classrooms in a number of small, one-room schools in predominantly Ukrainian communities.

Being a native Ukrainian teacher did not mean that Ted spoke Ukrainian at school—or even at home. Throughout the war years and well into the 1920s, a huge Anglicization movement swept across western Canada. Historian Bill Waiser likened the push toward British conformity to a crusade within Saskatchewan, a site of "missionary" activity where English-speaking churches worked in places with high numbers of continental European immigrants, such as the Canora-Yorkton-Kamsack triangle. Night schools, mission hospitals, and Boy Scouts and Girl Guides clubs popped up. Ontario schoolteacher J.T.M. Anderson, who would later serve as premier of Saskatchewan, became a school inspector in the Yorkton region. Schools became training grounds for British values, institutions, history, language, and empire.[2] Like Indigenous children in residential schools, continental European children were stripped of their language and culture, often ridiculed for the "ethnic" food in their tin lunch boxes, and forced to speak English, and English only, while on school property. Dark tales of isolation, physical punishment, and even beatings have passed down through some families.

As harsh as these measures seem to modern eyes, Ted Fedoruk himself was a product of similar training. Raised in a Presbyterian (not Ukrainian Orthodox) household and educated in English at high school in Yorkton and Normal School in Saskatoon, he no doubt accepted provincial mandates, expectations, and curricula. Whether his English skills were good enough for him to be awarded the $300 annual bonus given to English teachers in immigrant districts is unknown.[3] What is known is that Ted remained a teacher within similar immigrant districts throughout his teaching career. His teaching posts included the small country schools of Federhill, West Skalat, Krasney, Bridok, Lysenko, Chaucer, Scotland, Ebenezer, Fonehill, Okno, Phoenix, and Rivington.[4] Whereas Federhill, West Skalat, Bridok, and Kitzman (the spelling used in most history books) are within the small rural Ukrainian triangle of Rhein-Hamton-Donwell, other districts were a little farther afield. Krasney School District No. 1121 was southwest of Sheho, and Lysenko School District No. 494 was near Insinger, Saskatchewan.

If the school list for Ted Fedoruk is in sequence, then it is possible that he took the position at Krasney following his marriage to Annie and then returned a year or two later to teach at Bridok, south of Canora. A typical salary for a schoolteacher in the 1920s depended on the size of the school, the tax base of the school district, the decision of the school board, the length of the school term, and the training and experience of the teacher. Ted earned about $1,000 for his teaching in the Bridok School District in 1925 and 1926—a hefty salary in those years, and he was well able to support himself and his wife and to feel settled enough to increase the family.[5] At Bridok, the Fedoruks were close to Canora, where important events soon overtook Ted and Annie.

As spring rolled in not quite three years after their wedding, they were excited. All through the winter of 1926–27, tremors of change and anticipation bubbled in their household. No doubt hands rummaged through chests and closets at both the Fedoruk and the Romaniuk farms gathering small pieces of cotton and linen. Needles flashed, scissors snipped: Annie was expecting a baby. Ted and Annie planned to have their baby in Yorkton at the larger hospital where more experienced doctors would be on hand. Three years from marriage to baby is a long time for a couple from large Ukrainian families, and it's possible that there were some complications. But nature—both the baby and the weather—had other plans.

North American weather was unsettled that spring. A killer tornado ripped across Chicago, and others would wreak havoc in Mozart, Saskatchewan, and Vulcan, Alberta. Clouds churned, and precipitation led to one of the wettest springs on record in other parts of the northern Great Plains. In early May, a freak snowstorm, with strong winds and piles of snow, whipped through east-central Saskatchewan. Soon roads blew in and became nearly impassable: that is, what roads there were in 1927 in the heavy bush country north of Yorkton. Although every farm had horses, few had motorized vehicles. In the midst of the spring storm, Annie went into labour. Her medical team waited in Yorkton, but there was no way to get there. Instead, Ted turned north, heading for the regional centre at Canora.[6] There, on May 5, 1927, snowstorm and all, Annie gave birth to a daughter, Sylvia Olga Fedoruk. Celebrated at a christening at Annie's home church, Sylvia came to complete the Fedoruk family.

Having a baby in the late 1920s in rural Saskatchewan meant hard work for Annie: washing diapers and baby clothes by hand in tubs of water warmed on the stove, sewing and constantly remodelling clothes for a baby who, like all babies, grew quickly. Keeping a crawling baby, then a toddler, entertained and busy forced Annie to be resourceful. Toys probably would have been classics: a rattle, a teething ring, perhaps a teddy bear or doll as Sylvia grew up. From Bridok, Ted and Annie took over the Lysenko School, between Insing-

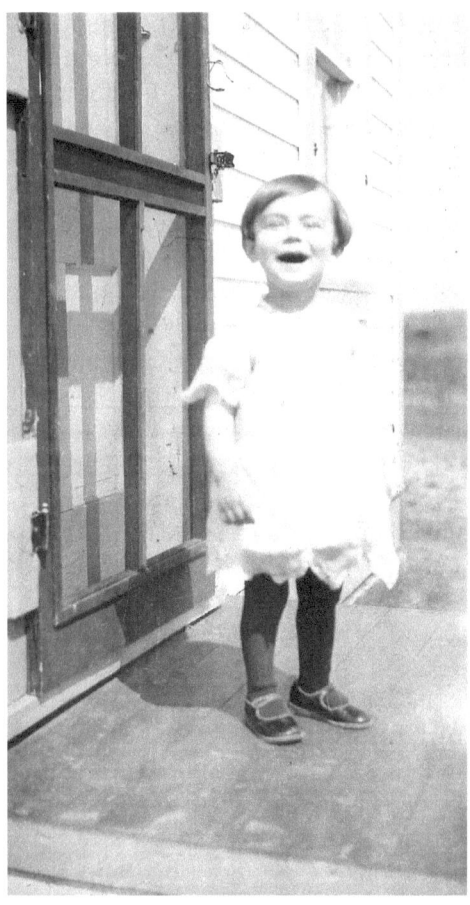

Two-year-old Sylvia, 1929.

er and Theodore, moving farther away from family members.[7]

Sylvia had dark, shiny hair that was rather straight, with only a few waves to be coaxed out. Her aquiline nose sat well on round cheeks, and she had laughing brown eyes. Full of fun and mischief, Sylvia grew into a girl who enjoyed stories, loved being outside and busy, and lived life at a full run. Only one story has come through from her early years. Ted and Annie went away for a weekend to attend a wedding, but for unknown reasons they elected not to take the young Sylvia. She was about three or four years old at the time—old enough to remember, and remember vividly, her stay at the neighbours'. What Ted and Annie did not know was that the neighbours were very poor. In the early 1930s, Sylvia's hosts were affected by the dire straits of a nearly ruined agricultural, economic, and physical landscape in western Canada. It had hit their kitchen particularly hard, devastating the garden at a time when the previous year's supply of canned and pickled vegetables was at a low ebb. There was little variety in their diet.

What they did have were onions. Lots and lots of onions. Sylvia ate onions at every meal for the entire time that her parents were away. For a young girl of Ukrainian ancestry, onions were likely common but probably not in that quantity. Her eyes burning from the fumes of raw onions, Sylvia battled between disgust for the pungent vegetable and hunger from her small tummy. The upshot of the weekend was that Sylvia developed what became a lifelong hatred for onions.

1. BLIZZARDS AND FIREWORKS

That aversion morphed into a pathological loathing that friends and family members—and later colleagues and chefs and communities—soon knew was no joke. If there were onions in a dish that she could see, then Sylvia would not eat it. Only her Ukrainian aunts were spared, but they soon learned to pulverize or otherwise hide the onions. Her refusal to eat them was stubborn and not always polite.

After Lysenko School, Ted took the family to the Wroxton-Calder region east of Yorkton. He took the helm at Chaucer School, north of the village of Calder

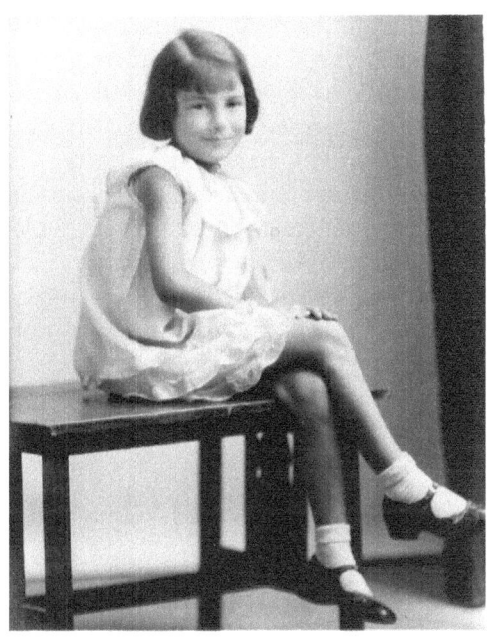

Sylvia, studio portrait, 1934.

and south of the village of Wroxton, on Section 16, Township 25, Range 32, west of the 1st Meridian. Chaucer School went by two other names—Toporoutz, or Toporowetz, No. 1666—but was renamed Chaucer by the time that the Fedoruks arrived. Many schools with original Ukrainian-sounding names were hastily renamed during the Great War and into the 1920s. After all, it was hardly patriotic to sport a foreign-sounding name, let alone one whose spelling was loose at best. The community bowed to the demands of Anglicization, changed the name, and painted a new sign over the door. It was there, at Chaucer, that Sylvia first went to school, side by side with her father.

In a one-room school, teaching was an art form. Ted, with about fifteen years of experience before Sylvia arrived in the schoolroom, was an old hand. But he had an ace in the hole: Annie brought an enormous amount of energy to the school, often as much in the thick of events as her schoolteacher husband. The Christmas concert, the annual sports day, and local spring and summer softball games became their specialty.

For most kids who grew up in rural Canada, the annual Christmas concert was a massively important event in the school year. Months of planning went into the plays, skits, tableaux, choruses, and small bits of fun. Plays and parts might be chosen as early as after harvest, with serious practice a regular part of the school routine. It wasn't difficult to see how the concert would impart lessons as part of the Anglicized Canadian curriculum. Skits and plays on British history, with kings and queens and treachery and bravery and sweeping costumes (possibly some mom's old robe), would transport the students to a different time and place. Oral diction, pronunciation, and proper elocution of English words pushed students to mastery. It doesn't take much to imagine some of the mothers in the audience, shining in delight at their children's performances but not understanding more than one word in three.

On the night of the program, the school would be packed with the entire community. Annie Fedoruk came into her element, designing costumes and choreographing elaborate staging. She was the ringleader and stage manager, keeping things organized and moving quickly and seamlessly behind the curtains. Ted Fedoruk was the concert master and emcee, directing the program and, for any music, accompanying the students on violin. Ukrainian local historian Theodore Onofrijchuk argued that "many a teacher was re-hired or fired on the basis of the performance of his class during the concert. A teacher may not have been very good at teaching all the other subjects, but he was considered by some trustees and parents to be an excellent teacher if he put on a good show."[8] Three hours later, children and parents both exhausted and elated, a certain jolly old man would arrive with paper bags filled with some candy, peanuts, a penny, and an orange. With a final carol and a rush to each sleigh or car for the trip home, the Christmas break could begin. In later years, Sylvia would look back on those one-room-school Christmas concerts with great fondness and nostalgia and a deep wish to share the simple joy of paper bags filled with treats with new generations of schoolchildren.

In 1935, the little family relocated to Scotland School, between Kessock and Wroxton. Scotland bulged with students; as many as seventy pupils squirmed and jostled along long rows of benches. Here, when Sylvia was a pupil, her father stood at the front, teacher and director and nurse and quartermaster and disciplinarian and song leader and janitor all in one. It's hard nowadays to imagine a rural one-room schoolhouse splitting its seams, with scents and sounds and sights. Today Scotland School is derelict, benches lying quietly along the walls, bereft of wiggling and farting kids learning to read and count. The hole where the stovepipe went through the wall is up high. Along the windows, hooks wait patiently for homemade coats that will never be hung again. In the cupboard, teacups have an imagined scent, hot chocolate on cold winter days.[9]

But in 1935 Scotland School was alive. With the first open patch of muddy ground in the spring, Ted and Annie would let the sports begin, hurling and chucking and sliding and hitting and catching. All schools would have annual sports days, and in some centres local schools would band together for one giant sports event. Generally held in June, these sports days would also draw a number of parents and as often as not became community picnics. Typical sports day events included classics such as foot races, long jump, triple jump, and high jump if the school had or could borrow or cobble together equipment for the day. Students knew to watch carefully for gopher holes or cowpies in the chosen sports field—the hazards of a rural sports ground. Other common events included ball throw, favouring those with a strong arm and a long reach. Tug of war, either between the schools or sometimes between children and parents, or between groups of parents, offered laughter and friendly rivalry. If the day was particularly hot, the adults might create booths with freshly cut boughs from poplar trees, offering shade for the watchers, picnickers, or those hand-cranking the ice cream. Ribbons were proudly worn, displaying achievements for all to see.

It was at these school sports days that Sylvia began to shine as an athlete. A woman who would later compete—in different sports—at the national level took her first steps on the path to athletic stardom on the playgrounds and sports grounds of Scotland School. By the time she was a teen, Sylvia could out-throw most of her classmates. The first flushes of talent, shown in ribbons proudly pinned, were the starting links in a lifelong chain of athletic excellence.

What really set the Fedoruks apart as teachers (and no school had Ted without Annie) was their commitment to playing ball. During the Second World War and through the 1940s and '50s, western Canada became softball and baseball crazy. "Baseball! God, if you came from the Prairies you had to remember baseball. There was nothing else to do. . . . Most towns, if they were big enough, and they had the surrounding farms and village to draw on, they had four teams, and there were some damn good teams. I've seen 10 teams playing, in the men's senior, on three diamonds, from 10 in the morning and when the last fly was caught just as the sun was going down, several thousand people would have watched."[10]

Donwell in particular was known for its exceptional ball team, one that could easily rival and rout city teams.[11]

Ted and Annie Fedoruk would load as many children as they could fit in a wagon, or perhaps Ted would borrow a farm truck, and off they would go to wherever the ball games were being held, at neighbouring schools or big, all-day tournaments somewhere nearby. On these days, Ted volunteered to be the umpire, keeping the kids moving on the field and judging and counting balls and strikes while Annie took on the real role: scorekeeper and coach for the team. Brought up at Donwell, Annie was a natural fit, coaching students through swings and misses, strategies, catches and throws, runs, slides, fakes, pop flies, and home runs.

With two parents as avid ball coaches, Sylvia, with her small but athletic build, was a natural. Soon she dominated in the infield, snatching balls from everywhere. It takes a skilled ball player to really own the infield: you need a dominant stance, the ability to be run over and get back up, speed, and agility to catch hard-hit line drives, blooper pop flies, piddly grounders, and accidentally overthrown balls, winging in from every direction, while racing base runners and beating them for the outs. But was Sylvia indeed a natural, or were her parents just doting and presumptuous? Any "teacher's kid" knows the layers of suspicion and the wisps of innuendo. Good grades are looked at askance. Did you earn that mark, or did the teacher (your parent) give it to you? Or, worse, did your parent-teacher help you—or do it for you—at home? Are you the captain because you deserve it? Where's the line between a good student who is a teacher's kid and a great student?

From the first day that Sylvia walked beside her father to sit in the front row as a pupil, Ted Fedoruk wanted to make sure that she would never be called the "teacher's pet." But what to do? He would have to mark her work, watch her learn and move through the grades, judge her performance. It was his job to coach, teach, call her out, throw hard fastballs, and make sure that he set difficult goals testing her ability to leap, make connections, and find the unknown. How would he make sure that she was deserving of her marks or athletic accolades?

Ted's solution was bold—possibly too bold. Sylvia was expected, right from the start, not just to perform well but also to outperform. Ted expected her to exceed her classmates in the classroom by at least 10 percent. She had to prove, again and again, that she was worthy of the marks that she got, that she had earned them.

Ted's intense scrutiny followed Sylvia into track and field and her ball glove. She grew up in an atmosphere of high expectations. There was no ease to be found at home either. Annie Fedoruk, still smarting from the sting of leaving school early, channelled scholastic energy through her daughter. Schooling and learning were the most important things. Annie expected, demanded, Sylvia's best. It's almost as if the mother was living her school life and expectations through the daughter.[12] With both parents demanding elite performance in scholastics and sports, Sylvia—as all children want to do—set out to meet, and even exceed, their expectations.

Luckily, she *was* a gifted scholar as well as a gifted athlete. From an early age, learning came easily to her. Sylvia soaked in her schooling and earned her way up through the grades. Later in life, her younger cousin Merylyn remembered Aunt Annie relaying stories about Sylvia as a schoolkid, fascinated with how things worked. Radios and small engines, wind-up cars, even bicycles drew her attention. She would find a few tools, and soon she'd have whatever it was apart to figure out its inner workings. The difference, Annie told Merylyn, is that Sylvia was equally good at putting it back together. She worked on it until it was as good as before or better. That mechanical mind, the ability to think in three dimensions and understand physics and mathematics, would resonate throughout her life. One of the drawbacks of her upbringing as an only child is that Sylvia never learned the give-and-take of sibling life within a household, the ability to push back or pull back, to make room for others, to wait and be patient. Expected to lead at school, and with no one to share that lead at home, or take a turn in the spotlight, Sylvia ended up with one setting: full on.[13]

A one-room schoolhouse in the heart of the Great Depression, probably short on books and supplies, with students in skimpy, made-over, hand-me-down clothes and shoes and slim lunch pails, could not have been expected to produce either a first-class athlete or a world-renowned scholar. Living at home with her family, on a teacher's salary that fell steadily throughout the 1930s (just as in every other school district in rural Saskatchewan scratched and bruised and torn by the economic blowout), would not have given Sylvia advantages. Saskatchewan residents' memories of the 1930s conjure up images of the dust bowl that wiped away crops and hope and deposited grasshoppers and despair, yet Sylvia's viewpoint was different: "The images of the dustbowl that characterize the period known as the dirty thirties didn't apply at all to our part of the province. Certainly there were financial troubles. But unlike the region to the south which relied heavily on grain growing, we were a mixed farming area and had various ways of obtaining the necessities of life."[14]

Ted and Annie Fedoruk maintained close ties to parents, siblings, and farms, and Sylvia would spend summers with her grandparents at the Romaniuk farm. Mischievous and busy, athletic and unafraid of mechanics or machines, she took particular pleasure in farm chores. The cream run—taking cream cans by buggy to nearby Hamton—was a staple. Every fall, if harvest came early and Ted could be spared from teaching, Sylvia loved working alongside the threshing crew.

Her mother, all green fingers and thumbs, grew fresh vegetables and fruits for a few extra dollars to stretch the family budget. No matter where they lived, Annie grew a huge garden plus a flower bed carefully built up around the teacherage. Sylvia learned gardening at her mother's side, digging and watering and hoeing. Annie's cabbages were particularly spectacular, monstrous heads sweet to the core. In the depths of the 1930s, when teacherage-to-fork substituted for today's farm-to-fork movement, Annie would take Sylvia along to Yorkton to sell cabbages to the owner of the local Chinese restaurant.

During the 1930s in Saskatchewan, thousands of teenagers were unable to afford to go to the nearest town to attend high school, instead taking courses through correspondence (with the help of the local teacher when possible). By the early 1940s, Sylvia had joined this group. Passing her grade eight with honours on June 30, 1941, receiving a certificate signed by her father, she took her grade nine primarily by correspondence, with some coaching by Ted. Sylvia chose typing instead of French as an extra course, a sensible choice during the war years when the Armed Forces soaked up typists by the thousands and university—where French was a prerequisite—seemed to be little more than a bold dream.

Sylvia's grade nine correspondence year showed a young woman with diverse interests. It is a fascinating report card, kept all those years in her personal belongings. What the report card does not show is Sylvia's later advanced skills in physics and mathematics. Of course, a grade nine general science course would have only a small physics component, along with chemistry, biology, and general knowledge, all without a laboratory, for no doubt Scotland School was not that advanced. Sylvia showed a predilection for memorization in literature and history—indeed, stellar marks in those subjects brought her overall average up substantially. She struggled more with composition and grammar, and they would dog Sylvia throughout her schooling, including at university. Whereas the mechanics of a radio or an engine or a toy kept her fascinated, the mechanics of the English language certainly did not. Typing, which she remembered choosing over French, isn't recorded in her report card, suggesting that it wasn't part of the local curriculum and available only via provincial correspondence courses. Nonetheless, Sylvia ended rural school life at the top of her class.[15]

Over all the years—the ball games and sports days, the Christmas concerts and daily learning exercises—one memory stood out for Sylvia Fedoruk in Canadian-maple-leaf red. In 1939, King George VI (who inherited the crown when his brother King Edward VIII abdicated the throne), along with his popular wife, Queen Elizabeth, paid a visit to the dominion. Daughters Elizabeth and Margaret were prudently left at home. Arriving in Quebec on May 17, the royal duo immediately wowed audiences by speaking fluent French. The king insisted on visiting all nine of the provinces, making whistle stops at major and minor sidings along the way. The royal couple criss-crossed the country and waved to as many as 2.5 million Canadians thronging to see them. When it was announced that the king and queen would have a whistle-stop visit at Melville, Saskatchewan, the Fedoruks acted. Ted and Annie

Sylvia, dressed to see visiting royalty in Melville in 1939.

believed that such an opportunity would come but once for the pupils at Scotland School. Plans fell into place. They borrowed a large truck, big enough to hold all of the pupils, and everyone dressed in his or her best. They left early to drive ninety-six kilometres from Wroxton to Melville, with plenty of time to park, rest, and jostle for position to see the royals.

They weren't alone. All day farm families, other school students, and thousands of other people poured into Melville from as far as 320 kilometres away. Painters slapped a WELCOME TO THEIR MAJESTIES onto the largest canvas available in the town: the side of the Saskatchewan Wheat Pool elevator. It is said that the local towns of Yorkton, Esterhazy, and Canora simply closed down for the day. No one was around anyway—everyone was in Melville.

It was a long, exciting day filled with crowds and anticipation. The train bearing their Majesties finally pulled in shortly after dark at about 10 p.m. A blue spotlight picked out the king and queen on the platform of the last car, and the crowd began to roar. The queen politely asked that the spotlight be turned and panned across the crowd so that she could have a good view of those who had come to see her in the dark. The monarchs were stunned. An estimated 60,000 people were roaring and waving, singing and shouting, crying and laughing. In fact, historian Bill Waiser noted that, in that moment, Melville had become Saskatchewan's largest city.[16] Sylvia was entranced. She spun and slipped and ducked and pushed toward the monarchs, trying to get as close to them as possible. The strong, lithe, twelve-year-old girl managed to get close enough to see their faces clearly. It was a moment that became etched with crystal clarity in her memory. As the monarchs gave a last wave and retreated, fireworks lit up the night sky and boomed across the crowd. Sylvia turned and slipped back to the others, her face turned up to take in the bright cascades.

As the fireworks faded and Ted and Annie rounded up their charges, night fell in earnest. The Scotland School crew were loaded back into the truck and stretched out with blankets and coats on makeshift beds, snug together for the trip home. As the stars twinkled, with the truck engine roaring, Sylvia looked up and sighed, believing that she had come as close to royalty as she ever would.

2. WALKERVILLE WONDER

THE YEAR 1942 MARKED A TREMENDOUS CHANGE IN THE life of Sylvia Fedoruk. The Ukrainian girl from Wroxton, Saskatchewan, born in Canora and raised in the Eastern European communities surrounding Yorkton, was moving.

In truth, many Canadians were on the move that year. Enveloped in a war rapidly spreading across the globe after the Japanese attack on Pearl Harbor in December 1941, the winter of 1942 brought a renewed, almost fervent, burst of war energy. As the United States shook off its military dust and flexed righteous anger, the war machine in Canada spun into overdrive. Thousands of men and women signed up to join the services, learning to fly planes or break down guns or climb escarpments or drive ambulances. Sylvia's world exploded outward. The Fedoruk family of Ted, Annie, and fifteen-year-old Sylvia moved east, crossing two provincial borders, to the industrial heartland of Ontario. Fuelled by money that the federal government was unwilling to spend during the Great Depression, the Second World War sustained an industrial economy bent on producing planes, trucks, tanks, and bombs. The national war machine pulled in supplies, raw materials, industrial knowledge, and—more than anything else—people. The Fedoruks moved to Windsor, Ontario, recruited by one of Ted's brothers, already in Windsor to take on some of the Ford welding subcontracts. The large Ukrainian connections spread across Canada meant that the Fedoruks left family members behind to join other family members.

Even with opportunity and a patriotic response to war, the real reason for the move was Sylvia. Ambitious, gifted, and full of energy, she needed and wanted more: a larger school, more classmates, more activities. If she was to finish high school, Sylvia would be moving that summer no matter what to Yorkton and the regional comprehensive school, like her father, or somewhere else. Ted and Annie valued education. If they stayed in Saskatchewan, the three would be split apart. If they moved to Ontario, they could remain together.

Windsor is Canada's southernmost city, located along the Detroit River.[1] The Fedoruks settled first in a cramped apartment, then moved to a small house at 1845 Westcott Road, in the East Windsor district, once known as Ford City.[2] Nearby neighbourhoods included Fontainbleu, Riverside, and Walkerville. Walkerville was the original industrial heartland of the Windsor region, where Hiram Walker had his distillery, creating the world-famous Canadian Club whisky. Whereas Wroxton in 1942 boasted fewer than 500 people, Windsor was a sprawling, blue-collar, industrial city with a population of well over 100,000—and growing every day. From a farming countryside, the Fedoruks entered a fully fledged industrial metropolis, with streetcars, time clocks, set work hours, excellent wages, and rush hours.

Ford City, as its name implies, was the hub of the Canadian arm of the Ford Motor Company.[3] Westcott Road ran just a couple of blocks from the Ford test track, where new cars were put through their paces steering and turning, braking and swerving, checking acceleration, speed, agility, and handling. The big Ford factory, across the street north of the test track, was running at full capacity to serve war needs. Instead of cars, the factory produced heavy trucks designed for war. Most of those in the new neighbourhood geared their days around shiftwork at Ford or support work for the workers. Secretaries, café workers, cleaners and janitors, babysitters, millwrights, engineers, riveters, shop floor workers, sheet metal workers, mechanics, and advertising agents rushed in, out, and all around.

The Fedoruks settled in. The house at Westcott Road boasted conveniences unheard of in a rural teacherage. Indoor plumbing and electrical power were staples in the larger urban centres and particularly in homes with access to Ford's large electrical plant. Annie, her domestic tasks eased by running water, oil heating, and electricity, joined the Windsor war workforce. During the war years, Ford flourished, as did all companies with supply, renovation,

2. WALKERVILLE WONDER

Postcard featuring Walkerville Collegiate Institute, 1931.

construction, or other contracts with Ford or tertiary companies throughout Windsor. Both Fedoruks were earning unprecedented salaries and considered a new goal: to send Sylvia to university.

As September 1942 began, Sylvia enrolled in Walkerville Collegiate Institute at 2100 Richmond Street. Built in grand Gothic style, designed by architects Pennington and Boyle, it was finished in 1922 at an astonishing cost of $600,000 and opened to great fanfare.

The school couldn't have been more different from the one-room Scotland School at Wroxton or the correspondence courses that had filled Sylvia's previous winter. Three storeys high, with a gymnasium, an auditorium with a stage for theatre productions, an indoor pool lovingly called "The Plunge," and a wood-panelled library, it had everything that an engaged and focused teenager such as Sylvia could want in a school. Its leadership came from the student council, named the Agora after the Athenian public square. Even the school's motto seemed to be created for Sylvia: "Nil sine labore," translated from the Latin as "Nothing without work." A cadet corps, formed during the early years of the war, boasted bagpipes and kilts and regularly won regional and provincial competitions. Walkerville Collegiate curried fierce pride in both students and staff. It was "renowned as one of the top schools in the province" and "consistently produced champion athletic teams."[4] Walkerville also had its gender divisions. There was a major area set aside for "manual" training for boys and another area equipped with "household science" paraphernalia for girls. And it was during that first fall at Walkerville that Annie Fedoruk had her first—and only—massive run-in with her daughter's educational instructors.

On Sylvia's first day at Walkerville Collegiate, the principal, looking to place the new student, did a snap assessment. A Ukrainian girl from a tiny rural Saskatchewan community, educated in one-room schools, with her grade nine by correspondence and no French-language training? She obviously should enter the household science stream, a commercial class meant to funnel students straight into the workforce, or possibly to end high school early, to be productive labourers (and probably new wives and mothers). Sylvia, they decided, was bound for household science, certainly not university material.

Annie was aghast. She was also enraged. With two incomes flowing in, she was determined—more than ever—that Sylvia would have the advantages and opportunities that she herself had never had, having been removed from school after grade eight. The next morning Annie played hooky from work. She marched to Walkerville Collegiate with Sylvia in her wake, aiming straight for the principal's office. By the time Annie was finished with the principal, Sylvia's scholastic direction had changed. The principal, with Annie looming over his desk, enrolled Sylvia in both grade nine and grade ten French and put her back in the stream for a senior matriculation suitable for university. Satisfied, Annie went off to work. Sylvia, ever the pragmatist, picked up her end of the bargain. She studied with fervour and determination. After all, learning a new language, for a girl with a reasonable conversational command of Ukrainian, wasn't all that difficult—and she was possibly as determined as her mother. Sylvia gained ground scholastically year over year, embedded in a large, diverse, and supportive school environment. She joined the school's leadership council, Agora, and served eventually as its vice-chair.

As was the case in Wroxton, Sylvia quickly became a major asset to Walkerville's many athletic teams. She learned to play and soon excelled at both basketball and volleyball, tearing through the more familiar track and field. In her four years at Walkerville from 1942 to the end of grade thirteen in 1946, Sylvia was on teams that brought back city-wide championships in basketball, volleyball, and track and field, at least one championship in each sport. She was just as engaged outside school and the gymnasium. Spring and summer saw Ted and Annie cheering in the stands after their shifts were finished, eating peanuts and hot dogs, and watching Sylvia play in city league ball teams, including the team that competed in the Women's Industrial Softball League Ford Championships in 1945, in which her team took home top honours.

The template of overachievement, established by the "teacher's kid" at Chaucer and Scotland Schools, was not an optional external push but a hard-wired part of Sylvia herself. There was no other way. Full

Sylvia practising ball, c. 1945.

on or not at all. A larger field of competitors meant that she had to work harder, reach farther. Her internal drive meant that she had little to no patience for partial or unfinished jobs. Nothing sloppy, no corners cut. If you were going to do it, do it well, and do it right. Given those qualities, school leadership on the Agora—and later other kinds of leadership—were fitting for Sylvia. Taking the position of Girls' Athletic President, she was lauded in the Walkerville Collegiate yearbook *The Blue and White* for her drive and energy: "Sylvia is one of those people who can't be outdone when it comes to accomplishing anything. She will tackle any job and doesn't rest until she sees it through. She has handled her executive position in a most efficient manner."[5]

On the flip side, though, her drive for excellence also meant that Sylvia carefully chose only those pursuits and interests at which she could excel. She curated her life, to an extent, to ensure that what she was doing she could do to a high standard. She was intensely

Sylvia, studio portrait, 1945.

competitive, which served her well in both sports and science. Occasionally, though, Sylvia would join something purely for fun. The school girls' choir practised every Tuesday afternoon on the third floor. At Christmas, the girls' choir would get together with the boys' choir to co-host a party, complete with games, box lunches, and a dance. Although Sylvia liked to sing, she did not pursue it rigorously, and that was rare for her.

Two teachers stand out in her academic career at Walkerville Collegiate. The first, Ruth McLaren, taught Sylvia grade eleven English literature. Despite a stellar record, composition remained her downfall. Miss McLaren told Sylvia that she would never be an author or a poet. It was obvious in the staffroom where her true interest and talent lay. Miss McLaren suggested that Sylvia consider a career in science. High school science instructor Howard Hugill had a dynamism and classroom presence that inspired Sylvia in her quest to immerse herself in science—particularly physics. Her drive to figure out how things work, to take them apart and put them back together, her innate talents in mechanics, got a fresh burst of energy. In the fully equipped science labs of a large urban school, Sylvia became bold, exploring the outer edges of science and math. The high seventies and low eighties that she brought in at Wroxton on those subjects were but a dim memory. Sylvia found her passion, and Walkerville teachers were happy to direct, support, and champion those scholastic abilities.

Her coming of age at Walkerville Collegiate must be nested within events in the wider Windsor and Ontario communities. By 1945, Ted was working with the firm of Smith, Kirkaldy and Dennison, and Annie joined Truscon Steel Company.[6] With both parents working in factories, Sylvia was exposed on a regular basis to the conversations and casual knowledge of local workers, experts with years of experience making and using machines. Windsor was a hive of craftspeople well able to deconstruct and reconstruct machines, use tools and dies, reverse engineer, and jimmy what was needed to do the job. Such trust in local expertise, in the ability to make machines do what one needed them to do, would serve Sylvia well at university and throughout her career. In her world, if you needed something, you designed it, and you built it.

As the war ended in spectacular fashion in 1945 with the dropping of two bombs on Hiroshima and Nagasaki in Japan, breathless stories of the destructive capabilities of nuclear energy splashed across the newspapers and bounced over radio waves. Yet, in the midst of grim news and dire warnings, hope emerged. Nuclear fission was making waves in Ontario, where by September 1945 ZEEP "went critical." The Zero Energy Experimental Pile (ZEEP) was a small nuclear reactor built at Chalk River, Ontario, the first such reactor outside the United States. Canada's own nuclear energy science coalesced around Chalk River.[7] Sylvia, about to enter her last year of high school, might not have known what those new advances would mean for her future career. But in Ontario a few more crucial seeds leading to her later career harvest of opportunities had been thoughtfully sown.

With the war over and men returning home, what was once a city geared to war found itself on the cusp of change. Women were asked to step back, to leave the factories and their jobs for the returning men, and to take up once more "their place" in the kitchen as helpmates to their husbands. Men who had war jobs also found their positions questioned. Why didn't you go overseas to fight? Shouldn't you step aside to make way for a veteran? It was a time of massive review—of family lives and what they meant, of a national war culture transformed back to a peacetime culture, of the city itself.

At the grade thirteen graduation at Walkerville Collegiate in June 1946, Sylvia Fedoruk crossed the convocation floor several times. In her four high school years, she had proven Annie Fedoruk's determined conviction. From Ukrainian roots deep in Saskatchewan's parkland, and educated in one-room schools, Sylvia had taken on a prestigious Ontario high school and brought home top honours. When she matriculated, she was the top female graduate, earning the Ernest J. Creed Memorial Medal. She received a Dominion of Canada scholarship worth $400—a princely sum at the time destined to open the way to the University of Toronto and the College of Engineering. The mechanically minded star student in math and science had her future firmly in sight. And no one worried about Sylvia entering the primarily male profession of engineering. Under the title "Things You Will Never See," her high school yearbook slyly declared that the most unimaginable event was "Sylvia Fedoruk taking orders from a man."[8]

That summer she continued to expand her horizons in the sports world. In 1946, Sylvia won a spot on the Windsor Esquires female fastball team, which operated in the international Michigan-Ontario fastball league. It was a hard-won position. Women's baseball, including softball and fastball, had become highly competitive. The Michigan-Ontario fastball league was at the crossroads between amateur and professional sport.[9] An international circuit with teams in Hamilton, London, Windsor, Lansing, Flint, and Detroit (three teams), the league was an upstart that—similar to the more famous All-American Girls Professional Baseball League featured in the Hollywood blockbuster movie *A League of Their Own*—set out, in some small way, to fill the void in professional men's sports created by the Second World War.[10]

The league used the larger city baseball parks, and as many as 2,000 fans crammed into the stadiums on game nights. Some of the women on the teams, such as Pauline Perron of Montreal, recruited by the London Supremes to play first base, crossed the line into professional ball. In addition to being offered a secure job at a local factory, Perron received cash for each game played. The Canadian amateur rules at the time didn't allow such shenanigans, but the realities of the time, with good Canadian players often emigrating south to the professional league in America, meant that rules were bent, broken, or ignored at will. Nonetheless, there was often a public backlash against women who had gone to play, for a few games or a season or two, down in the professional league and then returned to Canada. These women had to reapply to be reinstated to the amateur league—an application fraught with social, conventional, and public debates.

There is no record that Sylvia Fedoruk was ever paid as a player in the Michigan-Ontario fastball league, but most of the teams in the league had sponsors or used gate receipts and advertising to pay for team travel, accommodations, and meals. Even if she wasn't given part of the ticket sales per game, no doubt Sylvia felt that she was being "paid" to play ball—or, at least, someone other than her parents was paying for her to play. She was good enough, however,

2. WALKERVILLE WONDER

Sylvia's Windsor sports badges.

to be actively recruited to the All-American girls' league. The scouts watched and reported on the brown-haired, loud, and fiery player, and Sylvia would later recount, with some regret, an offer from the coach of the Flint, Michigan, team to move to the United States to play in the ladies' professional league. Her parents, however, were appalled. They could not imagine allowing Sylvia to travel alone to the United States, to be on her own, and to play ball for a living. Sylvia, they were determined, was heading to university.

Sylvia's 1946 fastball year, with thousands of fans watching in lit parks in evenings and on weekends in two countries, became another major highlight of her sports career. Historian Carly Adams noted that "sport provided an arena where women could develop intense relationships with other women and compete in physical activities where they could be aggressive, play hard, and shake off the social restrictions of traditional femininity."[11] During a time when and in a place where women were being cajoled back into more traditional roles and spheres, the Michigan-Ontario fastball league promoted and supported a group of athletic, driven, competitive women to go the other way. The team banded together, building a community of trust, fun, and friendship. Sylvia, probably playing her usual infield position, flourished.

Sometime during that summer, change crept into her home. Under social pressure to give up their jobs to returning servicemen, and with an entire war-built economy struggling to flip back to a peacetime footing, Ted and Annie Fedoruk faced their own choices. Despite watching their daughter enjoy a spectacular summer with the Windsor Esquires fastball team and anticipating the glowing promise of a place at the University of Toronto, the senior Fedoruks decided to return to Saskatchewan. At first, Sylvia didn't want to go. She tried to convince her parents to let her attend the University of Toronto. But Ted and Annie simply couldn't contemplate such a separation. Leave their only child, their much-loved daughter, behind? No.[12] Sylvia, with tears in her eyes, left behind the ball fields and teams, and the engineering dreams, crossing the many miles back west with her parents to Saskatchewan.

For Sylvia, Ontario had been a gift. Life in East Windsor and schooling at Walkerville Collegiate had shown the one-room-schoolteacher's daughter a world of possibilities, of scholastic achievement through hard work, of sports excellence, of international travel, and of the exciting possibilities of science. Walkerville Collegiate gave Sylvia confidence, leadership, scholastic pride, and poise, all the tools that she would need to make her mark in a varsity setting. Although she would later become one of Saskatchewan's most outspoken locally grown ambassadors, in truth her life would have been very different if the Fedoruks hadn't moved to Windsor. Sylvia would later note that "before we went to Windsor, there was no hope that I'd ever get to university, so I would have had some 'woman kind' of job," such as secretary or nurse.[13] Saskatchewan has good reason to be grateful that Sylvia went to Windsor, excelled at Walkerville Collegiate, dominated the Michigan-Ontario fastball league, and ultimately, that Ontario opened Sylvia's future physics path by investing in ZEEP.

3. RAMPAGING AMAZON

FRESHIE WEEK, UNIVERSITY OF SASKATCHEWAN, SEPTEMber 1946. Sylvia Fedoruk, stepping alongside the largest "abnormal" influx of postwar demobilized soldiers and farm and city kids ever to descend on the university, jumped into campus life. And what a jump. Her senior, tasked with outfitting Sylvia for freshie week, went through her own closet and Sylvia's closet and came up with the most outlandish outfit possible. Wearing a freshie beanie emblazoned with a white S for Saskatchewan and smothered in face paint, Sylvia proudly sported a plaid shirt, floral slacks, a dark apron, and rubber galoshes. Neither backpack nor book bag for Syl; she carried textbooks in a tin bucket emblazoned with her student number, 98135. Whisking down the leafy streets on a bicycle, her head held high, Sylvia joined other freshies similarly hazed, a wild ensemble of outrageous getups and competitive gentle shaming in the bowl in front of the administration building. From there, she joined in the Freshie Dance.

Sylvia's first week was a whirl of meeting people and finding her way around. From a rally at Griffiths Stadium to an All Varsity Dance, hectic energy set the tone. To remind the freshmen that college life was not all play and no work, September 28 was Workday, which all freshmen were expected to attend—no exceptions. Meeting at 2 p.m. at Griffiths Stadium, they engaged in a massive coordinated effort doing general cleaning, painting fences and bleachers, raking and tidying campus grounds, cleaning and putting in shape barns and buildings. The work connected students and campus. After all,

Sylvia as a University of Saskatchewan freshie, fall 1946.

when students know how much work is involved in maintaining facilities, they just might take better care of them and have a sense of ownership. *The Sheaf*, the University of Saskatchewan student paper, noted that "it isn't all work however, there's real fun to be had at Workday at the U of S. Everyone has a big time, dressed in old clothes, they really let their hair down and forget about the strenuous week of registration and first classes. It is a real chance to get acquainted and absorb some of the green and white spirit for which our university is noted. When the work's all done everyone meets back at the stadium for a feed, usually of apples and milk."[1]

Sylvia needed to squeeze some fun into her schedule. She was enrolled in Type C Arts and Science with an emphasis on natural sciences, and it's unclear why she didn't enter engineering, as had been the plan for the University of Toronto. It's possible that, coming so late, she could not secure entrance into what (at the University of Saskatchewan in 1946) was a college still reluctant to welcome women. Lectures commenced on September 24, and Sylvia jumped into her first five classes: calculus, chemistry, physics, English, and German. Walking into the elementary calculus class, Sylvia stopped. All heads turned to stare in her direction. Of seventy students, she was the only woman taking the course. Undaunted, with a toss of her dark brown hair and a flash of competition firing her determination, Sylvia calmly took her seat.

Every first-year student, except those in engineering, had to take first-year English, so Sylvia got set to plod through *King Lear* and composition. German would give her some competence in yet another new language, while chemistry and physics allowed for lab work and new adventures. A standard tuition of ninety dollars plus thirty-four dollars in student fees gave access to the library, skating rink, student societies, and labs, as well as accident and sickness benefits.

By October 8, all students had to report where they were staying; in case of an emergency, the university needed to know how and where to find each student. Sylvia settled into Mohyla Institute, at the time located at 401 Main Street in the old Empress Hotel, south and east of the University of Saskatchewan campus, not far from Nutana Collegiate. It was, after all, family tradition since her dad had stayed there in the early 1920s. The quickest ways to the campus were to bike or walk or take a bus. During Sylvia's tenure at Mohyla Institute, students were a "happy mix of high school, normal school and varsity," crossing ages and backgrounds, with a "structure somewhat like a very large family."[2] Its familiarity, good food, and protection meant much to Ted and Annie.

Mohyla had deep roots in Ukrainian language and culture. Students were expected to attend Mohyla events when possible, including Ukrainian language instruction, debates, public speaking, dances, and social evenings, including the famous Ukrainian Christmas carolling. Living in a Ukrainian residence would have been somewhat of a shock for Sylvia. After all, though she knew some conversational Ukrainian from extended family members and grandparents, the Fedoruks did not use the language at home. Cultural food, of course, would have been more familiar to Sylvia, a robust athlete and hearty eater, though onions remained a problem. The social aspect of dorm life helped to dissipate any feelings of homesickness—and, really, where was the home for her homesickness? Walkerville Collegiate and East Windsor? Wroxton? Or her parents' new house in the village of Rhein, so near grandparents and cousins and uncles and aunts? Sylvia would later recall with great fondness the structured program of study and work, good food, and discipline provided for and expected from Mohyla residents. Watching budding romances to building lasting friendships, trudging through the brutal cold the many blocks to the university campus when she missed the bus, receiving food parcels and letters from home, and even undergoing the dreaded initiations: these experiences would resonate with Sylvia as touchstones for her life and career.[3]

Sylvia used her spare time for sports. Freshettes—first-year women—were required to have medical exams and take two hours of physical education per week, beginning at the end of October.

Choices included either gym or modern dancing for one class, then one from a suite of activities including swimming, fencing, badminton, and basketball. Lockers were shared, and a copy of the student's timetable ensured that the physical education classes would have no conflicts. There was an official school gym uniform for girls: plain white blouse with short sleeves and dark green shorts, which could be purchased downtown at the Eaton's store, on the second floor, at the Ladies Ready-to-Wear counter. They also had to have white socks and running shoes. Beyond these basics, all freshettes were strongly encouraged to try out for "at least one sport in every season." Fall choices included track and field, tennis, and golf, and the university boasted its own swimming pool.[4]

Trying out for the track and field team, Sylvia soon caught the eye of coach Bob Shore. "There is plenty of good material, both new and old," noted Shore, watching the women's track and field team practise. The sports reporter from *The Sheaf* added, "In the javelin and discus throws Sylvia Fedoruk, another first year, bears plenty of watching."[5] Legendary track coach E.W. (Joe) Griffiths was also impressed. Sylvia, he saw, brought her intelligence to bear and used it to great advantage. What she lacked in size or speed or weight, for a woman tossing things, she made up in perseverance and brains. Sports weren't won by brawn alone. Her success, he said, was simply "a triumph of BRAIN over BRAWN."[6]

By October, the track and field women competed in an interfaculty match to see who would make the home team for the intervarsity track and field championships, held in Saskatoon. Sylvia easily made the team. "One of the more outstanding newcomers is Sylvia Fedoruk, who in practices has broken the inter-faculty record in the softball throw and has almost equalled the discus record." Her throw was 199.7 feet.[7] The University of Saskatchewan came to win its home tournament. Competing in discus, javelin, and softball throw, Sylvia took home three first-place medals for a total of fifteen points, contributing almost half of the thirty-six points that the team scored to win the trophy. Tossing a javelin 107 feet, she was just three feet seven inches short of the record. In ball, she bettered her own interfaculty record by a further two and a half feet. Sylvia was all about strength, though Griffiths knew that she didn't have the heft required to compete at the upper echelon of the elite level. Speed came from Betty Wilson, fellow coed, who outstripped all competitors in both the 60- and the 100-yard sprints, bringing home gold medals. All in all, the coed track and field team brought home five firsts in the eight categories and claimed the coveted Rutherford trophy presented to the top-scoring team.[8]

With track and field finished, Sylvia set her sights on basketball. Coach Ivan King held senior girls' hoop tryouts with both the senior Huskiette squad and its junior team, the Orphanettes. Some twenty-plus women attended the tryouts, including some "promising freshettes," reported *The Sheaf*.[9] As she had at Walkerville Collegiate, Sylvia made the senior team as a point guard. Her job was to be physical, be present, guard the basket, and be tough. With Charrie Tofstead as their manager, the team aimed to take back the Cecil Race trophy in the intervarsity basketball championship.[10] Their style of play was scrappy, fast, "scrambly," and often riddled with fouls. As a point guard, Sylvia was never a high scorer. Yet she was clearly a dominant player on the team. The Huskiettes practised five times per week, constantly honing their skills by playing in the city-wide leagues against the Orphanettes as well as Saskatoon teams the Elkettes and the Royals. They competed hard, aiming to bring back the Cecil Race intervarsity championship in Edmonton in February.

Despite a grinding athletic year shaped by season and sport, Sylvia's scholastics were also charging forward, embedded in a university looking to make a name for itself. The physics department was ambitious, aiming to build a physics research program unlike any other in Canada. Led by head Dr. Ertle Harrington, the department had a taste not only for pure research but also for applied research. His main interest and practice were in radiation and medical physics, but he was known as a glassblower as well. In 1931–32, Harrington, along with John Spinks from the chemistry department, built the first radon plant in Canada.[11] It was a closed glass system that allowed Harrington to extract radium gas from a radium bromide solution. A series of pumps would separate the hydrogen and oxygen, and the radon gas would be drawn into fine glass and then fine gold tubing. The gold tubing could be cut into tiny radon "seeds" for doctors to insert into small accessible organs such as the cervix, uterus, and tongue to combat cancer.[12] Radioactive gold radon seeds could radiate cancerous tumours in situ. The work was beyond experimental. Gold radon seeds became standard treatment for cancers that could be accessed and treated easily. The Saskatoon radon plant produced radon gas and gold seeds for many years, supplying Saskatoon and regional hospitals. Harrington's outstanding years of work drew close connections between the Department of

Physics and the provincial Cancer Commission, with Harrington often acting as a consultant and his students as technicians.[13]

Building on this history of applied physics research and connecting physics to cancer, Harrington wrote to Dr. Allan Blair, head of the Saskatchewan Cancer Commission, on December 18, 1944. In the letter, Harrington discussed the real need for a physicist to serve both the university and the Cancer Commission in a joint appointment. Blair agreed, and Harrington was given leave to find a suitable candidate. He cajoled Dr. Harold Johns to join the physics department at the University of Saskatchewan in 1945.

Born in Chengdu, West China, to educational missionary parents,[14] Johns returned to Canada for a B.Sc. in physics from McMaster University in 1936 and an M.Sc. and Ph.D. from the University of Toronto in 1937 and 1939.[15] Arriving in Saskatoon, Johns became part of the university's elite group combining physics, chemistry, and biology to look at cancer treatment. Since future research on radiotherapy was envisioned, half of his salary was initially paid by the Saskatchewan Cancer Commission in Regina, and his work went beyond the imaginary ivory tower to assess and build the mechanical aptitude of the Cancer Commission while also teaching classes and taking in graduate students in the physics department.

In the summer of 1946, just before Sylvia Fedoruk entered her first year of undergraduate studies, Allan Blair secured a travelling scholarship from the Canadian Cancer Society for Harold Johns to take a tour of leading radiation centres in the United States. On this tour, Johns saw and heard much that was new and exciting in the application of radiation physics to cancer treatment, including, at the University of Chicago, a 22-million-volt betatron. Johns ended the tour in Toronto, spending time with Dr. Gordon Richards of the Ontario Institute of Radiotherapy and taking an exclusive two-week course in physics and cancer treatment, presented by Professor W.V. Mayneord of the Royal Marsden Hospital in London, England.

Since Johns was the only professional physicist taking the class (the rest were medical doctors), he took extensive notes, which he later used as a guide to write his textbook *The Physics of Radiology*.[16] Professor Mayneord had spent the war years working in Canada at the Chalk River nuclear reactor looking for ways to create better medical isotopes. It was Mayneord who had determined that cobalt-59 could be turned into the radioactive isotope cobalt-60, which would replace radium, it was hoped, as a source of medical radiation. Johns, excited by the trip, returned to Saskatchewan. Blair asked him if he had seen anything that he would like to have in Saskatchewan. Johns said, yes, a betatron and a cobalt-60 unit.[17]

With Johns on board, the Department of Physics took direct aim at its first target: the purchase of a betatron machine. Harrington, along with Leon Katz, Newman Haslam, and Johns, produced a major report in 1946 designed to convince the powers that be (whether the university, the provincial government as the funder of both the university and the Saskatchewan Cancer Commission, or the federal atomic energy group at Chalk River) that the University of Saskatchewan should purchase a betatron. "Because of the increasing importance of the application of physics to medicine, the Saskatchewan Cancer Commission and the Physics Department have recently shared the services of Dr. HE Johns. During this past summer, . . . the desireability of obtaining a betatron for experimental work as a prelude to cancer therapy became apparent."[18] The report drew almost immediate notice. In December, Dr. W.B. Lewis, director of the Division of Atomic Energy of the National Research Council at Chalk River, came to Saskatoon to visit Harrington and the physics department. Lewis wanted to view the facilities and coordinate the U of S research team with those in Ottawa and Chalk River. The betatron program might get the green light, and Saskatoon, decidedly, was drawing notice.[19]

With the possibility of a betatron, and a clear connection between physics and nuclear medicine, Johns was on the lookout for good students to support a robust research program. The physics, math, and chemistry cohort that arrived on campus in the fall of 1946, full of mature students and returning soldiers, became a byword for years to come. They showed incredible promise. Sylvia's first-year physics class was co-taught by Harrington and Johns, and it was memorable. Excellent teaching, enthusiastic and smart students, and the odd explosion during each week's gruelling six-hour lab session made things interesting.

By December, Sylvia's classroom performance and grades had earned particular notice. The physics department had had exceptional female students before as well as a renowned female Ph.D., Luise Herzberg, the wife of Dr. Gerhard Herzberg, who would later become the 1971 winner of the Nobel Prize for Chemistry for his work on the structure of molecules, especially free radicals. Gerhard Herzberg had met U of S Professor J.W.T. Spinks while Spinks was in Germany in the early 1930s. By 1935, the Nazi crackdown on people of Jewish heritage forced the Herzbergs to consider emigrating. The University of Saskatchewan, on the advice of Spinks, welcomed the Herzbergs and did its best despite the Great Depression and the Second World War to support Gerhard's work. Luise was often frustrated and sidelined since her husband (and not she) had the faculty appointment, but nonetheless she both continued her own studies and worked alongside her husband in the physics department building the spectroscopy laboratory, occasionally teaching or taking on lab duties on a voluntary basis as well as being an active member of the physics society. The Herzbergs left in 1945, just before Sylvia came to campus, but Luise had made an impact on the faculty. The same year that Sylvia arrived, Norma Morgenroth successfully defended her physics master's thesis on acetylene. Thought to be the first woman to achieve a master's degree in physics at the University of Saskatchewan, Norma—along with her sister, Marian Shepherd, who would also receive a master's degree in physics in 1954—laid firm foundations and positive connections for female success in physics at the university.

Within that welcoming environment, Sylvia shone. Inviting the Mohyla resident to their house for a meal, Harold Johns and his wife, Sybil, set out to learn a bit more about this female student who had made such an impression on the university in both scholastics and sports. Over the course of the evening, both became more impressed. As Sybil served a lovely meal, she and Harold addressed Sylvia's future: what were her plans? As the conversation unfolded, Sybil, as much as or more than her husband, pointed out that women were welcome in medicine, and the burgeoning world of nuclear medicine, which combined physics with treatment of patients, could be a place unhampered by gendered stereotypes. Sylvia could make a place for herself in this world. Entranced by the possibilities of the research program laid out by Harold, Sylvia soaked in her future. In later years, the supper meeting became a foundational story of her career as a physicist, shared again and again with the media. Was the conversation that specific, or was it only in hindsight that it took on the proportions of legend? No one knows.

Two points are clear. First, Harold became Sylvia's physics mentor, but it was Sybil who had the foresight to consider and suggest Sylvia's position as a woman in medical physics and drew the outlines of the relationship. Second, Sylvia's skill was obvious and shone at the University of Saskatchewan. It is hard to imagine another university with the foresight to recognize and offer a

3. RAMPAGING AMAZON

potential research career to a female student after only a few months of lectures. The University of Saskatchewan, unlike the University of Toronto, was small enough to draw connections between the personal and the professional yet big enough for Sylvia's skills to be recognized. Thus, her future took shape. Canada's leading interdisciplinary team at the University of Saskatchewan was *the* place to study nuclear physics. Its growing application to the field of medicine meant that Sylvia could become involved in cutting-edge research and new treatment techniques. She went home for Christmas to Yorkton, enthusiasm and purpose beginning to flower and fruit.

There was one note of discord, though Sylvia didn't necessarily know it. Despite wholehearted support from the provincial government, the proposed betatron program had a hiccup. The atomic energy research leaders at Chalk River were not in favour of developing a betatron program alongside a civilian group such as the Saskatchewan Cancer Commission. General A.G.L. McNaughton, chair of the Atomic Energy Commission, demanded reassurance. Who would be in control of the betatron, the university or the commission? Divided authority leads to confusion, and the betatron was far too valuable to be left to the chance of a good working relationship. Harrington was quick to send reassurance in March 1947. Project direction for the betatron would be entirely in the hands of the physics department for nuclear research. Allan Blair, as head of the commission, also chimed in: "We are not at all sure how valuable or important the installation of a betatron would be to the actual treatment of cancer. All we do know on the basis of proven fact is that it might possibly be of some benefit in certain types of cases." As the physics team worked to secure permission, then funding, then housing for the betatron, its possible medical use as a treatment tool "was to be kept quiet."[20] The concerted Saskatchewan message became: get the machine to Saskatoon and *then* figure out how to use it for cancer research and treatment.

The oft-told story of Saskatchewan's purchase of the betatron outlines the visit by Harold Johns and Allan Blair to then Minister of Health and Premier of Saskatchewan Tommy Douglas. Without an appointment, the two men dropped in to see Douglas and tell him about the proposed betatron program. Since both were employees of the Cancer Commission—Blair as the head of the commission and Johns as physicist—they were immediately ushered in. They had so much already in place. Johns could offer a willing home in the physics department, support from the university with a room to house the machine, technical and academic support from physics and chemistry, as well as potential financial support from the atomic energy group at Chalk River. But they needed the province on board, too, with financial backing. A betatron was damn expensive, and postwar budgets had to be offset against a new government eager to make its mark in social engineering, including medicine. Douglas, without any consultation with finance or caucus, offered his carte blanche support.[21] The betatron program, even with its potential medical application for cancer treatment shrouded by a veil of polite lies, was a go.

In the meantime, Sylvia was on the road at a two-day meet at the University of Alberta in Edmonton in February. The University of Saskatchewan women's basketball team brought home an exciting final win, conquering the University of Alberta Pandas and the University of Manitoba Bisonettes in round robin play to bring home their coveted Cecil Race intervarsity trophy. In a wry note in *The Sheaf*, reporter and fellow Huskiette Shirley Nalevykin said that "hopes are high that Fedoruk will refrain from shooting from behind centre, and a special bulletin is being prepared to warn all players to duck for their lives in the event of Sylvia whooshing a pass down the floor."[22] Clearly, the hurling arm from javelin and ball was much in evidence.

As March moved into April and the university year ended, there were teas and suppers, farewells and final dances, in addition to serious studying for finals. Scholastics were a distraction from the end of the varsity basketball season. Coming back from their triumphant run in Edmonton and carrying the Cecil Race trophy, the team faltered in their own city league, ending the year with a loss to the Royals. No matter. Sylvia diverted her court energy into her studies and emerged at the end of the year at the top of her all-male elementary calculus class with an astonishing mark of 97 percent. English would drag in as her lowest mark, a mere 74, while German (80), chemistry (84), and physics (89) rounded out her year. At spring convocation 1947, she received one of twelve First Year Scholarships from the College of Arts and Science, finishing the year in third place, behind ties for both first and second.[23]

By then, change had come to her parents' household. Annie Fedoruk had always been particularly close to her younger sister, Mary Kulcheski. The Romaniuk family was an unofficial matriarchy, with their mother, Anastasia, at the head. As a result, there

3. RAMPAGING AMAZON

was a deep and loving connection and support system that on occasion tightened. As the war ended, Annie and Ted returned to Saskatchewan, where he once again took the helm of a rural school, this time one near Rhein called Kitzman. Then a major health scare rocked the two sisters: Mary was diagnosed with tuberculosis. At the time, it was a serious disease that required major changes in diet, exercise, and rest and usually included a lengthy stay in a sanatorium. Saskatchewan, long a leader in medical support, offered fully paid treatment for tuberculosis patients, and Mary spent time at Fort San, the sanitorium near Fort Qu'Appelle. Her two children, Dolores and Merylyn, moved in with Uncle Ted and Aunt Annie. On trips home from Saskatoon, Sylvia found not just cousins but almost siblings to spoil with treats and toys bought with scholarship dollars. Playing the role of big sister, she became close to Dolores and especially Merylyn.

Back at university in the fall of 1947, in her second year of a three-year B.A. degree,[24] Sylvia took intermediate calculus, a course of algebra and geometry, two physics courses (meteorology and climatology) both taught by B.W. Currie, organic chemistry, and a gruelling course in geology that involved a six-hour lab each week.

Sylvia became the women's arts and sciences representative on the campus newspaper *The Sheaf*, working in the sports department, writing articles for the coed sports pages tucked at the back of the paper. Sports writing requires an ability to brag and boast, cajole and entertain, with the occasional criticism tossed in for good measure. Sylvia soon learned not only to be present for athletics but also to think about how to tell the stories later to a wider audience. With wry twists, Sylvia herself captured much of her sports year, possibly writing under *The Sheaf* pen name of Effie Sinsmore, a play on Fedoruk as "eff."[25]

That fall Sylvia had a rival for the title of leading coed athlete: the tall, speedy, lithe Pat Lawson. National speed skating champ, provincial track champ, provincial junior tennis player, star swimmer and basketball player, Pat exploded onto the coed athletic scene. At the fall 1947 intervarsity track meet in Edmonton, Lawson and Fedoruk tied for points, each with thirteen. In fact, individually, they outscored the home team, which captured only seven points, and together they outscored the second-place Manitoba Bisonettes at twenty-two points. Pat took first in high jump and long jump and placed second in the 100-yard dash. Sylvia took first in javelin and softball throws and second to dominion champion (and fellow

Huskiette basketball teammate) Hazel Braithwaite in discus throw. Overall, the University of Saskatchewan smashed the competition, taking home a total of forty-three points and once again bringing home the coveted Rutherford trophy.[26] As track and field wound down, basketball geared up, with coach Ivan King putting his new team through their paces, getting ready to take on the Huskiettes' city competitors.[27]

On November 4, 1947, Dr. Harold Johns was the guest speaker at the Physics Club supper meeting. His topic was straightforward: "The Betatron Program at the University of Saskatchewan." He outlined to a large and interested audience the plan to bring a betatron machine to the university to study medical physics. Sylvia was a bright face and an eager set of ears in the audience. Built over the winter of 1947–48 by the Allis-Chalmers company in Milwaukee, Wisconsin, the betatron was due in Saskatoon sometime in 1948.[28] It could produce two different beams: an X-ray beam of 25 million electron volts and an electron beam of the same energy that could be brought outside the betatron using an external apparatus.[29] A betatron is designed to give electrons high energy. Electrons are accelerated inside a doughnut-shaped chamber creating a circular path with a magnetic field holding the electrons in orbit. The doughnuts were incredibly expensive, over $3,500 each. Once the electrons achieve the required velocity and then mass, they can be exploded out of the tube and directed at a target. "The bombardment produces X-rays of very high energy," noted *The Sheaf*.[30] The high-energy beams went more deeply into their target than regular X-rays, making them particularly important for cancer research and treatment. The ability of the betatron to penetrate body tissues, from three to five centimetres below the surface, while giving only a small dose to the outer skin tissues, made it a possible game-changer for medical physics. The rays were also considered "harder" than regular X-rays, with a shorter wavelength.[31] The betatron would be housed in a new annex being hastily built behind the physics department building and encased in concrete from three and a half to seven feet thick to minimize escaped radiation.[32]

While the physics department was preparing to create medical history, Sylvia was creating history in varsity sports. Basketball and track and field teammate Hazel Braithwaite was also a hockey player. In fact, she was the playing manager of the Huskiette hockey team. The team, under coach Elmer Berlie of the College of Engineering, had a problem. Braithwaite announced to *The Sheaf* that the team

3. RAMPAGING AMAZON

The Huskiette hockey team, 1948. Sylvia is in goalie gear on the right.

had a "dire need of a net-minder. Girls who are at all interested in playing between the gas pipes" were asked to find Hazel ASAP.[33] Maybe she took a good look at Sylvia's toughness and strength and talked Sylvia into the position. Perhaps Sylvia, watching Hazel take on two varsity sports *at the same time*, decided that whatever Hazel could do she could do too. Certainly, hockey was a new sport for her, and friends would later wonder if Sylvia could even skate. Certainly, the sports reporters expected not hockey but a "standout comedy feature." But Sylvia's competitive spirit rose to the occasion. When the Huskiettes opened their season on December 6, 1947, Sylvia—hampered by goalie pads and glove and stick and sliding out from the bench on wobbly skates—was between those pipes.[34]

The first opponent in the Saskatchewan Women's Hockey League was the Regina UCT Pats, and one could buy a ticket for the evening for a mere twenty-five cents at the Saskatoon Arena, which held 1,500 screaming and cheering fans in the stands. The game was described as scrambly and disorganized, but the girls made up for it with enthusiasm. Sylvia foiled a Pats breakaway and "played a nice game in goal" even though it was her first time.[35]

Winning was starting to come easily. The Huskiette basketball team, still stinging from losses to the Saskatoon Royals the year before, were ready for action. They came out on fire the first week of December, crushing both the Royals and the Elkettes. The sad state of the basketball courts at the university left them cold, however; it was best to watch the games at one of the local collegiates rather than on campus.[36] The basketball team travelled more in 1947–48, such as to Regina, where they played the Regina College Cougettes. The feisty Huskiette team sported an assortment of injuries: floor burns, one girl "favouring her magnum rearum," and Sylvia presenting "a battered nose and two distorted knees."[37] Since she went hard with two travelling teams for different sports, it's impossible to know which contributed more to her assortment of bruises or which took the majority of her time. Between games, practices, and travel, it's something of a miracle that Sylvia had any time left for studies.

As spring arrived, the hoopster team partnered with the coed curling and fencing teams to organize a massive intervarsity sports weekend, hosted by the University of Saskatchewan. For seventy-five cents, students could come out to watch curling, basketball, and fencing and then take in the huge Saturday night dance at the stadium swaying to Gordon King's varsity orchestra. With the campus still overrun with returned soldiers earning degrees, the ratio of men to women remained a problem. In one fell swoop, the coed sports weekend aimed to even the balance, bringing women from Alberta and Manitoba to round out the numbers—and compete in sports. In fact, so many women were coming that the Women's Athletic Board was worried. Would the women outnumber the men? Not to worry, the men declared. They were ready to do their part and come out, to dance and have a great weekend with their coed varsity cohorts. *The Sheaf* noted, with a touch of wry humour, "with all the talk about the part women should play in varsity life, the Saskatchewan gals are out to prove that the women's place is not in the kitchen."[38] When the weekend was finished, Sylvia and the Huskiette squad had once more brought home the Cecil Race trophy as the top team in western Canadian intervarsity basketball.[39]

Sylvia had also put her name in for the 1948–49 Student Council. The nominating committee commented that her stellar curricular record at the University of Saskatchewan since arriving in 1946 lined up well with her extracurricular activities—track and field, basketball, and now hockey, including both team and personal successes. Sylvia had worked for *The Sheaf* as a coed sports reporter and general journalist, and she served as both public relations officer and business manager for the Women's Athletic Board prior to her nomination as

3. RAMPAGING AMAZON

president. "She has proven that she can devote much of her time to many extracurricular activities and still maintain a high scholastic standing."⁴⁰

The early March elections might have offered an exciting evening of campus politics, but Sylvia Fedoruk couldn't wait around for the votes to be counted. She was in her alternate Friday space between the posts of the Huskiette hockey squad's goal at Rutherford Rink. In fact, Sylvia was geared up and just about ready to skate out to face the

Sylvia Fedoruk

Caricature of Sylvia from the 1947–48 Mohyla student yearbook.

also-undefeated team from Birch Hills when the news came of her win as the Women's Athletic Board representative on the Student Council. With no time to celebrate other than an awkward hug over her goalie gear, Fedoruk played her usual stellar game. After a scruffy battle with plenty of penalties for the green and white, the teams drew to a tie. The game, with an 8 p.m. puck drop, finished in time for the team and their many fans to skip over to The Ward-Heeler's Ball at the Cavern, a favourite pub for the varsity crowd. After what was no doubt a night somewhat short of sleep, Sylvia was in top form at the King George Hotel for the annual Women's Athletic Board luncheon on Saturday, a seventy-five-cent feast, in her new role as president-elect for the 1948–49 year. Her speech, reprinted in *The Sheaf*, said with glee that, "branded as a nest of rampaging Amazons, Saskatchewan can look to more fields to conquer."⁴¹ Sylvia, as the new coed president, looked ahead to adding—in a new gymnasium—badminton, archery, and volleyball to the slate of sports already on offer.

Despite a fast-paced winter, no doubt Sylvia watched with interest the addition being built at the back of the physics department building. New labs, darkrooms, and other rooms nested around the main addition, a large, thickly built room to house the university's new betatron unit. With support from the Atomic Energy Control Board, the cross-faculty team of Harrington, Haslam, Katz, and Johns aimed to start their research programs in the summer of 1948.[42] Sylvia wasn't quite ready to join them. Writing to her parents on March 17, she let them know that she would be staying on in Saskatoon for the summer, playing ball with the Hub City Ramblers, and working for the provincial government's new crown corporation, Saskatchewan Government Telephones. With an office job, "working an adding machine and typing," Sylvia would finally put her grade nine typing course to professional use. The job was five days a week, 37.5 hours, with a pay of ninety-five dollars per month. Sylvia got the job by being "connected playing ball and stuff I guess." She'd stay on at Mohyla through the summer, as a working student, and continue her B.A. in the fall.[43] She finished off the school year with her usual respectable marks in the high 80s, steady As in geology and organic chemistry, and over 90 percent in both math courses.

By July, Sylvia was a known hitter for the Saskatoon Ramblers. She joined an all-star team in the midst of success. The Ramblers had won back-to-back western Canadian women's softball crowns in 1946 and 1947, with Gil Strumm as their head coach. Sylvia had to show all her power and agility to make the team that spring. It was led by hurler Muriel Coben, whose portfolio included a year with the South Bend White Sox in the All-American Girls Professional Baseball League. Sylvia brought her bat, her infielding skill, and her mouth to every game. Depending on who was playing, she sometimes fielded at first base, sometimes at shortstop, sometimes at third. That year the Ramblers took down their Regina rivals, the Kappy Kaplan Regina Bombers, in a series of exhibition games that saw Sylvia smash three of four times at bat, including a home run. The Ramblers won the provincials to make a return run for the western title; however, despite Sylvia once again slugging some balls and racing the bases, the team was defeated by the Calgary Alexandras in a best-of-three series.[44]

When the Ramblers failed to capture the western title in the summer of 1948, Sylvia Fedoruk and her co-Rambler softball player and good friend Dorothy (Dot) George decided to have an adventure. With a few days clear in their ball schedule and some coordinated time off work, the two went fishing. Although Saskatoon does have a river running through it, it is not a fishing hotspot. Real fishing, the girls knew, could be found up north, way up north. Neither girl had a car; in fact, Sylvia had never driven one. Unruffled by

3. RAMPAGING AMAZON

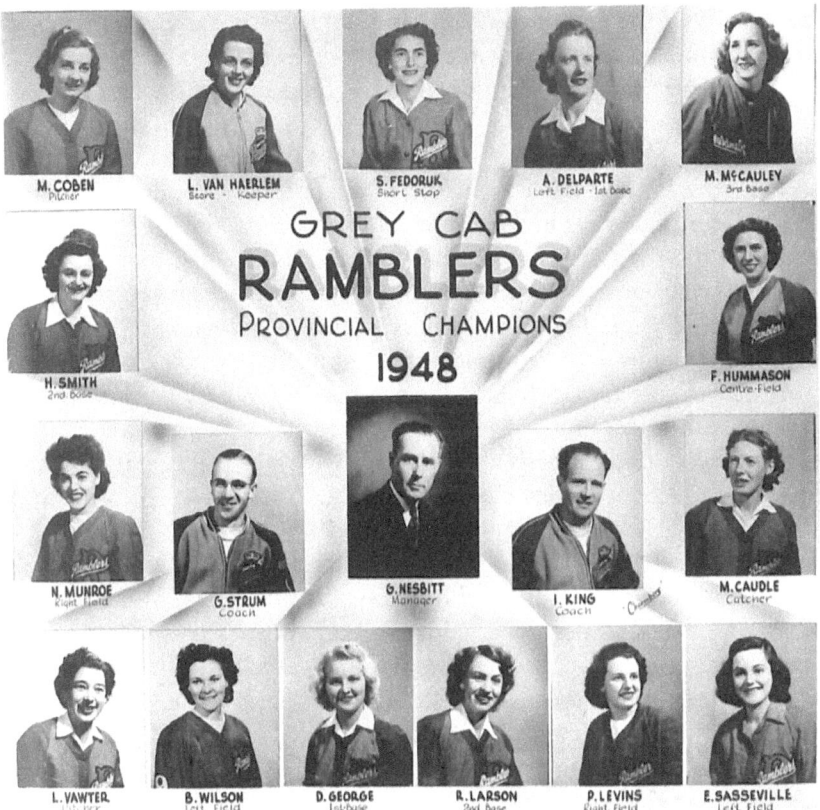

The Grey Cab Ramblers, 1948.

this minor irritation, the two girls packed rucksacks and stuck out their thumbs to hitchhike their way from Saskatoon north through Prince Albert and Waskesiu. That proved to be easy. Summer traffic to Waskesiu was steady, and the girls made great time. After that, though, things became rough. As they were walking toward Montreal Lake, evening began to fall hard. In the middle of the boreal forest, with no vehicles in sight and perhaps thoughts of coyotes or even wolves stirring their imaginations, the two girls stood looking at each other on a rather desolate stretch of road. Luck came around the corner in the form of a panel truck. The driver at first went past but stopped and backed up. Headed north to La Ronge, he gave the two grateful girls a lift. What followed was a week of excellent fishing, pulling in hungry jackfish and monstrous lake trout. At the end of the week, the same Good Samaritan truck driver happened to come by and trundle them back south.[45]

Sylvia was hooked. The northern fishing adventure had been such a success that the two women made a fishing trip an annual tradition. For the rest of her life, as she was able and had time, as soon as the ice had left the northern lakes, Sylvia would go north to fish. Her favourites included the La Ronge area, fishing the main lake and nearby lakes such as Besnard and Nemeiben, but by the 1960s Sylvia would book fly-in fishing trips to places more remote. As a student, though, she had limits to both her time and her budget. Every penny counted, and scholarship money, generous as it was, had to pay for Mohyla residence fees, university tuition, and essentials. Fishing drew out her ingenuity, hence the carefree plan to hitchhike. Later, her budget enlarged by a professional salary, Sylvia would happily pay the asking price to have a week of calm waters, biting fish, and convivial evenings.

The fall of 1948, Sylvia's last year for her Bachelor of Arts degree, began with less of a bang than her previous two years. Intervarsity track and field competition against the Universities of Alberta and Manitoba, once the leadoff to the year, had been cancelled, though the University of Saskatchewan track and field team was hotter than ever. With practices most afternoons, the team still drew a large cohort of willing tryouts and veterans. Sylvia continued with just two of her favourite events, ball throw and javelin, alongside fellow athletes Pat Lawson and Betty Wilson, competitors in jumping and running. The withdrawal and contraction of the track and field team from intervarsity competition indicated a general malaise at the university. Highly anticipated and expected work on the new university hospital and medical facilities had been stopped cold, mid-build. The new gymnasium and pool, announced with much fanfare in the spring of 1948, were little more than a concrete hole in the ground. Enrolment had declined drastically by about 500 regular students despite the clear presence of veterans still on campus.[46] Nonetheless, Sylvia entered her last bachelor's year with even more determination as the Huskiette basketball team kicked off tryouts and practices in September, weeks earlier than ever before.[47] Practising twice a week for two hours at a time—Saturdays at noon and Monday evenings—the team aimed for a high standing.

The betatron was finally installed in its new underground facility. Harold Johns was busy building a crew and feverishly outlining

3. RAMPAGING AMAZON

The betatron at the University of Saskatchewan.

a research program to bring the machine to full productive use. It was one thing to get the machine; it was quite another to become adept at using it, testing its abilities and limits thoroughly, and building various devices to utilize its possibilities. One of those developments was the creation of lead plugs to contain and aim the radiation; another was the use of a water phantom to test the depth of the dose. Both projects would lay the groundwork for later work on cobalt-60, just over the research horizon for Johns.

Sylvia's final year of her B.A. was more rounded academically than her second year, though it cost more: tuition had increased sharply, from $90 to $125, for one year of arts and science. Nonetheless, Sylvia's scholarships and summer work for Saskatchewan Government Telephones eased the financial burden. Courses in her last year included the History of Ideas, taught by University of Saskatchewan President J.S. Thomson. A requirement for Type C Math and Science majors, this course should be left to the third year of studies, the university calendar gently suggested. Sylvia also took Political Economics A with well-known Saskatchewan economist V.C. Fowke. These two courses were balanced by three math and three physics courses, including Functions of a Complex Variable, Differential Equations, and Boundary Value Problems, alongside The Principles of Radio, Experimental Heat, and Thermodynamics. All three of her physics courses were taught by Professor C.A. Mackay. Sylvia's course load showed no particular predilection for nuclear or medical physics—her training, in a B.A. course, was much more general. Specialization was yet to come.

By the time the Huskiette basketball team pounded the gym floor during league play, they had honed their game to a fine point. Using a strong zone defence and excellent guarding (with a contingent number of fouls), the Huskiettes were a team that believed the best offence was a good defence. In their opening game of the 1948–49 season, sporting one white and one green sock each, the team trounced the Orphanettes. Their only regret? That there was not enough room in the gymnasium to seat all of their fans.[48] As the year went on, it seemed that little could stop the team except their own "ragged" play if they became tired or the many fouls that they sometimes racked up. Aggressive but still mostly disciplined, the female hoopsters dominated the court.

They had reason to be disciplined. Coach Ivan King—in a move that today's coaches would never get away with—created an exclusive club for his team. It wasn't a club that any of the squad wanted to be in. To be presented with a badge for the Little Stinkers club meant that you had flubbed—and flubbed badly—either in a game or during practice. A missed pass, a trip, a failed block, a missed easy layup, a dead ball, any of them and more could bring on the unwanted prize: until the next practice or game, the singled-out unfortunate was forced to wear a small skunk crest on her uniform or a larger one smack in the middle of her back. Even *The Sheaf* noted with concern, "to you this may seem funny, but to the Huskiettes it is a very serious matter cause if any one of them manages by any miserable trick of fate to rack up three little stinkers, they are quickly given their walking papers."[49] The reporter, watching the women practise with something akin to awe, started to wonder, how would this team stack up against the Huskies men's basketball team? And Sylvia, that "shifty" guard, seemed to be everywhere at once, defending the basket with vigour. She and Lydia Yaremchuk acted as co-captains for the year, once more bringing home the Cecil Race intervarsity trophy and capping the season by breaking the seventy-point barrier at a game in Regina.

3. RAMPAGING AMAZON

Sylvia was front and centre in February 1949 as the physics department showcased the betatron in an open house to the entire campus community. Despite pretending otherwise to those at Chalk River, the Saskatoon crew was most excited by the machine's new potential application in treating cancer.[50] In fact, after months of delicate calibration and testing, including devising the new lead plugs, the Saskatchewan Cancer Commission was gearing up to allow Harold Johns and his new betatron staff to start treating cancer patients. In March, the first patient was selected for treatment. Unfortunately, the experimental nature of the betatron and its unproven role in cancer treatment dictated its use only as a last resort. The first patient chosen was very sick with an aggressive, end-stage cancer too deep for a successful operation. The doctors and technicians lacked confidence. Fourteen smaller dose treatments over a number of days brought no improvement to the patient, and she succumbed to the disease. They later wondered whether a higher dose might have helped more. The team continued with treatments on other patients, gradually accumulating knowledge of the machine and its power and in time increasing the per-treatment doses and their level of confidence.[51]

While Johns and the crew initiated clinical betatron applications, Sylvia had a quieter year on the sports front. She wasn't netminding for the coed hockey team or travelling around the province in blizzard conditions on a cold train to play in even colder arenas. But the Women's Athletic Board president had managed to bring in a sport from her Windsor days: volleyball. It was on the radar since 1946, and the Huskiettes pulled together a team late in 1948. Sylvia happily dropped hockey for a chance to bump, set, and spike. The new team did well in the intervarsity field, winning against the University of Alberta to capture the title. From today's perspective, an intervarsity championship between two universities that happen to be in different provinces carries much less weight than today's all-out national championships, but Sylvia was fortunate to be at the beginning of the intervarsity era, when multi-province championships were becoming part of the sports landscape. Today no one would expect a varsity athlete to compete and win in multiple sports with such ease, but athletes then were allowed such leeway and opportunity.

Convocation 1949 saw Sylvia haul in a proverbial bushel basket of accolades and awards. Her family arrived to celebrate her

Sylvia's convocation, spring 1949. Left to right: Dolores Kulcheski, Mary Kulcheski, Merylyn Kulcheski, Sylvia, John Romaniuk, Annie Fedoruk.

three-year Bachelor of Arts with a major in physics. Ted and Annie, with Dolores and Merylyn and Annie's sister Mary, along with Sylvia's grandparents, arrived in high style. All the girls got new dresses, Sylvia a long gown appropriate for the occasion. The family drove on dicey gravel roads all the way from Yorkton to Saskatoon, where they stayed in hotels and dined out for every meal—extravagances paid for with great pride. As Merylyn later recalled, "I remember the ceremony and wondered why my aunt was crying. . . . There was nobody sick."[52] Annie would have been crying and bursting with parental happiness. Sylvia was the first in their extended family to attend university, and the path to convocation had started when Annie had marched boldly and angrily down the halls of stately Walkerville Collegiate in Windsor and insisted that her daughter be put in the stream for university entrance. Perhaps Annie's own lost dream of schooling was fulfilled in part when Sylvia crossed the convocation stage.

3. RAMPAGING AMAZON

And cross it she did, not just once, to receive her degree, but "again and again and again!" remembered Merylyn.[53] At graduation, Sylvia earned the Copeland Scholarship presented to the top physics student, the Governor General's Gold Medal presented to the top overall student of the year, and the Spirit of Youth Award.[54] Of these awards, it's hard to say which one gave Sylvia the most pride and pleasure, but the Spirit of Youth Award best reflected her unique combination of athletic and academic talents. It has been noted often that she would have been a major contender for a Rhodes Scholarship to study at Oxford University—but at the time these scholarships were not offered to women.

Sylvia accepted a summer research position with the betatron program, funding coming from a research grant from the Canadian Cancer Association. The position carried a stipend of $100 per month for five months, starting after exams and continuing until her honours classes started in the fall.[55] Despite a cold response from the Atomic Energy Control Board and others at Chalk River to using the betatron for cancer treatment, its ability to penetrate to and radiate deep-seated tumours became its primary use.

Sylvia was a research associate when the betatron team made their first major breakthrough in the summer of 1949. One patient, a seventy-one-year-old shoemaker from Prince Albert, had a deep-seated tumour in his bowels, pushing against his spine. After consultations at both the Saskatoon Cancer Clinic and the Mayo Clinic in Rochester, Minnesota, his prognosis was bleak. As a last measure, Dr. T.A. Watson, the new director of the Saskatchewan Cancer Commission following the untimely death of Allan Blair, suggested that they try the betatron. The shoemaker agreed. In July 1949, he was brought to the north entrance of the physics department annex and then to the betatron room. Lying down on the treatment bed, he looked up to a huge mirror attached to the ceiling, which allowed the doctor, nurse, and technicians to see the patient while they were in a separate room—the machine was so large that direct viewing was impossible. Then they turned the machine on. "The building was rocked by a deafening electrical whirring,"[56] but of course the patient felt nothing. Radiation, even that caused by the betatron, cannot be felt. Each day for four days, they repeated the procedure: the patient was brought from the cancer clinic to the back door of the physics department building; down the steps and around the corner to the betatron room; laid down on the treatment bed; placed in the precise position required for best treatment, using a new position each time to allow the radiation to attack the tumour from all angles; then left alone with the ugly, squat, loud machine as it whirred electrons around the doughnut and sent them deep into his body. No improvement at first. But on the fifth day, something happened. The knot of cancer entangling his bowels and pushing on his spine released. He could feel it. For the first time in months, the patient could stand straighter, walk more easily. They continued the treatment for a total of fourteen days, and by the end the cancer had visibly diminished to less than one-fifth its original size. It wasn't a cure, but the treatment clearly bought two things for the patient: time and a better quality of life.[57]

Despite its abilities, the betatron had too many detractions. First, General McNaughton and the AECB had insisted that the machine be housed in the physics department building, but that created a logistical nightmare. Patients to be treated had to have cancer far enough advanced to require drastic and experimental measures, but they still had to be relatively able-bodied. Those kinds of patients were hard to come by. Second, they had to come by car or ambulance with a nurse and a driver and sometimes an ambulance attendant and a doctor, which increased treatment costs. Third, the machine was so large and bulky that placing patients properly to achieve the most effective treatment was difficult. The machine had little to no manoeuvrability. Fourth, the betatron itself, expensive enough to buy, was also expensive to operate. Each doughnut could be used multiple times but not indefinitely. A cost breakdown showed that each treatment cost about twenty-five dollars just for the betatron, not including transfer or personnel costs, which mounted.

Even with its many drawbacks, the betatron offered the Saskatoon team their first concerted use of high-voltage treatment designed for deep-seated tumours. They had calibrated the betatron to exacting standards, built and used a water phantom to measure the depth of the dose, created lead plugs to control and direct the energy beams, and had some idea of the needs of patients in a clinical treatment setting. These experiences proved to be invaluable as the team—technicians, research assistants, professors, and the Cancer Commission—turned their sights to cobalt-60. In many ways, it's sad that the story of the betatron has been overshadowed and all too often confused by that of cobalt-60. There is no way that the cobalt-60 team would have achieved international success without first learning to work with

3. RAMPAGING AMAZON

the betatron, even if the design and structure of the two machines were so different. The betatron was the groundbreaking scientific precursor to later world-shaking revelations.

Sylvia Fedoruk's three years spent completing her B.A. in physics occurred at a special time in the history of the University of Saskatchewan. Among the immediate postwar cohort of 1946, she was part of an impressive group of keen, intelligent students who together pushed and pulled each other up. Even so, in her first-year physics class with Harold Johns, Sylvia stood out. She didn't take another class with him during her degree, and it's a wonder that he remembered her. Nonetheless, when the time came to bring in promising future honours and graduate students to work on the betatron and the larger cancer research program, Johns pointed directly at Sylvia. His mentorship proved to be a beacon as she successfully joined the research team. By August 1949, as Sylvia was finishing her first summer as a research student with the betatron, the future was changing. Johns had requested a baked source of cobalt-60 from Chalk River to be used to treat those suffering from cancer. At his elbow, waiting eagerly to enter this new area of research, was Sylvia Fedoruk.[58]

4. COBALT BOMB

COBALT WAS THE "GREEDY PIG IN THE LITTER." DR. Harold Johns and his colleagues in the physics department at the University of Saskatchewan, including Sylvia Fedoruk, took on the task of designing the "presentation" of cobalt to the Chalk River, Ontario, plant. All of this was new ground. What size, shape, and weight of cobalt would best absorb radiation? "A miscalculation could mean 'cold' cobalt where the neutrons failed to penetrate."[1] The team designed a theoretical approach: cobalt pressed into a series of thin disks each about the thickness of a quarter or even thinner, that were then stacked together.[2] Nickel-plated and welded into metal capsules, each nucleus of cobalt-59 was expected to absorb an extra neutron while in the intense neutron radiation field inside the reactor. At Chalk River, in the ZEEP (Zero Energy Experimental Pile), three packages of cobalt-59 were placed into the NRX (National Research Experimental) reactor.[3] With its heavy-water system to slow and control the atomic chain reaction, ZEEP was the only atomic energy reactor in the world capable of making cobalt-60. In essence, cobalt-59 would absorb the radioactivity of the uranium until saturated, allowing the cobalt to "borrow" enough violence to destroy cancer tumours.[4] These capsules were expected to "cook" for up to five years to become the unstable and radioactive cobalt-60.

They didn't need five years. The Saskatchewan design proved to be so successful that the cobalt-59 discs "devoured so much of the uranium's output of atomic power" that other elements in the

ZEEP pile were "starved" and took much longer to activate than expected. The disc design was a resounding success.[5] The radioisotope produced in this process, intended for radiation therapy, gave off much more radiation as it decayed (emitting gamma radiation, the kind needed for therapeutic use) than did regular radium. The Canadian heavy-water system could "produce cobalt-60 about 100 times stronger than radium, and faster and in greater amounts than any other reactor."[6] The possibilities for cancer therapy were enormous. The greedy pig was welcome.

Radiotherapy in the mid-1940s was in its infancy, but both physicists and doctors already knew its limits. First, the depth dose, about ten centimetres on a 400 kVp X-ray machine, was considered woefully inadequate. Only the skinniest patients would have a hope of proper treatment; anyone heavy-set or obese could not be treated. Second, the rate of the dose was very slow. A patient had to remain still for at least half an hour, a nearly impossible feat, to get the required radiation to eradicate a tumour. Physicists around the world worked hard to find a way to create a radiation beam that penetrated farther and worked faster. One slight improvement came with the use of tin, copper, and aluminum filters, which increased the dosage rate on X-ray machines but not the penetrating power.

These dosage rate and penetration inadequacies were part of the reason that Professor Mayneord and others who knew what was happening at Chalk River were so excited by the possibilities of cobalt-60. As Johns later noted, it could produce about ten times the radiation, at about ten times the rate, from a unit a quarter of the size of the 250 kVp and 400 kVp machines.[7] The body absorbed cobalt rays differently too. In regular X-rays, bone and cartilage tended to suck up more radiation, which made it therapeutically dangerous. Cobalt rays were absorbed more equally by bones, cartilage, and other tissue, including less skin damage. Radiation sickness was less likely for the patient. Cobalt-60 produces more gamma rays, and fewer beta rays, than radium. Since gamma rays were the best curative rays, this point mattered. Finally, cost was always a concern. There was more cobalt than radium available, and Canada had the technology at Chalk River to turn cobalt into something medically significant at far less cost. "Cobalt worth one cent does the work of radium worth sixty-four dollars."[8]

In a world still reeling from the social, cultural, and psychological effects of the two bombs dropped on Hiroshima and Nagasaki in Japan, people wanted to know whether this new irradiated cobalt

4. COBALT BOMB

was really dangerous. Yes, it was. The small stacks of thin discs could be held in the palm of a hand—but if you did you'd be dead within minutes if not seconds.[9] Nonetheless, given its potential, it was time to find a way to successfully harness cobalt's possibilities.

In Saskatoon, Johns and his team were hard at work. For Sylvia, the requirements to study history, economics, and German, let alone English, were finished. Now it was all physics, all the time. In the winter of 1949–50, she took a total of eight courses in physics. Wave, Motion, and Acoustics was a lecture half-class with Professor W. Petrie that gave an introduction to vibration motion as the basis for sound and light. Theory of Measurements with R.N.H. Haslam included work on the interpretation of experimental data. In Optics with B.W. Currie, a lecture class with a four-hour lab each week, Sylvia learned the theory and use of optical instruments. Other classes were Spectroscopy with Currie and a combination lab-lecture class on Mechanics, Sound, and Light with L. Katz. Sylvia's final three courses of the year included Introduction to Quantum Mechanics with Haslam; Atomic Spectra and Atomic Structure, a master's-level course about multiplet and line structures of electron configurations with Petrie; and finally another master's-level course with Johns on X-rays in theory and experiment, X-ray scattering, and high-energy X-rays, including a detailed discussion of the betatron and other applications for medical physics. Her courses were a perfect complement to her work on the betatron team gearing up for cobalt-60.

Despite the growing intensity of her physics studies, Sylvia continued playing basketball. Following three wildly successful undergraduate years, including three years garnering the Cecil Race intervarsity championship trophy, the Huskiette basketball squad were "angels" on the University of Saskatchewan campus. "As basketball queens, these girls excel."[10] No doubt driven to let off some steam away from the physics labs, Sylvia let loose on the court. "Syl Fedoruk brought some comedy into the picture when, while checking a Royal, she stuck out her tongue, so surprising her opponent that the girl dropped the ball."[11]

Despite the joy in sports, Sylvia's main goal was to finish her honours program and go on to do a master's degree in physics. Studies and plans for the cobalt-60 unit were well under way, and the end of the 1949–50 year saw the Huskiette squad again win the Cecil Race trophy in intervarsity basketball. Sylvia carried her load of athletics and academics with ease. She dominated physics

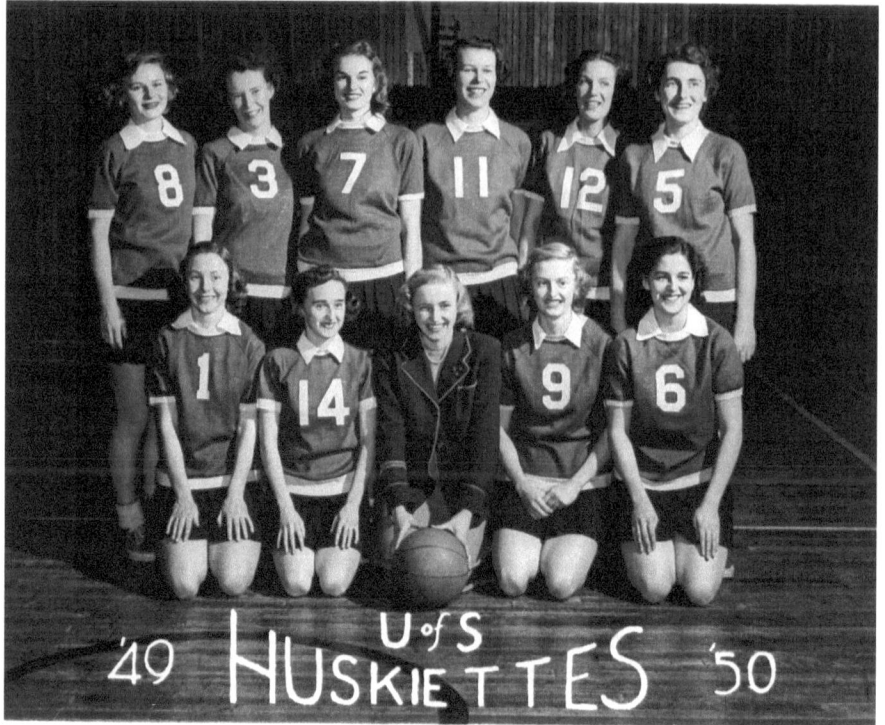

1949–50 Huskiettes basketball team. Sylvia is standing at far right.

courses, with marks ranging from 70 percent in Mechanics, Sound, and Light to 90 percent in Theory of Measurement, giving her an average of 82 percent and earning her high honours at the spring convocation with her four-year B.A. honours. In the summer of 1950, Sylvia didn't pause. As in the previous year, she accepted a research associate position with the university, splitting her time on research projects for the betatron and preparatory work for the incoming cobalt-60.

In her off time, Sylvia could be found with friends, riding her bike back and forth to Mohyla Institute, and going farther afield. She continued playing her style of loud infield summer ball with the Ramblers for the next several summers, throughout university and into her early professional career. In the summer of 1949, an exhibition game against the Harlem Queens travelling African American girls' softball team "overflowed the bleachers and nearly circled the playing field" at Cairns Field in Saskatoon.[12] The Queens had their usual travelling lineup, whereas Saskatoon fielded three of its

4. COBALT BOMB

teams—the Ramblers, the Clippers, and the Spartans—for three innings each. The Ramblers went first, and Muriel Coben struck out four and gave up only one infield bunt, but an error accounted for a run, and Saskatoon was down 1–0 after the first three innings. The Clippers took over and, despite being in last place in the Saskatoon league, had a tremendous three innings, with three runs and a pitching shutout, accounting for a 3–1 lead going into the top of the seventh inning, when the Spartans took over. Three hits and two errors led to three runs, and the game, a nail-biter with lots of action, ended with Saskatoon on the losing side. Nonetheless, it was "a fine evening's entertainment for the largest women's softball crowd" that Cairns Field hosted that year.[13] Despite the Ramblers' comparatively poorer showing against Harlem, the team was undefeated in round robin play. Yet it didn't clinch the provincial title.

Being around Cairns Field on sultry summer nights, Sylvia rubbed shoulders with everyone from scrubby local athletes to the likes of Gordie Howe, Saskatchewan's famous hockey icon. Howe took his salary from the Detroit Red Wings but spent his summers in Saskatoon playing ball for the Saskatoon Gems with holidays at Waskesiu Lake in Prince Albert National Park, where he regularly played in the Lobstick golf tournament. Howe was no pushover either. Despite a strict "no ball" warning telegram from his hockey boss, Jack Adams, owner of the Red Wings, Howe wasn't about to listen.[14] Saskatoon was a long way from Detroit, and Howe would regularly dust off his glove and join games despite the risks. Like Sylvia, he was an infielder, playing either first or third base. When he wasn't playing, he was a reliable umpire if one was needed. Cairns Field was such a central location that Howe purchased a house right across the road from the ballpark for his dad.[15]

Sylvia also spent some of her summer sunshine hours developing a new athletic passion: golf. Golf courses around Saskatoon were just being developed, and she took advantage of these early testing grounds and unconventional fairways. At a 1975 speech at the Holiday Park Ladies Golf Club, Sylvia regaled the audience with early memories of Saskatoon links. "Actually I too was a golfer at one time, my own career tightly linked to Holiday Park—at least the terrain that is presently called Holiday Park." In the late 1940s and into 1950, Sylvia noted, "the course was a favourite for me. Pedal my bicycle from Main and Victoria [the Mohyla residence] over to Ave H to pick up my friend Hazel [Braithwaite] and off we'd go out to the Sanitorium sand dunes for yet another tramp through the uncut fairways for a

63

Sylvia golfing, c. 1949.

game of golf."[16] In fact, the Holiday Park golf course wasn't officially opened until June 27, 1962, more than ten years after Sylvia and Hazel found it to be an open and appealing place to practise tee-offs, swings, and rambles with clubs.

On campus, Sylvia was a lab rat. Creating cobalt-60 from the discs of cobalt-59 was the first step, and the Saskatchewan team's solution seemed to be working at Chalk River. But the next part of the cobalt-60 project was even more critical. How would physicists and radiotherapists harness and direct that radiation safely to treat cancer? Unlike the betatron, which was designed and manufactured elsewhere and came to the University of Saskatchewan ready to be put to use, there was no machine anywhere in the world designed to handle cobalt-60, or to measure its output radiation beams, or to harness and direct its power effectively. Harold Johns set his team of colleagues and graduate students, including Sylvia Fedoruk, to work.

Johns first needed permission from the university, both to pursue cobalt-60 and to access much-needed funds to plan and build the machine, and the room, to house and direct the radiation. Unlike the betatron, purchased by the university with the blessing of Tommy Douglas for the exorbitant cost of $140,000 (not including the expense to build an annex to the physics department building to house the massive machine), Johns calculated that between $2,500 and $7,000 would cover the costs of construction of a therapy unit. The costs to house the unit could be factored into the new university hospital being built. Compared with the betatron, $7,000 was a paltry sum, and assent was soon given. Johns and his graduate student Lloyd Bates set out to design a therapy unit for the cobalt "bomb."

Unlike the unwieldy betatron, large and designed *first* to accelerate electrons to *then* be used potentially for the treatment of cancer, the cobalt-60 unit was designed specifically for cancer therapy in a clinical setting. As such, it had to be easily usable, nimble, and movable yet sturdy enough to handle

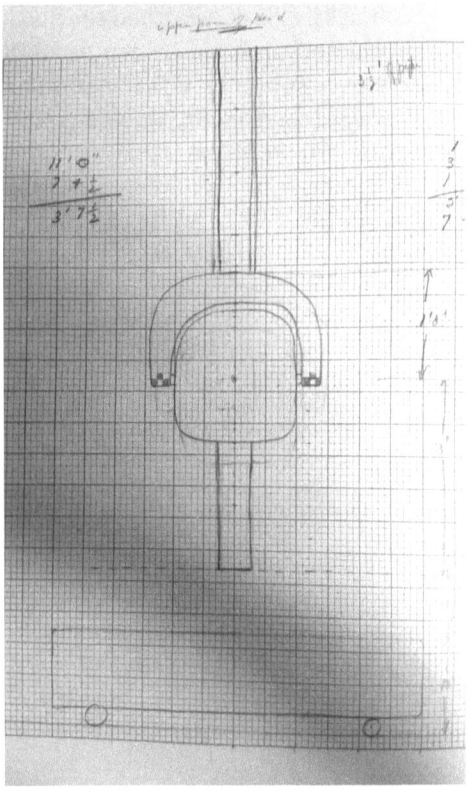

An early drawing of the cobalt-60 treatment head, showing measurements and a table underneath, from one of Sylvia's physics notebooks.

a bit of daily wear and tear. The team's experience with the betatron—unwieldy and awkward—came into play. There are early copies of the blueprints for the cobalt-60 treatment head in Sylvia Fedoruk's files in the University of Saskatchewan Archives. They show a head mounted on a u-shaped unit fixed on a track hanging from the ceiling. This mount allowed the unit to lift, lower, and move the heavy treatment head left and right, with a counterweight at the end of a cable in the next room to help balance and move the head. Bates and Fedoruk, among others, drew countless early and then more sophisticated designs as the team talked their way through the design process and discussed what would be the most helpful. Eventually, it was time to turn paper dreams into nuts-and-bolts reality.

Luckily, Saskatoon had the plucky and inventive Johnny MacKay, proprietor of Acme Machine and Electric Company. The grandson of a spinning wheel manufacturer and born near Scotsburn, Nova Scotia, MacKay took a course in machining in Trenton, Nova Scotia. He came west in the booming 1920s and took a position with John East Iron Works in Saskatoon. Six years later he struck out on his own, and by the time Johns came calling MacKay had built a roaring business. He was a renaissance man, by day a welder and fabricator, by night a clarinetist with the Saskatoon Symphony Orchestra, in which his wife performed as a cellist.

MacKay and his staff of six people carried on more traditional machinist work, as might be expected in a rural and agriculturally dominated province, helping farmers to repair and replace much-needed tractor, threshing machine, and, by the late 1940s, newfangled combine parts. But at night MacKay could be found at the university campus taking engineering calculus and drafting. He first came to the attention of Johns when MacKay came on board to help the physics department install the technical apparatus for the massive betatron. When Johns knew that the only way to harness the power of cobalt-60 was to design and build a prototype therapy unit, he naturally turned to the cool head and nimble hands of MacKay.[17] It was a partnership that proved to be successful beyond all hope. The cobalt unit was locally designed and built, and when finished the cobalt-60 bomb was used to treat and save thousands of Saskatchewan people through its many years of use. In fact, MacKay was able to capitalize on Acme Machine and Electric's experience. After the roaring success of the original cobalt-60 machine, Saskatoon became the manufacturing home of successive machines, each "a miracle of precision."[18]

While the cobalt-60 unit was on the design table and shunted around as parts and pieces in Johnny MacKay's Avenue A shop, the university had a different problem to solve. With the much larger radiation exposure of cobalt-60, campus engineers had to design and build a special room for the unit as part of the new hospital going up on the riverbank. Because of the potentially lethal exposure levels of the radiation, a room with concrete walls, lined with lead, was constructed in the cancer clinic wing on the ground floor of the new University of Saskatchewan hospital. A lead-shielded door led to the control room, behind an observation window with ten-inch-thick glass. No one except the patient could be in the room while the cobalt-60 gamma rays were bombarding the cancer; the

4. COBALT BOMB

machine had to be engineered to respond to remote control. Yet the room was on the ground floor, and there was a window. How would the engineers solve the problem of stray radiation? The simple solution was the most expedient: the construction crew built the laundry building a short distance away, and its walls would absorb the small amount of radiation that would go through the window when the cobalt-60 machine was in use. With "the greedy pig" soaking up radiation in Chalk River, the Saskatoon construction crews raced the clock.

In the summer of 1950, Sylvia was formally accepted into the master's degree program for physics, settling into her research. Johns supported her to apply for a scholarship through the Canadian Cancer Society, which she put to good use. Staying in residence at Mohyla Institute meant that Sylvia had to spend less time on domestic chores, which freed time for both physics and continued sports.[19] Although supportive, Johns—nicknamed The Whip by his graduate students—had stringent rules. The grad students were expected to produce work—even work at the master's level—exemplary enough to be accepted by a major international science journal. The stakes were high.[20]

The team at the University of Saskatchewan included graduate students such as Sylvia Fedoruk, Ed Epp, Doug Cormack, and Lloyd Bates. Johns's dual appointment with the Saskatchewan Cancer Commission brought experienced medical practitioners such as T.A. Watson, the new director of cancer services for the commission, into Sylvia's orbit.[21] Knowing that cobalt-60 was coming, and while MacKay, Bates, and Johns wrestled with the prototype, Sylvia had another task. Because they were building the entire system, Johns and his team also had to build all of the instruments to test the new machine's radiation output, depth dose rates, and other parameters. Sylvia's role was first to build, and then to test, all of the components that would eventually be used to measure the depth of the radiation dose that the cobalt-60 teletherapy machine could produce. It proved to be a daunting task.

Sylvia set out to find what depth dose measurements currently existed worldwide as her starting point. She found that in practice only two depth dose tables were available. The first table was a composite table created by Professor Mayneord in England. It simply averaged the tables of several different clinics and researchers throughout England, without testing or otherwise checking accuracy. The second table was created via instrument testing by the

Radiological Society of North America Standardization Committee. Sylvia would use those two tables to measure her own work against them for accuracy.

She was not starting her work completely from scratch—but close. Using a prototype similar to what had been used with the betatron, Sylvia carried the depth dose research much further and with far greater accuracy. Although the practical application of her work aimed to support the new cobalt-60 unit once it was complete and ready for testing, her specific task was both to create an apparatus that could be used to record measurements accurately and to test and publish the measurements. Her research records and her printed thesis give intricate details on her apparatus so that any other lab could recreate her instrumentation. These instruments included a DC-operated amplifier, an ionization chamber, a probe, a monitor system, and a recorder system. Her experiments actually took longer than her one year registered as a master's student. Sylvia calculated that the work covered the better part of three years, and the "major portion of time [was] spent in refining [an] experimental apparatus procedure."[22] In short, Sylvia included the instrumentation work to measure the betatron as part of the early work on the system to measure and calibrate the cobalt-60 unit—and she had started that work while still a regular undergraduate student. It was important to her and the team that her research was meticulously carried out and explained minutely to allow other researchers in other places to build similar units and reproduce her results.[23]

Whereas her summer days were spent in the labs in the physics department building, her summer evenings were spent on the ball field. The summer of 1950 saw Sylvia once again on the bench of the Ramblers, but the team appeared to be slipping a little, for the Clippers, who had shown their snazzy execution against the Harlem team the year before, led the standings. Sylvia continued to slug it out, such as when she brought in a three-run homer on July 22, 1950, winning the game for the Ramblers. Despite some good ball, the team was clearly struggling and ended 1950 in third place in the Saskatoon league. As before, when ball season ended, Sylvia went fishing. Johnny MacKay, the inveterate and nimble-minded machinist who worked with the University of Saskatchewan team on both the betatron unit and the cobalt-60 unit, was also a fisherman, and he joined Sylvia and some of her ball companions to go north, plying lakes and sprawling on the rocks to enjoy impromptu shoreline fare.

4. COBALT BOMB

Like the ball season, work also was not going smoothly. Sylvia huddled in the lab with Ed Epp and Richard Otto Kornelson, graduate students also working on aspects of cobalt-60 and depth dose. Epp worked on a ratio circuit to measure depth dose and defended his work a year after Sylvia in 1952. Kornelson worked on depth dose measurements in X-rays and how to calculate them. Both men were valued colleagues. Sylvia thanked them in her thesis acknowledgements, saying that "this thesis is a culmination of a problem undertaken with associates R.O. Kornelson and E.R. Epp, whose advice and contributions are gratefully acknowledged."[24] Others whose work drew from theirs included Doug Cormack, whose Ph.D. work focused on ionization chamber measurements in high-energy radiation, and L. Shenfield, whose B.Sc. in engineering physics focused on depth dose measurements in X-rays and referenced Sylvia's work.[25] The team atmosphere was important. Whether in a large laboratory working with others to solve a problem or on a basketball court or baseball field, Sylvia excelled when she was a member of a team.

Luckily, all of the graduate students had access to two critically important people. Bob Mauchel was the primary betatron technician and had a wealth of good ideas and support, and A.H. Cox, the university's shop instrument maker, was a machinist and gadget guru who had a complete shop in the basement of the physics department building. During her lab work that first summer, Sylvia spent most of her time constructing an ionization chamber that she called the "pancake design." Her early experiments were conducted to determine the effects of different thicknesses of the chamber wall. Frustration reigned. Fighting with faulty monitors, experimenting with different methods of mounting the cones onto the machine, and trying different types of diaphragms for widening or narrowing the field of exposure, Sylvia recorded her frustration in her notebooks, and her first several months of laboratory work involved a series of errors.

One of the constant problems was power supply. In Saskatoon in the early 1950s, the power supply was not reliable, nor was the level of power the same from one day to the next or not always from one part of the day to another. Draws on the power system could surge or wane, affecting instruments and measurements. A large part of every day before Sylvia began any testing went into checking her power supply. A typical notebook recording said that "at this point power failed—destabilization occurred and we can arrive at no conclusions."²⁶ The three slim notebooks reveal a frazzled, worried, and frustrated researcher. Much of her equipment, including the charging unit, was sent to the National Research Council lab for testing and repair. On the flyleaf of the notebook from 1950 is the following: "Problem of interpretation—all the work done up to Sept 1950. Found that when we plot our results versus fsd (focus to skin) we get very poor consistency."²⁷ In fact, the tables of measurements that Sylvia had built were not consistent with one another, nor were they consistent within themselves. In the end, all of her summer's research was thrown out. Johns, returning from a summer trip, dumped both Sylvia's and Epp's work in the trash can.²⁸ The data were far too inconsistent, he said. They had to dig deeper. Shocked and upset at losing so much time and work, Sylvia nonetheless agreed: she would never be satisfied with less-than-optimal results. Losing a whole summer of research work was a serious setback, yet she remained determined, even dogged, in her approach. The team refocused to solve the power issue first by using a DC unit instead of plugging into the inconsistent city power supply.

Sylvia swung straight into her final scholastic year in the fall of 1950, taking on a full load of physics courses to complete her master's work. In Nuclear Physics with L. Katz, she studied natural radioactivity, alpha and gamma decay, and applications of fission products to medicine. She also took a prototype course with Harold Johns in the Physics of Radiation Therapy, which concentrated on radium dosage, dosimetry, scattering, and absorption. This course would have been loosely based on the notes that Johns took during the summer course with W.V. Mayneord in 1946.

It's interesting to note the differences in marks between these two classes: Katz gave Sylvia 71 percent, whereas Johns awarded her 90 percent. In fact, checking her marks against professors, it's clear that either Sylvia didn't perform to her usual standard in any of Katz's classes, possibly because of the subject matter, or that Katz had a built-in bias against women, a bias that would come up again during her professional career. Sylvia also took Geophysics in the Atmosphere with B.W. Currie—a class that, while fulfilling requirements, was certainly outside her particular field of interest—and finished with a mark of 75 percent. R.N.H. Haslam took her through Theoretical Physics, in which she garnered 85 percent, while C.A. Mackay took her through Statistical Mechanics, which included classical and quantum methods to address thermodynamics and related fields as well as statistics. Sylvia again registered a mark of 85 percent. She also took on departmental work for credit, to show advanced knowledge of research work, as well as her own research for her master's thesis. Both her departmental work and her own work were geared to solving the problems of the cobalt-60 unit. Sylvia's course load for 1950–51 was her toughest yet.

Despite university rules demanding a focus on course work, sports were an exemption. In fact, in the fall of 1950, Sylvia competed once again in multiple sports: volleyball, basketball, and golf. She took home more intervarsity laurels, including from a punishing trip to Edmonton to golf in the snow. Saskatchewan golfers, it was noted, appeared to thrive under adversity.[29]

Sylvia also contributed coaching skills to incoming Saskatoon girl hoopsters. Ivan King and several Huskiettes created a basketball school for Saskatoon girls who wanted to learn or practise basketball. So many girls turned out that the course had to be divided into two groups. About seventy girls would come out every week, split across two nights to accommodate the interest. They would work on fundamentals and basic plays, including layups, dribbling, and skirmishing with senior players. It was a self-serving school for King, for no doubt he was busy shaping future potential Huskiette players.[30]

Despite a gruelling winter athletic schedule of both basketball and volleyball, in which Sylvia was both player and coach, her research work was finally making some progress. By March 1951, there were breakthroughs. On March 2, she reported that her amplifier, left running for three hours, had stayed steady. Almost in disbelief, she set it again. "Gad! Amplifier after 8 hours continuous use working like a charm. No drift whatsoever. Believe everything is working well enough to do experiments."[31] It's critical to note again that Sylvia's program of research meant *first* creating and developing the equipment to be used to conduct her research and *then* actually doing the experiments. Because the cobalt-60 unit itself was not finished, nor was the cobalt-60 finished cooking in the reactor, Sylvia's research testing was completed on a 22,000-volt X-ray machine housed at City Hospital in Saskatoon, whose output was equivalent to the anticipated output of cobalt-60. It has been a common but erroneous misconception that Sylvia completed her master's thesis research using the cobalt-60 unit or perhaps the betatron machine. In fact, her work predated the arrival of the former and did not use the wildly expensive latter.

Despite the breakthrough, the first two field experiments, done at Saskatoon City Hospital when the X-ray machine wasn't in regular use on Saturday, March 10, and Sunday, March 11, were disappointing. On March 10, Sylvia wrote "Don't believe. Obviously getting too small a reading at the surface."[32] That night she played with the Huskiettes against the Moose Jaw Pixies to vie for the provincial senior ladies' basketball championship, trouncing the Pixies 50–24. Sylvia was back in the lab the next day but couldn't take recordings because the amplifier didn't function properly. Once again she was thwarted.

March 14 proved to be the true breakthrough when Sylvia completed a linearity experiment for the new DC amplifier.[33] The experiment worked: the amplifier readings proved to be linear. The next day she changed parameters to test a new set of variables.[34] Again she ran a linearity test, meticulously graphed. Again the test showed that the amplifier was "~~perfectly~~ linear!!"[35] Sylvia, ever the scientist, did not believe in perfection, so she crossed out the word in her notebook. Nonetheless, she was clearly elated. By April 1, continued experiments were "most encouraging."[36]

On May 12, Sylvia was once again at Saskatoon City Hospital, ready to run more field experiments on her ionization chamber. She stabilized her readings by using a Brown recorder on the amplifier. It worked. With enough stable readings at hand collected during May and into June, cross-referenced and verified, Sylvia could finish her thesis. In it, she made a bold claim: the depth dose tables currently in use in both the United States and Britain were incorrect. Not *off*, not *miscalibrated*, or any other soft word but simply *incorrect*. Not only had she developed equipment whose accuracy could be scientifically plotted and replicated, but also her work proved that the U.S. Radiological Society tables were *not* reproducible or replicable. In short, the leading radiologists in the United States were treating patients based on measurements made with poor scientific protocols. It was a confident assertion from a young female researcher working in a university in western Canada.

As her thesis grew, precious piles of pages with data and argument carefully marshalled, Sylvia found ways to let off a little steam. In the dingy control room next to the betatron, in the basement annex of the physics department building, Sylvia shuffled, split, and deftly dealt out hand after hand of cards. On the floor, piles of screws, nuts, bolts, and other odds and ends spilled out in front of each player. Except for Sylvia, the players were all men, and all were graduate students. The scene was not raucous and rowdy, the air filled with jokes, banter, and sly wit. It was quiet, each player

4. COBALT BOMB

with an ear cocked and listening for steps, for movement, for someone to come down the long hallway. Discovery of graduate students wasting time playing blackjack and poker could be disastrous. If the sound of footsteps tapping closer and closer to the gamers' lair came, they had a plan: the players would pocket their playing cards and the dealer her hand and deck. The nuts and bolts and screws scattered over the floor? We're doing an inventory, sir. Ertle Harrington, head of the department, could swallow such sophistry since there would be no evidence of the betatron control room having become a gambling den and these loose bolts and nuts gambling chips.

Sylvia was a card shark, smart, astute, and daring. But in 1951 she had ulterior motives for playing and winning. Less than fond of a few fellow graduate students, Sylvia had been the target of a prank that veered into something frightening. Bob Summersgill, a fellow graduate student, had found her carefully typed thesis and spread it, page by page, all over the three floors of the physics department building. Lore provided by Sylvia's supervisor, Harold Johns, suggests that Sylvia retaliated by stealing all of the data notebooks of the other students and hiding them with smug perversity in the one women's bathroom. In that instant, the male cohort capitulated. All was returned. But Sylvia held a bit of a grudge, hence the card sharking. Playing against Bob and a few other students, her pile of nuts and bolts grew. They owed her, and soon it would be time to pay.

Sylvia's master's thesis, simply titled "Depth Dose" and a mere forty-four pages in length, including graphs and illustrations, was completed and successfully defended in July 1951. It provided sufficient data for clinical use, and its carefully calibrated and defended tables would become the standard for both creating the technical measurement components and calibrating clinical depth dose for cobalt-60 machines around the world. Yet her thesis was completed before the cobalt-60 machine was finished or the radioactive cobalt had even arrived in Saskatoon.

The cobalt was nearly on its way. A few weeks after Sylvia defended her thesis, the *Saskatoon Star-Phoenix* reported on July 30, 1951, that the city had received its precious shipment of cobalt-60.[37] The size of a stack of quarters, the cobalt-60 was housed in a hip-high lead container that weighed 2,000 pounds. The railway company, scared that the contents were in fact a bomb, and reluctant to carry anything stranger than grain, wood, or other raw materials, nearly refused the shipment. It was unwilling to place such a cargo on a westbound train. Harold Johns, frantic, was ready to travel to Ontario himself with a trailer to bring the precious cargo back to Saskatchewan. In the end, the Chalk River scientists convinced the railway to accept the freight, which it did with a couple of conditions: it had to go by express, to get it off the train all the sooner, and the University of Saskatchewan had to unload it.[38] The *Star-Phoenix*, anxious to both titillate and reassure its readers, showed a picture of the unloading and moving of the cobalt-60 to the university, with Harold Johns and Lloyd Bates in short sleeves and bare hands testing the outside of the lead case with a Geiger counter to ensure safety.[39]

By August, the new treatment room and the machine were somewhat closer to being ready, and the newspaper was on hand again to snap a shot of Harold Johns and Johnny MacKay carefully transferring the radioactive material into the head of their machine.[40] Once the cobalt-60 in its heavy lead case had arrived safely, the team "lugged" the lead case and lethal core "through the scaffolding of the half-finished hospital and into the bomb room."[41] Once there, it was manoeuvred into position beneath MacKay's completed treatment head. Then, wrapped in useless gowns and surgical masks, and with a Geiger counter measuring escaping radiation, the team threaded a rod down through the treatment head and into the lead travelling case. The rod was screwed into the metal cylinder with the cobalt-60 discs inside, and the cylinder was lifted swiftly into the treatment head "with scarcely time for a gamma to escape."[42] The team then hurried to finish the detailing in the room, move in the instrument panel, and start testing.

As usual, Sylvia's days were filled with a heady mix of science and sport, but ball was not going as well as Sylvia had hoped. The Ramblers, minus their star pitcher, Muriel Coben, struggled. They ended the year by losing the semifinal match to the Vanscoy Caps, whose play was led by the tiny but mighty Joyce McKee, whose great pitching caught the eye of many around Saskatoon's ball parks.[43]

In the meantime, Sylvia was ready for a much-needed break. By late July, she had cashed in her stack of blackjack and poker money from the guys. Once the cobalt-60 was in place in the treatment head, she cleaned out her lab office, once again hitchhiked to Prince Albert, and then caught a bumpy ride to the growing town of La Ronge.

In the 1950s, La Ronge was Saskatchewan's main northern outpost, the jumping-off point for prospecting, mining, trading, and fishing. As the fourth largest lake in Saskatchewan, La Ronge was teeming with fish, from the wonderful-eating walleye to the feisty

4. COBALT BOMB

jackfish to the huge, red-meated lake trout. The tourism boom had long since taken over lakes such as Candle, Emma, Christopher, Anglin, and Waskesiu, but accessibility was a problem for La Ronge. The tourism industry brought in but a trickle of money to the community. With the new Highway 2 finished in 1947 (using significant help from the conscientious objectors who spent their war years working in government parks), La Ronge was finally "open" for tourism. Almost immediately it changed. Within three years, by 1950, 3,500 anglers made their way to La Ronge during the summer season to try their luck. No fewer than fifteen new businesses designed to catch anglers opened for tourists. Camps, right in the town, multiplied. In 1951, Sylvia found herself in a town swarming with southerners intent on casting lures into the cold northern waters.

Fishing camps specialized in custom tourism services. Some were right in town, such as Red's, Pisipinook, and Lindy's. Others built camps around the lake. A secondary industry sprang up, picking anglers up at La Ronge at the docks and ferrying them to camps, either by boat to a La Ronge camp or by float plane to another lake. The fees at the camps were based on the services required: a cabin for three might cost between four and seven dollars a night, boat rental eight dollars a day, food two dollars per day, and tackle one dollar per day. A guide could be hired for about eight dollars a day. Shore lunch, for which the guide would find a good spot, gut a few fish, and fry them up, was a particular delicacy. It's possible that Sylvia spent her poker winnings in Red's Camp, one of the larger tourist fishing camps and one of the first to cater directly to the new tourism industry.

Sylvia planned and packed well: lots of money, necessary evening libations, warm clothes, and a friend or two along to share the journey and costs as well as someone to compete against in catching fish. Dorothy (Dot) George, a friend from Sylvia's years on the Saskatoon Ramblers ball team, often joined Sylvia on these northern jaunts. They returned home, full of northern air, just as the leaves started to think about turning.

Sylvia was officially hired on September 1, 1951, as an assistant physicist with the Saskatchewan Cancer Commission. Between defending her thesis in July and starting official work in September, aside from the trip to La Ronge, Sylvia had to move. No longer a student, she could not keep her room at Mohyla Institute. So she moved to 1027 Temperance Avenue, then by 1953 into the Braemar Apartments just north of the downtown core of Saskatoon and near City Hospital,

Sylvia as a professional physicist, 1951. (Note that the men's lab coat was too large for her.)

at 511 Queen Street, apartment 15.[44] Her good friend Hazel Braithwaite had moved into the next apartment. Sylvia began her professional career in Saskatchewan, working as a cancer physicist.

With her first paycheque, Sylvia put a down payment on a car and purchased a pack of cigarettes. The cheque represented her mother's dream for her daughter: a professional career with a steady income. That first cheque was $232.70 after deductions for income tax, staff fees, and union dues, more than double what she had earned as a graduate student. The car represented freedom. With better roads spoking in all directions from Saskatoon, Sylvia would be able to travel north, south, west, and east, head out on her own to ball tournaments in rural centres, and make weekend trips to Yorkton to visit her family. She had just one little problem: she had never learned to drive. Undaunted, she bought the car anyway and convinced friends to teach her how to drive. A favourite place of practice was the U of S campus, around and around the bowl in front of the physics department and administration buildings and the dormitories. In the early 1950s, car traffic could still access the bowl, making the endless loop from Convocation Hall west toward the chemistry department building and back again. Eventually, Sylvia gained enough experience to venture around the city and beyond.

With both her personal and her professional life settling in, Sylvia was unknowingly heading straight for national recognition. As the clock ticked down to the first use of the cobalt-60 bomb, her experimentation with amplifiers and ionization chambers continued. Sylvia tested radiation output of other Saskatchewan Cancer Commission treatments, including radiation "seeds," a procedure in which small seeds of radium would be inserted into or near a tumour. Her early ionization chamber designs, with improvements and tests by Harold Johns and T.A. Watson, eventually became a dosimeter used regularly in clinical practice by the Saskatchewan Cancer Commission to test radiation from seed therapy.[45] Her master's research notebooks, still a fundamental part of her work as a scientist, showed how Sylvia took her research on the X-ray machine to test and calculate depth dose and to design various treatment cones for use on cobalt-60 throughout the fall of 1951. That fall Sylvia convocated for the last time, crossing the graduation floor to receive her Master of Arts degree in physics. She was a physicist.

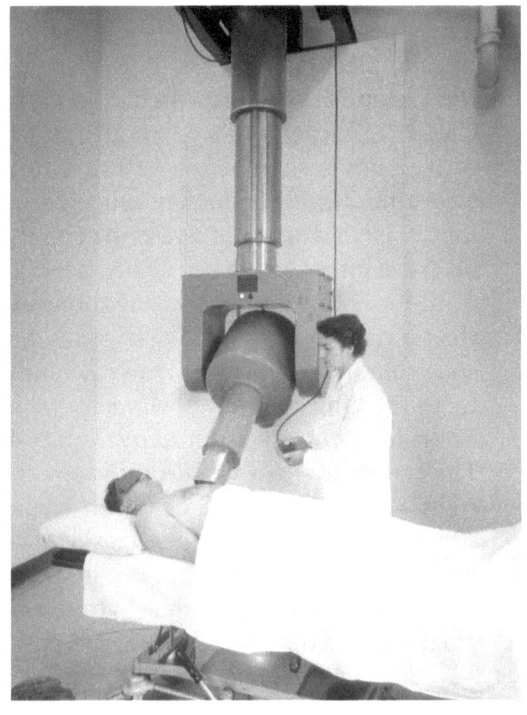

Sylvia with the unveiled cobalt-60 machine, 1951.

The official opening of the new cobalt-60 treatment room and therapy machine was planned for October 23, 1951. Premier Tommy Douglas was to lead the ceremony at the medical lecture theatre, cutting the ribbon to "release" the new cancer bomb. The vagaries of a Saskatchewan fall intervened. Stranded in Regina because of fog, Douglas, the minister of public health, T.J. Bentley, and the deputy minister of public health, F.D. Mott, were unable to attend the ceremony. Also slated to arrive but stranded in Regina was Mrs. Blair, the widow of Dr. Allan Blair, a man who had been instrumental in the planning and behind-the-scenes politics to secure the unit but had passed away before the big reveal. Douglas deputized Dean F.C. Cronkite, a North Battleford member of the Saskatchewan Cancer Commission, to take his part in the ceremony. Chancellor F.H. Auld and President Dr. W.P. Thompson snuck away from a meeting of the university's board of governors to attend the opening and give remarks. Dr. T.A. Watson, director of cancer services for Saskatchewan, presented a key to the new cobalt-60 unit to Cronkite. More than 200 people attended the ceremony and then walked down the narrow hallways to the new treatment room to view the cobalt-60 therapy machine in its thick-walled surroundings.[46] Sylvia was front and centre on the day, meeting and greeting all those interested in the new cancer bomb.

Even with such an exciting moment in her professional life, by the time that week ended Sylvia could toss off her professional persona to indulge in some royalty fandom. Princess Elizabeth, daughter of the king and queen whom Sylvia had been so excited to see in Melville in 1939, was on a royal tour of Canada with her husband. The couple stopped in Saskatoon. As they travelled in a motorcade right across the U of S campus, Sylvia, in the bleachers opposite Convocation Hall, waved alongside hundreds of others as Princess Elizabeth and her husband, Philip, Duke of Edinburgh, swept past. It was the second time that Sylvia was near royalty but certainly would not be the last.

One of the big newspaper stories in the fall of 1951 and the winter of 1952—vying with Korean War news, Princess Elizabeth's visit to Canada, and Elizabeth's father's illness—was the race to deploy the new cobalt bomb. It was a race that Canada was sure to win since it had not one but two Canadian contestants: Harold Johns and his team in Saskatchewan and Dr. R.F. Errington, Dr. A.W. Morrison, and Donald T. Green of the development division of Eldorado Mining and Smelting in Ontario. Their unit, which would be operated by Dr. Ivan Smith, director of the Ontario Cancer Foundation, and his team working in London, Ontario, was built and tested in Ottawa before being moved to London. Although some medical historians and journalists have portrayed this race as rivalry, the two teams were in close contact with each other and with both Chalk River and the national Atomic Energy Control Board, which served as the overseer of their combined efforts.

Each team designed and built unique machines to house and direct the radioactive energy. The Saskatchewan cobalt-60 unit relied on steel plates and an interior lead-encased wheel that could be turned on and off via rotation. Johnny MacKay, with Sylvia and the rest of the team, constructed a series of interchangeable lead plugs to direct the beams through larger or smaller fields as needed. These lead plugs were similar to what they had developed for the

4. COBALT BOMB

betatron. The Eldorado unit destined for London used mercury for its on/off mechanism. When the unit was in use, an air compressor blew the mercury away from the opening, allowing the radiation to escape from the treatment head. During a power failure or after use, the mercury would immediately gravity-feed over the opening, sealing in the radiation. Its field of therapy treatment could be changed by moving four lead blocks situated at right angles to each other into smaller or larger square or rectangular formations. Their cores were identical, two Saskatchewan-built stacks of cobalt discs radiated in the ZEEP reactor.

Both units were tested for depth doses using a DC amplifier and ionization chambers testing water phantoms—exactly the kind of apparatus developed by Sylvia in her master's research. It's highly probable that her own unit, or a replica thereof, was used to test both the Saskatchewan machine and the Ontario machine. Despite the significant differences in machine design, the two machines "were in excellent agreement" regarding depth dose measurements. No doubt the comparable data gave both research teams relief, since in science the ability to replicate an experiment is key to proving it.[47] It also showed that the two machines, despite different designs, could be used to similar effect.

The "race" essentially was two local newspapers crowing over which city was the first to deploy the new cancer bomb. The papers focused on the timing and testing of the units, particularly on how fast each group went from installation to treatment. The two cobalt units were developed differently. In Saskatoon, the same team that dreamed of, designed, and built the unit was also the team to test it and first put it into clinical use in treating patients. The London unit was built and tested by Eldorado engineers in Ottawa. It was then moved to London, installed, and put into use. In essence, it was the difference between building your own unit and buying one off the shelf. Medical historians also tend to point out that, in terms of the Saskatoon connection, the London unit had been created and tested in Ottawa by scientists and engineers Dr. A.W. Morrison and Don Green, trained at the University of Saskatchewan.

The Eldorado machine was shipped to London and installed on October 23, the same day that the Saskatoon machine was "officially" put into commission. The London unit, with less testing and calibration in situ, treated the first patient on October 27. Some medical historians, including C.S. Houston, have suggested that the London group did not take the time to properly calibrate their machine and that the rush to move straight from setup to first use was detrimental. The first patient treated in Ontario had an advanced form of cancer, and the treatment was not enough to halt the progress of the insidious disease.

The Saskatoon group, conversely, had a more methodical outlook. Two years of high-energy cancer treatment using the betatron had given the team confidence and experience and the ability to identify and choose patients whose forms of cancer would respond well to high-energy treatment. After all, they too—somewhat scared and unsure—had chosen an early betatron patient whose cancer had been too far advanced to treat and could hardly fault the London crew for their inexperience. Even so, the Saskatoon group took their time, looking through the list of patients and matching need with probability of success. Given the population difference between Saskatchewan and Ontario, there was no doubt a smaller pool of patients from which to draw. The first Saskatoon cobalt-60 patient was a forty-year-old mother who had advanced but not yet metastasized cervical cancer, well suited to the rays of the cobalt-60. She received her first treatment on November 8, 1951, with more treatments to follow. Radiation is carefully planned and always calibrated for each patient's body type, cancer, stage, and expected number of treatments—it takes multiple treatments to achieve clinical effect. Fate graced the determined and careful work of the Saskatoon team. Their first treated patient was cured of cervical cancer and lived for many years thereafter.

Despite the back-and-forth sniping of the two city newspapers about which team was the first to use the cobalt bomb, national attention swung like iron filings to a magnet to focus on Saskatoon when Eric Hutton, a reporter for the national weekly magazine *Maclean's*, ran an eight-page major investigative article on the Saskatoon cancer scientists.

Sylvia Fedoruk became the feminine face of the February 15, 1952, story, "The Atom Bomb that Saves Lives." Photographed in her lab coat efficiently running the remote control to show the movement of the treatment head, Sylvia was centre stage. Other pictures showcased Dr. Harold Johns; a partially naked Johnny MacKay gamely demonstrating how a patient would lie on the table during a cobalt-60 bombardment; Pauline McConkey handling the technician's controls from the adjoining room; and a picture, no doubt borrowed from the *Saskatoon Star-Phoenix*, from August showing the team loading the "hot" cobalt into the treatment head. Hutton's

4. COBALT BOMB

story proved that investigative journalists who viewed the larger picture could easily see that the story of Canada's cobalt bomb was centred in Saskatoon, where the leadership, knowledge, dedicated science, craftsmanship, and vision were undisputed. The reporter was also clearly enamoured of Sylvia:

> Dr. Johns' chief assistant was, and still is, personable 24-year-old Sylvia Fedoruk. Miss Fedoruk is undoubtedly the only Canadian girl ever faced with the alternatives of becoming an atomic physicist or becoming the country's top feminine athlete. Her ability to do either was never in doubt. Scholastically she has long since lost count of scholarships won, but "they averaged roughly two a year" for the past ten years. They were topped off by the Governor-General's Gold Medal for the outstanding graduate of the University of Saskatchewan in 1949. . . . In athletics Sylvia became individual high-point champion of the 1947 Dominion Track and Field Championships, held in Edmonton. She is acknowledged to be western Canada's outstanding girl athlete in every sport. "Except swimming," she insists. But actually her decision was made in high school, when the Fedoruks made a wartime move to Windsor, Ontario and Sylvia entered Walkerville Collegiate. There her science teacher, Howard R. Hugill, "made the subject so interesting that I decided to make science my career."[48]

In the wake of the *Maclean's* story, letters poured in with congratulations. Two in particular caught Sylvia's attention, and Sylvia kept them among her most prized life souvenirs. One was from high school English teacher Ruth McLaren, whom Sylvia credited with assuring her that science and math, not English, were Sylvia's strengths. Miss McLaren told her, "You are meant to carry a load bigger than most young people are capable of carrying, I am sure. I hope, Sylvia, you are having a happy life, and a pleasant one. It gives us all great pleasure to think of your success, and, too, it makes us feel that Walkerville had a wee bit to do with starting you on your career." Miss McLaren ended the letter by saying, "We are bursting with pride at your success."[49] Clearly, Sylvia had made as big an impression on Walkerville Collegiate as it had made on her.

The second letter was from Howard Hugill, her high school physics teacher, delighted to have one of his former students recognize the importance of high school learning. He said, "You credited me with having a share in influencing in you a liking for your chosen vocation. It gave me a real lift. Teaching at [the] high school level year after year can get pretty monotonous even under the best of conditions. An occasional acknowledgement like that, whether deserved or not, dissipates the pessimism that comes inevitably once in a while, when one asks oneself, 'I wonder if it is all worthwhile.' And you go on doing your best, such as it is, with renewed courage."[50]

Like Hugill, Sylvia enjoyed "a real lift" from the national recognition of her work on the Harold Johns cobalt-60 team. It marked both an end and a beginning for her: the end of her formal university training in physics and the beginning of a professional career as a physicist with the Saskatchewan Cancer Commission. Sometimes, just like her former high school physics teacher, Sylvia would face times of discouragement and doubt. But each year she received a Christmas card from the woman treated and successfully cured of cervical cancer as the first cobalt bomb patient. If ever Sylvia had moments of despair, those Christmas cards, sent from a woman whose life went from a terminal diagnosis to many years of zestful life, would lift Sylvia back up, and she could keep on working. The personal connection reinforced what would come to define her professional, sports, and leadership roles: Sylvia could do important life-saving and world-leading work right at home in Saskatchewan.

5. THE FRIENDLY ATOM

IF SASKATOON NOW HAD A "COBALT GUN," SYLVIA FEDORUK was the female gunslinger. Almost from the moment that the *Maclean's* article was released, the Saskatchewan Cancer Commission was inundated with desperate calls and frantic letters. People seemed to believe the new cobalt bomb would cure cancer and save lives—all types of cancer and all lives. People scrambled to bring patients to the cancer clinic for cures. No, Sylvia gently rebuffed them, cobalt-60 was *not* a miracle but "simply a very good X-ray machine" to be used in radiation treatment. It nearly broke her heart to read the pain and hope sent via pleading letters to the "cancer bomb clinic" at the University of Saskatchewan.[1]

If Sylvia was the gunslinger, then perhaps it was time to shoot a few of her own bullets. As assistant physicist with the Saskatchewan Cancer Commission (and the only full-time physicist), Sylvia was a major guest speaker when the Canadian Society of Radiological Technicians met at the Palliser Hotel in Calgary in 1952. Her message to the 150 or so convention delegates was one of caution. Contrary to the "unwise publicity" surrounding the betatron and cobalt-60 machines, neither could cure "all cases of cancer." Only time would tell doctors and physicists whether or not their machines were actually curing cancer or just fighting it back for a short time. Nonetheless, the signs were good. Since the installation of the cobalt-60 unit at the University of Saskatchewan, they were treating an average of sixteen people per day. Each person received multiple treatments of the high-energy X-ray per week for a period of three to five weeks. Another advantage of the cobalt-60 treatment, Sylvia noted to the gathering of radiological technologists, was its relatively inexpensive cost. With a Canadian nuclear plant able to create the cobalt-60 isotope and Canadian companies such as Acme Machine in Saskatoon able to design and build a usable treatment machine, about $13,000 would get a hospital an up-to-date cancer-fighting device. After the units in London and Saskatoon proved their abilities, Sylvia reported, a third unit was in the works for Vancouver.[2]

Her speech drew attention not only from the delegates but also from the local newspaper reporters, eager to hear about the everyday working of Saskatoon's groundbreaking path in nuclear medicine and the building of the cobalt gun. Always on the lookout for balance and a new angle, reporters were quick to frame medical isotope research and cobalt-60 treatment as the positive public corollaries to the fearmongering of the nuclear arms race. There was something good, they assured the public, to be found in the words *nuclear* and *atom*. Sylvia's own bosses, Harold Johns as senior physicist and T.A. (Sandy) Watson as head of the Saskatchewan Cancer Commission, told a Winnipeg audience in January 1951 that radiated cobalt "is a peaceful and useful product of atomic power," a strictly Canadian invention produced only in the Chalk River nuclear pile.[3]

While Sylvia's triumphant role on the Saskatoon cancer bomb team cemented her work at the university clinic and with the Cancer Commission, the Canadian public, and at conferences, the team's research was sending shock waves through the international scientific community. In the wake of building, testing, and using the cobalt-60 machine for clinical treatments, Sylvia was the lead or a contributing author on numerous articles published in world-renowned scientific journals in 1951 and 1952, including both *Nature* and *Science*. As expected by her supervisor, Harold Johns, his graduate students had to prove their academic chops via publication in leading journals. There were no journals more well known than *Nature* and *Science*, and for Sylvia to have publications in both during the early 1950s, as a woman and as a master's student, is a tremendous accomplishment.

World-shaking reputation aside, Sylvia was still Sylvia: fiercely intelligent but also full of fun and mischief. If the gunslinger metaphor has any traction, then it's only fair to point out that she did use the treatment head as a weapon—just not against people. It could be

5. THE FRIENDLY ATOM

Sylvia and Ed Epp demonstrating the water phantom.

rotated in such a way that Sylvia could send its beams through the north-facing window onto the gopher-infested grass between the cancer wing and the laundry building. Gambolling merrily in the sun, the poor gophers never knew that on occasion they would receive high doses of radiation therapy as Sylvia practised and perfected rotation, aiming, and calibration to move the treatment head into place and release the beams.[4]

The face-to-face and in-person learning of the conference circuit became part of her professional training. To take advantage of Saskatoon's leading international role on this new form of high-energy treatment, Johns coaxed a $1,000 travelling scholarship out of the Canadian Cancer Society, similar to the one that he had received in 1946. Sylvia conducted a two-month working trip to visit research hospitals across the United States and Canada, meeting physicists and clinicians to see and learn the latest treatment techniques and research trials related to cancer using radiation, including betatron accelerators and cobalt-60 machines. The money came from the John S. McEachern Memorial Fellowship Fund designed to support post-graduate study "elsewhere than in their parent institution."[5] The idea of cross-pollination and exchange was important in an era when research was intensifying at an exponential rate, but communication from one centre to another remained somewhat constrained, via official publications, letters, telegrams, and occasional phone calls and visits.

Sylvia used the bursary to take a grand tour of the leading North American cancer treatment institutes. At each stop, eager to learn what was new and interesting so that the Saskatchewan team could grow, she found that *her* knowledge was what these cancer centres wanted. What was supposed to be a learning tour became at least as much a teaching tour. Sylvia explained the science behind the Saskatoon story. "Probably the most important thing that I learned during this trip is that the work being done here in Saskatoon is of the highest calibre," she said in her trip report.[6] She proved to be popular, and made numerous valuable contacts, settling into the North American cancer research network.

In later years, Sylvia recounted the tour. Her interest was split between learning about high-energy radiation in the treatment of cancer and the growing use of radionuclides to diagnose disease. "It was an exciting time in the world of medical physics," she recounted in a retrospective speech to the 1989 dual conference of the Canadian Nuclear Association and the Canadian Nuclear Society. "High energy accelerators such as the betatron were being used to treat cancer; cobalt units were just beginning to be tested clinically; scintillation crystals and photomultiplier tubes were more readily available to university laboratories, and radiopharmaceuticals were beginning to appear on the market." At each stop, she met with leading clinical researchers, such as Dr. K. Corrigan at the Harper Hospital in Detroit and Dr. G. Bromnell at the Massachusetts General Hospital in Boston, where she was enthralled by work to measure thyroid uptake and to externally locate brain tumours. At Oak Ridge, Sylvia spent time with Dr. Marshall Brucer, with whom she discussed instrumentation and standardization, an area where her own master's work led the world stage.[7] The trip, even more than the *Maclean's* article and the academic publications in *Science* and *Nature*, launched Sylvia's career as a leading figure in radiation and cancer science developments. Going on research tours vaulted Sylvia from student to colleague, accelerating her professional role as an assistant physicist at the Saskatchewan Cancer Commission under Harold Johns and later as she assumed command of the physics services department. The trip marked a major change in her professional life. Work now came first.

5. THE FRIENDLY ATOM

As work commitments allowed, Sylvia chose to spend evenings and weekends at the baseball diamonds. When she did, her great energy still shone. By August 1952, the Ramblers "looked the club of old . . . as they tore loose,"[8] ending the season at the top of the heap and winning the provincial title. Joyce McKee had also jumped ship from the Vanscoy crew to the Ramblers, finding her place at second base and being an expert batter. The two women spent more time together, cementing a friendship that would define the next fifteen years of their lives. The 1953 season brought a repeat city round robin win, with Sylvia as a hitter and an infielder. But a season at the top of the standings was brought to a cold stop when the Saskatoon Clippers knocked off the Ramblers in three straight games to clinch the city title. They did not head to the provincials.

As winter rolled in, some of Sylvia's teammates from the Huskiettes yearned to be back on a basketball court. Several, including Sylvia and Pat Lawson, joined one of Saskatoon's "professional" female basketball teams, the Saskatoon Aces. The team romped and scored through a few winter seasons in the early 1950s, taking local and provincial championships.

At work, Sylvia's role as an assistant physicist morphed. Sylvia could be found testing equipment, developing new testing methods, researching protocols used elsewhere, keeping the labs stocked and running, and generally keeping things shipshape—in addition to publishing, travelling to international meetings, and participating in the field of medical physics. Her position was mobile. Sylvia went wherever there were high-radiation-producing machines that required attention. Travelling within Saskatoon between the original cancer clinic at City Hospital and the newly built cancer wing at the University Hospital, as well as down to the Allan Blair Cancer Clinic in Regina once a month, Sylvia was on the move. Her work turned to finding cancer treatment aids for breast and uterine cancer, including cervical and vaginal dilators and pelvic chambers. She was interested in the use of radiotherapy to prevent cancer surgery scar tissue from becoming cancerous, and she started work with radioactive iodine as a tracer looking at thyroid disorders.[9] Sylvia also got her hands dirty creating moulds for patients to wear to receive treatment over several days.[10] A keen eye on supplies and tools for the labs, from screwdrivers to steel tape, hammer to tin snips, showed her attention to detail. Her eye for organization set all Saskatchewan hospital radiation units at full service.

In 1954, with the Allan Blair Cancer Clinic in Regina feeling the pinch of being "behind" the University Hospital in Saskatoon, at least in terms of the latest in cancer treatment, Sylvia moved to Regina. Being in situ meant that she could concentrate on bringing that lab up to speed. One of the main items on the to-do list was to build a new cobalt-60 unit for the Regina Grey Nuns Hospital. With the Saskatoon unit in full daily clinical practice, Sylvia and the Cancer Commission team knew both its strengths and its shortcomings. Clinical practices, mechanical issues, stray radiation, janitorial needs—her experience was broad, and the commission sent her to Regina to help get things ready there.

By day, Sylvia was involved in her usual round of patient treatment plans and hospital administration, technical assessment, planning for the cobalt-60 treatment room, and working on her ongoing research program. But evenings were her own, so she sought out the coach of the Regina Govins. Neither the coach nor the team hesitated. Gil Strumm, then the coach of the Govins, was a regular fixture in Sylvia's life. He loved all sports, from softball and baseball to basketball, golf and curling, hockey and football, and he participated as athlete, coach, umpire, and volunteer, spending hours on committees, offering enthusiasm and support. Born and raised in Saskatoon, Strumm first saw Fedoruk in the Saskatoon league with the Ramblers and coached her in 1948. He spent most summer nights out at Cairns Field in Saskatoon, coaching, umping, and playing. On his transfer to Regina with Saskatchewan Government Telephones from 1949 to 1955, Strumm turned to coaching both men's and women's teams. In 1953, he coached at the World Softball Championships in Toronto.[11] Although good players with skill are the most critical component of a winning team, the coach takes a team from good to great. The Ramblers, without Strumm, hadn't been able to bring their team back to their glory days. In Regina with the Govins, he was clearly a major ingredient of a winning team.

Sylvia quickly earned a spot on the team. The Govins—sponsored by Saskatchewan Government Insurance (SGI), hence their name—had been Regina league, provincial, and western champs with a record similar to that of the Ramblers. Home league games were played at Central Park in Regina, and intercity games were played at Memorial Field in Moose Jaw. Central Park is one of Regina's oldest parks. From its founding in 1885, it has been Regina's mecca for baseball and softball. Throughout the 1940s

5. THE FRIENDLY ATOM

Regina Govins in Calgary, 1954. Sylvia is in the front, second from the left.

and '50s, ball scouts from the United States lurked in the bleachers, and many women who played "under the lights" found their way to the All-American Girls Professional Baseball League. Sylvia, now with a good-paying job, would never be tempted to join the league, but the presence of scouts in the stands kept the calibre of play high.

By June 1954, the Govins were on the field, and they were hot. As usual, Sylvia shifted from first to third base and short stop as needed, offering power and athleticism to the infield. It wasn't always easy going, though. In an article that Sylvia clipped and tucked into her Regina Govins files, the *Leader-Post* noted that "the grapevine has it that Gil Strumm, coach of the pace-setting Regina Govins, has discovered a new miracle breakfast food that seems to give his gals that needed spark when the chips are down." The reporter, despite asking, could not discover just what that was—only that it was *something*.[12] The team would get into tight spots, then rely on swift and sharp play, big hits, and good hurling by their pitcher to pull them through. It's possible that the new "spark" was Sylvia, loudly rousing her fellow players, "C'mon, gang. Get in the game!" Sometime during that summer the team also went on a team-building exercise, camping at Katepwa Lake near Fort Qu'Appelle with fishing, relaxing, eating watermelon, suntanning, and golfing. The off-field friendships no doubt helped the on-field play.[13]

There was determination and grittiness on the team that Sylvia clearly enjoyed. As was the case when the Ramblers were on top, the Govins had an amazing pitcher, Helene Sidaway, who threw a ball "with power and accuracy rivalled by few." Sidaway not only played for the Govins but also worked for SGI, managing work with two kids and a ball career.[14]

The Govins went into the western Canadian semifinal on the back of their 1953 ranking, not their 1954 winning streak, though they beat the reigning western Canadian champs, the Regina Legion, to earn their trip to the western semifinal. The winner of that semifinal, which pitted Alberta against Saskatchewan, was supposed to travel to Vancouver to vie for the title of western champion. But, with the vagaries of women's softball, the Vancouver team had run out of money, and the western title went to the Govins by default after their win in Calgary. With an unexpected holiday since they didn't have to travel to Vancouver, the Govins headed for Banff, touring the iconic region and relaxing in the hot springs.[15]

On their return to Saskatchewan, controversy hit. The Govins were slated to face Saskatoon's victorious Vanguards in a north-south provincial showdown to determine the Saskatchewan winner. The matchup was set to start about ten days into September. But a disastrous wet late summer held the ball season at a standstill, which had a ripple effect. In a shocking announcement on September 25, the Govins refused to meet the Vanguards for the provincial playdown. Strumm offered this explanation: "With some players unable to appear and others definitely not in top condition, we feel that we could not provide the public with the high calibre of softball which we have presented all season." It was a last-minute decision, throwing the series and the softball community into disarray. Several Vanguards players, who came from outside Saskatoon to play, were miffed since Strumm called late in the evening to let the other coach know of his decision to throw the match.[16] Others within the softball community called for suspensions against the Govins, but none was put in place. With no choice, the Saskatchewan Softball Association awarded the Vanguards the provincial title, but it was hollow. How could they carry that title without having a chance to face the western Canadian champions? The season ended for the Vanguards, and the Govins, on a sour note.

No whiff of this controversy can be found in either Sylvia Fedoruk's files or the writeup for the 1954 Govins team when they were inducted into the Regina Sports Hall of Fame. Mysteriously, the Govins apparently went from the south Saskatchewan championship to the western Canadian title *before* playing in the north-south Saskatchewan matchup for the provincial title. The official description of the team's dream year slides over the missing provincial playdown and certainly ignores the decision by the Govins to throw the title. Yet that controversy might explain why the 1954 Govins team has yet to make it into the Saskatchewan Sports Hall of Fame.

When summer ended, it was also time to say goodbye to Sylvia, who was returning to Saskatoon to take up her duties once more at the cancer clinic and the university and to return to the Ramblers. The Govins had a house party to give gifts and say farewell, which included a poem composed especially for the occasion:

> To Syl
> We sure do hate to see you go
> 'Cause you are one good kid
> We love ys' when you're smilin'
> And even when you blow your lid
>
> We're sad 'cause you are leavin'
> It just won't be the same
> Without that voice on third to yell—
> "Come on gang, get in the game."
>
> So when you get to Saskatoon
> Don't forget to drop a line.
> We'll want to know what's new up there
> And if you're feeling fine.
>
> Say a good word for Regina
> And the Govin gang, old dear,
> And if those guys don't treat you right
> Come back and share our beer.[17]

For Sylvia, even though she spent more time with the Ramblers, her one year with the Govins left an indelible mark on both her heart and her archive. It's almost as if her years with the Ramblers blended together, but her one year with the Govins stood out.

Her love for the Govins, though, didn't prevent Sylvia from doing battle with them on the ball diamonds in the memorable summer of 1955. That year was Saskatchewan's Golden Jubilee marking fifty years of being part of Canadian Confederation. The year-long celebrations included many sporting events, and fans of women's fastball had lots to choose from, including by August a provincial championship battle between the Govins and the Ramblers. It was a hotly contested best-of-five series, switching between the two rival cities. The Ramblers took it in five, using their home field advantage in Saskatoon to drub the excellent Govins in a 10–5 win. For Sylvia, it was a week and weekend of excellent ball, fierce competition, and friends everywhere she looked.

There was no time to rest. After taking the provincial championship, the Ramblers gathered their strength for the western softball semifinal series against the Vancouver Kerrys. On Labour Day Monday in Saskatoon, the Ramblers faced Vancouver for the first two of a best-of-three series, defeating the Kerrys in back-to-back games 12–3 and 12–0. Each was hardly a match. Although the Ramblers had played seven games in five days, they were not finished yet. The sweep took them to the western final series, which meant an overnight train trip from Saskatoon to Winnipeg on Tuesday night to play a best-of-five series against their rival namesake, the Winnipeg Ramblers.

It was a cold week to play a series in an unfamiliar ballpark, coming off a five-game weekend and an overnight train trip. With the temperature hovering at five degrees Celsius, the Saskatoon team lost their first game by a single point. Pitcher Shirley Coben was tired, and it showed. But stellar fielding, including double play after double play, supported relief pitcher Beth Britton. In the second game, with Britton at the helm, the Ramblers took the game 4–0, holding every Winnipeg rally firmly in check. Saturday saw back-to-back games. In the first, Saskatoon overpowered Winnipeg with a decisive 12–5 win, bringing the series to 2–1 in favour of the wheat province. Winnipeg rallied at the beginning of the next game, scoring early runs. Then Saskatoon roared back to a final score of 8–7, taking the series 3–1 to win the western championship.[18]

It was the end of an amazing eight years of high-level Saskatchewan ball for Sylvia Fedoruk, with back-to-back western Canadian championships playing for two different teams, the

5. THE FRIENDLY ATOM

Regina Govins and the Saskatoon Ramblers. The consecutive championships were a perfect high note on which to end her career. Sylvia hung up her cleats and ball glove, quietly retiring from ball while on the winning side of the ledger.

By the fall of 1955, she was appointed as a research associate in radiation physics at the University of Saskatchewan. The physics department still housed the betatron accelerator and was aiming to get its own cobalt-60 unit for research (not therapeutic) use. The university wanted, and needed, her expertise. The new dual appointment between the Saskatchewan Cancer Commission and the university echoed the duality held by her mentor and boss, Harold Johns. The Cancer Commission, whose money came from government funds, committed to a second Saskatchewan cobalt unit in Regina. Sylvia's stint in Regina in 1954 had laid the path, but the unit was not yet in place. Purchasing the cobalt from Chalk River, building a new cobalt bomb clinical machine, transporting and installing it, buying and installing lead lining in the treatment room, and ensuring that all other renovation and installation requirements were met took time. Minister of Health T.J. Bentley reported in 1956 that the new Regina unit would be a "half-unit," capable of working effectively using the partially degraded cobalt-60 from the original machine in Saskatoon. Saskatoon would get a new, charged cobalt-60 core from Chalk River, and the Regina unit would take the old cobalt-60 core.[19] When the latter unit was ready for installation, panic erupted. The lab didn't have all the needed equipment to lift the heavy unit into place. Sylvia, in her usual solve-the-problem style, promptly found a block and tackle set, threw it into her bright yellow car in Saskatoon, and made the trip to Regina in record time—two hours—on uncertain 1950s roads.[20]

The year 1956 marked two other major changes for Sylvia. Johns accepted a position as head of the physics division of the Ontario Cancer Institute at Princess Margaret Hospital in Toronto, leaving behind his Saskatchewan graduate students and colleagues. Although no doubt missing his insight and knowledge, Sylvia remained a physicist with the Saskatchewan Cancer Commission and took on a larger role with ease. She also accepted a promotion to lecturer in physics at the University of Saskatchewan. In 1958, that appointment moved to a lectureship in therapeutic radiology in medicine, though she retained a role as research associate with the physics department. The appointment to the Department of Medicine reflected the more established role of therapeutic radiology and cancer treatment at the University of Saskatchewan as opposed to the more experimental role of Johns. Sylvia's research switched to focus on better clinical applications and treatment.

Throughout the 1950s, Sylvia stretched and tested her professional wings. Her research interests in the expanding field of radiation physics moved from specific work on cobalt-60 to growing interest in measurement and performance issues as well as diagnostic scanning as a critical first step to treatment. For Sylvia, the ability to create and measure cross-comparable data scientifically was crucial. As a new field, medical physics was creating not only its own therapy machines and tools but also its own vocabulary, a new language of medical science. In her view, using precise vocabulary and measurements mattered. She aimed for consistency not only within one lab but also across treatment units and around the world. In the early to mid-1950s, Sylvia was the lead author or a co-author of twelve publications related to cobalt-60; thereafter, demand for her insights grew on the international stage. In 1956, she became a member of the International Society of Nuclear Medicine; in the 1960s, she would be the first Canadian elected to serve on this board as a trustee.

Although her professional life was steadily growing, building a national and soon-to-be international reputation, something was missing. Basketball, even with the Aces, had fallen by the wayside, and summer baseball was a younger woman's game—by 1957, Sylvia was turning thirty. It's not known exactly when she set foot in a curling rink, but when Sylvia returned from her stint in Regina in late 1954 she moved in with Joyce McKee, who soon figured largely in Sylvia's curling story. Joyce was a teammate on the Ramblers, and the two set up housekeeping at 612 1st Street East in Saskatoon, where they lived for twelve years, roommates and teammates. It didn't take long before Joyce pulled Sylvia into her favourite winter activity.

Curling was the winter pastime of Saskatchewan's summer ballplayers, with summers spent at the diamonds and winters at the rinks. Curling grew in prominence and professionalization with Saskatchewan's men's rinks regularly doing well at national bonspiels. Interest grew. Some of the women with whom Sylvia played ball, such as Joyce, came from fanatical curling families who spent weekends travelling to rural bonspiels in all types of weather.

5. THE FRIENDLY ATOM

Hailing from Asquith with a dairy background, the McKee family brought a sense of family and a deep work ethic to their favourite winter sport. Joyce set the Saskatoon men's curling world on fire in 1952 when, at the age of eighteen, she joined her father and two brothers in the Hub City men's league. This was not acceptable, many men thought. Men's curling was for *men*. There were traditions, a language, and a camaraderie that would be hemmed in by the presence of a young woman. The defiant stance of the McKee family was even more evident when they played.

Her dad, Mac, was there, but one of her brothers skipped the team, and Joyce—clearly the best shooter despite her short and slim stature—threw last rocks. The family entry into the Saskatoon men's playdown bonspiel, with Joyce on the roster, was met with uproar and indignation. No matter. Also curling in the women's league with Mrs. George Nesbitt, Mrs. Lou Hennigman, and ball teammate Miss Muriel Coben, Joyce deserted the Saskatoon men's bonspiel and entered the Prince Albert ladies' bonspiel, their rink taking the Grand Challenge, the prize for the largest score in one end, and laurels for being the best-dressed rink in the spiel. Muriel, just starting to pull back from her brilliant career as a pitcher with the Ramblers, was a powerhouse. "Apparently, she carries her pitching skill on the ice, too."[21]

Sylvia wasn't a curler. She might have been on a few rural sheets growing up near the Ukrainian village of Wroxton, where a curling club had been formed in 1919 to play the game on the local pond. The family's move to Windsor, Ontario, put a halt to any dabbling in curling. Her winters were taken up by thumping shoes and layups in basketball and sharp serves and spikes in volleyball, not by sliding down a curling sheet. Back in Saskatoon for university, the only ice that Sylvia played on was within the crease of the hockey rink, complete with pads and sticks and gloves as goalie for the Huskie girls' hockey team. In later years, she said bluntly, "I used to think curling was a bit of a funny sport. The University actually had a curling team at the time I went, but us basketball players didn't pay much attention to the sport at all."[22]

With Sylvia's full-time career as a cancer physicist, and Joyce's administrative career with Merlin Motors, neither could enter bonspiels during the week. Nor could they curl in the typical women's club leagues during weekday mornings or afternoons in which the time slots suited housewives. The prime-time men's leagues took up the evening slots. It wasn't until Saskatoon curling leagues started opening evening slots and ice sheets for professional ladies that Sylvia was able to get in the game. With draws at both 7 and 9 p.m., and four clubs going in Saskatoon—the CNR, Nutana, Hub City, and Granite curling clubs—one or two sheets would be available for an evening ladies' draw, usually at the Hub City club. Most women still curled in the larger afternoon draw at Hub City, Granite, and sometimes Nutana. All four clubs would make ice available, as needed, for large ladies' bonspiels or playdowns—sometimes under protest.

Sylvia entered Saskatchewan women's curling at a superb time. Local clubs had self-organized to create the Saskatchewan Ladies' Curling Association in 1948, hosting the hotly contested annual provincial championship. With Alberta and Manitoba also offering provincial ladies' playdowns, the associations soon moved to create a prairie-wide event, the first of which occurred in March 1953 in Regina. By 1954, British Columbia had joined, making for a true western playdown. As interest grew, eastern Canadian clubs, particularly in Quebec and Ontario, would visit the western playdowns as spectators or participants to gauge interest in a national ladies' curling association. By 1960, the Canadian Ladies' Curling Association had been formed.

Curling was a dynamic and popular local sport. Sports writers and commentators followed it keenly. The number of column inches dedicated to the "roar of the rings" easily rivalled that for hockey—and so it should. For the sheer number of people involved, curling outranked all other sports. From high school championships to ladies' to seniors' to men's provincial standings and hopefuls at the nationals, curling received aggressive attention. Even league play was covered in a daily roundup of the previous night's results and the current day's matchups. Bonspiels, such as the Hub City "Bond Spiel," took out large ads. With an entry fee of forty dollars per rink, a substantial sum in 1952, prizes ranged from $1,000 for first place in the A round to $100 for fourth place in the third event. Expecting 128 rinks to enter, Hub City would profit from the fees as well as admission and the lunchroom. A mere fifty cents would get one through the door for the whole weekend, and the lunchroom would be open all hours. For rural and small rinks without the new ice-making equipment, curlers took a chance on spring spiels. A chinook could quickly create a "slushspiel," with delays stranding teams for several extra days. Games shifted to midnight or 1 a.m. to guarantee a usable ice surface.

5. THE FRIENDLY ATOM

The 1950s saw changes to the women's style of curling. It was a time of transition as older women with long skirts and genteel pushes gave way to those with athleticism, long slides, pants and toe rubbers, and a takeout game. Joyce McKee, long used to playing top-notch curling alongside her brothers and father, would be a breakout player, transferring her skills to the ladies' league and ultimately creating a new path to change the game. Throughout the 1950s, the Hub City ladies' evening league saw McKee face off against many other skips, including some who would later join her on teams, such as Barbara MacNevin of Delisle. MacNevin became another Saskatchewan curling legend who skipped several teams of her own at the provincial and national levels.

McKee first won the provincial championship in 1954, soon after the four western provincial associations had organized a regional event. That year her rink consisted of Muriel Coben at third, Maisie Johnston at second, and Viola (Mrs. George) Nesbitt at lead. They won the city playdowns, took the northerns, then travelled to Yorkton to play against the southern winner, Mrs. E. Collins of Weyburn. Their best-of-three series was timed to coincide with the Saskatchewan Ladies' Curling Association annual meeting, giving the teams a full—and fully knowledgeable—audience as well as the requisite rounds of banquets and luncheons. But the February weather broke, and within hours the natural ice at Yorkton was virtually unusable—a "bonspiel thaw" was the prairie description. With the series just getting started and the western final already organized in Edmonton, Saskatchewan had to find a way to let McKee and Collins finish. In a panic, organizers decided to move the games to Regina to be played on artificial ice.

Saskatchewan's gendered curling issue arose. The only curling ice available already had a full slate of men's regular evening draws. The men refused to bump any of their games to free up the one sheet needed for the women's match. Instead, the second—and what turned out to be the last—game in the best-of-three series did not occur until 11 p.m., after the more important men's teams were finished and the men had gone off to quaff their beer. McKee didn't hesitate. She downed Collins for the second straight game, 11–6, finishing at about 2 a.m. Despite the pluckiness of taking the Saskatchewan title in the middle of the night, the McKee rink fared poorly in Edmonton and returned home without the western title, which went to Alberta's Dorothy Thompson.

In the 1958 Saskatchewan northern curling playdowns held at the Granite club in Saskatoon, McKee's rink was Muriel Coben, Barbara MacNevin, and Sylvia Fedoruk playing lead. Rural foursomes entered the playdowns alongside city teams. Well used to curling on natural ice, the rural teams gained an advantage when the Granite club's compressor unit, used to temper and cool the ice, gave out. Coupled with "unexpected balmy weather," the ice conditions quickly became "tricky." The McKee rink soon dropped out of the running, and the curling season came to an end.[23]

Living with Joyce reopened another world for Sylvia. The daughter of an avid gardener, Sylvia loved the little house on 1st Street for its north-facing entrance and its south-facing backyard, full of sunshine, ready for a garden in which to grow at least some of their own food. Every garden develops its own personality, its own *terroir* or character and sense of place. The soil, the air, the water, the amount of sunlight, surrounding plants and trees or open fields, the kind of honeybees, fertilizers, and cultivation techniques all affect what kind of garden it is, what can be grown in it, and how the produce will taste. Different types of seeds, even seeds bought from different growers, will make a difference. With gardening experience ranging from the Yorkton area to southern Ontario, Sylvia knew that gardens are about research and experimentation. The two professional women dug in. Joyce, with her farming background west of Saskatoon, was no stranger to gardens or the work involved in tending them. Pictures in the Sylvia Fedoruk collection show a sunny southern backyard with a cement flagstone patio, ready for alfresco drinks and barbeques, next to a luxuriant garden brimming with fresh vegetables and flowers. Friends remembered barbeques and picnics, and always loads to share when the crop came in, as long as no one expected Sylvia to eat the onions.

It's one thing to grow a garden, but what does one do with all of it? There was no way that the two, even with Sylvia's notable appetite, could keep up with their garden's bounty. A happy circle of co-workers and friends, some of whom lived more cooped-up lives in apartments without access to garden spaces, gratefully shared the bounty. The pair also became avid canners and picklers. Sylvia, with her deep Ukrainian roots, was known to her ball teams in the 1950s for her sauerkraut, leveraging the famous cabbage-growing abilities of her mother, Annie, into sour perfection. Snooping through each other's treasured recipe books, swapping

5. THE FRIENDLY ATOM

Joyce and Sylvia's backyard patio and garden at 612 1st Street in Saskatoon, July 1961.

recipes, and trying new ones, Sylvia and Joyce developed a happy kitchen companionship.

Sylvia's life map reveals epochs in which activities seem to have occurred naturally hand in hand. It is impossible to separate her dual professional lives of science and sport, which cannot be compartmentalized and instead should be considered together. As a university student, Sylvia was learning and experimenting, immersed in a range of subjects and sports. From English to track, chemistry to hockey, math to volleyball and golf, and physics to basketball, she was an unpredictable whirlwind. As she transitioned to a serious graduate student and then quickly to a full-time professional, her focus deepened. Her work on the team that learned to understand the betatron and then created the cobalt bomb was done with a high measure of excellence. The new practice of international travel and collaboration raised her profile. When Harold Johns left Saskatchewan, Sylvia entered some of her strongest professional research years. The betatron and the cobalt bomb taught her lessons in adversity, perseverance, designing and experimenting and machining, and investing in long-term research goals. The teamwork aspect was critical. Sylvia loved being on a team, whether in a science lab or cancer clinic or in baseball or curling. Reaching for both professional and sporting excellence, she shone.

From a cancer-fighting perspective, one lesson carved a new path for Sylvia's research interests. For the betatron and the cobalt bomb to have their best chances at effecting mitigation and cure, doctors and scientists had to find the cancer at a much earlier stage. From a research point of view, her interests swerved. If the 1940s were about the betatron and the 1950s were about the cobalt bomb, the 1960s saw Sylvia Fedoruk attack the problem at its source, designing nuclear scanning techniques to find cancer earlier. Her view of the friendly atom changed from a weapon bombing the cancer from the outside to a spy finding the cancer within.

6. PINPRICKS OF LIGHT

IN THE SUMMER OF 1959, SYLVIA FEDORUK TOOK HER FIRST major steps as an international physicist. Attending the International Atomic Energy Agency (IAEA) panel on medical radioisotope scanning, followed by the International Congress of Radiology conference, she aimed to create a strong Canadian female research voice on the international stage. Between these events, Sylvia visited cancer clinics using advanced medical physics equipment in both Britain and Germany. As usual, though, she balanced work with fun. On August 1, her close friend, roommate, and curling skip Joyce McKee joined her in Munich for a month-long European adventure.

Driving a rented car, the two young professional women—Fedoruk a scientist, McKee an administrative specialist—travelled south through Innsbruck to the muggy wetness of Venice, enjoying a classic gondolier boat ride, after which Sylvia swore mightily at the cost to use the bathroom facilities. On to the fashion capital of Milan, then back up the Como Pass, the two drove through Lausanne and Geneva, then across to Paris, Brussels, Amsterdam, and Dusseldorf. From there, they hopped back to Britain, driving north to tour through Scotland and, no doubt, sample the many boutique brands of scotch. After going back to London, they flew home to Canada at the end of the month. Sylvia's travel notebook, held in the University of Saskatchewan Archives, is a wonderful mishmash of serious scientific information from conferences and hospital visits and the everyday practicality of splitting, as evenly as possible, the costs of her trip with Joyce. If you need to know gas costs across Europe in August 1959, Sylvia's notebook is your source. It will also tell you the costs of beer, sweaters, postcards, and the use of a public toilet. Sometimes the two would lose count of who had paid for what and who owed whom.[1] But in the end both seemed to be satisfied that all was square, and they settled back into life in their shared house at 612 1st Street East in Saskatoon, in time to refocus on the upcoming winter of curling.

From the first few tentative slides and slips in the fall of 1954, by 1959 Sylvia had developed into a curler, capable of supporting Joyce in the rings. The *Saskatoon Star-Phoenix* called McKee "unconquerable."[2] Between 1956 and 1959, she had skipped her rink to an incredible forty-one wins in forty-three games in four years of the city bonspiel, with a single loss in each of 1957 and 1958. The February 1959 McKee rink of skip Joyce, third Muriel Coben, second Sylvia Fedoruk, and lead Donna Belding swept both the bonspiel championship and the grand aggregate honours for the fourth consecutive year. The bonspiels, though, were not tied to the provincial playdowns, yet the calibre of play was high and the number of rinks involved—eighty-six teams entered the Saskatoon bonspiel in late winter 1959—led to a spectacular week of curling. Nonetheless, when the northern playdowns opened immediately following the Saskatoon ladies' bonspiel, the McKee rink was nowhere to be seen. They had lost the city playdowns for the first time since the early 1950s. Sylvia and Joyce took time to shake off the sting of defeat with their month-long sojourn in Europe.

The 1959–60 McKee rink shook off their 1958–59 loss to make a major run for the provincial playdowns. The Saskatoon winner would compete in the northern playdowns. The southern and northern winners would then face off in a best-of-three match to decide which rink would head to the western championship. The two best rinks from each of the four city clubs, along with one from the Royal Canadian Air Force (RCAF) station, would participate in an eight-team double-knockout series (which simply meant that if you lost two games, you were out). The two teams from the Hub City club were skipped by Joyce McKee and Barbara MacNevin.

The McKee playdown rink had a shakeup after the unexpected loss in the 1958–59 season: McKee as skip, Fedoruk as third, Belding as second, and Coben as lead. The new rink put McKee in hot water. The ladies whom she brought to play at the city playdowns were not the same as those of her regular club rink: it was, in some

6. PINPRICKS OF LIGHT

ways, a hand-picked team. An unsigned letter from "disgusted women members" of the Hub City club called McKee a "poor sport" and warned that she should no longer expect cheering from her regular clubmates. McKee forged ahead. Even though it was the city playdowns, the women still had to work around the men's regular league and playdown schedules. Some nights saw a 6:30 game start at one rink and then a scramble and wild car ride across the city to another rink for a 9:00 game. Playing twelve ends, two more than today's usual ten, gave the women little time to rest. McKee had to fight the hardest against her Hub City compatriot Barbara MacNevin but squeaked out a hit and roll in the last end to take the game and propel her into the northern playdowns.

Joyce McKee with her high broom delivery style, c. 1960.

It was a sweet victory, and this time McKee thought that she had all of the pieces in place to take her rink as far as they could go. Although dominating bonspiels and playdowns throughout the 1950s, she had won the provincial title only in 1954. Newspapers argued that McKee was "always a strong contender, but never a champion."[3] The 1959–60 season marked her turn from not quite ready to ready. Her rink took the northern final, defeating teams with ridiculously lopsided scores and ending "years of frustration."[4] Undefeated and riding high, the rink was ready to contend for the provincial title. The hot McKee rink won the right to wear the provincial green against Pauline Klaudeman of Regina.[5]

The Saskatchewan team celebrated the provincial win alongside proud work colleagues. At Sylvia's desk at the cancer clinic, co-workers taped a large handwritten sign to the wall, WELCOME

CHAMPS, with a smaller one noting VICTORIA HERE WE COME! An effigy of Sylvia proclaimed "I'm the Third—My name is Sylvester," while a smaller sketch of a grumpy gorilla proclaimed "I'm the Skip!" to tease Joyce. Good-natured ribbing both masked and showcased pride in the provincial champs.

Change was coming to Canadian ladies' curling. A truly national round robin bonspiel, with teams from each province, was in the works for the spring of 1961. As a prelude to that championship, an "unofficial" Canadian champion would be crowned in 1960. The winner of the western championship in Victoria would fly to Ontario to engage in a best-of-three playdown against the eastern championship winner for a shot at a new national title. For McKee and Fedoruk, the stakes were suddenly a little higher.

The play in Victoria was hard and fast right from the first game, with all four teams fighting tricky "green" ice. Nothing was simple, and the Saskatchewan rink had to fight. Saskatchewan lost its opening game to Manitoba in an 8–7 contest that came down to inches in the last end. The next day Alberta ripped apart Manitoba with a commanding 20–3 win. In a round robin, McKee knew that she had to beat the Alberta rink. Luckily, there were many expat Saskatchewan people in the crowd cheering wildly. Fan support, coupled with the Saskatchewan takeout curling style, bolstered the team when they needed it most. In the stands, two men, Larry Marshall and Gordie Robertson, watched the McKee rink's power and precision with fascination, and their conversation was published in the Victoria newspaper. Marshall noted that McKee "would give anybody in our [men's] club a run for their money." Robertson replied, "But I wouldn't want to be the guy that played them. It would be too darn embarrassing."[6]

Journalists watching Saskatchewan and Alberta placed a slight advantage on the McKee team. If Alberta's Dorothy Thompson was the better game caller and shooter, her teammates lacked the fire and consistency of the ladies who backed McKee. Some saw a slight tendency for Saskatchewan to dominate early but then fall off toward the end of a game. McKee scoffed. Those lapses were just her being too careful after building up a lead—a mistake that she clearly did not intend to make in the last round robin game against Alberta.

And she did not. McKee, the "darling of the male curling experts by merit of her cool calculating skipping," downed Thompson 14–11 to take the western title.[7] It was a fitting climax, with Thompson easily out-curling the other seven ladies on the ice and bringing plenty of stones into play with her soft style and brilliant game calling. On the whole, the newspapers reported, the Alberta rink showed better curling percentages, but the Saskatchewan rink was better at clutch shots, particularly McKee's "happy knack of pulling off a big shot." Sylvia contributed by performing a perfect chip takeout of an almost frozen Alberta stone in the tenth end. The Saskatchewan team impressed the audience, who thought that the Saskatoon rink "was in a class by themselves."[8] With the win and new pins for their Saskatchewan curling sweaters, the rink geared up for the east-west showdown in Oshawa.

The McKee rink, 1960. Standing: Sylvia Fedoruk and Joyce McKee. Front: Muriel Coben and Donna Belding.

The east-west game pitted Saskatchewan against the Ruth Smith rink from Lacolle, Quebec. The western team arrived just as the Quebec rink swept the eastern championship unbeaten in round robin play. The Smith team also had a knack for pulling off big shots in the clutch: they had won three of their four games in the final ends with multiple counters. Clearly, Smith and McKee should have been—on paper at least—a good match. But the eastern champions were overwhelmed by the style of play of the McKee foursome.

Down east, ladies' curling remained primarily a morning and afternoon game for genteel ladies of a certain (older) age who played a conservative, slow, draw game with plenty of rocks in play. "Down there, curling is pretty expensive. There aren't too many clubs and the game itself appears to rank second to the social aspect of a membership."[9] The knockout style of play, long slides, and game calling of the western champions were so different that the eastern champions fell flat. Two straight losses of 11–3 and 8–5 decided the first, unofficial, east-west championship in a showcase of domination.

Brigadier General Jack Gow of the Royal Caledonians of Scotland was in the stands. A long-time curler, he was shocked at the skill level and playing style of the Hub City Saskatoon team. He told McKee that he had never seen the like. Saskatoon's knockout game was unheard of in Scotland. It would be nice to have a Canadian team tour the overseas bonspiels, he said. A cross-pollination of curling styles, and the suggestion of touring worldwide, would eventually lead to world ladies' curling championships as well as reciprocal visits of ladies' teams between Canada and Scotland. Clearly, there was much more to curling, and curling style, than had been explored.[10]

In the end, Saskatchewan took home the honours on both sides of the gender divide that year. Ernie Richardson's Regina foursome brought home the Canadian men's championship, while the McKee rink—even if an unofficial east-west win and not yet a full ten-province bonspiel championship—flew home with the Canadian ladies' championship in hand.

For all the lustre of winning, the season ended on a question mark. When asked whether the team would make a run for the championship again the next year, when the stakes would be even higher for the first official Diamond D ladies' championship, McKee demurred. She had no idea whether the same team would even be playing together the following winter. Time alone would tell. After all, it took a huge commitment to play elite curling, whether for professional women such as McKee and Fedoruk or for those with family or other responsibilities. Time to practise, to participate in hotly contested bonspiels, and then to travel to provincial, regional, and national playdowns took a toll. McKee and Fedoruk, unmarried and without children, faced perhaps fewer impediments than women with family ties. Yet professional lives required dedication and a supportive work environment. Few could successfully navigate both worlds.

Sylvia's international presence at the annual radiology congress and as a consultant with the International Atomic Energy Agency grew through the 1960s. By the end of winter 1960, just as the curling team returned from Oshawa and their championship win, Sylvia had received a letter from the minister of national health and welfare to become a member of the Department of Health and Welfare's Advisory Committee on the Clinical Uses of Radioisotopes

6. PINPRICKS OF LIGHT

as well as a physicist member of that committee's Executive Council. Sylvia, of course, accepted. It was the first step in her long career of national public service as a physicist.

One way to measure her productivity and influence as a scientist is to map her published scientific papers. Her two most prolific years of publication were 1952, following the installation of the cobalt-60 unit in Saskatoon, when she shared publication kudos for no fewer than five papers, and 1960, when Sylvia hit that impressive mark of five published papers once again. Most years her resumé reveals one to two publications, a more than respectable accomplishment for a career scientist. By 1960, her research interests had transitioned from treatment to diagnosis, to finding cancer earlier to better target and refine its treatment. Sylvia's burgeoning expertise in radiation scanning techniques led to work with colleagues in veterinary medicine. This group published four papers studying diagnostic scanning techniques to determine the limits of halothane use as an anesthetic on dogs. First discovered in 1955, halothane is now on the World Health Organization's list of essential human medicines.

On humans, Sylvia co-authored pioneering work on liver scanning with Dr. Donald Fee, a professor in the Department of Medicine at the University of Saskatchewan and a clinical associate at the cancer clinic. Fee, like Sylvia, was interested in seeing what was going on inside patients before any kind of surgery or radiation treatment was proposed. Published in the *New England Journal of Medicine* in 1960, based on two years of data and about 250 patients, the research showcased both Sylvia's engineering ability to adapt and modify instruments and her interest in explaining methodology so that others could replicate her work. The cancer clinic owned a Reed-Curtis Scintiscanner, which Sylvia and Fee modified. Instead of using it to scan the thyroid, she adapted it for photoscanning through an analyzer, along with an inverted cassette of red lucite and a light source. Once a patient was injected with radioactive rose Bengal dye, it would move through the healthy parts of the liver, but there would be no uptake in cancer metastases or scar tissue. The dye would be easily excreted from the body. Using Kodak Blue-Brand X-ray film and layering three sheets of film at once,[11] Sylvia found that she could take excellent scans of the liver, showing areas where the dye *was not* taken up, indicating metastatic sites or other problems. But, as with all photoscans at the time, there were limitations to either the resolution of the output or

Joyce McKee, Sylvia Fedoruk, Barbara MacNevin, and Rosa McFee, c. 1961.

the scan itself. "We hope that, with increasing experience and the substitution of a larger crystal and a focusing collimator, interpretation will be improved."[12] In essence, Sylvia was laying out research plans for the next several years.

As always, she unerringly balanced university teaching and research life with sports. Elite curling dominated Joyce's and Sylvia's domestic sphere heading into the winter of 1960–61. Still holding strong as third, Sylvia towered almost a full head above the diminutive McKee. But there was a change in the front half. Donna Belding had pulled away to form her own rink, while Muriel Coben, the oldest of the four, had stepped away from curling. McKee thus recruited Barbara MacNevin of Delisle, along with MacNevin's teammate, white-blonde Rosa McFee of Saskatoon. As usual, some of the toughest competition was right at home. The new McKee rink had to fight their way through a Saskatchewan ladies' field of 203 ladies' clubs with 4,300 members from north to south, east to west. Nonetheless, with the prize of a true national championship in their sights, the McKee rink went to work. Within the Saskatoon

6. PINPRICKS OF LIGHT

ladies' league circuit, it was soon clear that their stiffest competition came from their old teammate, Donna Belding.

In addition to full-time work and a hectic weekly and weekend curling schedule, Sylvia began to take on a larger role within curling administration. She became the president of the Hub City ladies' curling club, and in 1961 she was the committee chair working on the Saskatoon women's bonspiel. Prizes were both practical and a sign of the times: hostess chairs, walnut coffee tables, kitchen step stools, transistor radios, bedspreads, hair dryers, blankets, and Corningware dishes were in the offering. Banquet entertainment featured a program that looked at curling "fashion" over the past forty years. One item, though, caught everyone's eye. "Looking to the time of atomic energy when rinks would be heated by radiation was the model in the fetching pink bikini bathing suit, with fur collar and matching fur earmuffs, Miss Futurama."[13]

With so many entrants, the massive draw needed ice sheets at Hub City, Nutana, and Granite curling clubs over five days, handing the organizers a logistical nightmare. Travelling to and from three curling rinks to play, while spending every spare minute keeping an eye on the organizational side, Sylvia needed keen intelligence and good humour to keep up. At the end of the five days of play, as bonspiel president, she doled out the prizes, including the bonspiel championship, the grand aggregate for most wins, and the Butler Byers trophy to her own team.

The Saskatoon playdowns finished, McKee's rink advanced to the northern playdowns held at the Nutana rink in Saskatoon. The draw featured regional playdown winners from Springwater to Meskanaw, Nipawin to Kindersley. As expected, McKee dominated. Sometimes the games were wildly uneven, such as the drubbing of Foam Lake by a score of 17–0. Not all games were so lopsided, though. McKee's closest competitor was Nipawin's Myrtle Anderson, whose team of Zola Foster, Evelyn Raabel, and Kathy Hickley kept the games close. Anderson came close to ending McKee's run, matching McKee shot for shot. In a game of inches, each inch counts, and McKee, in some nailbiting ends that had those in the gallery on their feet, had to fight. A chinook broke the usual Saskatoon winter weather, and the teams dodged drips and even running water, opting to play early in the morning and late at night to counter the soft ice. McKee took the A event final from Anderson, knocking her to the B side, but Anderson roared right back. It took the McKee rink an extra end to put down the Nipawin foursome in the A-B final, in which they were often chasing, not leading, on the scoreboard. Solid shots from second Barbara MacNevin, with a shot percentage of 71, kept them in contention to the last rock. A miss by Anderson in the extra end made the difference, and McKee went on to the provincials.

The hotshots from Hub City had a faltering start. Because of the intense competition of the local and regional playdowns, the Saskatchewan final was a best-of-three series, with the northern district facing the winner of the southern district. Millie Binner's rink from Moose Jaw charged through southern play and met the McKee rink in North Battleford, site of the provincial playdowns. A headline in the sports section of the *Saskatoon Star-Phoenix* the next day reported, "McKee Loses First Game." The Binnie team of Vel Starrak, Dot Crippen, and Jean Baldenstone "outcurled the northern champions" to a heartbreaking loss of 10–7 in the opening Thursday-night draw. McKee curled an abysmal 50 percent.[14] Her rink went to bed angry and sad.

Yet the loss brought out the best from Sylvia, whose curling percentages rose as McKee's fell. Known for her pugnacious play, Sylvia, as usual, was the hardest on herself, pushing herself to rise to the occasion. She curled 80 percent and held that high average through the rest of the best-of-three series. On Friday afternoon, McKee's game improved, and Sylvia remained hot. Three major double takeouts, along with a raise guard takeout, kept her percentages high. The McKee rink downed the Binnie rink 11–7. "A pair of big ends by McKee at crucial times kept Mrs. Binnie under considerable pressure . . . and not once did the Saskatoon skipper relinquish the lead."[15] After supper, the two teams went back out onto the ice, and the Hub City foursome continued to pile on the pressure. Precise shot-making helped McKee to down Binnie 11–4 in the final and thus head to Ottawa for the first official Diamond D championship.

Legendary sports reporter Jack Kinsella marvelled at the new national championship: "Who would ever have thought . . . that the day would come when the female of the species contrived to compete in curling on a national basis, after the fashion of the Brier itself? . . . [If] the opening day's attendance is any criterion, there will be a lot of unwashed dishes in the sink this week." Sexist commentary aside, the basic question was would the curling be interesting to watch? Some teams, such as from Alberta and Saskatchewan, were "surprisingly good," Kinsella admitted. "In the west, it seems,

6. PINPRICKS OF LIGHT

everyone curls, and curls well."[16] Festivities kicked off with the highest level of pomp and circumstance: Governor General of Canada Georges Vanier and his wife, Pauline, met the lady curlers for tea at Rideau Hall.

At the Hunt and Golf Club, pipers led the ten rinks onto the ice for the opening ceremonies. Then the teams began to play. The opening draw of the week-long round robin bonspiel pitted McKee against her Alberta nemesis, Dorothy Thompson of Edmonton. The Edmonton rink, described as "all business girls," missed beating McKee "by an eyelash."[17]

Sports reporters described the way that Sylvia and Joyce curled: "Polished and schooled . . . long slides, broom hand held aloft, faultless footwork. The Saskatchewan skip and third wear man-tailored trousers and low shoes with toe rubbers, and when they're delivering rocks they kick off the rubber on their sliding foot. So the skip glides right out to the hog line, then straightens up at the last second and steps legally over the line."[18] At the end of round robin play, the McKee rink was awarded the first official Diamond D trophy as the undisputed winner, going nine wins and no losses through their first truly national event.

McKee, Fedoruk, MacNevin, and McFee shone with accomplishment and pride. McKee told Kinsella that it was the culmination of thirteen years of curling over 13,000 ends. Everyone curled in small-town Saskatchewan, she noted. Skill came from playing the game a lot, she said with modesty. The real secret, though, was togetherness, for a team to "get along well together," McKee declared.[19] Curling finished, the Saskatchewan foursome took time to visit the House of Commons for Question Period. Henry Jones, MP for Saskatoon, rose on a point of personal privilege and acknowledged their presence, to loud clapping from the house.

Travelling back through Toronto, they stopped at "Eddie Shack's house," Maple Leaf Gardens, to take in a game between the Leafs and the New York Rangers On their return to Saskatoon, their home curling club, Hub City, hosted a special banquet in their honour. They also visited Regina. The team was piped into the Legislative Assembly by Eldon Johnson, MLA from Kerrobert-Kindersley. Premier Tommy Douglas called their victory "a proud day for Saskatchewan. We honour your performance and we wish you continued victory." Presented with a silver tray each to commemorate the success, they were feted at a dinner right in the legislative building.[20]

The McKee rink win was a standout for the women's curling world, and its success held pointers for the 150,000 Canadian women registered in the dominion ladies' curling association.

First, start young, even if you are so small and weak that you have to put two feet in the hack, and two hands on the rock, to push it hard enough to get it down the ice, especially on the rough, less than perfect, and rather frosty natural ice found in so many rural curling rinks.

Second, if you can, learn in the "prairie curling hatchery," where you have to play more games and play more like the men than the eastern women. McKee's strength and compact agility, swinging the forty-pound curling rock back before rocketing forward out of the hack, caused a sensation.

Third, pick your rinkmates for compatibility rather than skill. With so many league games, fun bonspiels, serious bonspiels, and multiple games on a given day, the team must, above all else, like each other. All that ice time made for a battle-hardened McKee team, but in the end they relied on her for her precision shot-making. They—and the spectators—were so used to McKee making difficult shots that when, from time to time, she missed one it caused more of an uproar than the amazing shots.

Fourth, youth is an advantage. "Rinks finish stronger over a long bout of curling packed into four days"[21] if they have youth, vigour, and athleticism. In other words, if a team views it more as sport than as recreation, they will have an advantage.

Fifth, practice is essential. Again, like athletes practising basketball shots on an empty court, or golfers working the driving ranges and putting greens, the McKee rink invested in regular practice to work on draws, hit the broom, or make precise takeouts.

Today's curlers will probably read these pointers with heads nodding, but in the early 1960s the western Canadian women's style of play, with the McKee rink firmly at the top and in command, transformed Canadian women's curling. It moved with alacrity and sharpness from a genteel way to pass the time to a full-on sport.

As Sylvia drew further into the world of curling, she quickly became intrigued with memorabilia. Curling offered large trophies for teams to hoist in triumph and stand behind for pictures; small trophies, one for each teammate to take home; crests to decorate team sweaters and outfits; and the hot collector item, curling pins to commemorate the home rink, the association, the event, the team, or the sponsors. Sylvia began bringing home pins from each bonspiel,

6. PINPRICKS OF LIGHT

each championship. As she and Joyce travelled the province, and then the country, the collection grew. At first, the ladies would use the pins as decorations on their curling sweaters. Joyce, the most senior curler with the most bonspiel and provincial decorations, carried the heaviest load. Yet the collars and lapels of the rest of her teammates began to gleam and glitter.

Sylvia's Diamond D pin, 1960.

As the ladies began to compete and win at the national level, a switch flipped inside Sylvia, likely because of the first Diamond D pin. She took a close-up photograph of this illustrious pin, capturing its image for posterity. Soon after the team travelled to a summer bonspiel held in Dawson Creek, British Columbia. There, she recalled, "I became fascinated by the wonderful handmade pins and badges displayed by curlers in the Yukon country."[22] From then on, Sylvia developed a mania. Instead of merely wearing pins offered as prizes at bonspiels and by curling clubs, she began to buy, trade, and collect pins. Soon she had too many to wear. By the early 1960s, her collection numbered in the hundreds and included a rare pin from Scotland crafted in 1747. It was the beginning of a lifelong eccentric hobby.

The 1961–62 season saw the Joyce McKee rink in Hub City league play, once again at their high standard. Sylvia, meanwhile, stretched her administrative wings to include taking on the role of president of the Saskatoon Ladies' Curling Association, affiliated with the provincial and new national apparatus. Saskatoon had more clubs in play too. In addition to Hub City, Nutana, Granite, and CNR, there were clubs in operation at Exhibition, Sutherland, the University of Saskatchewan, and the old RCAF base. These changes meant more ladies involved and more experience across a broader range of ice and club conditions. After all, just like today, clubs could become known for their catering or bartending abilities. A good hamburger or a good beer or perhaps a gin and tonic would be well appreciated, and the regular administrative work involved in running a local club had its own demands. Both on and off the ice, the Hub City foursome were busy.

But something was different. That difference became apparent at the annual Saskatoon ladies' bonspiel, an event that—for many years—McKee had dominated. The bonspiel had ninety-six entrants, its highest ever, in January 1962, a split of twenty-nine out-of-town entries and the balance drawn from within city limits. An intense week of curling was planned, starting with a Monday-morning draw. With a few days to go before the opening draw, in a phone call late Thursday night to bonspiel headquarters, McKee withdrew. Although she could have drawn on Barbara MacNevin and Rosa McFee, Sylvia Fedoruk was unavailable. That week she was in Winnipeg for a national conference on medical physics. As her career in physics gained strength, it was clear that Sylvia had to make some tough choices, and curling sometimes had to come second. Although Mary Bannister was ready and able to join McKee for the week, the team chose to sit it out instead, watching from behind the glass in the spectator seats.[23]

The withdrawal did not matter for the larger goal of once again earning the right to represent Saskatchewan, for the McKee rink was already qualified to play in the Saskatoon playdowns, but there was a certain expectation that the rink would play in the local ladies' bonspiel, and the withdrawal was seen as a rebuff. The 1962 Saskatoon ladies' bonspiel battle was long and hard, with as many as five teams in the running for grand aggregate champion. What mattered was that the Saskatoon ladies' bonspiel fell the week before the Saskatoon playdowns. McKee and her team, rested and prepared after a week of watching their opponents, and with Sylvia back from her conference, were ready.

McKee won the Saskatoon playdowns and advanced to the northern playdowns for the sixth time in seven years.[24] By the end of the second day at the northerns, the rink had an aggregate score of 54–12 in four games. The McKee foursome even beat the formidable Myrtle Anderson rink from Nipawin, making it look unreasonably easy, downing them 10–2. They also thumped Yvonne Lindberg of Dundurn by a score of 20–3. McKee walked away with the northern championship.[25]

The north-south playdown was in Yorkton against the Regina squad of Addie Bright, with Jean Fitton, Gwen Pedenson, and Audrey Pells. The McKee rink came out flying, sitting at a cozy 6–0 after just three ends. Nonetheless, Bright fought back with

6. PINPRICKS OF LIGHT

determination and counted here and there to bring the score close to a tie, but the McKee rink wasn't to be denied. It emerged from the Saskatchewan playdown run victorious over the Reginans and headed into the 1962 nationals as the odds-on favourite.[26]

The Canadian women's Dominion D championship opened in Regina on February 26, 1962, with high expectations for the home-grown Saskatchewan foursome and reigning two-time national champions. To accommodate the number of spectators, the championship needed to be held in a place with lots of seating. The largest Regina hockey rink was converted into curling ice, and all was ready. The McKee rink started hot, opening with an 8–2 victory over Fern Irwin of Ontario, and following with an 11–2 drubbing of Vera Reed of Alberta.

With a crowd of about a thousand people cheering, things looked promising. Then came some stumbles. Cold weather, hovering at forty degrees Celsius below zero, kept crowds light for the second day of the draw. The cold weather created a few tricky patches on the ice sheets as well, which took some getting used to. Saskatchewan defeated Newfoundland in the morning draw, but a nailbiter game against Ina Hansen of Kimberley, British Columbia, brought despair. The McKee rink, to their shock, faced a 9–2 deficit after five ends. They fought back, bringing the game to an even score after five ends. But McKee was light on her final draw despite desperate sweeping by MacNevin and McFee. They needed that draw to score two points to force an extra end, but in an upset that rocked the house McKee lost 11–10. Nonetheless, after some stern reflection, the McKee team came back. They downed Pearl Carter of Nova Scotia 9–3 and backed that win up with a 12–4 victory over Phyllis Pinder of Newfoundland.

In a round robin format with no playoffs, the only way that Saskatchewan would remain in contention would be if someone—anyone—beat Ina Hansen of British Columbia, who had earlier defeated Saskatchewan's home rink. And that did not happen. The McKee rink watched in heartbreak and agony as—despite a fantastic week of curling—they came up short. Hansen won all of her games and took home the Diamond D trophy, with the 8–1 record of McKee dropping her to second place. It's an indication of the loss that in Sylvia's personal histories and scrapbooks much is made of the first two appearances and wins at nationals, whereas the 1962 run for the championship, with its lone defeat on Saskatchewan home ice, barely rates a remark. There were such high hopes heading into the national final, the excitement of planning the bonspiel in Regina, and a home team at the top of their game. But the round robin structure left no room for second chances. The team wouldn't be visiting the legislature or listening to speeches or receiving prizes and accolades. The trip back to Saskatoon was quiet.

A true scientist learns to channel both elation and disappointment into something constructive. If grit and tenacity did not bring results in sport, they might in science. Sylvia walked away from the Regina loss and threw herself fully into a new cancer scanning research program.

Preliminary work on liver scanning led her to believe that a new scanning machine with a larger crystal would help to create better scans with more accurate results. A crystal converts radiation into light. When a patient is injected with a radioactive tracer element, such as iodine 131 (I-131), the element concentrates in the organs. Sensitive to the gamma rays given off by the radiopharmaceutical in the tissues, the crystal would give off scintillations or fast flashes of light. The gamma rays would be focused through collimators, which would contain and direct the gamma rays to allow only those travelling in the right direction to be seen by the crystal. These gamma rays, read as pinpricks of light within the crystal, would be "seen" by a photomultiplier, essentially electric tubes on the back face of the crystal, which would transform the light into electrons, "multiplying" it. Depending on the size of the scintillation of light, the camera would detect where in the crystal the light sparked. The larger the crystal, the more photomultipliers were necessary for the camera.

Information from the photomultipliers would pass to recording devices, such as a solenoid and tapper similar to a Morse code tapper, or later through an oscilloscope to other recording outputs. These recordings would show the size and shape of an organ, letting the doctors and technicians "view" it without surgery to see if it was a normal size and shape or displayed irregularities or lesions. The same basic principles, including scintillation crystals, are still used in modern medicine's expensive computerized tomography (CT) and positron emission tomography (PET) scans. It's important to remember that the machines made from these crystals—scanners, cameras, and so forth—were not themselves radioactive like the cobalt-60 unit, which needed to be in its own lead-lined room. These crystal scanners and cameras would read radioactive trace elements injected into the body to allow for better diagnostics. The heads themselves were encased in lead to shield the detector from stray radiation and keep diagnostics clear and correct.

6. PINPRICKS OF LIGHT

To get a larger crystal, Sylvia wrote to the crystal division of the Harshaw Chemical Company of Cleveland, Ohio, for specifications. A major chemical company specializing in a broad array of scientific supports, including chemicals and catalysts for industry, its background work supported the Manhattan Project of the 1940s that brought forth the atomic bomb. One of Harshaw's departments specialized in growing sodium iodide crystals for use in optical instruments, scintillation scanners, and cameras. "These crystals ... start off as molten sodium iodide, and they slowly pull the crystal up through an oven that warms and then cools it and that grows it as a single crystal. But growing one of that size is not easy. Then it has to be sliced. They were cut with a wet string in a very, very dry environment."[27] Sylvia, probably with money from the National Cancer Institute of Canada, bought a crystal about the size of a large softball.

Her growing interest in diagnostic scanning techniques and the purchase of new, larger crystals led to the development of two important machines between 1960 and 1965 at the University Hospital cancer clinic in Saskatoon: a whole-body rectilinear scanner (1962–63) and a scintillation camera (1965). To fully engage in this new work, Sylvia needed a catalyst. Master's student Trevor Cradduck was a graduate of the University of Bristol, had undertaken a two-year graduate apprenticeship at General Electrics Corporation UK in Coventry, and was a specialist in medical electronic engineering, particularly in its use for medical physics. He could combine an understanding of the technicalities of physics with the worlds of electronics and image capture. It was one thing to inject tracer elements and take a scan; it was quite another to *view* that scan in such a way that it would help a physician to diagnose, and then treat, illness. In 1962, Sylvia was promoted to assistant professor; at last, she could supervise graduate students.[28] Cradduck was co-supervised by Sylvia and Doug Cormack, who had been her fellow graduate student under Dr. Harold Johns, earning a Ph.D. and joining the faculty at the University of Saskatchewan. Being Cradduck's supervisor, as well as sharing an office, Sylvia and Trevor became close colleagues and friends.

The new whole-body (moving) rectilinear scanner once again required the machinist skills of Johnny MacKay of Acme Machine and Electric in Saskatoon. Funded by a grant from the National Cancer Institute of Canada, the machine was large and heavy and required its own room. The detector head and its shield weighed

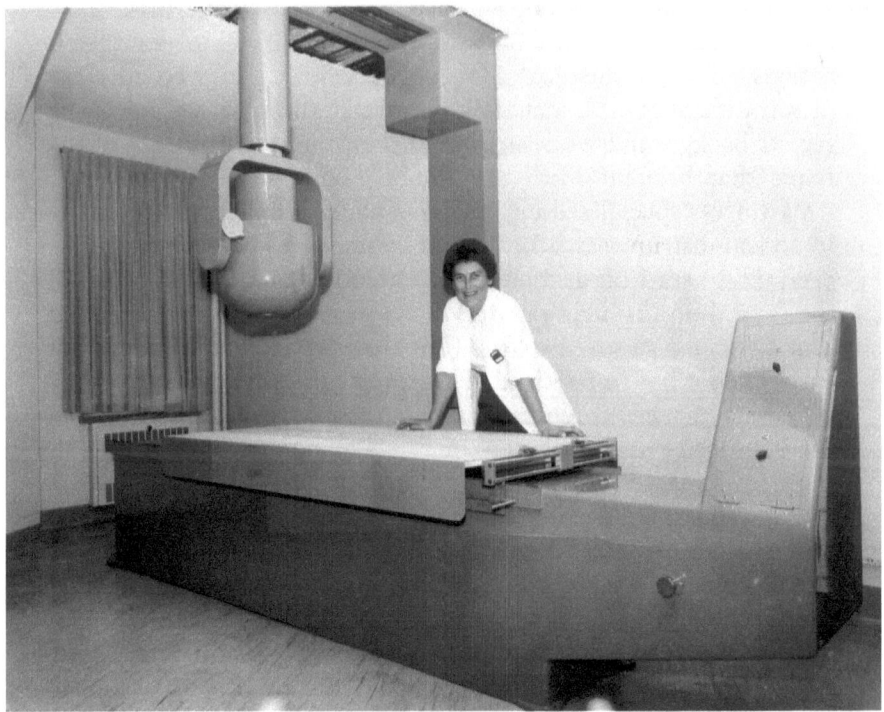

Sylvia with the completed rectilinear scanner, 1962.

about 1,750 pounds and operated on a transverse carriage above the patient, with a counterbalance cleverly hidden near the wall. The unit looked much like the original Saskatoon cobalt-60 unit—after all, MacKay's machine shop had made them both. Not only the detector head would move; during operation, the bed was also designed to move. Between the moving scanner head and the moving bed, the two mimicked furrows in a field, taking measurements in a methodical, preset graph.

Sylvia had considerable experience working with MacKay as the machinist on call for hospital and university high-tech machines, so she also knew his faults, one of which was that Johnny moved at his own pace. To compensate, Sylvia would send Cradduck down to Acme once classes were finished for the day just to hang around and be visible. It was a way to make sure that things got done eventually. Cradduck noted wryly that his master's degree took longer than usual in part because Johnny was tough to hurry along. Then again Sylvia was also known to have her thoughts wander from work

6. PINPRICKS OF LIGHT

commitments. During baseball's World Series, she would lug a television set into her office so that she wouldn't miss a single inning.[29]

Cradduck described the rectilinear scanner in a paper read at the Tenth International Congress of Radiology in Montreal in August 1962: "First of all, why was it considered necessary to build yet another scanner when so many are already in existence, both commercial and otherwise?"[30] The new Saskatchewan version used a much larger crystal that increased detector sensitivity, using a collimator to "look" more deeply into tissue to find deep-seated tumours. Whereas a thyroid is close to the skin, major organs such as liver or kidneys or pancreas are deeper.[31] Increased scanner sensitivity allowed technicians to give a much lower radioactive dose (but of higher energy) to the patient. Second, building their own machine meant that they could use it for whole-body profile scans. And third, they wanted better data handling, picture forming, and information storing for the resultant data. In building their own data capture, Cradduck and Fedoruk and the team were able to separate the scanning process from the imaging process.[32] The team could make changes and improvements as they went through testing and use, much as they had with the cobalt-60 unit and the liver scanner. Cradduck successfully defended his master's thesis on the scanner design and display capture in October 1962. He immediately began work on a doctorate, again with Sylvia and Cormack as his co-supervisors.

The Montreal conference in 1962 at which Cradduck presented his and Sylvia's scanner design led to a new trajectory for Sylvia. Following the conference, Harold Johns (now working in Ontario) invited four former students to visit his family cottage at Lake Boskung, Ontario. The former students, now colleagues with their own research interests and abilities, went there to help entertain and impress his international colleagues. At the lake, Johns hauled everyone out onto the water to go water-skiing. All of the visitors and colleagues were soon skimming over the water with ease and style. Except Sylvia. A non-swimmer, she was uncomfortable in the water, and no matter what she tried she could not get the two long boards parallel and pointing straight ahead. She fell, fell, and fell again, sucking up lake water before finally admitting defeat. As she would later note, "I failed, but that didn't matter."[33] Her lack of grace on the water had no impact on her intelligent mealtime and evening conversations, and by the end of the lake visit Sylvia had been recruited to join a task force for the International Commission on Radiation Units and Measurements

Sylvia with Vera Pezer as the Astronuts, c. 1960s.

with the International Atomic Energy Agency in Vienna. For a woman working at a small university in western Canada, it was a prestigious invitation.

Photographs from the 1960s show a different Sylvia. Whereas the 1940s and 1950s showcased a fresh-faced and athletic young woman, by the 1960s she had developed a mature personality. The pictures show her taste for cigarettes and even the odd cigar, and drinks were always at hand. If the intervarsity wins of college more or less matched the regional baseball titles, the national curling scene brought a significant leap toward presence and success or failure. Celebration and camaraderie can be found in the photo collection. Sylvia also loved dressing for fun, entering the spirit of a funspiel or Halloween party with great zest and laughter. Her social energy needed to find outlets, and though work was consuming and challenging, her personal life was just as full.

Back in Saskatoon after the Lake Boskung trip and gearing up for Trevor Cradduck's Ph.D. work, Sylvia worked with Trevor to design a scintillation camera. The rectilinear scanner was a moving detector scanner; the new scintillation camera was stationary. The crew had the option of purchasing a predesigned unit from Nuclear Chicago, a firm that had developed and was commercially marketing such medical items. The Saskatoon team found the Chicago camera inadequate and decided again to build their own. First was the purchase of a crystal. Once again working with the Harshaw company, Sylvia ordered a stunning crystal eleven inches in diameter and half an inch thick, about the size of a dinner plate. This time she and Trevor split construction forces. Johnny MacKay and the local crew

6. PINPRICKS OF LIGHT

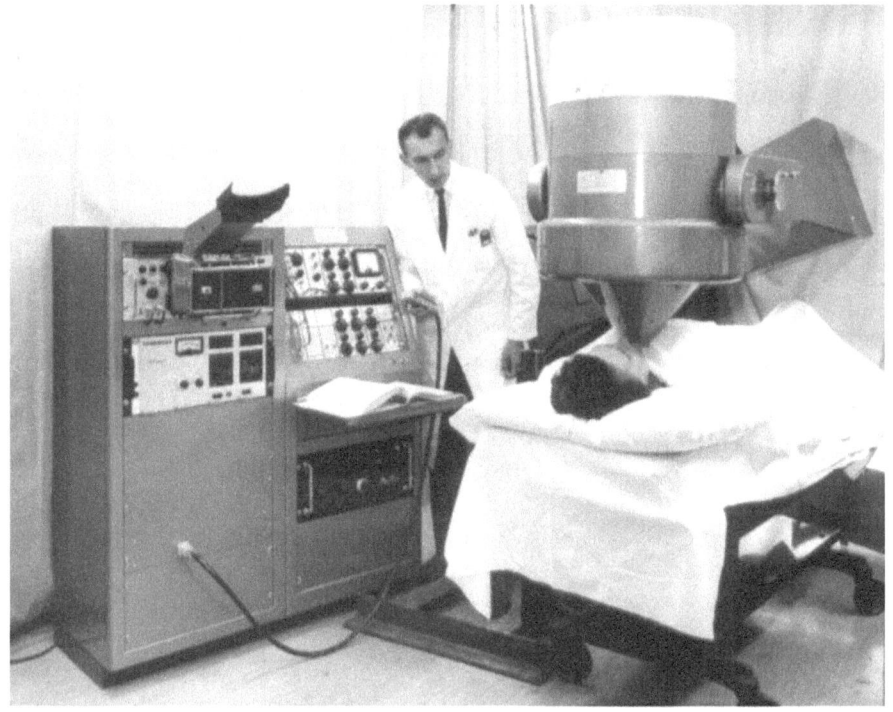

Trevor Cradduck with the scintillation camera, c. 1965. The photo depicts a pinhole collimator, no longer used.

at Acme built the housing and the collimators. The electronics were developed by a commercial firm, Nuclear Enterprises, in Winnipeg, well used to building such precision instruments. Its chief physicist, Dr. W.B. Reid, had also been a graduate student of Harold Johns.[34]

Both the whole-body rectilinear scanner, the first of its kind in existence, and the new scintillation camera, the first gamma ray camera in Canada, were soon in operation at the cancer clinic. The camera, at a cost of $20,000, was built using the financial bequest of the estate of Benjamin J. Schurr of Swift Current, who had passed away from cancer in 1961. At 1,000 pounds, the camera was substantial. In comparison to the whole-body scanner, though, it would be more versatile and efficient, so they hoped. The rectilinear scanner could only look at small areas at a time, up to thirteen millimetres. It took a while to cover a larger area, moving back and forth across a patient's body while the patient reclined on the bed. The new scintillation camera, with a much larger crystal lens, could photograph a larger area in less time. It also could be moved, taking pictures either vertically or horizontally, depending on which part of the body was of interest.³⁵

Johnny MacKay was there for the process of mounting the camera. As Cradduck explained,

> the scintillation camera that we built, we needed something to mount it. At that time, the Caesium treatment unit in Regina had reached the end of its life. So we took that base to mount the scintillation camera. Doug Cormack, Syl Fedoruk, Johnny MacKay, and myself went to the Grey Nuns hospital in Regina to extract the mounting and bring it back up to Saskatoon. The camshaft of Syl's Buick broke when we were on our way down south. Doug and Johnny MacKay and I managed to get to Grey Nuns ourselves. Syl arrived later, being towed. We had to take the mounting unit out through a window of the Grey Nuns. They hired a truck with a crane on it. We took the window out and put the crane through the window. The unit was so heavy that the truck began to tip. Johnny MacKay and I stood on the front bumper of the truck to hold it down. We weren't having much effect, but we tried. Once it was out through the window, the crane could lift and change the centre of gravity, and everything was fine. Health and safety would have been tearing their hair out if they'd seen us on the bumper of that truck, lifted right off the ground!³⁶

In Saskatoon, the housing and camera were wheeled down the corridor from the loading dock and put together in the F wing of the University Hospital.

Sylvia and Trevor's work on scanning techniques earned Sylvia a spot on the presentation panels at two major international events. In April 1964, she travelled to Athens, Greece, for the *XI Congresso internazionale di radiologia*. In Athens from April 17 to May 4, Sylvia mixed work with tourism, visiting the wonders of ancient Greece, including Delphi, where the Oracle once lived.

She returned via Vienna to London, where she stayed for several days at the Strand Palace Hotel. Sylvia was inundated with letters from home. Olive Gordon, a long-time friend and curling colleague, sent a missive with Saskatoon curling news. Brenda Clark, a cancer clinic co-worker, sent a breezy note from the "stool parade" at the clinic, where she was checking stool samples for Chromium 51, a synthetic radioactive isotope used in cancer detection, and watching the pile of mail on Sylvia's desk threaten to topple to the floor. Three letters from Joyce McKee reveal a mix of domestic news, shared interests in politics and hockey, and a frank admission of loneliness. The warmth between the two women, coupled with domesticity, indicates that they were closer than mere roommates. After all, they played sports together, took most holidays together, and cooked, gardened, cheered, and attended events together. Their intertwined lives operated, in effect, as one unit.

The international junket to Greece and London wasn't Sylvia's only major trip that year. An invitation to São Paulo, Brazil, in 1964 for the *I Congresso internacional de biologia e medicina nuclear* took Sylvia away again in August. It was a massive undertaking. Flying from Saskatoon to Winnipeg, Toronto, and then New York, Sylvia finally boarded Varig Airlines for the jaw-dropping flight from New York to São Paulo. Leaving Saskatoon on August 31, Sylvia travelled across the equator and across seasons, leaving late summer and arriving in late winter. All of her trips to date had been to various places in North America and Europe; South America was a whole new continent and experience. The congress arranged and paid for her expensive flights as well as her accommodations and some of her more appealing meals. Sylvia kept the handwritten menu from La Popote, a restaurant in São Paulo, where she was served escargots de Bourgogne, filets à la Moutarde, pommes Lyonnaises, fromages, glaces, café, and two kinds of wine, Meursoult 1959 and Moulin à Vent 1957, along with French liqueur. Gone for nearly a month, Sylvia returned to Canada at the end of September, having visited numerous hospitals and cancer centres, attended a major congress, and created lasting international collegial connections.[37]

Cradduck's dissertation work combined two of Sylvia's favourite physics passions: creating a completely new instrument and then measuring its parameters and possibilities. Under her guidance, his doctoral work not only investigated the scintillation camera but also argued for new ways to cross-compare stationary cameras and moving scanners. The work broke new ground in developing reliable measurements and vocabulary regarding spatial resolution, sensitivity, and distortion as objective parameters for comparison. Using their original whole-body rectilinear scanner and the new stationary scintillation camera, Cradduck and Fedoruk moved the goal posts to create a whole new way to measure and compare the many commercial and privately built scanners and cameras being sold commercially around the globe. Sylvia's work with the whole-body scanner and scintillation camera was even more impressive than her team work on the cobalt-60 bomb ten years before, from a scientific if not a patient outcome point of view. The scanner work showcased both her technical abilities and her vision, breaking new ground at the international level on standardization, quality, reproducibility, and training.

Cradduck won his doctorate in September 1965, but it wasn't an easy fight. He defended his dissertation and then left the room. On his committee, in addition to Sylvia and Doug Cormack, were a number of people from both physics and engineering. If medical physics had been well received when Harold Johns had been around, its stature had slipped in the university scene. Some of the grumpier old guard wondered whether medical physics was really physics and whether it was worth a Ph.D. Sneaking into the atmosphere was the knowledge that Sylvia herself, despite her energy and expertise, did not hold a Ph.D., the reason that she had to share co-supervision with Cormack. Cradduck, as Sylvia's graduate student, was on the receiving end of an old-guard viewpoint that women were not good at physics. The dean of engineering looked around the room and then spoke. If you won't give this work a Ph.D., he threatened, I will. The physics old boys, led by the same professor who had refused to grant Sylvia decent course marks, backed down. Cradduck went on to a long and successful career.[38]

On the domestic front, Sylvia's new pastime and passion for collecting curling pins had a major impact on household decorating. Joyce and Sylvia redecorated their shared "den" as a curling shrine. On the wall hung curling hats, side by side. Trophies, large and small, from useful platters to dust-collecting monstrosities, sat squatly around the room on top of every horizontal surface, from the hifi to coffee tables to shelves jutting from the walls. On the walls, in wood-framed, sturdy display cases, Sylvia's growing collection of curling pins gleamed. By 1965, the collection was large enough to earn attention in Saskatoon. Sylvia put a selection on display in a downtown jewellery store window, accompanied by a beautiful caption in calligraphy: "These curling pins are part of an outstanding collection of over 1,500 belonging to Syl Fedoruk of Saskatoon." It was an homage to a pastime that brought together Canada's curling history as viewed through art.[39]

6. PINPRICKS OF LIGHT

The early fall of 1965 saw Sylvia once again travelling overseas, this time to Harrogate in North Yorkshire, England, and then to Rome. Arriving in London on September 5, she was in Harrogate by the next day, travelling by Pullman railcar. Staying at the "old, huge, draughty but oh so comfortable" Hotel Majestic on the third floor, Sylvia spent a day getting over jetlag and rehearsing her paper before the First International Conference on Medical Physics opened. From breakfast to high tea to evening wine and cheese parties, Sylvia's travel diary is full of temptation and regret: "Gad diet is shot!" she wrote, "wow the calories!" The conference was not a roaring success. Sylvia, to her horror, faced a technical failure. Her slides, carried carefully from Canada, were too large to fit into the projector provided. She had to give her talk without any accompanying visuals. "But anyway talk I suppose okay but flub a question from Brownell," she recorded.[40] As usual, Sylvia was her own worst taskmaster. Not to have given her best presentation at such an illustrious gathering—opened by none other than Professor W.V. Mayneord, considered by many the "godfather" of medical physics and a mentor to Dr. Harold Johns—caused Sylvia anxiety. Then, to "flub" a question nearly brought her to tears. She longed for nothing more than to get back to her room and crawl into the bathtub to relax and settle down. Her anxiety was still so bad the next morning that she played hooky and went for a guided tour with other conference attendees and then to a pub before returning to the conference in the afternoon to chair a session. The rest of the conference went more smoothly, and Sylvia embarked on a hospital tour to Edinburgh, Oxford, and London before travelling to Rome for the annual radiology conference.

The view of the Alps as they flew over them, Sylvia recorded, was tremendous. Rome was impressive. The sense of history, the size of the buildings, and the stupendous number of people astonished her, let alone the food and wine. Figuring out the subway system was tricky, but she was able to get from her hotel to the congress with no major trouble. Her paper there, delivered on September 22, seemed to go much better than at Harrogate; the slides worked, and Johns, in the audience, "told me he was impressed, whatever that meant."[41] As the congress continued, Sylvia was just leaving for the night when she ran into a group of colleagues from Hammersmith hospital in London. They pinched several bottles of champagne—and two glasses—from the reception room and walked through Rome to the Trevi Fountain. Tossing three coins in, the group sat and drank, sharing glasses until the bubbly was all gone. Sylvia was a popular companion. Her travel diary records numerous meetings with colleagues from around the world. As at any conference, not all of the papers presented were up to her standards. Some were good, some were excellent, but some were "bloody awful." After listening to a few of the awful ones, she wrote that "my conscience wasn't bothering me about moving anymore." Clearly, there had been tempting offers, perhaps a few international invitations trying to woo Saskatchewan's brown-eyed science dame to positions overseas. But Sylvia refused. Saskatoon remained home. As usual, her friends back home in Canada kept in close contact with her. Mail came from Brenda Clark with plenty of work questions and commentary, and from Joyce McKee, who noted that "I miss you lots—even if we fight all the time you're home." Sylvia flew home to a gaggle of friends at the airport eager to hear about her Roman adventures.[42]

If she was no longer on teams winning at the provincial level, curling remained an important part of winter life. Joyce and Sylvia could be found playing for high stakes at major curling bonspiels, including cash spiels in the early 1960s and the Calgary Rose Bowl in 1965, the last year that the two played together.

Back at work, Sylvia would have moved forward with a research and technical program on scanning techniques, but disaster struck. The scanner room could get very warm at times, with electrical machinery, the camera, collimators, and recording equipment. A staff member—no one seemed to know just whom—opened a window to let in some air but forgot to close it for the night. A severe weather change swooped across Saskatoon, plummeting the temperature to well below freezing. The fragile and precious sodium iodide scintillation crystal froze and then shattered. And with its shattering came the end of Sylvia's active research projects, including designing and building from scratch new cancer investigation instruments. Commercial production outstripped anything that Sylvia could manufacture locally, and competition drove costs down. As a public hospital operating under the universal Medicare system, costs mattered. Her days as an inventor came to an end.

Nonetheless, even as her research program faltered, Sylvia's experiences and insights were needed more than ever on the international stage. As a working member of the international task force on scanning, Sylvia's supervision of Cradduck's work on the whole-body scanner and the scintillation camera helped to bring focus to

6. PINPRICKS OF LIGHT

the larger issue of standardization. The task force was charged with creating a report aimed at opening a clear discussion on ways to standardize measurements across machines and around the world. There were five people on the task force from Canada, the United Kingdom, and the United States. "This was when the real fun began," remembered Craig Harris, at Duke University in Durham, North Carolina.[43] W.J. MacIntyre was in Cleveland, D.E. Kuhl was in Philadelphia, and J.R. Mallard was in Aberdeen, Scotland. The five would meet mostly via mail, then at major meetings in conjunction with international radiology conferences, to pursue their work. Most of the crew, for example, was in Rome in 1965 when Sylvia presented some of the Fedoruk-Cradduck cross-comparative work and pitched her coins into the Trevi Fountain.

Just as her professional life accelerated into an international role, so too the shattering of that scintillation crystal mimicked another shattering in Sylvia's life. After twelve years of sharing a small bungalow with Joyce, Sylvia moved out. In April 1966, she gathered up her curling pins and trophies, jars of sauerkraut, clothes and hats, and all the debris of twelve years in one domicile and relocated to apartment 11 at 1801 7th Street East. Sylvia was well advanced in her professional career; she no longer needed to scrimp and save by sharing living space, as she had when first starting out. As Joyce's international letters indicated in 1964 and 1965, the two were experiencing an inexorable change. Domestic bickering hampered what had been a close relationship. Sylvia's work and travel schedule, with long, gruelling, international trips, also created distance. As recounted by friends, Joyce and Sylvia could be chalk and cheese. The boisterous Ukrainian girl from north of Yorkton (where almost every bale stack hid a cache of moonshine) was aghast when Joyce, the scion of a rather staid teetotalling Baptist family, would hide the booze bottles if her sister came to visit. Such duplicity, Sylvia thought, was completely underhanded.

She had her own issues with alcohol. Sylvia needed—craved—release. First visible during times of celebration with her ball team or at the curling rink, it's clear from her files and photographs, her day-timers and household grocery lists, that she had an occasional propensity to overimbibe. An evening of conviviality could degenerate. Some quietly suggest that Sylvia was in fact a social drunk and sometimes, when coupled with the more blunt aspect of her personality, could be a mean drunk. It is possible that she and Joyce had too many disagreements over this issue to find a workable solution.

Another factor in, or result of, their domestic split was Sylvia's decision to idle back on professional competitive curling. Although still enjoying the high skill level of the Saskatoon women's league, Sylvia turned her attention to building the game, taking larger administrative roles. In 1965, she was elected (along with Olive Gordon) as one of two first women directors of the Hub City Curling Club. In 1966–67, following Joyce and Sylvia's domestic separation and curling split, Sylvia harboured hopes of making it to the provincials with her own team. A letter from Sylvia's father brought a reminder that there was more to curling than winning: "How is your curling coming along? Don't be disappointed if you do not win Sask. Championship. To have fun and pass time is more important often than trophies."[44] Sylvia's path diverged sharply from Joyce's path. McKee went on to rebuild a new nationally winning rink from the Rose Bowl winning team, including Saskatoon curling sensation Vera Pezer, along with Lee Morrison. To replace Sylvia, Jennifer Falk came on board.[45]

In addition to an increased interest in curling administration, Sylvia began offering herself as a photographer and feature writer for national curling magazines, attending both men's and women's national playdowns. A 1967 feature on Sylvia published in the Montreal *Gazette* showed a slimmer Sylvia at the Diamond D playdowns, camera around her neck, and, for the first time, her iconic short haircut. It seems clear that she began to leverage her role as a woman most effectively by being less like a typical woman: no domestic ties, no feminine frippery or hairstyle, immersed in work, keeping up with the men in drinking and carousing, travelling extensively, and pursuing her own interests. Her style and outlook at the curling rink echoed increased managerial and leadership roles at work, including pursuing business management and leadership courses to support both her Saskatchewan role at the cancer clinic and her international position with the International Atomic Energy Agency. She kept her oddball mania for collecting curling pins.[46]

Notwithstanding the change in her domestic situation, including relearning how to plan and cook for just one person, Sylvia needed concerted attention on her work with the task force for the International Atomic Energy Agency. A couple of subgroup meetings during the writing phase in 1966 and early 1967 in Vienna and Heidelberg took the project from conception to completion. In Vienna, the group worked hard during the day and relaxed in the

6. PINPRICKS OF LIGHT

evenings with wine and adventures. One evening excursion took the crew right across the communist Iron Curtain. They decided to drive to Bratislava, Czechoslovakia, for supper and beer, passing the dour checkpoints just for the adventure. One member, Craig Harris, bailed out of the car before they went through the first checkpoint. Contracted to the U.S. Atomic Energy Commission, his American passport and visa wouldn't let him cross. The poor man was left to wait for the rest of the group to return after they had wined and dined on the red side of the curtain.[47]

In 1967, the task force met in Heidelberg, and there Sylvia shone. "We worked hard all day and sometimes well into the night. When one of us proudly read something we had written, [Sylvia] would say, 'I don't understand it; explain it to me.' Then we'd realize we didn't understand it either and would work on it until we did. Many of [Sylvia's] contributions to the report were based on [her] insistence that it be readable."[48] Heidelberg also offered opportunities for evening shenanigans. When one of the men accidentally spilled a glass of slivovitz over the only draft of the report, the rest of the team simply bent down and lapped it up—no point in wasting good alcohol! The late-evening work and the need for good beer and food led the hapless crew to mistake their car for a battering ram. The only bar open was across the river. The international crew, exhausted from a long day and in need of immediate sustenance, aimed for directness, not obedience to traffic laws. They slammed their rented station wagon over an ancient stone bridge, long closed to traffic, as the quickest way to get to the bar. A Heidelberg policeman, stunned that anyone would drive a car over such an ancient structure, merely stood there gaping as the crew left the dented car and sprinted toward warmth, beer, and food.[49]

Delivered in 1967, the task force's report set out standards for comparative measurement of scanners and cameras, based on sensitivity and resolution. These standards were in place until into the 1970s, when technology leap-frogged their work and companies began to self-standardize outputs. Sylvia's international experiences led to additional work as a consultant in nuclear medicine with the International Atomic Energy Agency in Vienna in 1966, 1968, and 1969, from which Sylvia gained an international reputation and perspective that would be of use in the Canadian scene.

Despite her professional accomplishments and world-leading reputation in radiation technology, Sylvia could not win the one battle that mattered the most. In the spring of 1968, she was preparing to attend the IAEA Panel on Dosimetry Requirements of Radiotherapy Centres in Caracas, Venezuela. Planned by the Atomic Energy Agency in Vienna, the conference was meant to shepherd a new era of proper cancer clinics across South America. It was easy enough, by the late 1960s, to purchase cutting-edge technological machines to fight cancer. What was missing was a suitable level of personnel. There was a major shortage of trained medical physicists and technologists. As the chairperson of Canada's medical physicist association and the head of physics services for the Saskatchewan Cancer Commission, Sylvia had this issue close to her heart.[50]

Life intervened when she received a phone call. Her mother, Annie, was sick. It turned out to be ovarian cancer, that deadly silent killer that remains the most lethal form of cancer for women. By the time that it was discovered, Annie's cancer was well advanced. Sylvia moved her mother to Saskatoon to try chemotherapy treatment at the cancer clinic. Sylvia was in the right place at the right time to pull strings, if necessary, to get leading-edge or extra treatment for her mother. It was to no avail. Despite chemotherapy and radiation treatment, Annie Fedoruk passed away on November 14, 1968. She was buried in the Yorkton cemetery, and Sylvia experienced personal loss far worse than she had to date. Her pain was acute; to compensate, she threw herself into work and volunteering to fill every moment.

Her mother's death marked the end of a particular era for Sylvia. Although Annie did not finish school, she was a major role model for Sylvia and one of her most important champions. It was Annie who insisted that Sylvia not only obtain an excellent education but also turn that education into an established career. In the midst of her mother's cancer fight in 1968, Sylvia was promoted from assistant to associate professor in therapeutic radiology and continued her work as the director of physics services for the Saskatchewan Cancer Commission. In October, a month before her mother's death, Sylvia was appointed a member of the provincial Radiological Health Committee, reflecting the continued importance of radiological imagery and radiation therapy to both cancer and the larger Saskatchewan health system. Even in the midst of personal pain and tragedy, Sylvia's professional life shifted almost inexorably from research to administration and leadership.

As Sylvia buried and mourned her mother, there was a concurrent shift in Canadian life. The so-called swinging sixties brought a renewed women's movement in which professional women such as

6. PINPRICKS OF LIGHT

Sylvia with her parents, summer 1968.

Sylvia received increased attention and targeted support. The irony is that she never needed it. Following the advice long ago given by Sybil Johns, Sylvia had been able to carve a professional career path at the crossroads between physics and medicine, in the new area of medical physics in which gender mattered less than research or administrative ability. Nonetheless, her accomplishments must be tempered by a reminder that Sylvia, by choice, was not a typical woman. Unhampered by typical domestic expectations of marriage and motherhood for women, she could leverage natural talents in ways and in a time when others, perhaps equally gifted, simply could not. Her gender might not have mattered, but her choices certainly did. Yet, in a backward irony, her gender as a woman mattered to others, particularly those looking to build leadership teams that reflected new goals for gender inclusion. As Sylvia Fedoruk moved toward the new decade, her gender became a springboard into new and interesting national roles.

7. WE CALL THIS MEETING TO ORDER

IN 1951, WHEN SYLVIA FEDORUK WAS FINISHING HER MASTER'S degree and the cobalt-60 unit was being installed in Saskatoon, she was living through a summer of change. Moving out of the Mohyla residence and settling into her own apartment in Saskatoon, she was about to start a professional career as a physicist. Money was tight. Sylvia made a little extra cash by playing poker and blackjack against fellow graduate students, but every dollar counted. Hers was not the only domestic situation undergoing change that summer. Her graduate supervisor, Harold Johns, and his wife, Sybil, were expecting a baby. All of the physics colleagues viewed that impending arrival as an event to anticipate and celebrate. The physics crowd started a sweepstakes on the baby's due date. Cash began to flow, bets were laid, and in a race that no one (including Sybil) had much control over, Sylvia ended up picking the right day. Instead of keeping the much-needed cash, she quietly tucked the winnings into an envelope and handed it to the Johns for the new baby.[1] That style of quiet, open-handed financial generosity became one of Sylvia's private hallmarks.

Generosity should be counted in more ways than money. Sylvia had other major gifts, offered to local, provincial, national, and international entities. Her second gift, after generosity, was time. Unlike most other women with consuming domestic responsibilities, Sylvia had the precious gift of time. In a society built on volunteer hours dedicated to creating spaces for arts, sports, charities, worship, health, and leisure, time was no small gift. Sylvia gave freely of her time to the things that she enjoyed and the things that she aimed to help.

Her third gift was energy. As shown in her university years and moving into research roles at the university, the cancer clinic, international committees, and sports leadership, Sylvia was a master multitasker. Filling days to the brim, slicing time into pieces, and pouring energy into each minute, she could go from working to cheering, planning to organizing, travelling to presenting, cajoling to wheedling to demanding. If she had ten minutes free, she would find a use for them and cross another item off her to-do list. It gave her a focused outlook, organized and thoughtful. Day-timers spilled over with notes, jots, underlines, cross-outs, big loopy circles, and lots of checkmarks.

Her fourth gift was good humour. The descriptive word used most to explain Sylvia is *warm*. Slightly zany when with her closest friends, wont to have a drink or two (or several) in good company, Sylvia deployed humour and genuine caring in equal measure. Willing to see the ridiculous in situations, able to bring a humorous jest into tense negotiations, she brought many otherwise awkward meeting moments through to agreements. Elta Brown, a colleague at the cancer clinic, noted that "I shall never forget the meetings that would have disintegrated into something akin to chaos had it not been for your steadying influence, made possible by the respect your colleagues held for your scientific background and administrative good sense." Sylvia was calm but commanding when necessary. Elta Brown added that "the leavening agent . . . was a gentle humour that was dispensed at appropriate times and in the appropriate dosages."[2]

Her last gift was an astonishing intellect. Sylvia learned fast. She took up French with no prior experience and excelled in it, then later added a smattering of German to her basic Ukrainian. In first-year calculus, Sylvia wiped the floor with the other sixty-nine classmates—all men—and averaged at least two scholarships per year throughout high school and university. Her gift of intelligence was more than rote memorization or simple understanding. Sylvia had an incredible ability to achieve higher-order thinking, to take existing knowledge—whether in science, board leadership, or sport—and find new ways to expand it, apply it, track and compartmentalize it, and make it more usable in new directions. At work, Sylvia paid attention to detail. "I recall how her responsibilities were fulfilled to the maximum degree," said Fred Wigmore, who would serve as chairman of the Saskatchewan Cancer Commission and, in some ways, Sylvia's boss. "Any problem was investigated, checked and double checked." Thoroughness was her watchword. But ultimately Elta Brown bestowed the most important compliment. Despite her lauded intellect, Sylvia could make those around her "appear more talented and competent than they really are."[3] Self-deprecating and comfortable with her own achievements, Sylvia had a gift for shining light on others.

She always kept a finger on the pulse of her staff. Sylvia knew, often first, if someone was in trouble or experiencing difficulty. Always she would help. The cancer clinic staff would sometimes meet socially at the curling rink, her other major home. During one of these social events, Sylvia checked in with two new staff members just arrived from the United Kingdom, right before Christmas. The two young women, reeling from the Canadian cold and with little money in their pockets, had underestimated almost everything about Canadian costs and requirements. "Syl, you SAVED us!" one recounted. Realizing their dire straits, Sylvia quietly passed them a wad of cash, enough to get them through and have a Christmas until their paycheques arrived. "That was the first inkling that Sylvia Fedoruk is someone pretty special."[4] At the cancer clinic, a warm generosity of spirit led Sylvia to keep a drawer of change to help fill the parking meters of the terrified patients undergoing treatment. No one would get a parking ticket on her watch if she could help it.

By the 1970s, Sylvia's natural athletic brawn was mostly a memory. Although Sylvia still curled and golfed, photographs show a woman in her mid-forties who had settled comfortably into a more generous body. On occasion, though, she made a valiant effort. With her good friend, pharmacist Irene Bell, Sylvia took a ski trip to the Rocky Mountains in February 1971. She and Irene had met in the mid-1960s, and Irene was central to Sylvia's relocation from her apartment on the east side to a new posh and expansive space in one of Saskatoon's newest downtown highrises at 325 5th Avenue North. From there, it was a quick walk over the bridge to her work at the cancer clinic in the University Hospital. Both curlers and golfers, the two built a friendship that would last for the rest of their lives.

Eager for new adventures and determined to conquer a new sport, Sylvia bought all her downhill ski equipment, from skis to boots to poles, so that she could not "chicken out." By the time she reached

Sylvia with a lake trout, Costigan Lake, 1971.

the top of the ski lift, she realized that she was in deep trouble. "I had never been on skis before," she noted, "and I fell off the lift at the top." In total fright, absolutely unable to conquer herself, Sylvia was stuck. Once you're up there, how do you get down, except ski? But skiing down, on legs that refused to cooperate and a mind full of fear, was impossible. "I got to the bottom though—on the back of a motor-toboggan."[5] Why would Sylvia suddenly, in her mid-forties, decide to take on skiing as a new sport, especially after the debacle on the water at Harold Johns's lake cottage? It's possible that some of her friends, such as Irene, were already avid skiers and that Sylvia wanted to join them. She also might have had too much confidence and thought that she could use that old adage, mind over matter, to suddenly become a skier. It also could have been because Sylvia was a committee member for the Canada Winter Games held in Saskatoon in 1971. Although she was there to serve the curling and ceremonial committees, downhill skiing was about to become Saskatoon's next big thing. Just south of Saskatoon, on purpose for the games, the "pimple on the prairies" ski hill at Blackstrap was being built. Perhaps Sylvia and her friends had high hopes of swooshing down the slopes close to home on reasonably warm Saskatchewan Saturday afternoons in winter. Humiliated and chastened, Sylvia quietly sold her brand-new downhill ski equipment, opting instead for the less risky cross-country version. Less chance, she noted, of breaking a leg. After all, it was about moving your body in any way that you could—at least that was the main point of Canada's ParticipACTION movement, of which Sylvia was a City of Saskatoon Formation Committee member.[6]

7. WE CALL THIS MEETING TO ORDER

Summer would see Sylvia, often with good friends Dot George and Eileen Joss, heading north. A favourite haunt was Keighley's camp on Nunn Lake River, then operated by Bob Keighley. Another was Costigan Lake, a fly-in camp with incredible fishing. At Costigan Lake, Sylvia won the Master Angler award from the Saskatchewan Anglers Derby. Fishing one of the deep bays of Costigan Lake, she pulled out a twenty-two-pound six-ounce lake trout. The fish was registered, and Sylvia was included in the province's annual report.

When not fishing, Sylvia had a set of golf clubs at the ready. As soon as golf courses opened the fairways and greens, she could be found on the links and in the clubrooms. With experience as a competitive varsity golfer, she wanted to test her skills and challenge both herself and others, and this desire drew her to provincial-level competition as an adult. One of her favourite yearly events was the Lobstick golf tournament at the legendary Waskesiu eighteen-hole course. Begun in 1933, the Lobstick remains one of Canada's premier match game golf tournaments. Her golf skills were good enough to get Sylvia to the Lobstick tournament, and she participated in it many times. The pressure of golf was different from that of team sports. It was an individual game, and Sylvia found that it brought out *too much* of her competitive streak. She was always mad at herself, a flaw that did nothing to contribute to either enjoyment of or growth in her play. Friends noticed that her golf game would improve or go all to hell depending on her golfing partner for the day. If Sylvia was with a non-competitive friend, then the golf was so-so; if there was real competition walking alongside her on the links, then her game improved immensely.[7]

Despite summer golfing and fishing, her favourite sport remained curling, and Sylvia gave time, energy, and organizational ability to local clubs and then the Saskatoon-wide curling league. Sylvia still participated in club play two nights a week, and the occasional weekend bonspiel, but she was increasingly drawn by the administrative and decision-making aspects of the larger provincial and national curling organizations. Her ability to see the larger picture beyond the local rink allowed her to build the game not just for friends or even Saskatoon but also for all Canadians. Sylvia led a lasting change to women's curling at the national level, developing professionalization, inviting media, and addressing friction and opposition. Winter evenings were filled with meetings and letters and phone calls. She watched as the Canadian Ladies Curling Association (CLCA) organized and ran national playdowns, and she became a regular attendee, both on and off the ice, during the 1960s. A typical winter trip for Sylvia involved travel to the national women's and men's playdowns, even when she was not competing, a habit that she held well into retirement.

Within the national-level CLCA, Sylvia climbed the ranks. By 1970, she was second vice-president. By 1971, her dedication to the game paid off when she became the president-elect.[8] The new job came with a major perk. Sylvia became one of the Canadian women chosen to travel on behalf of the CLCA to Scotland for a grand curling tour. Such tours had been regular events for about seventy years, with teams or groups of teams travelling to the other country. On November 4, 1971, twenty Canadian women curlers—two from each province—arrived in Glasgow. Three full weeks of curling ensued, with an itinerary that criss-crossed Scotland and took them from city to small country rinks as far north as Inverness and Aberdeen and as far south as Stranraer and Lockerbie.

It was a moving bonspiel of massive proportions—people, geography, travel, rink times, games, and social events. Sylvia kept a detailed diary and scrapbooks of the trip, both gruelling and fun. By the end, Canada had sixty-nine wins, fifty-two losses, and seven ties, and Sylvia's team had nineteen wins, six losses, and one tie. Her team was Jean Snowdon of Alberta, Saskatchewan Ladies Curling Association Secretary Agnes Pittman, and Sylvia Schacter of Quebec. Fedoruk, as usual, was severe on herself, even in what was meant to be more a social than a competitive tour. She hogged an important guard stone in one game and moaned, "Lost the game on that shot." Bett Law of Scotland caught her eye: "She has copied Joyce McKee's style down to the original backswing." The diary is filled with commentary on the rinks and amenities. The Falkirk rink, for example, "is large enough to hold 6 sheets of ice with dividers and has one end used for figure skating," full of whirling and jumping bodies as the ladies played. In many places, the rinks were old wooden converted skating rinks, and the ice was less than ideal: swingy, as much as fourteen feet, with not enough pebbling and some strange runs. Nonetheless, Sylvia's team soon got used to each other and started winning games, specializing in a few astonishing come-from-behind wins and even a seven-ender.[9]

In most places, there was an inordinate amount of ceremony. Clearly, the local women had invested in organization. Players were often piped in by bagpipes, haggis was a regular item on menus, and a formal meet-and-greet with the mayor and other lords and leaders constituted various civic receptions. The women took regular breaks to be tourists, visiting Loch Lomond and Loch Ness. One day they stopped at the John Haig and Company malt whisky plant in Markinch. "Talk about racket with that many bottles clanking about," Sylvia recorded.[10] The plant produced 25,000 cases per day, with a dozen bottles in each case. A complete tour of the whole operation ended in lunch and sampling. Sylvia bought two bottles to take home. A flu bug ran through the ladies, and Sylvia caught a massive cold, wheezing and coughing through much of the social round of food, drinks, travel, curling, and trading badges and pins. Sometimes they stayed with local billets, sometimes at hotels. When billeted, Sylvia took advantage of any pets, romping with happiness with any and all dogs. They decided to festoon the rear of the bus with messages for passing motorists, just to add to the frivolity. Late nights with lots of jokes and visiting, it's clear that Sylvia and the Canadian crew enjoyed every minute of the tour. The final banquet took place on November 24, with "about 165 giggly women at the banquet from all over Scotland." The final grace was a typical Scots mix:

> Be thou our ship through out life's game
> And syn we're sure to win
> Tho slow the shot and wide the aim,
> We'll soop each other in.[11]

By the end of the tour, each curler had thrown eleven tons of granite, walked seventy-three miles up and down the ice, and travelled 1,600 miles in Scotland over the twenty-one days. Sylvia stayed a few more days in London, going to plays at Drury Lane and seeing Agatha Christie's *The Mousetrap* before writing a thank-you note to Queen Elizabeth II expressing gratitude for the Scottish and English warm hospitality during her trip, enclosing a tour pin and brochure. She flew home on December 2 and later received a gracious acknowledgement from Buckingham Palace.[12]

By the time that Sylvia returned to Saskatoon from the Scottish tour, her competitive—and international if friendly—curling days were behind her. Turning her attention to administration, Sylvia was a major part of the negotiations leading to the Macdonald Tobacco Company's becoming the new national ladies' curling sponsor. There had been an acrimonious split with Dominion Stores and their Diamond D national sponsorship in the late 1960s.

The CLCA had managed for a few years with no sponsorship, but such a move was unsustainable. To grow the sport and set it on a solid foundation, the CLCA needed a sponsor for its premier annual event, the Canadian ladies' championship. The Macdonald company was a good fit. It had been sponsoring the men's brier for years, was familiar with curling and its traditions and expectations, and did not attempt to control either the governance or the decision-making, unlike Dominion Stores.[13] What Macdonald did ask for, though, was discretion. As Sylvia later recounted, Macdonald's senior executives made a policy decision: "'Make sure that the fellow representing the Macdonald Tobacco Company at the Lassie can never be accused of getting any of the women in trouble'— That is why the two elder statesmen, Bill and Jack, were given the job rather than the younger, more virile fellows who work the Brier."[14] Sylvia's role in leading and handling the negotiations and the firm relationship between the CLCA and Macdonald Tobacco cannot be overstated. Sylvia had a way of dissolving tough situations and easing things through. In some ways, the strength of Canadian women's curling, with so many world championship and Olympic Games winners, can be traced to her determination to put ladies' curling onto a professional, sponsored footing aligned with that for men.

The 1972 Canadian Ladies Curling Championship was held in Saskatoon, where Sylvia was the centre of a whirlwind of organizational activity and active cheering. As president and local host, she had the ability and a growing network of contacts to develop not just a bonspiel but also a whole program of events that included local and provincial dignitaries. The championship in Saskatoon was particularly exciting, for the city had a hometown rink: skip Vera Pezer, with Lee Morrison, Sheila Rowan, and Joyce McKee. The foursome dominated round robin play and took home the championship in front of a wildly enthusiastic crowd.

In many ways, 1972 was one of the busiest years of Sylvia's life. During that year, Sylvia was appointed to or assumed positions at the national level in both sport and science. Given her excellence in international committee work for radiation science with the International Atomic Energy Agency, and her early 1960s advisory work with the federal minister of national health and welfare on radioisotopes, Sylvia once again found herself leading at the national level. In 1972, she was appointed as one of the first female members of the Science Council of Canada.

Created by federal statute in 1966, the Science Council in some ways mimicked the President's Scientific Advisory Committee in the United States. Sylvia was a good choice for the council since it had published a major report on the atomic industry in Canada. Her one-time physics nemesis, Leon Katz, had been part of that report, as had colleagues at Chalk River. Katz's polite disdain for women in physics did not ring loudly in the 1970s, with a strong women's movement and a concurrent shift in social attitudes. That Sylvia was selected to join the council should come as no surprise. She was quick to capitalize on the appointment in a way that offers a good lesson to women looking for career advancement. Sylvia made sure that the president, vice-president, dean of medicine, and other leaders at the University of Saskatchewan received formal notice of her appointment to the Science Council.[15] Recognition mattered.

After the excitement of the ladies' curling championships in Saskatoon, Sylvia was back at work at the cancer clinic, aiming to complete a new project. After twenty-one years of continuous service, the original cobalt-60 machine was set to retire after treating 6,728 patients. The radiotherapy department was in full renovation mode, expanding to absorb multiple new machines. "The new radiotherapy department includes a betatron suite, two cobalt rooms, and one high-voltage therapy room, completely underground to protect against possible dangers of radiation."[16] Incorporating a betatron into the hospital setting made the vision of Ertle Harrington, Harold Johns, and the rest of the Department of Physics team a reality. Here was a betatron *meant* for imaging and treating humans, and right in the hospital, instead of across the campus in the back basement of the physics department building.

Media attention concentrated on the new cobalt unit. Special structures, mechanisms, and electrical systems were needed, including a wall seven-and-a-half feet thick to protect against radiation. This was a far cry from the first-floor room where Sylvia learned to use the machine by radiating hapless gophers. The size and weight of the new unit caused some consternation. The hospital's building team had to create a special hatch in the roof to get it down to its new underground cavern. All in all, the new cobalt unit and its installation cost $1.1 million—a far cry from the paltry few thousand dollars needed in 1950.[17]

Purchasing a commercial cobalt unit meant that some of the fluidity and knowledge that came from designing and building one's own machine was lost. Instead of making the machine perform to the cancer clinic's needs and expectations, it became a matter of learning what the machine could and could not do. Sylvia and the cancer clinic technicians soon came to learn the ins and outs of the machine, improving their technical manipulation of it. Throughout the 1970s, it became clear that the technical expertise needed to run commercial machines related more to computer programming than to machining or hand-calculating the physics according to Sylvia's precise depth dose tables. Peter Dickof, who came to work for the Cancer Commission at Regina's Allan Blair clinic in 1979, brought his computer expertise and spoke of that transition: "When I got there, all the equipment was being purchased from manufacturers, but we were writing the software for them. There was this attitude of just doing stuff yourself. That was clearly back to Sylvia's long continuity with that past."[18] Local modifications of commercial machines would keep costs down as well as lead to useful local outcomes. But the days of local modifications were numbered.

That summer Sylvia went as far north as she could go in Saskatchewan, to Grease River Lodge, less than half a mile from the border with the Northwest Territories. Her travel diary from this trip reveals that the lodge was operated by Slim and Hap Cave.[19] It was located on a series of connected lakes, including Scott, Premier, and Wignos Lakes, which drew anglers across the border into the Northwest Territories. With no commercial fishing and no other camps, the lake was a northern getaway of the most remote, and pristine, kind. A fly-in camp was different from a tourist camp in the town of La Ronge. In the former, anglers flew in with little more than their clothes and favourite tackle box and rod. All else, from food to boats and gas to guides to accommodations, was provided. Slim and Hap Cave recommended plenty of fishing tackle, no doubt because the rocky outcrops and underwater reefs would slice and steal lures. They also recommended lead core fishing line since the trout were big and the jackfish hungry.

A guide would prepare a large, eighteen-foot, high-walled boat with a twenty-horsepower motor, packed and ready to travel out to the good fishing spots early in the morning. Shore lunches were a specialty, and the fishers would be brought back in the evening for a "delicious meal prepared by first class cooks, served family style and all you can eat."[20] With accommodations in oil-heated cabins with a 110-volt lighting system and single beds, the camp could hold ten guests per day. Guests were reminded to bring rain gear, warm

7. WE CALL THIS MEETING TO ORDER

clothes, a camera and film, and all their own alcoholic refreshments. Any fish caught were filleted, packaged, and frozen for transport.

Sylvia drove to Waskesiu to stay with friends. From there, along with Dot George and Eileen Joss, she drove to La Ronge and boarded a plane to Uranium City. There an Otter float plane took them to Scott Lake. Arriving at four o'clock in the afternoon, they started fishing right away, catching four trout, including one that tipped the scale at fifteen pounds, and a six-pound pickerel. The next morning they were up by 6:00 a.m., ate breakfast at 7:30, and then headed out. The jackfish and trout bit well, the women found, and by the end of the day they tallied the largest fish: a fourteen-pound jackfish and a sixteen-pound trout. Each day was similar: get up early, eat breakfast, and get out on the lake. The women loved catching the big trout, but all revelled in the fun of hauling in hungry and feisty jackfish. One day Sylvia landed a dozen jacks hiding and feasting among some lily pads, in less than an hour. The next day they concentrated on trout, a "bonanza," she exclaimed, fourteen trout in total on a "beautiful sunny day lots of fun. Trout running across water." Another day of trout fishing, and then Thursday, because of a "poor morning for trout—one four-pound and three piddly ones," the women opted to catch jackfish: "Great Fun!"[21]

But it was a good thing that the trip was almost finished: the women ran out of booze on their last night—a calamity according to Sylvia in her travel diary. They left after spending one last morning on the lake, fighting in a seventeen-pound eight-ounce lake trout. The flight home took the women to Uranium City, where they had a quick tour of the Eldorado mine, then on to Stony Rapids. A flight to La Ronge brought them back to familiar stomping grounds, and they took advantage of Red's Camp to fish one more time before driving to Waskesiu. Then Sylvia went home to Saskatoon.

With so much fish, though, Sylvia had a storage problem. She left the fish at her local Safeway grocery store in its meat locker while she tripped over to the Hudson's Bay Company to buy a freezer. After it was delivered and set up in her apartment, Sylvia retrieved her fish and invited a load of friends over for a fish fry. With the gas for the trip north, the flights in and out, and buying a freezer when she got home, the fishing trip was not a cheap adventure.[22]

Nonetheless, Sylvia was a single woman with a substantial professional profile and an income to match it, and northern fishing was one of her favourite ways to spend quality time every summer. Hap Cave wrote "Many thanks. It has been a pleasure having you girls as guests."[23] Soon after their Grease River Lodge/Scott Lake adventure, Dot George and Eileen Joss, together with good friends Audrey and Murray Coben, built a cabin at English Bay on Lac La Ronge. Sylvia became a regular guest and would spend a week at English Bay every June, as her schedule allowed, to fish with Eileen and Dot.

Although curling, fishing, and golfing occupied much free time, with work and national leadership events taking more time, Sylvia still found something missing. She filled that personal gap with Tinker, an all-black "Heinz 57" cross between a poodle and a spaniel, with curly hair and floppy ears. He came into her life in 1971 as a puppy after Sylvia and Irene Bell visited the pet store in the Grosvenor Square Mall on 8th Street. Tinker and Sylvia lived first in the high-rise apartment block downtown. Owning a dog was a major adventure for her. When Sylvia was the child of a rural schoolteacher in the 1930s, a dog would have been both beyond their household budget and impractical since they often lived in rural teacherages. The move to Windsor, Ontario, during the war years with two parents working shiftwork and Sylvia engrossed in school and extracurricular sports meant a continuation of the non-dog limitation. Back in Saskatchewan for university and living in the Mohyla residence, again filling her days and evenings with studying and extracurricular activities, Sylvia still could not accommodate a dog. Once she was working as a professional physicist, it might have been possible to get a dog, but once again sports dominated her life. Summer ball playing meant days and evenings away from home practising and playing. Winter curling meant the same. It wasn't until Sylvia pulled back from more competitive sports in the later 1960s and established her own household without Joyce McKee that she had enough free time in mornings and evenings and on weekends to consider owning a dog.

Tinker taught Sylvia the joys of daily faithful companionship and responsibility. Daily walks were now necessary, and she took Tinker out and about regularly, stretching her own legs and trying to stave off or at least hold in check the weight gain that came with her reduced sporting activity. But Tinker also brought change. As a high-rise apartment dog, he soon learned that his mistress returned just after he heard the sounds of the elevator rising and stopping on their floor. In happy anticipation, he came to associate elevator sounds with Sylvia and began to bark—a lot. And he couldn't be broken of the habit. In some desperation, she decided that, since she couldn't stop the barking, she'd have to move.[24]

When Sylvia began living in apartments, her gardening diminished substantially. Thankfully, on summer weekends, along with her cousin Merylyn's son Michael and later accompanied by Tinker, she would travel the many miles east from Saskatoon to Yorkton to visit her father and aunt and uncle in their mirrored homes across the street from each other on First Avenue. Both the Fedoruks and Mary Kulcheski grew extensive gardens. Michael, Mary's grandson and Sylvia's cousin, remembered Annie and Ted's garden: "They had a huge,

Tinker, 1973.

huge garden. At least it seemed so to me. To a six year old, you look at it and go, wow! They had green thumbs. They could grow anything."[25] With a barking dog and a yearning to have her own garden once again, Sylvia started scanning the classifieds.

She bought her own house at 49 Simpson Crescent in the Greystone Heights area of Saskatoon in October for $26,000. It was ideally situated. Since it backed onto Greystone Heights schoolyard, Sylvia could take her beloved Tinker for regular walks, with plenty of space in the schoolyard or on the green verge along 14th Street, backing the University of Saskatchewan agricultural plots. A bungalow with a backyard large enough for a west-facing garden, the house gave Sylvia enough room to entertain friends and family, host guests, and finally put down roots in a place that she owned. By 1974, Sylvia and her dog had settled in. Their Christmas letter concluded thus: "Tinker, my 'Heinz 57' pal continues to run the household and manages to eat as well as his mistress."[26] Domestic contentment reigned.

Tinker much enjoyed the companionship of Sylvia's young cousin Michael, a schoolkid at Greystone Heights right behind Sylvia's backyard. Sylvia always knew when Michael was passing by since Tinker would announce the event with enthusiastic barks and a run to and much tail-wagging by the fence. Michael would reach over the fence or come into the yard for a visit. He also became the secondary support system for the dog, taking him for walks around the schoolyard or just letting him out for a pee if Sylvia was occupied with meetings or other concerns and couldn't get home for lunch. By the time Michael was in grade five, his classroom was in the wing closest to Sylvia's house: "If I stood in my classroom, I could wave to her in the dining room. It was that close."[27] When Sylvia and Michael and Tinker travelled to Yorkton, Tinker's road treat was an ice cream cone from Dairy Queen; he would hold the cone gently between his paws and lick it with great enthusiasm.[28]

The house did have its faults. The Greystone Heights area was not, in fact, a "heights" but a "depths." In May 1974, a massive rain storm pounded the city. Sylvia was aghast: there were four inches of water in her basement, and she "had to work pretty hard and fast to move everything up to the main floor. Many Saskatonians were not as lucky with their possessions—some homes had so much water in the basement that the main floors buckled."[29] Over the years, a host of other floods, from rain or spring runoff or broken pipes, would see Sylvia doggedly hauling boxes and furniture up the stairs to salvage what she could, spreading things around upstairs, in the garage, or out on the lawn to dry. She soon learned to keep important treasures up off the floor or stored in good plastic containers; otherwise, she ran the risk of losing something critical. Despite water perils, 49 Simpson Crescent gave Sylvia her most enduring home.

The new house also gave her the space to display her by now massive collection of curling pins. Sylvia travelled annually to take in both the Brier and the Lassies, and her baggage could make airport handlers groan. One suitcase for clothes and necessities, and one for the part of her curling pin collection that she was willing to display or sacrifice on trade, accompanied her across the country. Travelling across Scotland with the Canadian-Scottish women's tour in 1971, she gleefully bought, traded, and acquired pins from the many leagues and rinks that they visited, from Aberdeen to Lockerbie.[30]

In 1974, *Saskatoon Star-Phoenix* reporter Jean Macpherson came calling to the house on Simpson Cresent. What was Sylvia's obsession all about? she asked. Happy fellowship, the excitement of the chase, and the artistic appeal of each piece, Sylvia explained. The collection, Macpherson reported, showcased "intricate patterns and imaginative designs. Some are gold, some are silver; there are copper badges, bronze, other metals, and some in cloth, wood,

7. WE CALL THIS MEETING TO ORDER

and plastic." With the earliest Canadian pin dating from 1807, for the Royal Montreal Curling Club, Sylvia's collection included a few rare treasures, such as a pin from the Governor General's Curling Club and the King of Sweden's Curling Club. Others, Macpherson noted with much admiration, were works of art, with ribbons, tartan, chains, and even one with a blue heron feather. With almost 3,000 pieces in her collection by 1974, there was satisfaction in the chase, in trying to get complete runs of pins from major national bonspiels such as the Brier.[31]

Pin collecting and trading led to many new friendships. "You meet so many people through the hobby," Sylvia told Macpherson. "Last month I was in Montreal on an engineering conference, and it turned out the president of the association of engineers was a fellow I'd traded badges with for years." She even had a charm bracelet, heavy with one complete set of pins. Another year she pulled out her pin collection and hooked them all onto her curling sweater, just to see how many she could fit on. It was encrusted: all across the lapels, shoulders, down the arms, and up and down the back, including the pockets. "I couldn't move!" she laughed, it was so heavy by the time she was done.[32]

With meticulous detail, Sylvia went beyond collecting to careful recording. Numbered and described, her pin collection eventually exploded beyond what her curling sweater, or even her walls, could hold. By the time she moved into her own house at 49 Simpson Crescent and Macpherson came to visit, only the cream of Sylvia's collection was visible. It was mounted on dark velvet and displayed in heavy wooden frames, and her basement den walls were completely covered. The rest of the pins were put away, bagged and boxed and stored—but still documented—waiting for her imagination to create a new way to collate, frame, wear, or display her collection. Sylvia wrote and submitted a short article to *The Curler* newsletter in the early 1970s, which worked as an advertisement for her curling pin obsession. "The true collector gets the most satisfaction when the unusual badge is found or the collector meets an unusual person with such a badge," she opened the piece. Those unusual people in the Canadian curling pin trade included Ren Fortier and "Bingo" Christie, whose deaths she lamented: "The Brier will never be the same without these colourful characters." Ren traded Sylvia a prized St. Pat's Curling Club pin, and Bingo traded her a Grey Goose Curling Club pin, in the shape of a flying grey goose. "Anybody willing to trade with Trader Syl?" she asked hopefully.[33]

Her professional life took another major step forward at this time. Her appointed position on the federal Science Council in 1972 was superseded by a new national appointment that made news across the country. Effective May 1, 1973, Sylvia was appointed the first female member of the Atomic Energy Control Board of Canada (AECB). The AECB was established under the *Atomic Energy Control Act* in 1946, an act designed to set the federal government firmly in the lead, and in control, of nuclear technology in Canada. It was a matter of intense national security. The act was broad and powerful. It gave the AECB power to seize intellectual property, control or suppress information, expropriate companies or private property, and create crown corporations, among other powers. The act, in effect, put nuclear technology under civil regulation. Two crown companies were set up almost immediately. Eldorado Mining and Refining (later Eldorado Nuclear) was purchased by the federal government in 1943 to take federal control of uranium production in Canada, and Atomic Energy of Canada Limited (AECL) was created in 1952 to take over the Chalk River project. One of the first projects created by Eldorado, and taken over commercially by AECL, was the Ontario cobalt bomb, the fraternal twin of Saskatoon's cobalt-60 unit. The AECL would also develop the Canadian CANDU (Canada Deuterium Uranium) nuclear reactor technology. So, with Eldorado, Chalk River, AECL, and the AECB, Sylvia had long worked with the people and entities that controlled Canada's nuclear destiny.

By the 1970s, the AECB had settled into its role as regulator and supervisor of the development and use of nuclear energy in Canada and as the country's agency of contract for the international community. Its primary concern was safety. In this new federal position, Sylvia shone. The five-person board was small enough to be nimble but drew enough professional firepower to be effective. Under board leadership, the AECB had an operating staff of well over 150 people, but even so the board's list of responsibilities was long: regulating and monitoring uranium exploration and mining, nuclear fuel manufacturing, nuclear power plants, transportation of radioactive materials, radioactive storage and remediation protocols, heavy-water plants such as Chalk River, radioisotope use in hospitals, radioactive research at universities, and international nuclear trade.

Nuclear research and power production, activities that took up the bulk of Eldorado's and AECL's time, had increasingly come under fire through the 1960s. By the 1970s, protests—in newspapers, letter-writing campaigns, and marches—were common. But there was clearly room for convincing in either direction. Norma Bicknell, a member of the Local Council of Women in Calgary and one of Sylvia's former classmates, convinced her women's council not to sign a local petition banning all nuclear research. If Sylvia Fedoruk is on the Atomic Energy Control Board, Bicknell said, "I am convinced she makes the best possible 'watchdog.'" In other words, with Sylvia as a guide, Canada had nothing to fear.[34]

Yet at first she nearly refused the position. Her first reaction was negative. Was she being asked only because of her gender? Was it therefore a token appointment? But she soon came around. There was no way that, given her stellar national and international record, her appointment could be token. It was, instead, "recognition for the years of work I have done in the field,"[35] particularly in the area of nuclear medicine, an area under AECB jurisdiction. In fact, the offer was probably based on both gender and her stellar record, but it was an offer that Sylvia really couldn't refuse. It required high-level security clearance because of the nature of the role, but that only added to its cachet.

The AECB position was demanding and consuming, with board meetings every two to three months, more if there were special issues or disasters, requiring airplane trips to Ottawa or elsewhere. The salary for an AECB board member was $125 per diem up to a maximum of $3,000 per year, all expenses covered (e.g., flights, hotels, and meals). So the position wasn't a money-making one, yet it did offer recompense for time spent. Next to her work at the university and the Saskatchewan Cancer Commission, it was her longest-serving appointment. Sylvia was a member of the AECB board from 1973 to 1988. Yet in all that time she never took the board chair position. Her intelligence and influence stayed in the background. Soon after her 1973 appointment, and not coincidentally, Sylvia was awarded a full professorship at the University of Saskatchewan. Even though she did not hold a Ph.D., her international and national work, reputation, and position demanded nothing less from the university.

Sylvia was an AECB board member through some of its most interesting and challenging years. The construction and startup of several Canadian CANDU power stations, at places such as Bruce, Pickering, Point Lepreau, and Darlington, focused the board's attention. Radiation problems and remedial cleanup at Port Hope and Port Granby from the Eldorado plant's waste and debris brought the AECB under fire by 1976 for not taking a more active oversight role.³⁶ A radioactive leak from a natural 3,000-foot-wide band of radioactive ore under the town of Elliot Lake also made the news. The vein produced radon gas in unacceptably high quantities.³⁷ Issues of contamination, cleanup, and responsibility sparked a massive outcry in Canadian newspapers. The Canadian nuclear industry, critics charged, was little more than a nuclear old boys' club, a "cozy network" of relationships that connected the AECB, Eldorado, and AECL. How, they wondered, could the AECB be a regulatory agency for the other two entities? One was created to regulate atomic energy, one to mine it, and one to sell it—but where was the distance among them when people and influence moved back and forth with such ease and secrecy? The relationship between the AECB and Ontario Hydro was similarly rife with controversy. As the builders and operators of the new nuclear power plants, the two often had a thorny relationship but kept it as much as possible from the public eye. The attitude was that the public just didn't need to know since more often than not the public didn't have a good understanding of the technical aspects of nuclear energy production. As a result, the public was often cut out and had little policy-making input, and only rarely would the AECB host public meetings to address concerns.³⁸

The publication of critical information was a sticking point for the AECB since the nuclear industry distrusted the media and vice versa. Miserly information would often backfire and lead to breathless reporting. In 1979, a select committee of the Ontario Legislative Assembly studying Ontario Hydro affairs, particularly safety at the new nuclear power plants, revealed a showdown via letters between the AECB and Ontario Hydro. The Control Board wanted significantly increased safety procedures for fuel failures; Ontario Hydro shot back that its safety record was exemplary and that these new measures were expensive and not required. The controversy revealed by the letters showed Ontario Hydro trying to influence the AECB, with the latter coming across as less of a sharp-toothed watchdog with real bite and more of a tiny poodle, yapping in the corner.³⁹ "Control? What Control?" screamed headlines.

Nonetheless, Sylvia thoroughly enjoyed her work as a member of the AECB, despite—or perhaps because of—the public controversy. Nuclear energy, she knew, would always inspire public interest. As soon as she joined the board, her office in the cancer clinic received a new filing cabinet that could be locked. AECB board notes and records, as a matter of national security, required secrecy. In her yearly Christmas letters to friends and family, Sylvia exuded enthusiasm for what she saw, experienced, and helped to lead.

> The highlight of the year [1974] had to be a visit to the Nuclear power complex under construction on the shore of Lake Huron near Kincardine, Ont. The Bruce Nuclear Power Development presently has in operation the Douglas Point Generating Station and two 800 ton Heavy water units. Four 750 Megawatt nuclear power reactors are under various stages of construction and plans include a further four units to be completed in the 1980s. In addition, the Heavy water facility will be enlarged to include 8 units. The visit was most exciting and I continue to marvel at what man can accomplish when government establishes a policy of "full steam ahead."[40]

Ever the scientist, Sylvia could not resist giving a scientific and jingoistic overview, even in her chatty Christmas letter.

Her brand of intelligence and wry ability to see humour and irony were a big help in her AECB work. Sylvia would later remember a time

> when members of the Board went underground to tour two uranium mines at Elliott Lake, Ontario. Although mine regulations called for no smoking below ground, there were cigarette butts throughout the stopes. This was at the time when there was great concern about the relationship of radon gas (which is emitted during the radioactive decay of uranium by-products) and lung cancer. Following the tours, a meeting was held with union representatives from the United Steel Workers of America—the sixteen reps who gathered for the meeting were complaining about a miner colleague who had just been diagnosed with lung cancer which ... beyond any doubt to them was due to the radon gas in the mines. "What are you going to do about it, Board members?" they asked as they sat around the table in a blue haze, enjoying a good smoke.[41]

Although Sylvia might have raised an eyebrow at the irony of union reps blaming radon gas for a colleague's lung cancer while blowing clouds of blue cigarette smoke, she nonetheless championed miners' safety, particularly working conditions in uranium mines and exposure over time to radiation. In 1975, she flew to northern Saskatchewan to view the up-and-coming mine at Cluff Lake. Along with a doctor, another member of the AECB, and the Saskatchewan chief inspector for mines, she was there to view and assess the site and its proposed safety protocols. Met by Jean Claude Chauveau, the executive vice-president of the French-owned Amok Limited, Sylvia asked some hard questions about monitoring of an ore site where the ore ranged in radioactivity across spots and even within a small area. Production aimed to start in the spring of 1978 contingent on the completion of the all-weather road. Sylvia took extensive notes on the plan to extract the uranium ore, what the mine would look like, how the shifts would be run, and how the mine would be built to keep occupational health and safety front of mind. Rotating the miners among sites, shifts, and areas of radiation was critical to ensure that no miner was exposed to levels beyond defined limits.

The company setting up the new mine at Cluff Lake had to consider all aspects of the mining program, from pit to plant to storage building to wet storage to tailings. The mine needed the all-weather road to bring in reagents, mostly sulphuric acid. "Hot uranium ore doesn't need much doctoring," Sylvia noted. Just how hot was another matter: "Amok had just removed 20 feet of over-burden to expose a very rich body of uranium ore. [Sylvia] was down in the pit and was very excited with the very high readings being recorded by the radiation detector. However she was standing too close to a pump that was extracting water that was seeping into the pit that her fortrel pant leg completely shrivelled up (from the heat of the pump manifold, not from the radiation)."[42]

Sylvia's shrivelled pantleg notwithstanding, Amok's originally planned timeline spoke to the special requirements of building a massive mine in northern Saskatchewan. First and foremost, the company had to build a winter road in 1975–76 to haul up big equipment and construction materials. Construction of the mine would take place over 1976 and 1977. The original winter road would need finishing to convert it to an all-weather road by the end of 1977 in order to open the mine in the spring of 1978. Her visit to the mine gave Sylvia a sense of the place and space and intent of the project, which would serve her well as the AECB, as well as the province, navigated the legalities of the mine's creation.

Uranium development in Saskatchewan caused a furor in the province. There was already production of uranium ore at Eldorado's mine in Uranium City. Was there enough demand for another mine and increased production? The province created the Cluff Lake Board of Inquiry, headed by Mr. Justice E.D. Bayda. It began in April 1977, and Sylvia was on the witness stand on the first day, representing the AECB and its views on Canada's uranium development.

The Cluff Lake Board of Inquiry moved from Regina to Saskatoon, then to Uranium City and other northern towns, to hear diverse viewpoints on greater provincial uranium development. Amok, in an attempt to sway public opinion, created a mobile model of the mine site to showcase uranium mining and miner safety procedures.[43] The inquiry revealed bitter and divisive social and environmental concerns across the province, splitting those in favour of development against those who argued that uranium development in general and Cluff Lake in particular would cause social and environmental disaster.

Florence Poorman, a journalist for the *Saskatchewan Indian*, reported that Amok promised 50 percent First Nations hiring at its northern mine, but there was much skepticism about this promise. She noted a number of concerns raised by the Bayda inquiry, including "the probable disruption of the northern way of life, should an all-weather road be put through to Cluff Lake. An influx of tourists, campers, hunters, fishers, and the like, and while there are paper promises of the number of native people that could, or should, be employed by the mine, there is no guarantee that this must come about. And . . . there is nothing to ensure that ANY of the monies generated by the mine, either directly or indirectly, will remain in the north to benefit the people of the area whose land it is."[44] Although the Bayda uranium inquiry set a precedent by going into small northern communities to open the dialogue on the impacts of uranium development, ultimately the report would support uranium development in the province.[45]

When not travelling in Canada on AECB business or working at the cancer clinic, Sylvia could be found in her west-facing garden. Through the years, she experimented with a range of produce to see what grew well and what she and her friends enjoyed eating. There wasn't much use growing Swiss chard or turnips if no one wanted to eat them. Potatoes and carrots, tomatoes and cucumbers were staples, though she also grew corn, squash, zucchini, and peppers on occasion. The garden wasn't large since Sylvia also wanted space for a few trees and perennials, a bit of grass, a herb garden with basil and other fresh herbs, a patio for barbequing and eating, and space for her dog to run. Every inch had to count. Close friend Vera Pezer suggested that Sylvia's garden represented her personality: if Sylvia could do or grow something well, then she would; if it didn't work out, then she quickly dropped it. One year she grew horseradish, which she turned into horseradish sauce, but that experiment was not repeated—whether because one year's bounty was enough for many years or because it wasn't successful is now unknown.[46] Michael Vann, Sylvia's cousin and frequent visitor, said that her garden was therapeutic. Sylvia had inherited her mother's green thumb and enjoyed growing things in her own backyard. She also filled her house with all kinds of plants. If Sylvia was away, which was frequently, then Michael was drafted to water the plants. The houseplants added splashes of green around the rooms and offset the enormous collection of art that Sylvia scattered across her walls and on any available horizontal space. From pictures and paintings to sculptures, pots, and wall hangings, Sylvia kept an eye open for pieces to add to her collection or to buy for special friends.[47]

Her activities in the garden extended and enhanced her cooking, one of her known talents. The barbeque would run all summer and into other seasons when possible. No one who visited Sylvia would ever go home hungry. There was always good food and plenty of it. In fact, if you visited, you'd probably not be hungry for *days*, for Sylvia would send you home with all of the leftovers. In a strange twist, probably because she spent so much time travelling, Sylvia rarely kept leftovers in the house. Meals shared with friends or family became meals *given* to them. Everyone would go home with copious leftovers, enough for several days.[48]

Despite her board membership with the AECB, Sylvia's day-to-day life remained closely tied to the cancer clinic and the university. The year 1976 marked the twenty-fifth anniversary of the cobalt-60 unit, and Sylvia was pushing for recognition of it. In a letter to Tony Dagnone, then an associate executive director of the University Hospital, she put forward a plan: "I believe that the University Hospital and the Saskatchewan Cancer Commission should celebrate the 25th anniversary of the birth of the Cobalt 60 era here in Saskatoon in part by announcing that the first machine will be permanently displayed in the University Hospital." Sylvia wanted a museum-style display of the Saskatoon cobalt unit, a piece that would capture provincial pride in being the first worldwide. The London unit, after all, was on display in the Museum of Science and Technology in Toronto. An early unit in the United States had been moved to the Smithsonian Institution, she noted. The Saskatoon unit? *In storage in the laundry building.* Something, Sylvia said with vehemence, should be done. But the hospital didn't budge. It would take another ten years, and a project with Sylvia at the helm, before the original Saskatoon cobalt-60 unit would go on display to the public in the foyer of the new cancer clinic.[49]

As the Bayda inquiry moved along in 1977, Sylvia's personal world took a difficult hit. As a cancer researcher and treatment leader whose mother had succumbed to the disease, Sylvia was no stranger to the peril and pain of a cancer diagnosis. Yet, unlike the miners whom she had met in Ontario, she had walked the path away from cigarettes, knowing their link to cancer. In the early 1960s, pictures of Sylvia at the curling rink or sharing an evening with friends showed cigarettes poking out between her fingers. But there was no sign of cigarette use after her mother's death. Life itself, no matter how cleanly lived, could be sideswiped by cancer. In a cruel stroke of irony, Sylvia's father, Ted Fedoruk, received terrible news. After battling poor health for years, including high blood pressure and a few hospital stays, he was diagnosed with inoperable stomach cancer in 1977 at the age of seventy-nine. Sylvia's handwritten notes for 1977 reported in May that "Dad doesn't look well." In late June, while Sylvia was in Ottawa for an AECB meeting, she wrote "bad news from Yorkton." By July 1, she was back in Saskatchewan and in Yorkton with her father, spending time with him until his death on the morning of July 17. Sylvia chose Bailey's Funeral Home, a few blocks from her parents' house, for the funeral service, but it was conducted by Father Zuzak of the Holy Trinity Transfiguration Ukrainian Greek Orthodox Church. Ted Fedoruk was laid to rest next to Annie in the Yorkton cemetery. His death was hard on Sylvia but almost welcome. Being an only daughter, stretched between career commitments and national leadership, meant that Sylvia felt some guilt when her father's letters pulled on her heart strings. "When are you coming?" Ted would ask. In another letter, sending Sylvia a card for her birthday, he wrote "Your gift will wait until you come to see me."[50] With his death, the pull to Yorkton softened, and her mailbox no longer filled with cute birthday or Valentine's or Christmas cards meant for an eight-year-old girl.

Following her father's death in 1977, Sylvia received an unexpected invitation—one that she, a lifelong fan of the royal family, could not ignore. Along with 400 others from across Canada, Sylvia received a crisp embossed invitation to attend a dinner reception in Ottawa for a Tribute to Young Canadians Who Have Achieved Excellence in the Arts and Sciences. The Chateau Laurier reception would be presided over by none other than Her Majesty Queen Elizabeth II and her husband, Prince Philip, as part of their visit in 1977 to Ottawa to celebrate the queen's silver jubilee of twenty-five years on the throne. "Young" was defined as under the age of forty, but apparently no one had looked at Sylvia's birth certificate. Sylvia had, in fact, turned fifty that May. Nonetheless, for her role on the Science Council and as the first woman on the AECB, she was among the "nattily attired" guests, who included performers, artists, scientists, journalists, and many from Canada's Indigenous community. "Many of the people present said they weren't sure why they had been invited," the *Star-Phoenix* noted. It seemed to be a hurriedly strung-together party, haphazard in concept and execution.[51]

With 400 people milling about the room, would Sylvia actually get to meet the queen? Or would she be just another Canadian looking longingly as the regent of the realm floated along at the far end of the room, surrounded by protocol agents and discreet secret service protectors? Actually, she did. With the United Forces string band providing background accompaniment, the queen circulated around the room and spoke with many people, including Sylvia. They chatted about her work at the cancer clinic and with the AECB, particularly uranium development. The queen proved to be a knowledgeable conversant, quick to ask probing questions and pointing out convergence with nuclear and uranium issues in England. She then offered both thanks and congratulations to Sylvia for her work before moving on. A tangible result of the Ottawa banquet was the first of Sylvia's major Canadian medals signifying great accomplishment. In November, she received a Queen's Silver Jubilee Medal.

What's interesting about this meeting with the queen is how quickly it was forgotten. A little more than ten years later, when Sylvia became the first female lieutenant-governor of Saskatchewan, the *Star-Phoenix* wrongly proclaimed, "At last, Sylvia Fedoruk may get to meet the Queen."[52] The writer just assumed that Sylvia hadn't, and she modestly chose not to offer a correction. But in truth—from her first trip in the back of a truck in 1939 to wave at Queen Elizabeth and King George, to Princess Elizabeth and Duke Philip's visit to Saskatoon in 1951, to her many visits to London, where Sylvia would watch the changing of the guard and gaze up at Buckingham Palace, a wave on the streets of Yorkton when the queen's motorcade went through in 1967, Sylvia's personal letter of thanks to the queen after the wildly successful Scottish curling tour, to her attendance in Ottawa for the queen's jubilee—Sylvia had always been moving toward royalty.[53]

As the 1980s rumbled into view, she found herself looking backward more often than forward. With reunion events for softball and basketball, her early athletic career drew fond memories and nominations into various local and provincial halls of fame. Sylvia relished the camaraderie.

At the Husky-Huskiette basketball reunion weekend in 1980, Sylvia gave a speech in which she could finally dare to call Huskiette basketball coach Ivan King "Ivan the Terrible." "For those of you that are meeting Ivan for the first time, you're in for a surprise—this mild, affable senior citizen was a terror as a coach—flying chairs, loose hairs, spilled water bottles and instructions became large bursts of shouts—good thing he isn't coaching today—the University gym would be violating our city noise pollution bylaw." Terrorized, the senior girls would get back at their coach the only way they could: by in turn terrorizing the freshettes on the team. "The posh Kensington Hotel in Edmonton was never the same after that memorable night of pounds and pounds of unfrozen Jackfish tucked neatly in the beds of the rookies—in retrospect this man [Ivan King] welcomed initiation—it allowed the veterans to vent hostilities they held toward their coach—too bad we didn't have the guts to get even with him directly."[54]

Sylvia's frank and funny speech captured both the spirit of Ivan King as a coach and the camaraderie of the Huskiette team. Through the years, friendships developed on and off the courts would weave through Sylvia's life. Women such as University of Saskatchewan colleague Pat Lawson (who served with Sylvia on the local ParticipACTION committee), Mayor Cliff Wright's wife, Betty (who had been a teammate), and friend Peggy (Wilton) McKercher (who would later encourage Sylvia to put her name forward as University of Saskatchewan chancellor) were in the audience laughing and nodding at her revelations.[55]

Sylvia meeting Liberace, c. 1978.

Sylvia's name could once again be found in academic publications, again with an eye on the past. Sylvia and University of Saskatchewan radiology colleague C. Stuart Houston turned their attention to medical history, particularly the history of radiotherapy research and nuclear medicine in Saskatchewan. After all, Sylvia was on the ground at the beginning of Canada's development of nuclear medicine as a student of Harold Johns, working with both the betatron and the cobalt-60 unit. With an eye for detail and an appreciation for Canada's—and more particularly Saskatchewan's—leading role, Sylvia, with Stuart's unflagging support for cataloguing medical history and its many firsts, made several key contributions to Canada's medical history.[56]

Her board accomplishments and abilities led Sylvia to the chair of Saskatoon's Centennial Auditorium when it faced dire financial difficulty. With great ambition, the board led an effort to rejuvenate the auditorium as a venue for conferences and trade events in addition to its central role as the city's major arts and performance venue. Sylvia relished the many concerts and events and would often take Michael Vann along. He remembered seeing some of the major acts of the era, including Anne Murray and Liberace, of whom Sylvia was a particular fan.[57] She wrote to him, and received from him, signed Christmas cards for years.[58]

When her term on the Centennial Auditorium board ended in 1982, the farewell included a written toast in the form of a poem from the rest of the board:

> Not so very long ago, when Syl was in the chair
> The Budget Boys cried "Deficit," red ink splashed ev'rywhere
> Quietly determined, Syl made all their dreams come true,
> Said, "Red pens now are out of style—we write with black or blue!"[59]

Bad poetry aside, it's clear that Sylvia's time at the helm helped to steer the auditorium out of financial difficulty and into an innovative new role within Saskatoon.

At work in 1982, Sylvia found herself back on the front lines of cancer care. Over eighty staff at the two cancer clinics (the Saskatoon clinic in the University Hospital and the Allan Blair clinic in Regina) walked out on strike. As members of the Saskatchewan Government Employees Union, they were looking for parity wages with other health-care workers and walked out August 11 after talks stalled. Walking out was not an easy choice: cancer clinic workers, on the front line of patient care, loved their patients. And their patients loved them. During the strike, some cancer patients and caregivers walked the line in solidarity or gave other support to the striking workers.[60] Sylvia, as the director of physics services, was pressed into service as a radiotherapist to fill the gaps in the urgent care team, along with her entire physics staff. Even so, the number of patients who could be treated by the remaining skeleton crew plummeted. From a typical fifty to sixty patients treated a day, Sylvia and the other management staff could handle about half that number. The Regina clinic was in the same position. Such massive reductions meant triage, to the point of sending patients outside Saskatchewan for much-needed treatment.[61]

In Saskatchewan, health care is a political issue. Given the seriousness of the strike, which threatened essential and critical cancer care of some of the province's most ill patients, the new provincial government under Grant Devine's Progressive Conservatives swung into action. First, the health minister, Graham Taylor, recommended a conciliation panel to work through the issues. This proposal was accepted by the Saskatchewan Healthcare Association, acting on behalf of the Saskatchewan Cancer Commission, but rejected soundly by the union. With fear escalating, in the middle of the summer recess, the legislature was called back into session. Telegrams and registered letters went out to all MLAs, many of whom were on vacation. With the support of the NDP opposition, the cancer clinic staff were legislated back to work.

The strike would have been a matter of some distaste to Sylvia. Working side by side with radiotherapists for more than thirty years, she had been an early leader in ensuring that radiotherapy was a recognized career, with proper training and support. Without parity wages, there was no way to keep qualified workers at the clinic. For Sylvia, that struggle was real. And make no mistake: she believed in wage parity. In the staff rooms and meetings, in the hallways and casual chats in the parking lot, Sylvia—who always kept a finger on the pulse of the staff—would have seen and understood the immense frustration. There had been no contract for almost a year, negotiations had stalled, and the union had clear grievances. Yet all of the staff knew first-hand the importance of their jobs. Cancer patients are frightened to the bone, sick, and starving for hope. It would have been a wrenching decision to take strike action, and Sylvia knew it. Nonetheless, she breathed a sigh of relief when the full team came back to work.

Although the strike was over, all was not well on the home front. Tinker was twelve years old, and the signs were clear. While Sylvia was away up north in La Ronge on a fishing trip, Tinker passed out. On February 14, 1983, Valentine's Day, her faithful mutt died. Sylvia was not one to mourn overly long. She missed the doggy companionship and the excuse to be outside walking. The pattern of a day is different when there is a pet to look after, to feed and care for, to take for walks, talk to, and welcome you home after a long day at work.

By April, Sylvia was ready to search for a new dog. On April 19, an ad in the paper announced puppies for sale, and the next day she drove to the farm north of Sutherland to have a look. She wasn't all that impressed, yet something must have intrigued her, for she visited the farm again on April 28. By May 3, all reticence was gone, and she picked an all-black male spaniel-poodle-cross pup. On May 11, Sylvia visited the farm yet again, and this time the pup had a name: Charli. She didn't take him home. Instead, she waited until May 26, when Michael was back from university and available to come along to pick him up. Michael remembered that the name was supposed to be Charles, which sounded more dignified, but it soon changed. "Charli was the runt of the litter, the smallest of the pups. Nervous about leaving. I scratched around his tail region, holding him, talked to him. To the very last time I saw him, he would back up into me so I would scratch his tail region. That's what he associated with me."[62] Replacing twelve years of companionship with Tinker with a new relationship with Charli took a bit of finesse, and Sylvia developed the habit of connecting the old name with the new one. Thus, Charli Tinker was brought to Simpson Crescent.

As a cockapoo, Charli was a designer cross between a cocker spaniel and a poodle. Just under knee height, furry and black, he had a regal and imposing handlebar mustache that would have been the envy of many Victorian-era men. Spoiled and loved, Charli is the best known of Sylvia's doggie sidekicks. Sylvia insisted that Charli learn some of the tricks and ways of Tinker, especially Christmas presents. Tinker had developed a knack for opening presents, understanding which ones were for him. "She practised presents with Charli before Christmas when he was a puppy," Michael noted. "He would go to the tree and sniff around and leave the present alone if it wasn't for him. He enjoyed Christmas, lots of treats, new toys. He had fun. The tradition had to continue, Tinker could do it, so Charli had to learn." One item changed, though. Whereas Tinker's favourite treat was ice cream, Charli preferred French fries. "Burger King got to know Sylvia really well," Michael remembered. "She'd go through the drive through for fries for Charli."[63]

One final development in Saskatchewan's cancer treatment story drew Sylvia's attention. By the early 1980s, the University of Saskatchewan, the provincial government, and related decision-makers concluded that Saskatoon's cancer clinic, despite its upgrades and new equipment in the early 1970s, was no longer adequate. Planning got under way to develop an entirely new cancer clinic adjacent to the University Hospital on the bank of the South Saskatchewan River near the new Diefenbaker Centre. With the new clinic ready to break ground in 1984, Sylvia received one final workplace appointment. P.H. Peters, the executive director of the new Saskatchewan Cancer Foundation, appointed her as project liaison and coordinator in charge of ensuring progress on building the new clinic. No one knew better than Sylvia the building requirements to safely contain the radiation given off by the cancer-fighting machines such as cobalt-60 units or betatrons or linear accelerators. With her known affable, detail-oriented, but no-nonsense style, she was an excellent choice to serve as the go-between for multiple and sometimes conflicting interests, which included not only the contractors for the project (Ferguson Folstad Friggstad, known as 3F) but also the University Hospital, the University of Saskatchewan, the Saskatchewan Cancer Foundation, and the Meewasin Valley Authority in Saskatoon, responsible for developments along Saskatoon's riverlands.

Sylvia followed a policy of "no surprises." Trading her lab coat for a hard hat and boots, she was often seen in and around the new building, chatting with the construction crews and watching the building rise. Bringing out her trusty camera, Sylvia recorded the construction of the building. The role of the project liaison officer was described as "a euphemism for an unusual individual who can skilfully, diplomatically, but firmly steer a conglomerate of architects, engineers, academics, and bureaucrats into building a first-class research and treatment facility."[64] Soon it became apparent that the building of the new cancer clinic would be her swan song and farewell to a long and illustrious career. As she navigated meetings and issues, settling disputes and foreseeing problems before they could mushroom into poisonous toadstools, Sylvia decided that her work as the director of physics for the Saskatchewan Cancer Foundation, hand in glove with her work as a full professor of oncology, was ready for sunset and closure. She had worked full time for thirty-five years. The official sod-turning ceremony for the new Saskatoon Cancer Clinic was March 10, 1986. That day Sylvia sent in her letter of resignation to the dean, College of Medicine, requesting retirement effective December 31, 1986, with the status of professor, Division of Oncology.

For those who thought that the upcoming retirement of Sylvia Fedoruk meant that she was getting ready to rest, there was news, in fact lots of news. The Saskatoon YWCA voted her as one of three Women of the Year in a nomination that described her as "equally at home with northern residents of fishing villages as she is at a banquet with the Queen of England."[65] Sylvia also received the province's highest honour, the Saskatchewan Order of Merit, along with fellow recipients Chris Sutter, Saul Cohen, Phyllis Tynney, and Lyall Gustin. The lavish meal in the Regency Ballroom of the majestic Hotel Saskatchewan in Regina, hosted by Lieutenant-Governor F.W. Johnson, fed the guests seafood paté, chicken Florentine, and creamed La Ronge wild rice. Sylvia was asked to give the response to the toasts on behalf of all the recipients. Selected from 164 nominations, the five recipients "all accept the award with the greatest of pleasure. All of us are extremely proud of Saskatchewan and it is a somewhat humbling experience to realize that our province feels the same way about us."[66]

In the audience for the Saskatchewan Order of Merit investiture was Sylvia's special cousin Merylyn, along with husband Garry and son Michael. As Sylvia's name was called, there was an accompanying speech outlining her list of accomplishments. Her family was taken aback. "Did you know about that?" they asked each other in whispers, heads swivelling. Another accomplishment was read out. More head swivelling, more questions. "Did you know about *that?*" Despite being Sylvia's closest living relations, the Vann family had not really understood the depth and breadth of Sylvia's professional and leadership roles. Modest and unassuming at home, Sylvia was never one to brag or boast, to the point where her family sat shocked with pride, listening to a litany of her accomplishments.[67]

As the countdown to the opening of the cancer clinic and the closing of Sylvia's working career ticked, letters began pouring in. Her retirement would be an important affair, and colleagues around the world sent laudatory messages.[68] Speakers at the retirement banquet cast eyes and minds forward. For such a woman, they wondered, what could possibly be next? Lloyd Skaarsgard pointed out, with wry humour, "Examples like yours, I'm afraid, make the goal of 'Equality with Women' very difficult to achieve . . . for men." Sandy Watson suggested that a larger role would suit Sylvia: "It is easy to see who the next Governor General will be when Madame Sauvé retires." But Fred Wigmore, past executive director of the Saskatchewan Cancer Foundation, hit the mark with his prescient comment: "Sylvia should probably also have a zenith. It would seem to be appropriate to suggest that her many admirers and supporters should ensure that she become the first Lady Lieutenant Governor of Saskatchewan."[69]

"Quietly determined," the description of Sylvia given by the Centennial Auditorium board, could be the most accurate description of her leadership style. From her work to bring the Macdonald company on board to support the Canadian Ladies Curling Association national playdowns, to her work on the Science Council and more particularly the Atomic Energy Control Board, to the way in which she shepherded the Centennial Auditorium from red to black, as well as leading staff and other personnel at the cancer clinic through acrimonious strikes and construction, her keen intelligence, forthright observations, astute decision-making, all leavened with humour and grace, made Sylvia a welcome voice at board tables from the local to the national level.

Her leadership style was about vision, not simply about maintaining the status quo. Sylvia did her best work when there were big problems to solve. Whether as part of the team working on the cobalt bomb, through her work on scanners and cameras, as the president of the CLCA when it needed a new source of sponsorship, with the challenges of the AECB, pulling the Centennial Auditorium out of enormous debt, or liaising the building of the new cancer clinic, Sylvia was indeed quietly determined. She was interested in knowing *what* you wanted to do and then figuring out *how* to do it. For Sylvia, leadership drew from the positive, her belief that from something small could come enough power to make exceptional change. It was the energy itself, and how people chose to use it, that mattered. Radiation, the product and result of atomic energy, was the negative side, the warning, the danger. But even then her perspective went the other way. Through her work at the cancer clinic, Sylvia saw first-hand how many lives were saved or extended with medical intervention through radiation. Even if dangerous, it just needed to be aimed in the right direction. Sylvia Fedoruk was ready to take her leadership and vision in a whole new direction.

8. MADAME CHANCELLOR

IN THE LATE WINTER OF 1986, AS SYLVIA FEDORUK BEGAN TO count down the days to retirement, a group met at her house. Their purpose involved a pen, a special piece of paper, and signatures. Seven friends, all graduates of the University of Saskatchewan, decided to put Sylvia's name on a nomination form. The nomination was not for political appointment. Peggy McKercher, along with others from Sylvia's basketball and curling past, eagerly inked their signatures to nominate Sylvia as a candidate for the chancellorship of the University of Saskatchewan. Then they waited.

It was an unusual election, Sylvia would later recount. It did not include kissing babies, making stump speeches, or planting signs on lawns. It only took seven signatures and some luck. The university added her name to a ballot filled with an august field of fellow graduates: John Egnatoff, Mike Kindrachuk, and Jack McFaull. Egnatoff was a Saskatchewan political figure and educator, with ties to both the Liberal Party and the Department of Education at the University of Saskatchewan. Kindrachuk was an educator, serving as an elementary school superintendent for many years, and held roles in multiple volunteer organizations. McFaull was a Saskatoon leader, well known to the University of Saskatchewan as an idea man on the Board of Governors, interested in governance, investment, strategy, and growth. Nonetheless, the campus alumni community, spread across the world, dutifully marked and returned their ballots. The victory, and yes, she would often say that it was sweet, went to Sylvia. The University of Saskatchewan secretary, Iain Maclean, dutifully informed all nominees on May 1, 1986, and began the process of ushering Sylvia into her new role.

She began formal work as chancellor on July 1 and was immediately engulfed in a much higher number of public functions, meetings, receptions, luncheons, and dinners than ever before, some of which took her out of the province. This rapid increase "represents a departure from my regular life-style," she wryly suggested to Iain Maclean's secretary, Jean. In a two-page memorandum sent to Iain's office, Sylvia outlined an almost shockingly busy schedule, which included everything from press conferences to concerts with the governor general, appearances at telethons, ribbon-cutting ceremonies, graduations and convocations, curling socials and bonspiels, and speeches to the international bowling tournament and the Beechy Agricultural Fair. Receptions at which she had to give a formal or an informal speech drew particular attention on the memo, and Sylvia noted that "the underlined are dates when I was expected to open my mouth and put my foot in it."[1] Although a popular speaker at sports events and in the nuclear industry, Sylvia would more often speak her mind first and then think later.

As chancellor of the province's largest university, Sylvia immediately became a major figure in provincial political and social circles. Invitations flowed in. During her first fall as chancellor, she was invited to the opening of the legislature, the Christmas extravaganza of the lieutenant-governor, and the Christmas soiree of the University of Saskatchewan president, and she received Christmas cards from the premier, the prime minister, and the governor general.

The one drawback of being a chancellor is that it's an unpaid position, and in 1986 there wasn't even an office. The old Convocation Hall and Administration building were in the midst of a massive renovation and building bee. Sylvia, undaunted, kept her centre of operations in her office in the University Hospital, where, despite her retirement as the head of physics services, she remained in a part-time project management role to finish the liaison work building the new cancer clinic near the Diefenbaker Centre. A morning here, an afternoon there, bookended by chancellor responsibilities and continuing work as a board member with the AECB, Sylvia's post-retirement world changed a little but kept the university as the centre of her whirlwind.

The formal investiture of Sylvia Fedoruk as the new chancellor took place at the fall convocation on October 25, 1986. Since she

8. MADAME CHANCELLOR

Sylvia Fedoruk, chancellor of the University of Saskatchewan, official portrait.

was meant to preside over the convocation, her investiture came first. With the audience braced for and somewhat dreading a droning, self-important speech full of solemn questions and answers, with everyone draped in archaic formal regalia, the event was a delightful surprise. The investiture of Sylvia as chancellor of the university was both heartfelt and moving.[2]

Sylvia, when she spoke, clearly pushed her voice through tears of joy and great thankfulness for the opportunity to preside at the convocation as the new chancellor. At the podium, she drew the audience in with stories of her own first month at the university some forty years earlier. Back then "freshies" were matched with seniors and made to cavort for a whole week down the hallways wearing freshie beanie caps and performing menial tasks. Standing on the convocation stage and waving her original freshie beanie emblazoned with an S for Saskatchewan, Sylvia spoke of many years of close personal and professional association with the University of Saskatchewan. Her senior might have forced her to carry her books around in a bucket, but she was glad that she had stuck with it—look at where it had brought her, from freshie to chancellor, in forty years. The audience roared in appreciation. The investiture finished, Sylvia stepped gladly into her new role, conferring degrees on the graduates.[3]

After a winter of balancing project management, AECB duties, and new chancellor roles, by the spring of 1987 Sylvia was looking for a break and to have a little fun. One of her most enduring and entertaining summer calendar events began in the early 1980s and remained a blacked-out spot in her day-timer to the end of her life. The event, on the surface, was a golf tournament, one that fulfilled all of her needs: playing golf, enjoying camaraderie, and being part of a team. The "Slobstick," as it was called, was a parody of Saskatchewan's classic Lobstick golf tournament and was held at Waskesiu.[4] The Slobstick's roots were in curling, among people whom Sylvia knew. In the early spring of 1971, the Saskatchewan ladies' curling team of Vera Pezer, Joyce McKee, Lee Morrison, and Sheila Rowan won their first Canadian ladies' curling championship. What better way to celebrate that win and kick off summer than to have a celebratory fun weekend in Waskesiu, with golfing, barbecues, and much laughter? The curling foursome found other Saskatoon curling friends up for the same weekend. They joined forces for visiting and golf, and the annual Slobstick was born.

Some of the organizational traditions began in that first year. The basics were covered: bring your own sleeping bag, crash in a friend's cabin, have ample supplies of food and liquor, golf (whether you like it or not), be willing to play practical jokes, participate in skits, and tell stories and sing songs (and someone please bring a ukulele). On the deck at the end of the weekend, they said, "Should we do this again?" The answer was split second and loud, bouncing off the nearby trees and billowing out over the water: "*Yes!*" Sylvia wasn't a participant in the earliest years, but by the 1980s she became a fixture at the Slobstick.

The Waskesiu golf course was popular, which meant that the Slobstickers had to accept whatever tee times they could get—even if it meant being on the course Sunday morning at 7:42 after carousing Saturday night. A more civilized start time of around 10:00 was to be appreciated. Six bookings of four golfers each would support twenty-four golfers on the course, one group after the other in loud, cheerful companionship. Golf hazards on the Waskesiu course vary from classic water and sand traps to huge evergreen trees, including the iconic lobstick. Other hazards include wandering elk herds and thieving red foxes with a penchant for collecting and running off with your well-hit ball. Slobstick attendees paid green fees to the organizer, brought clubs, and rented carts. "The Lobstick Golf and Tennis Club Inc. continues to accept our entry because we are symbolic of a superior level of golf," teased the invitation to Slobstick XVII in 1987. Alcohol wasn't allowed on the fairways and greens, "but these restrictions do not apply between approximately 3pm and 10am."[5]

As indicated in the Sylvia Fedoruk fonds, from the sheer camaraderie to the teasing and fun, the actual golfing was secondary. As the Slobstick expanded over the years, with multiple women joining, including Mona Finlayson and friends Irene Bell and Doreen Fairburn, it became a movable party. The Sylvia Fedoruk video and photo archives contain a large number of still images and VHS videocassettes from the annual Slobstick. Sylvia worked one year to curate, scan, and compile a history of the tournament from 1971 through 1995. It's possible to trace both the expansion of the Slobstick from a small circle of friends to a larger circle of as many as thirty people and the changes over time in clothes, hairstyles, and events. An all-women weekend, the Slobstick built deep friendships. "New jokes are welcome and old jokes are tolerated providing they're funny!"[6]

The Slobstick was a yearly reunion. "The renewal of friendships and the mystical Waskesiu, that is what keeps bringing people back," explained Doreen Fairburn.[7] The women indulged in a great time with insider jokes, funny costumes, special shirts, skits and musicals, hula events, and much laughter. Some years there would be costume competitions, and the Waskesiu links were resplendent with crazy outfits and decorated golf carts. Evening games included skits, with much planning and stealing and contriving to create character costumes—everything from tea towels to curtains to newspapers to sundresses could be sacrificed. One year the post-barbecue skit was in celebration of the retirement of Doreen. The skit, put together by Mona Finlayson, had Slobstickers portraying people from all over the world. Sylvia's group portrayed the USSR, and Mona explained to me that Sylvia "always liked to have a chance to proudly display her Ukrainian heritage in a fun way" and adopt a deep Ukrainian baba accent. Be that as it may, the skit involved hectic entrances onto and exits off of the deck, with hurried costume changes in the cabin before dashing back out for the next scene. Sylvia, playing a staid Ukrainian baba, swept out from the cabin onto the deck, proudly wearing her babushka. What she had forgotten, though, was her pants. The now-cool northern night swiftly goose-pimpled her legs, and she looked down in shock, then dissolved into fits of giggles and guffaws of laughter along with all the rest of the cast and crew. No one who recalled this story could remember if they managed to finish the skit.

Lots of food, especially barbecues filled with meat or fish, scented the evening air. Sheila Rowan, a tall, left-handed, first-base ballplayer who was teammates with Vera Pezer as the champion pitcher on the Saskatoon Imperials and played third on their Canadian championship curling team, used her left hand with dexterity, flipping burgers and steaks with equal ease in her role as Stretch the Barbecuer. One year a fox snuck up to the cabin and, when the ladies had their backs turned, made off with a mouthful of steak. The women, undaunted, when the meal was finished, calmly set out a few more pieces for the hungry fox to enjoy. Coffee and alcohol, in about equal amounts, fuelled the fun. With multiple women bringing food options from salads to main courses to desserts, the barbecue potlucks were a feast. Sylvia's famous "Syl's Dills" added the contralto sourness to the flavour profile.

Friday night typically saw visiting and reacquaintance, but there were a few special excursions. One year the women rented the fully licensed *Neo-watin* paddlewheeler for a private trip around the lake.

The Saturday-night parties, though, became legendary. Several of the women became adept at the ukulele, which features prominently in pictures and videos in the Fedoruk collection, even accompanying the women on the paddlewheeler excursion. By the early 1990s, someone mounted a sign, "Women's Healing Lodge," beside the door of the main cabin, a tongue-in-cheek view of the purpose

8. MADAME CHANCELLOR

The Slobstick women on Waskesiu's paddlewheeler, 1990. Sylvia is second from top left.

of the weekend's activities but one that, in truth, was not far off the mark. Men were strictly verboten.

In 1987, Sylvia's Slobstick invitation came to "Emminent Chancellor,"[8] a nod to her new role at the university. The Slobstickers got together to decorate a golf cart for her use on the fairway. Covering the cart with the oldest and ugliest gold bedsheet that they could find, they also stuffed a much-washed Princess Margaret souvenir satin pillow for Sylvia to lean on in high perch. A sign on the cart completed the look for "Her Enemance." The wry and sly wit, with deliberate misspellings poking fun at Sylvia's election, masked a deep sense of pride for several of the Slobstick women, also graduates of the University of Saskatchewan, signatories to the nomination form, and delighted in her astonishing chancellorship win.

Following on the heels of her elevation to the Saskatchewan Order of Merit and the chancellorship, Sylvia received another call: she would be inducted as an Officer of the Order of Canada. The honour is kept for those who have made real, identifiable contributions to Canadian culture, science, sport, or society. Other inductees that year included country and western singer and television star Tommy

Hunter, Olympic sprinter Ben Johnson, Saskatchewan Cree artist Allen Sapp, and Edith Simpson, dean emeritus of the Department of Home Economics at the University of Saskatchewan. The Order of Canada is the second highest civilian order after Canada's Order of Merit.[9] The Order of Canada admits three ranks of members: Companion, Officer, and Member. Sylvia was appointed an Officer of the Order of Canada in a lavish ceremony presided over by the governor general on April 29, 1987. Sylvia and a guest could travel to Ottawa for the ceremony, expenses to be reimbursed by Rideau Hall. She had a conclave with her family: Sylvia could take only one person. Who would go with her? Consensus chose Mary Kulcheski (her mother's sister, mother to Sylvia's special cousins Merylyn and Dolores). Mary had never been to Ottawa.[10] The two had a wonderful time, attending ceremonies and conducting a whirlwind tourist romp, before Sylvia put Mary on the plane home while she went off to AECB meetings.

Back in Saskatoon working part-time in her hospital office, Sylvia faced a desk piled high with architect's renderings, site schematics, letters, meeting notes, and other items for the cancer clinic, along with invitations, schedules, and event organization details for the chancellor, with the locked AECB cabinet in the corner. Once a month, when the phone bill came in, Sylvia would sit down and calculate which phone calls were for the cancer clinic, which for the chancellor's office, and which for the Atomic Energy Control Board. Sorting out and submitting bills to their respective owners, Sylvia was the centre of a three-pronged whirlwind. She was reappointed to the AECB in 1987. The position didn't conflict with her chancellorship—if anything her new role was a bonus and a feather in the AECB cap. The board took great pride in issuing a press release on her reappointment that listed her as Miss Sylvia Fedoruk, OC, and Chancellor of the University of Saskatchewan.[11]

Working with architects and construction crews, Sylvia was finally able to build cobalt-60 history and commemoration right into the new cancer clinic. She had tried but failed ten years earlier to get the University Hospital to dust off the original cobalt-60 bomb from its spot in the back of the old laundry building and create a museum display within the hospital. By 1987, with an accommodating budget and a willing construction crew, Sylvia could create commemorative space. The original cobalt-60 unit was mounted into the ceiling of the foyer of the new cancer clinic, a visible display of the past at the point of entry into the new clinic.

8. MADAME CHANCELLOR

The University of Saskatchewan also kept Sylvia busy working crowds, shaking hands, and giving speeches at the opening of a series of new university buildings. In fact, despite a major provincial economic downturn, the university was in the middle of a building spree. In 1986, Premier Grant Devine gave the go-ahead for the university to start construction on a new Department of Agriculture building. Renovations and major additions to both the Department of Geology building and the Administration building were well under way, as well as the new cancer clinic. The geology department building opened in 1986, the new Administration building in 1987, and the cancer clinic in 1988, while cranes soared and whirled around the growing height of the new agriculture building.

The opening of any new building on a university campus is a time of speeches, congratulations, and political manoeuvring. Sylvia, as chancellor, excelled at the first two aspects but was wary of the third—she had never been one to join or advocate for any particular political party. Nonetheless, she gave a speech at the opening of the new Administration building. Handwritten by Sylvia on a pad of paper, apparently at the last minute, the speech extolled the "wonderful fall Saskatchewan morning" in which to celebrate the opening of a "very functional and attractive building." She mourned the "mothballing" of the original College Building and looked forward to its restoration so that it could once again take its place as the head of the university's magnificent bowl. As a sign-off, she recommended that everyone take a look at archivist Stan Hanson's pictorial exhibit, which showed the evolution of the university through its buildings, and she issued a call to the politicians: "In the not too distant future, Mr. Minister, we expect to have approval for a new Fine Arts building and a new Physical Education and Athletic complex."[12]

With both a Saskatchewan Order of Merit and an Order of Canada, and sitting as the head of the University of Saskatchewan convocation, Sylvia enjoyed elite invitations. Queen Elizabeth II and Prince Philip came to Saskatchewan in 1987 soon after the opening of the new Administration building. Sylvia was among the nearly 1,000 attendees at a luncheon at the Centennial Auditorium in honour of the queen's visit but did not, at that time, get a chance to greet the queen personally. As a volunteer for Saskatoon's bid to host the 1989 Jeux Canada Games, Sylvia was also invited to attend the queen's ribbon-cutting ceremony at the new canoeing and rowing facilities on the banks of the South Saskatchewan River. Her role was simply to fill out the crowd. Once the queen and prince left, Saskatoon returned to normal and shifted into winter. On November 28, 1987, Sylvia—along with Joyce McKee and other members of their winning Saskatchewan curling teams from 1960, 1961, and 1962—were inducted into the Saskatoon Sports Hall of Fame.[13]

Not all of the requests coming to Sylvia needed her presence; sometimes her opinions were enough. The Saskatoon Library wrote to her on August 17, 1988, asking for help. In preparation for a display of *Local Celebrities' Favourite Books*, the library was hoping for her contributions. Sylvia considered, then sent back the following.

> *Seeking a Balance: University of Saskatchewan 1907–1982*, by Michael Hayden
>
> *Why Shoot the Teacher?*, by Max Braithwaite
>
> *The Cruel Sea*, by Nicholas Monsarrat
>
> *Klondike*, by Pierre Berton
>
> *Karsh Canadians*, by Yousuf Karsh
>
> *The Wit and Wisdom of John Diefenbaker*, edited by John A. Munroe
>
> *Saskatchewan: A Pictorial History*, by D.H. Bocking
>
> *Saskatchewan Government: Politics and Pragmatism*, by Evelyn Eager
>
> *The Canadian Encyclopedia*
>
> *Historic Architecture of Saskatchewan*.[14]

Sylvia's book choices offer a high dose of Saskatchewan and Canadian history and political commentary, along with photography, historical fiction, historical fact, and a touch of humour. All except *The Cruel Sea* are distinctly Canadian books, and only two are novels. Her tastes clearly ran more to the factual and nonfictional, though it's possible that this list was skewed. Knowing that schoolchildren and other library visitors would see her recommendations, Sylvia would have created this list with an eye to education rather than fun.

Being chancellor wasn't just about giving speeches or cutting ribbons or accepting accolades or giving book lists. Sylvia was automatically a member of the board of governors. She was chancellor during a time of extreme fiscal restraint and cold relations between the university and the provincial government over finances. These restraints exacerbated faculty negotiations during 1987 and led in part to an acrimonious strike in 1988. Although Sylvia didn't have an active role in the negotiations with either the government or the faculty association, she was acutely aware of the situation as it unfolded. The 1987 board meeting minutes held in the University of Saskatchewan Archives reveal university strategy vis-à-vis government funding. Facing a major budget shortfall, the board held a private strategy session that considered multiple possible ways to balance the budget, from cutting internal expenses on administration and maintenance to eliminating programs, increasing both domestic and foreign student fees, and reducing library appropriations by sharing purchases with neighbouring institutions. Such measures might balance a budget but would lead to deteriorating faculty and staff relations and declining student enrolment. These internal measures were aligned with external measures that included a major public relations campaign to incite support. The board of governors, with the chancellor sitting as a member, was a major player in strategy and politics with an astute ability to guide public opinion.[15] Sylvia was learning fast.

In a 1987 board of governors meeting, in a move to try to appease the faculty and avert major job action, Sylvia moved that "the University accept the use of binding, final-offer arbitration as the means of resolving salary scales and professional expense allowance levels for 1986–1987."[16] Her motion was not enough. In March 1988, the University of Saskatchewan faculty walked off the job. For the first time in its almost eighty-year history, the university was in crisis, with just over half of the faculty in revolt: the strike vote registered 424 in favour of job action and 412 against it. With the end of classes and exams looming, the university convulsed. Bitterly divided, administration and the faculty association couldn't come to any agreement. Neither could the professors. Some walked the picket line; others deliberately went public with their non-support and continued holding classes for and administering exams to their students. Professional colleges, such as veterinary medicine and engineering, stood in stark contrast to the College of Arts and Science, in which more faculty joined the strike. That the faculty were not united was problematic. The public wasn't as supportive as the faculty might have hoped. The University of Saskatchewan pay rates were clearly on par with salaries at other prairie institutions, and university parents and students across the province asked tough questions. Would students lose a whole year of classes if they couldn't take their exams to finish courses or graduate?

The provincial government stepped in. Faculty were legislated back to work two weeks after walking off the job, with a promise of binding arbitration. Students—and their parents—breathed a sigh of relief. Exams went forward, and the academic year was saved.[17] From Sylvia's perspective as the head of convocation but also as a long-time faculty member, the issue would have hit close to home, pulling her sympathies in multiple directions.

During her term as chancellor, Sylvia received a most welcome, and astonishingly apt, invitation. The University of Windsor, in honour of her accomplishments in the field of nuclear medicine, wished to confer on her the honorary degree Doctor of Science at its early June convocation. Sylvia was met at the airport and taken on a driving tour of her old haunts, including Walkerville Collegiate and the house where the Fedoruks used to live. The University of Windsor did its homework and presented her with something of a homecoming, including inviting some of her old teachers and school chums to attend the special convocation ceremony. Sylvia was touched.

Asked to give a convocation address, Sylvia combined current events with history and a message for the students. Speaking about her chancellorship, she described how the "job can be symbolic, or it can be pretty demanding. I now regard myself as the official cheerleader of our University. . . . In fact, inside a period of one year, there were some 143 functions, dinners, meetings, and speeches, that I took part in." On achieving success, she told the graduands, "I never really turned away from a new challenge, nor turned down a request to participate on committees, first locally, then nationally and international[ly]—nothing ventured, nothing gained." On being a woman, Sylvia told the crowd that she was lucky in that both her parents and influential and perceptive teachers had had "the confidence that a female can do as well as the male in our society." She ended the speech with a challenge to the audience and to herself: "One is never too old and one is never too young to

8. MADAME CHANCELLOR

contemplate a better human condition. One should never be too strictly bound by convention and tradition. One should never be restricted by established policies and practices. Mankind and womankind have a potential to progress and to grow, and that is dependent on personal philosophies, personal principles and personal efforts of individual members of society. . . . The key to happiness is having dreams. The key to success is making them come true."[18]

There is a simplicity to her message that belies a deeper understanding of other people's experiences, particularly those of women. Her claim—repeated in dozens of speeches at dozens, even hundreds, of events and reported both in print and on television—was that she wasn't a feminist. Sylvia simply did not believe that affirmative action or similar advocacy work was necessary; instead, people's own skills and abilities should be enough to lift those people to the tops of their own mountains. But in truth Sylvia *was* a feminist, though she was not a bra-burner marching down streets waving placards. What she believed was that men and women deserve equal opportunity, equal pay, and equal respect. More than miffed on multiple occasions when men with equal or inferior education had been offered higher positions or more pay, Sylvia believed that women should be treated as equals, not as different.

Although she would continue to declare her antipathy for feminism, by 1987 Sylvia had read enough research reports and publications as chancellor of a major university to know conclusively that there was an imbalance built into the very structure of academia and society. In a June 1987 speech to the Saskatchewan Women's Institutes, she relayed this new understanding. "There's this philosophy that men and women have different brains and that females just can't grasp mathematics," she reported in an obvious huff. That was bunk, she said, pointing to herself as an example. The solution, she argued, was to support young women to enter non-traditional careers, particularly math, applied science, and engineering. The speech indicated that Sylvia had capitulated. Mounting research on how women too often had been actively excluded had eroded and fundamentally changed her earlier insistence that men and women are equal.[19] Not equal enough, she had decided. For the rest of her life, Sylvia actively supported conferences, programs, and other events that encouraged the participation of women in science in general and women in physics in particular. She had received mentorship and support in her own career, and now she offered her hand to young women coming into science and math.

The musings on women's career limitations and roles revealed Sylvia's own academic regret. Despite her opportunity and academic intelligence, Sylvia had never attempted to earn her Ph.D. Although she showcased excellence in research, publications, and accomplishments, she ended her career path much where she had started it: as a physicist with the Saskatchewan Cancer Commission and a professor at the University of Saskatchewan, though she did rise through the professorial ranks. She didn't jump from city to city, climbing a professional ladder out of Saskatoon to Chalk River or Toronto or even Vienna. Instead, Sylvia chose to build strong ties to place, forging a commitment to Saskatoon and Saskatchewan, her in-depth work on cancer imaging and treatment, and a peerless sports career and selfless third career as a volunteer and leader. As a response to that commitment and a lifetime of achievement, the University of Windsor honoured Sylvia with her own Doctor of Science degree. Finally, and without any dissembling or guilt, Sylvia could claim the title of doctor.

Throughout her term as chancellor, she continued working as a consultant, occasionally at the hospital but primarily at the new cancer clinic, in addition to continuing her role on the Atomic Energy Control Board. Her day-planner was packed with luncheon and breakfast meetings, flights to and from Ottawa, and committee work for the Jeux Canada Games. Early in 1988, Sylvia wrote in capital letters in her day-planner "LAST DAY from June 1/51 to April 30/88," recognizing that at last, between using up her holidays and relinquishing her consultant work, she was finally finished her working career.

Sylvia snuck off north for a quick fishing holiday on the May long weekend but was back in Saskatoon to preside at the convocation. Two days of convocation, then a third one in Regina, all the while making sure that her garden was rototilled and ready for planting and her lawn mowed. That spring Canada Post issued a stamp to celebrate the cobalt-60 work, and Sylvia was delighted to receive one. Life was still very busy: a mix of professional work as chancellor, volunteer work on the Brier committee, work with the AECB, a new appointment to the committee studying national Centres of Excellence, a provincial appointment to the upcoming committee studying health innovation in Saskatchewan, her garden, and her personal life, which included lots of meals with friends and family, funerals, weddings, dentist and doctor visits, and shopping (preferably for food, computer equipment, or a new camera). It was a full schedule, with few down days. Little did Sylvia know that the pace of her life, instead of winding down through true retirement, was about to escalate.[20]

Accolades and honours such as appointments to the Saskatchewan Order of Merit and as an Officer of the Order of Canada represent a degree of achievement attained by few. To those honours, a third came. In 1988, the Most Venerable Order of the Hospital of St. John of Jerusalem (known simply as the Order of St. John) elevated Sylvia to the rank of Dame of Grace. Part of the St. John's Ambulance Foundation, its work embraces volunteerism, humanitarian work, health care, and research. To achieve the rank of Dame of Grace, Sylvia had to meet the criterion of demonstrated leadership at either the national or the provincial/regional level, "in a position carrying major responsibility."[21] Her work as the first female member of the AECB, head of the national women's curling association, on multiple other federal and provincial boards as a volunteer or scientist, as well as numerous international roles, in addition to her stature as chancellor of a major western Canadian university, were more than enough to convince the Grand Prior to support Sylvia's elevation. The Order of St. John is one of six major Canadian honours, alongside the Order of Canada. Sylvia now had three major Canadian and Saskatchewan honours.

If there is a lesson to be learned about the chancellorship of Sylvia, it is that cultivating a commitment to place, to a university, its host city, and its people becomes its own reward in the end. The bond between Sylvia and the University of Saskatchewan grew and changed as she moved from student to faculty to chancellor. Coming into the sphere of the board of governors, the president, and the university secretary, she developed a wide circle of influential colleagues across the campus and in the larger public, beyond her familiar stomping grounds at the hospital and cancer clinic or even in physics. As the "head cheerleader"[22] for the university, Sylvia Fedoruk broadened her perspective and influence. She moved into the circle of what some might call the "Saskatchewan Establishment," filled with alumni of influence, institutional prestige, financial investment, strategy and power brokers, among provincial leaders both political and financial. From there, her bond to the university and to Saskatoon would expand and strengthen to encompass the entire province.

9. THE HONOURABLE LEFT-HANDED GOVERNOR

No dream is too small to go unnoticed. No goal is too big to be realized.[1]

LATE JULY 1988. THE TELEPHONE RANG AT 49 SIMPSON Crescent. On her way out the door to chair a business meeting at the university regarding funding for the new agriculture building on campus, Sylvia Fedoruk was in a hurry. After a barked hello, she stopped cold. On the other end, to her astonishment, was a senior cabinet minister in Prime Minister Brian Mulroney's government in Ottawa. He got right down to business. Her name had been put forward as a possible candidate to become the next lieutenant-governor of Saskatchewan. Was she aware that her name had been put forward? Yes, Sylvia responded, she'd heard a few rumours but hadn't dared to believe them. Was she interested in such a position? Sylvia, taken aback in surprise, drew herself together and stood tall. Yes, she said, she would be interested. "Okay," the minister replied. "You need to stay close to the telephone, and if the prime minister should call then you're the chosen candidate. If there is no call within seven days, then that's it. It won't be you. Oh, and one more thing: you can't say anything about this to anyone. You are sworn to secrecy." Sylvia thanked him and ended the call.

What a predicament. With a busy social schedule as chancellor, Charli needing walks, grocery shopping, and all the other intricacies of daily living, it wasn't particularly realistic to stay close to the phone in 1988. Cell phones in every pocket wouldn't happen for some time, so instead Sylvia made sure that her answering machine was set and did her best. The secrecy was actually the harder of the two charges. Who wouldn't be bursting with such incredible news? Wouldn't it be an added feather in the University of Saskatchewan's cap that a graduate and retired faculty member, and its current chancellor, would possibly be the next lieutenant-governor? It's hard to imagine how Sylvia got through the meeting, let alone the next several days. In some ways, it was lucky that her immediate family was very small: with no siblings and both parents passed away, her closest relatives were her cousins Dolores and Merylyn and their families, who were also living busy lives and hopefully wouldn't notice a bit of silence from her corner. But Charli, her cockapoo, was a good listener, so Sylvia told him. His discretion was perfect.

It was a long, almost cruel, wait. The phone didn't ring, and didn't ring, and didn't ring for the full seven days. Sylvia decided, "Well, that's it. It won't be me." She went to bed and had a good sleep but woke in a daze at 6:30 on the eighth morning: the phone was ringing. In her nightgown, she answered it. On the other end was the distinctive voice of Brian Mulroney. He was impressed, he said, with her credentials. But his wife, Mila, was very, *very* impressed. Would Sylvia be willing to serve as the next lieutenant-governor of Saskatchewan? Sylvia said yes, yes, and yes again, almost before Mulroney had finished asking. Soon after, the phone rang again. This time it was Premier Grant Devine, calling with congratulations. It wasn't a dream, Sylvia decided. This was really happening.

Sylvia told that story, with few variations, every time she was asked about how she had come to be the lieutenant-governor. The surprise, the trepidatious waiting, Charli as listener, the early morning phone calls. It's a good story—but it doesn't match her daily day-planner, which acted somewhat as a diary. Kept in the University of Saskatchewan Archives, the day-planner reveals hidden details, some of which are interesting enough to matter. The "senior minister" whom she never named in public? None other than her old family friend, Ramon (Ray) Hnatyshyn. Sylvia had long known the Hnatyshyn family. Ray's mother, Helen, had been a teacher in the Wroxton area when Sylvia's father was also a teacher there. In the late 1970s, when Helen received an honorary degree from the University of Saskatchewan, Sylvia gave the introductory speech. Ray Hnatyshyn, at the time, was the MP for Saskatoon West and the minister of justice. In fact, he called first on July 21

9. THE HONOURABLE LEFT-HANDED GOVERNOR

to get her thoughts on the idea of becoming lieutenant-governor and incidentally to ask for a list of chancellors of the University of Saskatchewan. Sylvia compiled the list and called back to tell him. That list, after all, put her among some of Saskatchewan's best and brightest, from Emmett Hall to John Diefenbaker. Hnatyshyn said, "I'm going to put your name forward to be considered as lieutenant-governor. I don't know what all is involved, but I'm certain that you would enjoy the job." Sylvia agreed. Two days later she met Ray downtown at the Saskatoon Farmers' Market during her weekly pilgrimage. When she got home, bags heavy with fresh vegetables and other delights, he called again. He told her to "be available for telephone on Monday," she wrote. Monday came and went with just a meeting of the board of governors finance committee but no phone call.[2]

Sylvia in the meantime was starting to wonder what she might have gotten herself into. A lunchtime trip to the university bookstore unearthed a reference to a book by Evelyn Eager on the Saskatchewan government. It wasn't an encouraging picture. A new lieutenant-governor, she read, "is given scant assistance in learning his duties" and even has to ask for permission to leave the province. "I can tell you that I was beginning to hope that the Prime Minister would not call," she would later tell the Canadian Club of Saskatoon.[3] A Tuesday filled with board meetings and lunch saw Hnatyshyn call twice. Wednesday morning Sylvia sat in her professor emeritus office at the clinic "waiting for a call." She was home by lunch, and Michael Jackson, Saskatchewan's chief of protocol, phoned "re: Sept 7/88"—the future date of her installation as lieutenant-governor. But she had not yet received a call from Ottawa. But Thursday morning, July 28, both the Prime Minister's Office and Grant Devine called, and all became official.[4] So she did, in fact, wait a week between her first call from Hnatyshyn and the official call from Ottawa. But Sylvia wasn't exactly hung out to dry: Hnatyshyn kept in close contact with her, and the protocol office called with a date. It is all too human to tell stories in a way that instills a touch of drama and suspense—and Sylvia's public version was manna for the media.

With protocol offices in high gear issuing press releases, Sylvia barely had time to call her family. Soon newspapers, and television and radio stations, tracked her down, and Sylvia was dashing from home interviews over the phone to studio interviews downtown. Michael Vann, her cousin Merylyn's son, was driving from

Calgary back to Saskatoon with a friend, listening languidly to the radio as the miles rolled by, nowhere near a telephone. Hearing the announcement, Michael hollered "What?!" His jaw had dropped in astonishment. His buddy was nonplussed. "You know her?" "Yes!" Michael said, "She's my cousin!" "And you didn't know about this?" "NO!" Michael's shock approached anger as he wondered why she hadn't told him. But shock/anger quickly became pride: cousin Sylvia would be a fantastic lieutenant-governor.[5]

The media, apparently, agreed. What was it, pundits speculated, that had led to this appointment? Sylvia's extensive and impressive career as a medical physicist? Her Ukrainian background? Her many and varied sports careers and successes? Or was it her gender, making Sylvia the first female lieutenant-governor of Saskatchewan? All of the above, they seemed to decide, with a large dose of her well-known humility and warmth thrown into the bargain. Saskatchewan people crowed that Sylvia was deserving and completely non-partisan. This was an appointment based on merit and merit alone. Before Sylvia had a chance to catch her breath, Saskatchewan celebrated.

Her work began long before the official investiture. Decision-making and organizing filled every moment. The day after speaking with the prime minister and accepting the appointment, Sylvia went to Regina. Meetings with the speaker of the house, with Michael Jackson, and with Irene White, who would be Sylvia's future personal secretary at Government House, and lunch at the Diplomat, one of Regina's toniest restaurants, filled her day.

Then Sylvia had to divest responsibilities and resign from all committees, from Jeux Canada Games to the Atomic Energy Control Board. It wouldn't do to be accused of either favouritism or conflict of interest in any role. The exception, approved by Governor General Jeanne Sauvé, was that Sylvia could retain her post as chancellor of the University of Saskatchewan until the next university election cycle, which would be in 1989. Sylvia also had to make decisions about her house, yard, and garden as well as think about where she'd live in Regina. One thing was non-negotiable: Charli would accompany her, and the province would just have to make the best of it.

Sylvia's investiture occurred on September 7, 1988. The day was overcast and very windy but without rain. Arriving at the legislature in the Government House landau pulled by two Clydesdales with a driver and a red-serge-attired RCMP officer up on the box,

9. THE HONOURABLE LEFT-HANDED GOVERNOR

Sylvia wore a modest dark blue skirt and suit jacket, emblazoned with her three major Canadian honours. Hair freshly trimmed in her signature pixie bowl style, she was accompanied by an RCMP honour guard and aides-de-camp up the stairs and into the legislative building and down the hall to the legislative chamber. Then the party waited.

Inside the chamber, Speaker of the House Arnold Tusa from Last Mountain–Touchwood stood. He informed the chamber that the lieutenant-governor designate and her party were about to enter. Everyone rose. Sylvia, accompanied by aides carrying her commission of appointment, entered the chamber to the tune of the royal anthem, "God Save the Queen." It was a tune that Sylvia would come to hear countless times, in hundreds of places across Saskatchewan, over the next five and a half years. Then the clerk of the Executive Council read out her commission of appointment, executed by Harvie Andre, registrar general for Canada, and signed by Jeanne Sauvé. Sylvia then swore the oath of allegiance to Her Majesty Queen Elizabeth II and the oath of office to the Province of Saskatchewan, administered by E.D. Bayda, chief justice of Saskatchewan, who had conducted the Cluff Lake Inquiry when Sylvia was a new AECB board member back in the 1970s. She then directed that the great seal of the Province of Saskatchewan be given safe custody with the provincial secretary.

Ramon Hnatyshyn, the minister of justice and attorney general for Canada, rose to give greetings to Sylvia from the government. He was the perfect mix of government leader and old friend, and of course he had been a significant supporter—and secret instigator—of her appointment. Premier Grant Devine then spoke of the office of the lieutenant-governor as essential to the autonomy of the province and integral to parliamentary democracy. More importantly, he spoke of the connection between her new office and the "communities of people and families and cultures," where Sylvia would be a symbol of unity and humanity, hope and loyalty. As the patron of so many of Saskatchewan's voluntary, artistic, and other worthy causes, the lieutenant-governor is a symbol of "those crucial elements which give our society heart and compassion and sensitivity." Devine made a special point of drawing a clear connection between the crown and First Nations Peoples in Saskatchewan. Finally, he separated her duties and predicted how Sylvia would handle them. She would, he said, carry out her constitutional duties with "dignity and wisdom," and she would travel all over Saskatchewan with

Sylvia (centre) with Grant and Chantal Devine, Roy Romanow, and Speaker Arnold Tusa, 1988.

"warmth and enthusiasm" to inspire people.[6] The chamber exploded with resounding agreement.

Then Sylvia rose to speak. Clearly overcome, her voice trembled, but she pushed through the cloud of emotion. Traditionally, the first speech by the new lieutenant-governor helps to set the tone and lay out priorities. Each lieutenant-governor designates certain causes on which she or he will concentrate energy. Sylvia opened her speech by expressing trepidation about the appointment. On the one hand, she was deeply honoured to have been chosen; on the other, she was "apprehensive of my ability to carry out all of my responsibilities effectively." Honesty, humility, and excitement were audible in her voice. "If I were to single out one area in which to focus my attention most particularly, it would be our province's children." Sylvia had hinted to the media prior to her installation that children would be the focus of her term of office: "You know, it's funny, I'm a spinster, yet I can relate to children and I feel I have a message for them."[7] She looked forward to travelling the province,

9. THE HONOURABLE LEFT-HANDED GOVERNOR

particularly the northern regions and schools, to deliver the personal story of a young woman from a rural one-room school and how, through education and determination, anyone could build a good future. Again the chamber erupted in agreement.

As Sylvia stood on the front steps of the legislative building to receive military honours, the wild wind "threatened to rip the many flags from their poles." She was honoured with a royal salute from a 100-person military guard of honour and a fifteen-gun salute from the artillery. "It's not often that you have 15 guns fired off in your honour," Sylvia later told reporters, but she worried a little about what the geese in Wascana Park thought about all the noise. The official party and all guests then ducked back inside out of the fierce wind to celebrate the occasion with a tea hosted by the speaker of the legislature. Emerging about 4 p.m., Her Honour climbed back into the landau to leave the legislative grounds and be whisked back to Hotel Saskatchewan to rest and change for the swanky evening installation dinner at the Saskatchewan Centre of the Arts. Her first day was a triumph of precision planning, pomp, and ceremony.[8]

Sylvia soon settled into her new office just down the street from her old one at the Allan Blair Cancer Clinic. For thirty-five years, her job at the Saskatchewan Cancer Commission had taken Sylvia back and forth between Saskatoon and Regina, directing the physicists at both clinics. This time she went a few hundred yards farther down Dewdney to arrive at one of the oldest buildings in Regina: Government House.

Government House as we see it today was constructed between 1890 and 1891 on the bald table of prairie not far from the territorial government buildings. The brick structure replaced the original Government House, "a single-storey wooden structure, painted red, cobbled together from portable houses built in Ottawa and Montreal and transported to the site." This original structure was well known for its wretchedness, which in winter was legendary. Sir John A. Macdonald gave a candid description to the House of Commons of a building in which, despite seventeen stoves going continuously, the water in a jug would freeze.[9] The new two-storey brick house, with fifteen bedrooms for servants, the lieutenant-governor, and family and guests, a billiard room, drawing and dining rooms, as well as kitchen and cooling rooms, was created with the most up-to-date amenities available, including its own well with running water, electricity from the Regina Lighting Company, indoor flush toilets, central heating, and a telephone.

Government House was home to the territorial lieutenant-governors, starting with Joseph Royal and his family, who moved in October 1891. Provincial lieutenant-governors received appointments after the birth of Saskatchewan in 1905. The house was continuously occupied, and assiduously expanded or renovated numerous times, including extensive work on the grounds to plant trees and create gardens on the bald prairie, building and renovating outbuildings such as stables, and changes to the house itself, including adding a conservatory and connecting it to the new city water supply. A ballroom was built where the original south-facing conservatory sat, and the conservatory was moved to the west side. The house was the site of ceremonial and social functions for the province, including welcoming the king and queen on their cross-Canada tour in 1939 with a lavish meal in the ballroom with the province's elite.

But political change brought all that to a screeching halt. Almost as soon as he took power in 1944, Tommy Douglas and his Cooperative Commonwealth Federation (CCF) Party declared Government House an unnecessary expense and a relic of a bygone age. Despite vocal opposition from the Board of Trade, Royal Canadian Legion, historical societies, and local judges, the house was closed, and most of the furnishings were auctioned off for a mere $6,000 to a group of about 400 people eager to buy history for a few dollars. Sitting lieutenant-governors, when in Regina, took up residence and office space in the Hotel Saskatchewan. Government House was leased to the Department of Veterans' Affairs and served as a rehabilitation centre for returned servicemen, with over sixty residents. In 1958, the veterans moved to other quarters, and after some debate the Adult Education Division of the Department of Education took over, renaming it Saskatchewan House. In 1964, it became the Regina Vocational Centre, but the buildings and grounds continued to deteriorate. Rumours of possible demolition grew. Groups such as the Chamber of Commerce and Regina Council of Women began to press for rehabilitation, gaining national recognition via the Historic Sites and Monuments Board of Canada in 1968. Throughout the 1970s, support grew, and the provincial NDP government of Allan Blakeney, successor to Douglas and the CCF, which had closed the house in the first place, made an about-face in 1978 to financially support restoration work.

Restoration and refurbishment required much time, skilled tradespeople and historical researchers, and planning. There was

9. THE HONOURABLE LEFT-HANDED GOVERNOR

great effort to track down the original pieces of furniture and fixtures, which had dispersed throughout the province and across Canada and the United States. Hard work and much money brought the house back from a crumbling mansion that had undergone too many modernized renovations to a semblance of how it looked between 1898 and 1910, the home of Lieutenant-Governor Amédée Forget and Mme Forget. It was a "creative restoration." Government House now functions primarily as a museum, but its ballroom and other rooms are used for major local or provincial events. The north end of the original house, what was once the kitchen, scullery, servant's hall, and pantry, as well as the sun porch, were converted into new permanent offices for the lieutenant-governor. No longer would visiting heads of state, provincial bureaucrats, and even royalty have to pick their way down the halls of Hotel Saskatchewan past last night's supper trays and the housekeeping cart to get to the lieutenant-governor.[10] The office was officially opened July 1, 1984.

Although Government House no longer serves as a private residence, the offices, ballroom, conservatory, and museum operate as the legal and social "home" for sitting lieutenant-governors. They continued to reside in Hotel Saskatchewan and later in a condominium bought by the province, which allowed Government House to separate its ceremonial role from its domestic function. By 1985, just three years before Sylvia's arrival, Government House had been restored as a combination of historical preservation and modern functionality.[11] Once again, the pride of place and a sense of history and pageantry leveraged the lieutenant-governor to provincial notice.

From the day that she swore her oath of allegiance and her oath of office, Sylvia put her life into overdrive. There couldn't have been a more prepared candidate. With great enthusiasm, she dove right in.[12] Two days after her installation, Sylvia attended the City of Weyburn's 75th anniversary celebrations as her first official visit. The day had been long in the planning, with "feverish last-minute adjustments, and perhaps more than a few silent prayers."[13] Arriving in her long black limousine from Regina, she joined a cavalcade of antique cars bearing federal and provincial politicians and the mayor, led by a pipe band. Sylvia popped out of the limo to see over 2,000 people waiting and cheering. The schoolchildren, she would later note, were particularly happy since her visit had automatically given them a day off. Her remarks for the day were given directly to the children in an outdoor speech at Jubilee Park. First she explained to them what a lieutenant-governor does. Then she reminded them of her own humble beginnings: "I started out just like you." Telling stories about the royal visit in 1939, she mused about the connection between herself as a girl cheering among the crowd at Melville to that day in Weyburn as the queen's representative. "If you want to get ahead," she encouraged them, "you must set goals for yourself." Following speeches and band music, Sylvia went on a walkabout among the crowd. As she chatted and visited, an aide asked one young boy, "Who do you think this lady, Sylvia Fedoruk, is?" The boy lifted an eyebrow with a knowing expression and breezily replied, "Oh, she's the new left-handed governor!" It was a splendid introduction for Sylvia to the joy and enthusiasm of crowds, the instant and warm personal connections, the many funny stories from each community, her stock stump speeches on education and goal-setting, and the ceremony of her new office.[14]

If Weyburn's civic celebration showed more of a country welcome with antique cars, a parade, pipe bands, and an open-air grandstand, the next night Sylvia was at a lavish, over-the-top, urban "night of nights" as the premier, Mayor of Saskatoon Cliff Wright, and Sylvia, along with other dignitaries, attended the opening of the new Saskatchewan Place arena and concert venue just north of the airport in Saskatoon. With Saskatchewan composers Billy Andrusco and Martin Janovsky providing new music, and the Saskatoon Symphony Orchestra filling the air, attendees enjoyed superb performances by Saskatchewan Express and skating guest Toller Cranston. Even so, the crowd, estimated at an anemic 2,600 paid guests, hardly topped the crowds at Weyburn.[15] But for Sylvia the size of the crowd never mattered. The enthusiasm of the reception, as she slowly became comfortable with the new vice-regal role, was all that mattered.

Her official duties kicked off in two such different communities and events, but Sylvia soon learned to swim along with the current. As chancellor, she attended functions but essentially served as her own—unpaid—organizer and office assistant. There wasn't a special office or car or plane or even much protocol to consider and no attendants. With the role of lieutenant-governor, the scale and pace of precise organization rose exponentially. Working closely with the provincial protocol office led by Michael Jackson and under the care and direction of Irene White, her personal secretary, volunteer aides-de-camp who served as her unofficial security officers,

9. THE HONOURABLE LEFT-HANDED GOVERNOR

carriers, and message bearers, as well as drivers and pilots and other staff, Sylvia was the hub of a mostly smoothly turning wheel that criss-crossed the province east to west, south to north.

One of her most anticipated events in the fall of 1988 was the opening of the new cancer clinic in Saskatoon. As a long-time employee, central figure in its construction, sitting chancellor of the university, and now lieutenant-governor, Sylvia was a proud and fitting member of the audience at that opening. She wiped a few tears of joy and pride from her eyes as the building received its consecration. The honoured guests toured the building, walking right beneath her specially constructed cobalt-60 exhibit mounted in the ceiling.[16]

Soon planning began in earnest for vice-regal events. As is the case with every new lieutenant-governor, invitations and requests arrived from non-profits and charities that had enjoyed past patronage from Government House. It was Sylvia's choice to accept or decline, shaping her support and eventually her legacy. Pat Langston, who worked in the Government House office as the receptionist and messages and congratulations secretary, noted that Sylvia took her time making every decision: "She was a very thoughtful, steady person who never made a decision and never did anything on a whim. She studied it carefully before she did it."[17]

Having a woman as the new lieutenant-governor created a few ripples of change through the province on a level generally unseen. All corporations, non-profits, and charities operate under provincial law, with constitutions and bylaws. If the group enjoyed the patronage of the crown but lacked the foresight to imagine a sitting female lieutenant-governor, then every "he" and "him" had to be formally changed and constitutional language altered to reflect the new reality. Even the Provincial Council of Women, a group whose purpose was to promote women's interests, was caught flat-footed by this problem.[18]

Sylvia's interest in Saskatchewan's youth and northern regions set an agenda of heavy travel. Sylvia wanted to visit schools, as many as possible, to meet with children and youth. Her cousin, Merylyn Vann, provided critical advice. As a superintendent of the Saskatoon school division, she noticed that lieutenant-governors were more well known and understood to schoolchildren in and near Regina. As Merylyn's son, Michael, remembered, "For years, they had the kids from the area into Government House. Mom was talking, does it have to be just kids from Regina area? That got expanded to a broader range of kids coming down. It's living history, it has sights and sounds and smells, it's good to put all that together."[19] As the pace of engagements increased, the staff workload expanded. Invitations rose, and over time the part-time office staff became full-time and then increased again.[20]

Irene White, Sylvia's personal secretary, carried some of the most interesting burdens. There was no such thing as a typical workweek. There might be breakfast meetings and a busy day right up to evening social events, weeknights and weekends, not to mention paying attention to what the government was up to and which legal documents might be arriving. A day might start in Regina but then end in another city. Irene and Sylvia logged many hours together by limo and plane, touching urban and rural, northern and southern, First Nations and settler spaces across the landscape.

Wardrobe was a major area of contention. If Sylvia had her way, she'd be in casual slacks and comfortable shirts every day, nothing fussy, nothing too tight. She'd worked thirty-five years in slacks and a lab coat and, at the end, a hard hat and muddy boots as she walked the work site for the new cancer clinic. But protocol for a sitting lieutenant-governor dictated otherwise. Dresses and skirts and tailored suit jackets were expected, along with the odd hat, some "glitzy" outfits for dressy evenings, and in general a major spruce-up to Sylvia's usual wardrobe. In fact, from September 6, the day before her installation, clothes became such an issue that Sylvia started to make notes in her day-planner: luncheon (green dress), military inspection (black dress, navy walking coat), meetings (white and red two-piece summer outfit), Saskatchewan Place opening (lamé). One can feel her relief at a Sunday-afternoon Huskie football game (Sunday slacks and U of S sweatshirt).[21] With all of those skirts and dresses and lamé came the dreaded nemesis of Sylvia's existence: pantyhose. Countless times there was loud swearing as Sylvia pushed tough, strong, working Ukrainian girl gardening and canning fingers through yet another pair of flimsy pantyhose. Eventually, in total exasperation, she bought herself a pair of cotton gloves to wear while wrangling her legs into delicate hosiery.[22]

Merylyn in Saskatoon, along with Irene in Regina, doubled as clothes consultants and personal dressers. Sylvia was no shopper, at least not for frippery and finery. She was a "Walmart and Costco rat," Merylyn's husband, Garry, chuckled.[23] But these venues didn't have the styles needed—except for pantyhose. Grimly, Irene or Merylyn would steer Sylvia around the shops and try to

9. THE HONOURABLE LEFT-HANDED GOVERNOR

direct her purchases, suggesting and selecting and cajoling to get as many new outfits as possible before Sylvia lost all patience and took off for a coffee and a treat. There was a shopping excursion only if they were lucky. As often as not, Sylvia would call and say "I have need of your services." Personal shopping services, she meant. Merylyn—and after her death Garry's new partner, Carol Walker—would trundle off and bring home three potential outfits, or shirts, or suits, or whatever else might be needed. Sylvia would try them on at home, and the rejected outfits would be trotted back to the stores, without Sylvia ever setting foot in them. Irene, a smart dresser with hair and nails always done and looking immaculate, had quite the job bringing a recalcitrant Sylvia to heel. It was not that she was obstinate; she just didn't see clothes as particularly important or interesting, and the new styles of suits, dresses, and pantyhose were a far cry from her own comfortable wardrobe, hanging lonely in her closet back home in Saskatoon.

If the lieutenant-governor position was paid like the chancellor position—a salary of precisely zero dollars—then likely the wardrobe makeover wouldn't have been as transformative or encompassing. Money, though, was not an issue. When Sylvia started as lieutenant-governor in 1988, her federal public salary for the position would have been about $70,000 per year and increased with inflation.[24] Unlike the men who had previously occupied the position, a female lieutenant-governor bore a new and different weight of social expectation. As her day-planner filled with notes, it's clear that there was a makeover happening, whether Sylvia wanted it or not. Recognizing that her new role carried certain expectations, she learned fast.

Irene was also in charge of monitoring and directing menus. It was protocol for the hosts to ask about the lieutenant-governor's food preferences and allergies, likes and dislikes, and Irene told every group in Saskatchewan, from all points of the compass, of every ethnic background and culinary experience, "*Do not use any onions.*" She might have had to repeat this notice if the menu contained soup or stuffing: "*Please remember, no onions.*" Because, heaven forbid, if the message didn't get through to the right people and there were onions, Sylvia simply wouldn't eat the food. And that, of course, was a major faux pas by the hosts. On the flip side, if staff were having a party or it otherwise seemed appropriate, Sylvia might bring a jar of her famous Syl's Dills, which always drew rave reviews.

Sylvia started her Regina sojourn living in Hotel Saskatchewan. The previous lieutenant-governor, Fred Johnson, had been a Regina resident and could stay in his own house. Appointees prior to him had lived, while in Regina, at Hotel Saskatchewan since the closure of Government House. Sylvia, a single woman with a dog, needed something different. On the advice of Gordon Barnhart, then clerk of the legislature, the province purchased a stand-alone bungalow condominium unit not far from the legislature, in Lakeview Place. The provincial government was in charge of furnishing the house and building a dog run out back, and Sylvia and Charli got their keys on October 28. They soon settled in. A flagpole, newly installed out front, flew the vice-regal standard. A second flagpole went up at 49 Simpson Crescent in Saskatoon, to be flown whenever Sylvia spent a night in her own home.

Charli accepted the mantle of vice-regal companion with alacrity, spoiled and cared for by aides-de-camp and secretaries. But two things did not sit well with Charli: uniforms and Sylvia's limousine. The limo would arrive to pick her up for work, and Charli went crazy with barking, both at the long black beast and at the uniformed driver. Nonplussed by Charli's outrage, everyone learned to simply ignore the dog. If the day was extremely busy with in-town engagements, Charli stayed home—but let his mistress know, in no uncertain terms, that he objected to this ignominy. If Sylvia was away overnight or for several days, Charli went to a kennel. During her years as lieutenant-governor, Charli spent a lot of time at various kennels in both Saskatoon and Regina or with friends able to take in the happy black dog for overnight visits. On office days, Charli went along, sweeping through the halls at Government House or sitting under the desk as Sylvia worked. Staff kept doggie treats and biscuits and bones on hand, and a water bowl, for their vice-regal consort. Christmas videos show a dog soaking up the winter sunshine on his favourite chair, glaring at the camera like a teenager as if to say "Get lost, Mom," and opening Christmas presents with great dexterity and abandon, shredding wrapping paper with teeth and delicately separating boxes from paper.

When Sylvia moved to Regina, she took along a few fun items, such as her camera and her new camcorder for home movies. She took the camcorder to Government House and took her "audience" on a tour of the new working digs. From the front door, she videoed the large receiving room on the right-hand side of the corridor, with a fireplace and north-facing windows. The receiving room doubled

9. THE HONOURABLE LEFT-HANDED GOVERNOR

Sylvia and Charli, official portrait, Christmas 1988.

as Sylvia's office; her desk sat scrunched into a corner by the fireplace, facing out toward the door. Off this room, there was a bathroom, with that most modern piece of technology, a working pull-chain toilet. Another door led to the old scullery and back kitchen. Across the hall were her hard-working office staff, one of them with a typewriter on a tea trolley for a desk. Having her desk in the receiving room was a bit of a logistical nightmare. With files and letters

Sylvia and schoolchildren decorating the Christmas tree at Government House, c. 1988.

strewn about as Sylvia worked, some of which were private or important legal documents such as orders-in-council, security was a bit of a concern. Kitchen and cleaning staff could come through at any time, or cigarette smoke could drift in from the back rooms. Eventually, Sylvia moved her office down the hall and across the corridor, facing east on the same side as the imposing front entrance. That room remains the private office of the lieutenant-governor.[25]

The first Christmas at Government House, Sylvia opted for old-fashioned rural traditions, including hosting a tree trimming with a cohort of young children at Government House, using over 400 handmade ornaments from local schoolchildren. After the tree was decorated and a few rousing carols rang out, each of the children went home with a brown paper bag stuffed with an orange, ribbon peppermint candy, peanuts, a few chocolates, and a shiny new loonie. This classic rural Christmas tradition would continue every year that Sylvia was at the helm. In photographs, she sticks

9. THE HONOURABLE LEFT-HANDED GOVERNOR

up from the middle of a group of children, an owl above the chickadees. It's hard to tell who was having more fun.

In early January 1989, Sylvia was the secret guest on the hit Canadian TV show *Front Page Challenge*. It was filmed on January 7 but aired later in the spring, and she relished the back-and-forth question-and-answer banter after the panellists—Betty Kennedy, Holly Preston, Pierre Berton, and Allan Fotheringham, along with host Fred Davis—had finally guessed her identity. Berton fired off a series of questions about poker, which Sylvia answered with great fun, giving as good as she got. Others asked about her cancer work, her roots north of Yorkton, and how she got called to be the new lieutenant-governor. Then Berton issued the last salvo:

> PIERRE BERTON: How many hands do you shake every week, Your Excellency?
>
> SYLVIA FEDORUK: Well, just a few days ago, I shook 998 hands during the New Year's Day levee, from two to four o'clock in the afternoon.
>
> PIERRE BERTON: You have to have, you have to have a technique for that so you [Sylvia: Yes], so you don't put your arm in a sling. What is your technique?
>
> SYLVIA FEDORUK: The technique is you shove your hand in there first. And then they can't squeeze. I learned this when I was chancellor. I had my hand really bruised the first time. [much laughter]
>
> PIERRE BERTON: You break the other guy's hand [Sylvia: That's right!] before he can break yours! [laughter and clapping, Sylvia laughs].[26]

Although Sylvia clearly enjoyed the "people responsibility" of her job, she never lost sight of the first priority of the lieutenant-governor: ensuring a functioning responsible government. Her primary duty was to hold a pen and sign her name. In her office, there would be orders-in-council, directives from the lieutenant-governor given on the advice of cabinet. Cabinet holds the ability to make some day-to-day working decisions so that it is not always necessary to have the legislature in session.

Orders-in-council cover a wide range of government operations, such as appointing provincial board members for crown corporations and crown agencies and judges and other major officials, signing and amending lease agreements and operating agreements, securing project funding, making minor changes to laws, programs, or regulations, and dealing with a host of other changes to government operations or decisions. In a typical month, a lieutenant-governor might sign as few as twenty, or as many as sixty or more, orders-in-council.

Another major duty is to visit the legislature to give royal assent to bills that have been read, debated, and passed by the members. In general practice, the clerk of the legislature will let the Office of the Lieutenant-Governor know when there are several bills to be passed at once, to streamline operations and reduce the number of times that the lieutenant-governor must be present. Generally, a lieutenant-governor visits the legislature several times over the course of a session, depending on its length and the number of bills successfully debated and passed. A few times Sylvia arrived at the legislature only to find that no bill required her assent; for whatever reason, things didn't pass as expected or were sent back for more work.

One of the most important official duties of the sitting lieutenant-governor is to prorogue (end) a session of the legislature and to open a new legislature by reading the Speech from the Throne. Each time there is an election, the leader of the party able to ensure support from a majority of the MLAs is invited to form the government, called a legislature. Each session of that legislature is counted: the first session of the twentieth legislature, the second session of the twentieth legislature, and so forth until the next general election.

The normal operating procedure for the legislative assembly is for a session to be "adjourned" until such time as the speaker of the house recalls, on the request of the government, the members of the Legislative Assembly to return. An adjournment acts like a recess; background business, such as committee work and unpassed legislation, remains on the agenda. A session can pick up where it left off, without a new Speech from the Throne, once the members are recalled. An adjournment can last for a few hours, a day, a weekend, a few weeks, or even several months. The members of the legislature do not need the lieutenant-governor's permission to adjourn; it is entirely at the members' discretion and falls under majority motion rules.

9. THE HONOURABLE LEFT-HANDED GOVERNOR

Adjournment is different from *prorogation*, a constitutional term with a specific meaning. Whereas the Speech from the Throne opens a session, prorogation terminates (ends) a session of the legislature. A session can only be prorogued by the lieutenant-governor, acting on the advice of the first minister (the premier of the province). All unpassed legislation, with the exception of private members' bills, dies on the order paper, and all committee and background work outlined in the Speech from the Throne is automatically finished, since, once prorogued, there is no sitting legislative session.

Sylvia standing next to the speaker's chair, 1989.

Legislative custom dictates that a session is adjourned when the members are released for long periods of time. Members may be recalled at short notice for an emergency, such as a strike or a natural disaster. A session is usually recalled and immediately prorogued just at the start of what will then be a new session. The time between a prorogation and the next Speech from the Throne is, typically, only a few hours.

Sylvia became the lieutenant-governor of Saskatchewan while the second session of the twenty-first legislature was adjourned. As such, her first official working act in the legislative chamber after her installation in September 1988 was at 10:04 in the morning of March 8, 1989. Sylvia entered the chamber, sat on the throne, and announced the prorogation of the second session of the twenty-first legislature, which had been opened with a throne speech by her predecessor, Fred Johnson. She exited after a mere five minutes, and the assembly stood prorogued until two o'clock that day. In the afternoon, Sylvia once again walked into the chamber to open the new session with the throne speech. In a gesture to the important roles played by both sides of the house (the government and the opposition), it was her practice—and no doubt that of other lieutenant-governors before and after Sylvia—to enter the house on the government side, greeting members with warmth, and, once her duties were finished, to exit the house on the opposition side, again offering personal greetings and nods. Roy Romanow, then the leader of the opposition, remembered Sylvia as a woman of substantive presence and intelligence every time she visited the chamber.[27]

The Speech from the Throne, written by the government, opens each new legislative session and outlines the government's goals, directions, and particular initiatives for that session. Written in the first person, the speech places the lieutenant-governor as the head of the government—"my government" will do this, "my ministers" and "my first minister" (the premier) will do that. Members of the Legislative Assembly generally meet in fall and spring sessions over the course of a twelve-month period, though emergency sessions may be called when necessary. During her term as lieutenant-governor, Sylvia presided over the end of one session, the start and finish of five sessions, and the opening of a sixth one, some of which ran across multiple years.[28] Once the Speech from the Throne is given, members of the Legislative Assembly debate the speech, which takes priority over all other business for up to seven days. Then the speech is passed, and the assembly turns its attention to the tasks set out in the throne speech and addresses a wider range of issues as they arise.

Sylvia's first throne speech was thirty minutes long and outlined Premier Grant Devine and his Progressive Conservative government's plans and initiatives for that session. The speech outlined a number of recognizable initiatives, including creating the Saskatchewan Pension Plan, Grasslands National Park, Wanuskewin Park in Saskatoon, and an extensive litany of environmental initiatives. Sylvia also announced, with some excitement, the July 1989 visit of Prince Andrew and Sarah, the Duke and Duchess of York, whose five-day visit would "focus ... on children, our native peoples, and the North."[29] Sylvia's personal thrill in delivering her first throne speech, and the announcement of a royal visit, would have been obvious to all in the room.

After the throne speech, Sylvia could relax for a bit and go off to Waskesiu on a holiday. The Slobstickers struck again. Not quite a year in office as the province's highest civil servant, Sylvia Fedoruk

9. THE HONOURABLE LEFT-HANDED GOVERNOR

nonetheless attended her now-annual Slobstick golf tournament retreat in 1989. The ladies, with many years of pranks and fun to boast of, were ready. Sylvia might have thought that she was now something special, but the Slobstick girls were ready to mock her. Decorating a golf cart, as her new "regal ride," even more extravagantly than they had when she had become chancellor, the women crafted a tiara and drove Sylvia around the town, with much hooting and hollering. She took it all in good fun.

The royal visit of Andrew and Sarah was the longest royal stay in Saskatchewan to that point in time. Stopping first in Prince Edward Island and Quebec, along with a brief visit in Ottawa, the couple then flew to Prince Albert and embarked on a northern tour that included Nipawin, La Ronge, and Meadow Lake before heading south through Saskatoon and Swift Current, ending in Regina. Sylvia flew to Prince Albert to be there when the royal couple touched down on July 20, with a civic reception. It was a short visit. The duke and duchess turned north, and Sylvia returned to Regina. She travelled on July 24 to Swift Current to be on hand for their visit to the agricultural research station. July 25 saw Sylvia ready in Regina for the visit of the royal couple to Government House, where they had lunch before leaving the province. Sylvia's day-timer notes "Lunch for Andrew and Sarah," as if it was an everyday occurrence. Local artist Trudy Teneyke created teddy bears outfitted with RCMP red serge suits, which lined the road outside Government House. Sarah took one of the bears back to London. Following lunch and a rest, Sylvia and the royals arrived via the landau to the legislature for a sunset ceremony before the Duke and Duchess were taken to the airport.[30]

When you're the lieutenant-governor, you're *always* the lieutenant-governor, even when you're up north, staying with good friends Irene Bell and Doreen Fairburn at their cottage at McPhee Lake and enjoying a round of golf. A message could come through at any time from Irene White. In August, resting and relaxing from the royal visit and enjoying some quality golf time, Sylvia got a message while on the golf course: drop everything and drive to Prince Albert. Irene White met her there, flying in a government plane, with a critical order-in-council to sign immediately. Her signature in place, Sylvia started to drive back to McPhee Lake when her car's alternator blew. Friends found her stranded and gave her a ride back north. Sylvia was on the phone most of the next day, and it was soon clear that the legislative session was about to wrap up back in Regina. Sylvia was needed. A friend drove her to Prince Albert, where she picked up her car and drove to Saskatoon, then flew to Regina. After nine o'clock in the evening on August 25, Sylvia visited the legislature, after the late-summer sun had already set. Sitting on the throne, she gave royal assent to fifty-three bills, then withdrew. A drive from Waskesiu to Saskatoon, then a flight to Regina, all for six minutes in the legislature—that's the importance of royal assent, as the axis and hinge of parliamentary democracy. Dwain Lingenfelter, then an NDP MLA for Regina Elphinstone and president of the New Democratic Party, rose to wish everyone "a pleasant summer, what's left of it."[31] Clearly, the session had been long and gruelling.

Sylvia's yearly schedule had two major events routinely blacked out, and no official functions could be scheduled. One was the annual Slobstick golf tournament on a late May or early June weekend, where Sylvia could relax with old friends, golf, and mostly forget about duties and obligations. The other was her annual trip north to pull in some frisky northern pike and deep-swimming lake trout. Fishing brought contentment, and every spring Sylvia would yearn to toss a few lures into northern waters. Her love of the north and of fishing folded neatly into her new role.

The call of the north helped Sylvia to usher in a new event in the lieutenant-governor's schedule. September 1989 saw the first of what would become her annual northern tour. One of her first recommendations as lieutenant-governor was to create a special series of awards for northern students. Then Sylvia herself would fly throughout the north to hand out the awards. It was a way to combine multiple interests and goals: students, schooling, and northern Saskatchewan. It also brought to action Merylyn Vann's astute point: it isn't right if only the kids in and near Regina get to see and visit with the lieutenant-governor. All kids, no matter where they live and go to school, have a right to meet the queen's representative.

The northern tours presented certain logistical problems for the vice-regal party. Flying sometimes in a Twin Otter, other times in a small float plane, the group criss-crossed the north, from Cumberland House to La Loche, La Ronge to Deschambault, Pinehouse to Fond du Lac and Athabasca and Black Lake and Wollaston, depending on the year. Sylvia would be accompanied by a small retinue of an aide-de-camp and her secretary, Irene White, a few government members from the Department of Northern Education, and of course the pilot.

9. THE HONOURABLE LEFT-HANDED GOVERNOR

Each leg of the tour would have a guide in charge of local logistics such as ground transportation, lodging and food, as well as getting the group safely to and from events. Irene, always impeccable, was sometimes aghast at the occasionally bare-bones offerings. In one place, flush toilets were not an option, and the "restroom" was a shack with a five-gallon pail in the corner, its lid replaced by a toilet seat. Sylvia, on the other hand, never flinched and didn't care in the least—it got the job done, it was more comfortable and private than squatting in the bush, so what more could you want?[32] Other stops were more lavish and often included accommodations at various fly-in fishing camps. In each community, the welcome was warm, the drums and dances full of energy, the food excellent and fresh (and often made by home economics or work experience students), and the students delighted to receive awards directly from the lieutenant-governor. Her rapport with the kids, chatting about pets and regular life, helped to create a bond that, Sylvia hoped, would help them to hear her message: stay in school, she would say, because it will give you more options later. Scheduled within each trip would be a few hours of stolen bliss, off the beach or out in a boat with a fishing rod, angling for a hungry jackfish, a grayling, or an elusive tasty trout.

With a schedule filling and Sylvia popping in and out of government planes and limousines, crossing the province by air and land, she needed a cadre of professional support staff, including drivers, pilots, and of course aides-de-camp. Aides were expected to have military or police training, were usually retired, and needed references to apply for the prestigious—but unpaid—position. Vetted, aides also needed approval by the lieutenant-governor through an interview. Before her term even started, Sylvia spent days meeting and interviewing potential aides-de-camp, for long days and many miles, as well as a certain measure of personal discretion and protection, required Sylvia and the aides to get along. She was the first lieutenant-governor to hire female aides-de-camp, a tradition that has continued. Government House developed a cadre of available aides-de-camp from across the province, not just Regina but also Saskatoon, Moose Jaw, and eventually Yorkton, North Battleford, and Prince Albert. Local aides-de-camp able to meet Sylvia meant that the Regina crew didn't have to travel as much, which suited everyone.

Sylvia shared the stunned ecstasy of a province that watched its Saskatchewan Roughriders make it through the playoffs game by game and arriving—unbelievably—at the Grey Cup final in 1989.

She watched the game at what she laughingly called "The White House" (her condo in Lakeview), and her day-planner records the Rider win over the TiCats in the "last 2 sec" of the game.[33] The next day Sylvia hurriedly bought a Rider scarf to wear proudly as she joined many others at the airport to welcome the winning team home. Two days later she was at the legislature for the Riders' reception and welcome. Their storied ending to the year somehow mirrored Sylvia's own climb, from one-room school to lieutenant-governor: if you try hard enough, you'll get there.

By her second Christmas at Government House, Sylvia was fully settled. She'd been in the post for a year, moved through the cycle, and earned the respect of the legislature. Adjusted to the new pomp and ceremony, she brought her whole self—scientist, proud Saskatchewanian, and volunteer—to her role. One of the rewards of being lieutenant-governor is the creation of a personal coat of arms. Sylvia's, delivered in 1989, recognized her science career and connection to Saskatchewan. Sylvia also developed a warm working relationship with Premier Grant Devine, who visited Government House on a regular basis, first to call as the premier on the lieutenant-governor and then to chat about a wide range of issues. Her intelligence and thoughtful opinions offered frankly were great feedback for a sitting premier not always able to keep a pulse on regular opinions outside his cabinet or the media. Sylvia was more in the community, and across the whole province, than anyone in the government.

Sylvia also earned respect and great love and support from the people of Saskatchewan, particularly children. After all, she would say, of course they love me; when I come to visit, they get time off school! With no children or grandchildren of her own, Sylvia looked on all Saskatchewan schoolchildren as honorary grandchildren.

An annual event that changed and expanded under Sylvia is the Government House New Year's Day levee. A Canadian custom, it grew out of an early fur-trade practice in which traders and others nearby would visit a fur-trade fort on New Year's Day to toast the factor or governor. In turn, they might hear the state of affairs of the region, country, or world and, in some cases, renew their pledge to trade at that establishment. Alcohol and the firing of muskets to make as much noise as possible, as well as some singing, were often part of the day. This fur-trade custom was adopted by British colonial governors, then by sitting governors general and lieutenant-governors. In its earlier years in Saskatchewan, the New

9. THE HONOURABLE LEFT-HANDED GOVERNOR

Year's Day levee tended to be an adult-oriented event. But when Sylvia took the helm, she deliberately opened it up to children, adding events and activities that they might enjoy. For many families in and near Regina, or those willing to travel a few hours, the New Year's Day levee at Government House has become an annual tradition, almost a ritual. Local volunteer clubs gear up weeks in advance to prepare food, and Government House staff mark it as one of the most important events of the calendar year. The levee in 1990 saw 1,250 guests at Government House, and Sylvia needed eight aides-de-camp on hand to help manage the crowds.

Early spring brought members of the Legislative Assembly back to Regina for a spring session. Once again Sylvia entered the chamber in the morning and sat to deliver the short speech for prorogation, giving a brief overview of what legislation had been passed during the session. A notable legislative piece included amendments to *The Saskatchewan Human Rights Code*, to protect "individuals with disabilities, whether they be caused by learning disabilities or mental illness."[34] Her speech brought about prorogation, and she exited the chamber.

Returning at 2 p.m., Sylvia sat on the throne to deliver her second Speech from the Throne for the Devine government and open the fourth sitting of the twenty-first legislature. At forty-one minutes long, it would be her longest, and to read it today in the Hansard record it's easy to see why. Responding to severe economic challenges in the province, the speech is a rambling, pleading, and meandering screed that declares, with great hyperbole, "the world has declared economic war on Saskatchewan."[35] A throne speech is usually declarative, bold, and decisive. This particular speech contained apologies that the Devine government had "moved too quickly and without adequate prior consultations." To address provincial woes, Devine created Consensus Saskatchewan, a new agency built to travel the province, allowing Saskatchewan people to have their say on what should be done to address the economic morass. With a core group of "one hundred citizens from all walks of life," Consensus Saskatchewan would solicit ideas, then make specific recommendations "on how best to take Saskatchewan through the next decade and into the next century."[36] In essence, the speech said *we've made mistakes; tell us how you'd like us to fix them.*

Devine's rural base had been hit hard by drought, low commodity prices, and rural out-migration; this session looked for ways to meet the rural crisis by dispersing government services out of Regina and into rural service centres across the province, supporting Community Development Bonds, and promising local stabilization. Austerity measures to address the fiscal deficit included ministerial salary rollbacks, government hiring and spending freezes, departmental consolidation, travel restrictions, and, for Saskatchewan residents, eliminating the gas tax rebate program. The speech promised a budget, as was the custom. As always, the Speech from the Throne ended with "I leave you now to the business of the session, with full confidence that you will favourably discharge your duties and responsibilities. May Divine Providence continue to bless our province and guide this legislature in all its deliberations. God save the Queen."[37] Little did Sylvia know that it would be her last throne speech until December 1991. She exited the chamber and went back to her people and personal responsibilities.

Sylvia also took a trip east to Ontario, where the University of Western Ontario in London bestowed another Doctor of Science (*honoris causa*), an honour that she accepted with grace and gratitude. Trevor Cradduck, her former graduate student, had been central in securing this honour. A backyard barbecue was planned following the convocation, and Sylvia was late. One organizer, grateful for the tardiness, swooped around, setting out the fanciest glasses and china plates, whisking away the plastic and Styrofoam. After all, Sylvia Fedoruk was a lieutenant-governor. When she finally arrived, clad in her comfiest sweatpants and beat-up sweatshirt (she had stopped to change out of the dreaded pantyhose), she walked in, snagged a beer from the cooler, and took a long, satisfying chug. "Oh, I needed that," she said, before moving past the organizer, beer in hand, to find friends. The dainty organizer was gob-smacked to see the queen's representative so perfectly at home with a beer in hand.[38]

A summer of public events, including her now second annual northern tour in September, brought Sylvia to October 1990 and her first major scandal as lieutenant-governor. News broke that she had written a cheque for $200 to the PC Canada Fund, the coffers of the federal Progressive Conservative Party. Her donation appeared in the Elections Canada register, released in 1990 for the 1989 year. A sitting lieutenant-governor must, at all times, be non-partisan in politics. In the event that a lieutenant-governor must choose a party to act as the government in a minority house, neutrality and impartiality are critical. Sylvia was aghast and ashamed and immediately said, "It was a stupid thing to do. . . . I haven't been very proud of myself."³⁹ Although never a member of any political party, Sylvia had made political contributions to both the federal Conservative and Liberal Parties in the past, as a way to show her "belief in the political system" as a whole.⁴⁰ She couldn't recall how the donation had happened but assumed that she had sat down and written the cheque in response to a letter requesting support. Sometimes the simplest of mistakes arises from the most mundane tasks.

Political science professors across the country cast criticism, calling the action "highly improper, if not worse," bringing the crown "into disrepute and . . . danger."⁴¹ Public opinion was mixed. After all, Sylvia had been lauded as a refreshingly non-partisan appointment. This story cast shade on her character and on the appointment, and there were a few rumblings that perhaps she should resign. Premier Grant Devine, though, was a staunch supporter. "She's a great person for Saskatchewan. She's a great role model for young people." Publicly stating that he hoped people would give her "the benefit of the doubt," he also hoped she would not resign, and certainly he would not suggest that she do so. "For all I know," he went on, "she's contributed to everybody. She certainly hasn't been partisan."⁴²

Bob Pringle, an NDP MLA, expressed disappointment in the contribution but adamantly claimed that it wasn't about the amount or the party to which the donation was given. His issue was the principle of non-partisanship, and he said that only Sylvia could decide if her poor decision changed the "integrity of her office."⁴³ A few letters to the editor in both Saskatoon and Regina reflected the wide range of public opinion, from "to err is human" and "forget about it" to calls for her resignation or even the abolition of crown representatives across Canada.⁴⁴ In the end, though, it was a dervish in a teapot. Sylvia did not resign, and the incident was dropped.

No matter how much Sylvia loved being the lieutenant-governor and living in Regina, come Christmas time she wanted to be home in her own place at 49 Simpson Crescent in Saskatoon. Christmas followed a regular pattern. Christmas Eve at Merylyn and Garry Vann's house with their son, Michael, where they would eat a traditional Ukrainian meal with perogies and cabbage rolls as main courses. Christmas Day was a movable gift opening, with some at Sylvia's house and some at Vanns' house, then sliding a turkey or ham, or both, into the oven at her own house to host the Vanns for a classic Christmas meal. Boxing Day was generally a visiting day, but no one was expected to cook: food was Chinese, ordered in, with friends and family. The Golden Dragon got the call in 1990, with steamed rice, mushroom chow mein, egg rolls, dry garlic ribs, deluxe vegetables, fried shrimp, and sweet and sour pork. And *no onions*.[45]

The year 1991 would prove to be one of the busiest of Sylvia's appointment. It marked a major reflection on history and accomplishment as the defining theme, with the 100th anniversary of Government House. Government business, though, dominated. On April 11, the legislature resumed sitting from the previous June adjournment, but in a major departure from expected practice there was neither a prorogation of the previous session nor a new Speech from the Throne. Instead, the provincial legislature made a change to its rules and procedures for the election of a speaker of the house. The convention had been that the speaker was a de facto appointment by the premier of the sitting government, which carries the majority vote. In the spring of 1991, the Legislative Assembly changed its protocol to allow any MLA to declare his or her candidacy for the position and the clerk of the legislature to conduct a secret ballot vote. This move brought the rules and procedures in line with those of the federal house and a few other provincial legislatures.

The sitting speaker, Arnold Tusa, gave his resignation. It was somewhat of a hollow change. By the next morning, April 12, only Tusa had put his name forward as a candidate. Sylvia entered the chamber briefly to command the house to elect a speaker. She left, and Tusa was acclaimed to the position. He took the speaker's chair. Sylvia re-entered, and he relayed his election to Her Honour. She acknowledged the election, in full confidence that the house would be "conducted with wisdom, temper, and prudence" and pledging her ready access.[46] She then withdrew, and the legislature moved on to routine proceedings.

Although the election rather than the appointment of a speaker was a fascinating historical side bar for legislative historians, it didn't really overshadow the real problem: with no prorogation of the last session and no new Speech from the Throne to open a new session, the Devine government continued to operate under the intentions and aims outlined in the throne speech from more than a year before—the wandering, angst-filled speech that had pushed blame for the province's woes onto everyone else and called for consensus throughout Saskatchewan on what to do. Clearly, the government was in trouble. Opening salvos of the day from the opposition centred on the new provincial sales tax, which elicited

9. THE HONOURABLE LEFT-HANDED GOVERNOR

numerous petitions and delegations against it, as well as a somewhat damning report by the provincial auditor general on provincial department finances and spending choices. Electoral reform, including the fact that several vacant constituencies had not held by-elections, combined with a proposed and much-contested bill to change electoral boundaries, had the chamber hollering.[47] The spring session proved to be raucous.

With a fractious legislature in which members were yelling across the floor, a more peaceful and celebratory event took place under the auspices of the University of Regina. It bestowed a new honorary degree on Sylvia Fedoruk, among hundreds of graduands surrounded by excited siblings and parents, a Doctor of Laws (*honoris causa*). Given her role as head of state for Saskatchewan and representative of the queen, this honorary degree recognized Sylvia's growing knowledge of Saskatchewan's political and legal systems. That knowledge would soon be tested.

By June, the Devine government was in a political corner. Nearing the end of its constitutional five-year mandate, with no budget passed and no election called, chaos and divisive rhetoric stormed through the chamber and the media. By June 12, the government was planning its exit strategy. Brian Barrington-Foote, the deputy minister of justice and deputy attorney general for the province, began a series of discussions with Sylvia about ending the spring session *without* passing a budget or even interim supply bills. Instead, the government formally asked the lieutenant-governor to consider signing special warrants to fund the government. When Sylvia asked to see the legal documents on which this path would be supported, her notes of their conversations, which can be read in the University of Saskatchewan Archives,[48] reveal that it was "not incumbent" on the lieutenant-governor to view the legal documents because she would be "taking advice" from the premier. In other words, Barrington-Foote and the Devine government wanted Sylvia to take their advice without reading, for herself, the legal documents. She was clearly angry.

Devine would ask her to prorogue the session and continue the work of the civil service by signing special warrants. By June 15, Barrington-Foote had asked for additional legal opinion on the decision and let Fedoruk know that the government would pursue this path. Sylvia shot back with a question. Are you acting in the best interests of the province? And, she told him flatly, she was reluctant to sign warrants "if they prorogue to avoid examination of the estimates in the legislature." In other words, if the government moved to prorogue the session to avoid answering questions about a budget, she did not support that. Moreover, Sylvia insisted that she would follow this course only if Devine asked her directly to do so.

With dissent rising both in the opposition and even in the Progressive Conservative Party, NDP MLA Dwain Lingenfelter rose on June 18 to call for a motion of non-confidence. Such a motion stopped the legislature cold. The government didn't have enough people in the legislative chamber that day to defeat the motion and so walked out. The division bells rang for almost an hour, and behind the scenes there was much scrambling. At four o'clock, the house reconvened with a filibuster from two government MLAS who took the floor, while Grant Devine called on Sylvia Fedoruk at Government House. Back in the chamber, where the filibuster was ongoing, at five o'clock the speaker called a supper recess until seven o'clock.[49] The sigh of relief was audible.

Sylvia kept point form notes of her meeting with Premier Devine on June 18. She started with sympathy: how are you holding up? "Okay," she recorded as his reply. "Caucus staff very supportive." But he had concerns about the health of some of his members. He was calling on her, he said, for a couple of reasons: for royal assent on bills at seven o'clock that evening and for "a break," asking her to prorogue the government for the "health and safety" of the members. Security, Devine said, was required. There were "unprecedented threats" to both his family and cabinet members. The storm inside the house had spilled over across Regina and into the media, and both the Devine family's house and those of sitting cabinet members had been targeted. Anger and fear prevailed. Devine told Fedoruk that they needed to prorogue the session to create a cooling-off period "for the summer." She told him, with typical directness, that she "had problems about warrants," but she wanted him to know that she was prepared to take his advice. In return, he promised not to abuse the prorogation, and he understood that the lieutenant-governor's office "must not get involved in the political consequences." In grim acquiescence, the conversation ended.[50]

Promptly at seven, Sylvia entered the legislative chamber, "her face like a thundercloud."[51] Stalking down the aisle and sitting on the throne, she first gave royal assent to nineteen bills, none of which was a budget. Then, acting on the request of Premier Devine, she prorogued the session, effectively killing all future debates,

9. THE HONOURABLE LEFT-HANDED GOVERNOR

motions, and bills, including the motion of non-confidence, the budget, and the bill to move government offices into rural ridings. There was also no election writ. Sylvia agreed to stop the government cold. There was no warmth in her voice, manner, or presence. Rising and sweeping steely eyes around the room, the lieutenant-governor walked out. The decision to prorogue the session clearly "went against her personal judgement."[52] But, as promised, she acquiesced to Devine's direct request and read out the prorogation.

Some people in Saskatchewan were outraged and staged a protest not in front of the legislature but in front of Devine's house.[53] With no budget passed, the only option left to keep the government working—and salaries and operating expenses of the many civil servants looked after—was for Sylvia to sign special warrants. And that, it turned out, skirted a major constitutional crisis. Behind the scenes, and recorded by Sylvia, there were continued conversations about the issue. A four-page letter from Barrington-Foote to Fedoruk admitted that there were two potential legal conclusions. The first was that the government was within its rights to ask for prorogation and special warrants, and such was its recommended course. But, he admitted, the second potential legal conclusion was that "special warrants are not available at all, as these expenditures were foreseen and therefore should have been provided for." All of the conversations revolved around whether or not the argument put forward by the government was "reasonable" as a legal interpretation. In the absence of anyone spearheading a court challenge (which the opposition NDP chose not to pursue), Fedoruk was bound by convention to acquiesce to the premier's request.[54]

Special warrants are an exception to the basic rule of law (hence "special") that government expenditures *require* legislative consent. In other words, there must be a budget debated and passed by the house. Typically, if a budget is particularly problematic and requires more time to investigate and debate, it might not be passed until after the new fiscal year has begun on April 1. In that case, a session will vote to pass one-twelfth of the budget, or one month's worth of proposed expenditures, a process known as "interim supply," until the budget receives final approval. In 1991, interim supply bills had been passed to take the government into early July. The special warrants exception permits a lieutenant-governor, at the request of cabinet, to approve expenditures under certain limited conditions. In normal practice, a special warrant is issued if, toward the end of a fiscal year, a department runs out of money and requires a top-up or there is an emergency situation such as a fire or flood.

One aspect of a special warrant is that by convention it is used only when the house is not in session (adjourned, prorogued, or dissolved for an election). If a session is only adjourned, it is easier to recall the house, expecting it to introduce and pass motions. If prorogued, a whole new session must be put in place, which includes a Speech from the Throne. Special warrants had been used numerous times in the 1980s, at a far higher rate than at any other time in Saskatchewan history. In the spring of 1982, when the sitting NDP government submitted a budget, the election writ dropped within a month. With the house dissolved, government expenditures were authorized using special warrants, the right tool in that instance.

However, after the new Devine government was convened in 1982, it passed neither a budget nor interim supply bills. Instead, it strategically passed special warrants only when the house was not in session. An *Appropriation Act* (budget) was finally passed in 1983, almost a year after the Conservatives took office. Nonetheless, political commentators conceded that it could have been just a novice administration learning to find its feet. The situation was slightly different in 1986–87. In the fall of 1986, Devine and his Conservative government won a second mandate. The Speech from the Throne that December outlined its priorities, and after a few weeks the house was adjourned. It did not sit again until June 1987, months into the new fiscal year. In that case, again, special warrants were used to finance government operations, though there was an increasingly loud call from media pundits and academics to the lieutenant-governor's office to force Devine back into the legislature to introduce, defend, and pass a budget. Frederick Johnson declined to do so.[55]

In 1991, the situation was again different. With a prorogued house and no passed budget, there was no other legislative option for the government to operate than special warrants signed by Sylvia. The media and people in Saskatchewan in general roared in outrage in opinion pieces in newspapers, and Sylvia became the target of a call that had seemingly grown through the years, questioning the use of special warrants in non-customary ways. A protest formed outside Government House on June 26 by a small group calling themselves the Concerned Saskatchewan Citizens of Regina, who called on Sylvia Fedoruk to stop signing the warrants and to call an election. The protesters met with Irene White, Sylvia's personal secretary, but Sylvia did not greet them.[56] Another protest at Government House in August, which included two busloads of people, also missed Sylvia, busy playing golf at the Lobstick tournament in Waskesiu, losing the sixth flight by one putt.

Behind the scenes, though, Sylvia and the Government House staff were in an uproar. It was an unprecedented constitutional predicament, and while she might have been able to force the issue she wasn't sure if convention, or the law, would allow such use of her powers. Each of the two major political parties sought legal opinions, but only one, that of Merrilee Rasmussen, became public. In her opinion, the government's actions in using special warrants for political expediency and not necessity were illegal and unconstitutional. The Conservative government's opposite legal opinion, given to Sylvia but not released to the public, supported its right to use special warrants.[57] The NDP, with an election imminent but not yet called, was unwilling to take the matter to court.

As a measure of mitigation, the Devine government issued strict orders to its departments to ask only for one month's allocation at a time, similar to an interim supply bill. As well, government staff were clearly told to limit expenditures to the bare bones, with no out-of-province travel, no new initiatives or program enhancements, and no discretionary spending. Such actions were a sign that the Conservative government had no intention of abusing the special warrants to initiate new programs without legislative consent.[58]

Nonetheless, pressure mounted, and anger turned on Sylvia. Even if signing the special warrants seemed like the right path at first, the length of time elapsing inexorably dragged her into a deeper political quagmire. Dale Eisler, the *Star-Phoenix* political editor, argued that the deepening crisis cast Fedoruk and the Office of the Lieutenant-Governor as "a pawn in a political game." After all, it was the Conservatives' decision to prorogue the legislature and then let weeks go by without calling an election, and these actions were increasingly viewed as political decisions to shore up the party, not to support good governance of the province. Sylvia became more and more incensed.[59]

It was clear that the legal opinion provided by Rasmussen wouldn't be viewed as non-partisan, and Sylvia, ever thoughtful and determined, flew to Ottawa. She sought the advice of old friend and, at that time, Governor General Ray Hnatyshyn, as well as previous clerk of the Legislative Assembly of Saskatchewan Gordon Barnhart, now clerk of the Senate in Ottawa. It's not known what Rideau

Hall offered as counsel, but Barnhart remembered their lunch as an exchange of views and thoughts on the roles and conventions of the Office of the Lieutenant-Governor. The position is meant to advise and to counsel and to warn, but ultimately, even though the office has the power to go against the advice of the premier, by convention it rarely exercises that power.[60] Sylvia herself, in speeches at high schools, had explained the role of the lieutenant-governor as that of a fire extinguisher: be highly visible, in bright colours and strategically located, but hopefully never used. "The fact that they are not used does not render them useless—and there are severe penalties for tampering with them."[61] Did Sylvia believe that Devine's government was "tampering" with crown powers via special warrants? The fire extinguisher is an interesting analogy, leading to an important question. In the end, Sylvia decided that it was up to the electorate to decide which government it would support. She would sign special warrants until the election occurred.

In the meantime, her public appearances continued to be frequent, particularly with the 100th anniversary of Government House. Yet Sylvia experienced disappointment too. The royal tour of the Prince and Princess of Wales to Canada that summer was forced to bypass Saskatchewan because of the provincial constitutional crisis. On July 29, in a face-to-face meeting with the premier in her private office, Sylvia told Devine that she felt cheated about missing the royal tour. Under some pressure to address the public over special warrants, she told him that she would not issue a public statement. Advised against it by the governor general, Sylvia told Devine that such a statement would connect her office directly to a political debate. After all, there were two conflicting legal opinions on the whole affair. Devine recognized that the situation might hurt her personal reputation "a little" but didn't believe that it would diminish the role of the lieutenant-governor overall. Sylvia was not impressed by this delineation between her personal reputation and that of her office. It remained, from her perspective, a lousy situation.[62] One major legal opinion was clear: an elected legislature in Saskatchewan had a constitutional limit of five years. Sylvia could not sign any special warrants to continue the existing government after that five-year period ended. Devine had to call a fall election.

Government House hosted its official birthday bash over two days in September. Sylvia took a break from political and constitutional angst to indulge in historical fun. Wearing a floor-length green sateen skirt and jacket accented in blue, worn over a collared blouse

9. THE HONOURABLE LEFT-HANDED GOVERNOR

and cameo broach, Sylvia played dress-up along with hundreds of attendees who wore historical costumes to celebrate a late-summer picnic. RCMP officers dug out replica North West Mounted Police uniforms of the era, and 1890s music played. A massive outdoor garden party, complete with speeches, music, and food under a warm September sun, gave Saskatchewan and Regina a historical party to remember. A few weeks later a swanky moonlight ball in the Government House ballroom went to the wee hours, a celebration reminiscent of many generations of swishing ball gowns and handsome tailored suits swaying to and fro across the floor.[63]

Soon after the celebration, things began to move on the political front. A series of meetings throughout early September gave Sylvia some indication of change on the way, and her day-planner and personal file are filled with meetings and phone calls with Brian Barrington-Foote, captured in handwritten notes. It was time to call an election—but once again it seemed to Sylvia that the government was veering wildly from basic protocol and precedent. Learning on September 6 that Grant Devine intended to announce an election date without her signature on the writ, she expressed her outrage to Barrington-Foote: "Why not do it in the usual way—why mess with every basic rule—HAVE ALREADY WITH WARRANTS." Her handwritten notes, underlined and capitalized, show anger, which no doubt was tossed verbally at the deputy attorney general. The government responded that it would issue statements saying that it *would be* asking the lieutenant-governor to sign the election writ. Announcing time delays in this way "sounds like the LG is involved in election planning. Cannot condone this at all!" In another note, Sylvia scribbled "as it is, I am accused of being in PD's [Premier Devine's] back pocket." Clearly furious, she questioned the mood of both the province and the legislature: "Who is to say that PD maintains the confidence of the elected members of the legislature?"[64] Faced with the righteous ire of an intelligent lieutenant-governor who knew that her first minister was not acting in the provincial interest, the government appeared to back down.

Anything official, including signing the order-in-council to drop the writ on the election, had to wait until Sylvia finished her 1991 northern tour through La Ronge and Camsell Portage and contended with wind and snow on Lake Athabasca while she fished for grayling. She also toured through La Loche, Buffalo Narrows, and then Île-à-la-Crosse before heading back to La Ronge and then on to Cumberland House, where after handing out awards she got a tour of the Saskatchewan River Delta and managed to catch some jackfish before changing plans and flying immediately back to Regina.

The next morning, early on September 20, 1991, Premier Grant Devine asked Sylvia Fedoruk to dissolve the legislature and call an election. With "a snarly public in the mood for change," and the NDP "light years" ahead in the polls, October 21 was set to be a testing day for the Devine mandate.[65] Would the public support the Progressive Conservative government's unabashed and extensive support for rural and farm issues, or would its skirting the edge of a legal precipice over special warrants and proroguing the legislature, not to mention its unwillingness to call by-elections, or its intention to bring in a harmonized 14 percent provincial and federal tax, be its downfall? Either way, the outcome made little difference to Sylvia, in the middle of her term as lieutenant-governor. She wanted the election, followed immediately by a budget bill, to ease her own constitutional crisis as a lieutenant-governor forced to sign special warrants to keep the provincial civil service in paycheques.

Roy Romanow and his NDP MLAs blew into power, taking fifty-five of the sixty-six seats, with Devine relegated to opposition leader status and Liberal Lynda Haverstock taking her seat—the only one for the Liberals—in the chamber as leader. Contrary to popular expectation, the NDP did break the Conservative hold on rural ridings, winning twenty-five of its fifty-five seats in primarily rural regions.[66] Sylvia's day-timer refers to the election as a "total wipe out."[67]

On a freezing first day of November, Romanow walked into the premier's office and was sworn in, surrounded by political allies and his family. Sylvia was there too to wish him a warm welcome and drink tea, as per custom. With an office, and the legislative building, full of celebrations, a Ukrainian choir, and members of the media, it should have been a glorious day. But Sylvia had something important on her mind.

Crooking her finger at Romanow with sober conviction, she said, basically, *we need to talk*. Taking the new premier to a corner of the room, Sylvia said—in no uncertain terms—that she expected her new first minister to help solve the immediate constitutional crisis of special warrants. Call in the legislature, she said, and pass a budget. Romanow was taken aback. After all, it should have been a day of celebration. But Sylvia was adamant. Again the new premier demurred. He was not comfortable, he said, passing the existing

9. THE HONOURABLE LEFT-HANDED GOVERNOR

estimates budget until he and his new government had had a chance to open the financial books and do a complete review. "I said I just can't do it. I can't enact this budget and take responsibility for it," Romanow recounted.[68] Sylvia stood her ground. "You can pass the current proposed budget from the Devine administration and change it on the fly," she said. "I'm not willing to continue to sign special warrants when we have better options. The constitutional crisis is real, and both the prime minister and the governor general are worried. This cannot go on." Romanow nodded. He would see what he could do. Both satisfied, the two rejoined the party.

It was a pivotal moment for both Romanow and Fedoruk. Their relationship, previously cordial but more distant, changed dramatically. Romanow had come face to face with Sylvia's vaunted intelligence and authority. A woman of substance and presence, Sylvia Fedoruk had asked Roy Romanow, in no uncertain terms, to lead Saskatchewan out of its constitutional crisis.

On December 2, just over a month after the election, Sylvia entered the legislative chamber to deliver the throne speech opening the first session of the twenty-second legislature. It was a short speech—ten minutes—but it started off exactly as Sylvia had requested. "The primary work of this session," she said, "will be to provide supply for my government for the remainder of the current fiscal year." Noting the "fundamental tradition" that "public funds must be appropriated by the legislature, and that members have the right of grievance before supply," the new government would vote for interim supply on the basis of the previous administration's estimates. "This will end the need to fund the ongoing operations of government through special warrants."[69] There is no doubt that these comments gave Sylvia great satisfaction and relief. But the speech went one step further: it established the Financial Management Review Commission, an independent and non-partisan commission to review, in depth, the province's financial records and public accounts. The intention was that the review would give a firm base to a new budget going forward.[70] The short session, just three weeks long, adjourned the early morning of December 22 when Sylvia entered the chamber past midnight and gave royal assent to sixteen bills plus a budget that would take the government through to the end of March 1992. All breathed audible sighs of relief.

Roy Romanow had cut his political teeth under Allan Blakeney, who had established a precedent of regular meetings with the sitting lieutenant-governor. Grant Devine had also been a regular visitor to Government House, though some of the meetings had been less warm. Romanow took the tradition from occasional meetings to regular monthly meetings. With no published agenda or minutes or recordings, these meetings served as sounding boards for sitting premiers, and a non-partisan avenue for lieutenant-governors, out in public across the province, to bring views and comments back to the premier. Usually surrounded by partisanship and political manoeuvring, premiers tended to value the perspectives and opinions offered, grateful as well for a safe place to raise concerns or discuss problems.

As the Saskatchewan Financial Management Review Commission under Don Gass began to issue preliminary reports, Romanow and Fedoruk would meet. How is it going? she'd ask. On the positive side, they joked that the Ukrainians were clearly taking over: Ray Hnatyshyn as governor general in Ottawa, Sylvia Fedoruk as lieutenant-governor in Saskatchewan, and Roy Romanow as the new premier. But politically and financially? Not well. Engulfed in a financial crisis of epic proportions, Saskatchewan—along with Newfoundland—faced the real possibility of bankruptcy.[71]

The federal government watched intently, with no small degree of worry. After all, if one or two provinces ran aground, the country's credit rating would also slip drastically. The storm in the Saskatchewan teacup threatened to slosh over the provincial borders. On top of Gass's findings,[72] an RCMP fraud investigation into how government ministers and MLAs reported earnings and expenses rocked the legislature on both sides of the house.[73] Tempers ran high, stress stalked the corridors, and everyone felt the screws tighten. The Romanow government was working within this atmosphere to come up with its own budget, based on the commission's findings. No one liked what the numbers were saying. An austerity budget of shocking proportions looked imminent. It was "very difficult to convince the caucus, let alone the public. We were all under tremendous pressure. And we knew the budget would be horrendous, with cut services and increased taxes."[74]

Romanow led a three-day budget meeting with his caucus, bringing in officials from each department and showing slide after slide of the dismal numbers and proposed deep cuts to services and rises in taxes. Caucus rebelled. "They said we didn't do it, and we shouldn't take responsibility for it. I couldn't get it passed through caucus," Romanow recounted. That's when he lost his cool. He told

9. THE HONOURABLE LEFT-HANDED GOVERNOR

caucus that "it's obvious that we aren't going to be able to come up with a workable budget. And if we can't do it, the people of this province are owed a government that can create and pass a budget." He stormed out and headed straight back to the premier's office. "Call Sylvia Fedoruk," he said. "I'm going to report to her and ask her to do a writ of execution for a new election and government." Sylvia was available. "We printed up the documentation, and I went over to Government House. And there she was, typical Syl Fedoruk, in command. Authoritative in her presence."[75]

Romanow recounted to the lieutenant-governor the horrendous budget, his caucus rebellion, and his plan to call a new election. Over the next two hours, Sylvia listened and quietly poured drinks. She then looked Romanow in the eye and said, "I'm not signing this," referring to his request to call a new election. Firmly, she insisted that the new premier do what he had been chosen by the electorate to do: "It may cost you the government, but it is your responsibility. As lieutenant-governor, I'm not going to follow the advice of my first minister. I won't sign that writ." Romanow, recounting the story, noted that "the biggest part of the discussion was her calm cool, not panicking. Cool intellectual argument about duty and responsibility and how it should be done. It was probably the biggest factor. My sense of duty was refreshed."[76]

Romanow conceded, nodding quietly. With renewed conviction but no small amount of trepidation, he returned to the legislative building and went back to the caucus meeting. If caucus continued to revolt and refuse to put the budget to the floor of the house, or chose to defeat its own budget on the floor by voting against it, then there would be an election and probably a defeat. Gearing up to confront caucus, Romanow was about to speak but was smoothly interrupted by Glenn Hagel, the MLA from Moose Jaw. As Romanow recounted, "he said, 'Mr. Premier, before you say anything, I wish to report that in your absence the caucus has met, and we've agreed to endorse this budget wholeheartedly and without reservation.'" Romanow's jaw dropped in shock and relief.[77]

In some ways, it was the end of his personal leadership crisis, but it was only the beginning of a painful road through fifty-two rural hospital closures and other severe austerity measures. There was blowback from the opposition, occasionally from his own government, and certainly from the public, particularly rural voters. "My monthly or more regular meeting with Sylvia was in the mode of intelligent advice, firm advice, supportive advice, understanding my position, but most importantly a validater of what we were doing. Not ideologically. Just in the sense of trying to pull the province out of fiscal difficulty."[78]

Sylvia forced the issue, pushing Romanow back to caucus, refusing to sign the writ for another election so soon after the previous one, and in essence choosing the rockiest path forward through rural hospital closures and public agony. As painful as the choice was, and with great regret for those whose lives would change, Sylvia would support no other solution given her upbringing. Hard choices are a part of life, and financial security was non-negotiable. If that was the situation, then the only option was to find ways to address the province's fiscal standing. Romanow has stated unequivocally that, "if there is any credit for helping us out of that 1990s dilemma, her role in advice and consent is understated but absolutely pivotal to us pulling it through."[79]

It is fascinating to compare the two crises and Sylvia's responses to the two very different requests from two sitting premiers. On the surface, the stormy acquiescence to Devine's request to prorogue the government and sign special warrants seems to have been weak, whereas Romanow's memory of Sylvia's graceful but firm refusal to accept his request to call an election seems to have been strong. Yet there is more to both stories. Sylvia was defending her perception of the duties of the lieutenant-governor. In the case of special warrants, she knew that her office would bear the brunt of the pressure but that she would do what was needed to make sure that no one went without a paycheque. The electorate would have the opportunity to consider the government's actions and vote accordingly. In the case of Romanow's request for a new election, her refusal reinforced the very words that Sylvia had said in the December 1991 throne speech: the government's job is to put forth a budget, and it's the right and responsibility of *every* sitting MLA, on both sides of the house, to voice a grievance with the budget. Where Romanow saw a revolt and potential political crisis within his caucus, Sylvia saw debates and hard choices, *precisely* what governments are elected to undertake. Her refusal forced Romanow back to caucus, and Sylvia was prepared for the fallout, whatever form that might take.

She opened the second session of the twenty-first legislature on April 27, 1992, with a Speech from the Throne that outlined the Romanow government's—and Sylvia's—belief that "a community that lives beyond its means will not long prosper." People

9. THE HONOURABLE LEFT-HANDED GOVERNOR

in Saskatchewan faced "an overwhelming debt that threatens our economic stability today, and jeopardizes our hopes for economic recovery tomorrow. . . . Our children did not create this debt. We have no right to burden them with it." Despite typical political showmanship that wrongly put all of the fiscal blame on the previous Progressive Conservative government, the truth was nonetheless sobering: "Today, Saskatchewan people are burdened with the highest per capita debt in the nation."[80]

Even as Sylvia ended the throne speech with the usual exhortation, "God Save the Queen," that innocuous statement carried new meaning. Behind the scenes, Government House was gearing up for what might have been the most important meeting in Sylvia's life: a personal visit to Buckingham Palace and a private audience with Queen Elizabeth II. Each sitting Canadian lieutenant-governor is entitled, during his or her five-year appointment, to one private tête-à-tête with the reigning monarch. If dresses and pantyhose were the bane of Sylvia's existence, she had to add one more: hats. Protocol dictated that Sylvia must wear a hat to meet the queen.

This time Sylvia couldn't send a personal shopper. She had to go to the mall herself and buy a hat. Off she went. There was one shop that carried hats, and a nice blue one was in the window. Sylvia stomped in and asked to try it on. With her big brain and Ukrainian background, she was no ethereal waif. She had a big head, and chances were poor that the hat would actually fit. Jamming the hat firmly down over her pixie locks, Sylvia looked in the mirror and nodded. The saleslady nodded too. It fit, it looked good, and Sylvia liked it. Done. She plunked down her money and sailed out. The whole transaction had taken less than ten minutes, and Sylvia was ready to meet the queen.

Flying with her personal secretary, Irene White, Sylvia arrived in London to stay on the seventeenth floor of the London Hilton, overlooking Hyde Park and Buckingham Palace gardens. On May 5, her sixty-fifth birthday, she watched the Changing of the Guard, visited the House of Lords to get her bearings ahead of the official state visit to the opening of Parliament, had a tour of Westminster Abbey, and in the evening went back to the abbey to hear the choral evensong. In a postcard home to friends Irene Bell and Doreen Fairburn, Sylvia wrote, "Not often have I been to a church service on my birthday but the evening service at Westminster Abbey was really very exciting! Sat in the pews where the choir sits for coronations and weddings."[81]

May 6, 1992, saw Sylvia Fedoruk attend the State Opening of Parliament, at which Queen Elizabeth II in full ceremonial robes entered and read the Speech from the Throne. Sylvia sat near the Duke and Duchess of Kent, while Irene White sat next to Norma Major, the wife of British Prime Minister John Major. That afternoon Sylvia was ushered from the Hilton via limousine through the gates at Buckingham Palace. As tourists and Londoners along the road gawked and stared, trying to get a glimpse of the queen's visitor, Sylvia and Irene were whisked with legendary grace and honour into the palace and up to the receiving room. Following the protocol officer's strict instructions, Sylvia greeted Her Majesty, and the two settled in for a visit that lasted over half an hour. Propriety dictated no personal questions, but the queen had been well prepped for Sylvia's visit and knew about her work in cancer therapy and as a past member of the Atomic Energy Control Board of Canada, as well as her varied sports career. The thrill of having a private audience was "awesome," Doreen Fairburn recorded, from a phone call to Pat Langston in Government House, which acted as a go-between and message-taker for Sylvia while overseas. Doreen was asked to call Merylyn and Garry Vann to let them know "all's well."[82] Whisked back to their Hilton hotel, Irene and Sylvia had just enough time for an evening meal before attending the smash musical *Miss Saigon*. Sylvia spent the rest of her time in London touring, including a visit to Canadian High Commissioner Fredrik Eaton, with a luncheon at Macdonald House on Grosvenor Square, before embarking on a swing through Edinburgh, Aberdeen, Stoke-on-Trent, and Wales and returning to London and flying home on May 19.

In some ways, Sylvia's visit to England, though long awaited and much anticipated, operated under the radar of Saskatchewan's media. After all, hot political stories from hospital closures to fraud investigation and charges dominated the news cycle. Sylvia's trip was somewhat out of step with the provincial mood—there was an ugly undercurrent regarding the cost of Canada's constitutional monarchy via its governor general and lieutenant-governors and a risk of backlash from disgruntled Saskatchewan citizens: You're closing our hospital but sending Sylvia to meet the queen? Really!?

Government House chose modest, even austere, circumspection. And even Buckingham Palace, the soul of perfection, could get things a bit wrong. The court circular for May 6, 1992, read thus: "The Lieutenant Governor of Saskatchewan (Her Honour Mrs. Sylvia Fedoruk) was received by the Queen today."[83] Sylvia always

9. THE HONOURABLE LEFT-HANDED GOVERNOR

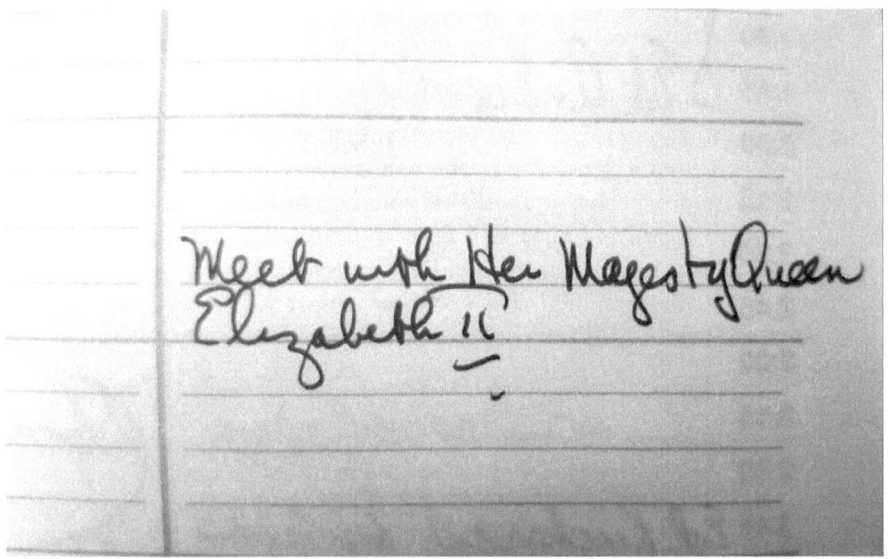

Sylvia's desk diary notation: "Meet with Her Majesty Queen Elizabeth II," May 1992.

went by Miss, never Ms., and certainly never Mrs. Nonetheless, she returned from the trip to England as a jubilantly renewed monarchist, eager to continue her work in Saskatchewan as the queen's representative.

Despite a busy itinerary that might see as many as five events squashed into a day, Sylvia was able to maintain some balance between professional work and personal life. Some of her closest friends in Saskatoon orchestrated a surprise arrival for a belated sixty-fifth birthday party at Government House in the ballroom, aided and abetted by Sylvia's Government House staff. "It was a hoot," Pat Langston remembered. Her friends were "no saints," and they'd all known each other for a long time. With much laughter and camaraderie, the group listened to Sylvia's stories from Britain, gave Sylvia a gentle ribbing about being so la-di-da, and helped to celebrate the milestone marking official "old age." Sylvia's summer, between official duties, was peppered with visits north to Waskesiu and McPhee Lake and La Ronge to golf and fish and visit with friends and relax. Charli was a great fan of northern trips, with lots of long walks through the boreal forest, swimming, and being with Sylvia (and not in a kennel). As always, with the legislature in session, Sylvia would spend a good part of her time in Regina, signing orders-in-council and giving royal assent to bills as they passed. On

August 28, she was in Regina to give final royal assent before the house adjourned.

The September 1992 northern tour, her fourth such tour, saw Sylvia handing out personal achievement awards to numerous northern students, from La Loche to Cumberland House to Fond du Lac. The northern tours always brought a unique sense of adventure for the Government House staff and aides-de-camp. One year the Canadian Shield was particularly unrelenting, giving Sylvia's southern prairie–trained driver some consternation—after all, nowhere on the shield is it flat, and parking can be tricky. One time the driver badly misjudged the angle. The female aide-de-camp opened her passenger-side door and promptly rolled out of the borrowed half-ton truck and onto the stone and moss. Sylvia, laughing, clambered out with ease, completely nonchalant. The northern trip was split in two by a quick flight south to Saskatoon for Sylvia to attend the historic Treaty Land Entitlement Framework Agreement signing at Wanuskewin.

While Saskatchewan First Nations were working hard to find paths through issues of treaty land entitlement and racism and to bolster their connection to the crown, other Saskatchewan residents also had reasons to protest and push public leaders. The international AIDS crisis had reached a fevered pitch around the world, including in Saskatoon, where community members were succumbing to and dying from AIDS. Students in the Department of Art and Art History at the University of Saskatchewan joined a new worldwide movement, Day Without Art, on December 1. Structured to coincide with World AIDS Day, Day Without Art showcased the impact of the AIDS crisis in general and on the artistic community in particular, and the artistic and scholarly community at the university chose to participate.[84] To signify the importance of mourning and action, the group invited Sylvia to speak at Convocation Hall, giving extra credence to the scope and depth of the AIDS crisis. Government House agreed, and she was set to appear.

In a way, it was rather amazing that Government House agreed to the speech, since the AIDS issue was fraught with social controversy. Attending and speaking at Day Without Art showed that Sylvia and Government House deliberately supported what some at the time considered a highly controversial topic. At that time, AIDS was widely considered to be an issue that only affected gay men and the larger homosexual community. To speak at an AIDS event was next to supporting a public stance on homosexuality.

Several members of the government under the previous premier, Grant Devine, had been openly hostile to gay and lesbian issues and viewed homosexuality as aberrant. The sense was that, if you must be homosexual, do so quietly. Don't flaunt your proclivities in any public form. When federal MP Svend Robinson came out as gay (the first Canadian politician to do so), Devine was quoted as saying "I don't want my children saying this [being homosexual] is a reasonable, normal thing to do."[85] For Sylvia to attend Day Without Art would have been a significant departure for Government House and a signal of support for Saskatchewan's homosexual community. She was set to drape a black cloth over a picture created by local young artist John Harelkin, who had died from AIDS in the summer of 1992. Draping the picture would symbolize bleakness and absence.[86]

Although some of the organizers were delighted that Sylvia would be in attendance, others were not. A student protest movement, led by a young graduate student named Christopher Lefler, was set to appear at the event. The group, looking to garner wider support, asked friends and acquaintances to join their protest. They wanted to ask Sylvia, as a political representative, why Saskatchewan had yet to enshrine gay and lesbian rights into *The Saskatchewan Human Rights Code* and why—as a researcher herself—she did not push for more research dollars to investigate AIDS.[87]

The protest took the form of an artistic installation called *Masquerade*. The plan involved the protesters arranged inside Convocation Hall wearing black T-shirts declaring "We are all HIV positive" on the front and "She Kills Me" on the back. Each would carry a bouquet of dark-haired dolls with hair cut in a style mimicking Sylvia's iconic blunt cut. No words, no raised voices, just silence and a statement. Organizers were horrified as Lefler and his team unfolded their plans. The planned protest was viewed by moderates to be far too outrageous, too politically charged, and too personal. In an attempt to de-escalate the situation, both the head of the art department and the university president met with Lefler. His response was stark: "I've lost no fewer than twenty-five friends to AIDS. The protest [will] go forward."[88] Glenn Hubich, a performance artist from Regina, worked with Lefler on the art protest, along with three others. It's probable that someone from the university (possibly the president or secretary's office, the art department, or simply a concerned organizer) sent a message of warning to Government House to let the lieutenant-governor know about the rogue art protest planned for her Day Without Art speech.

Although Sylvia's day-timer does not reveal any warning, there were other issues at play. Sylvia had been having health concerns throughout November, including a stress fracture in her foot that required crutches and medications, in addition to heart trouble, high blood pressure, and trips to doctors and even emergency room visits. On warfarin to control blood clots, she wasn't feeling her best. Rather than drive to Saskatoon for the Day Without Art event, Sylvia decided to fly, but at the airport she "chickened out," as she recorded in her day-timer. A brutal wind, with a nasty squall of snow and rain in Regina, meant that neither driving nor flying was a good option.[89] Since Sylvia did not attend the event, because of her health, the weather, or the protest, Lefler and Hubich's organized public stance lost its strength. The protest went forward, but it was hollow. Lefler and Hubich lashed out through the media. "She has the power to shut the legislature down if something is not done," Hubich charged. Lefler said that just talking about AIDS doesn't stop it.[90]

Lefler and Hubich, in their comments to the press, overestimated Sylvia's power to influence government direction. As shown in the 1991 special warrants constitutional crisis, the lieutenant-governor's office might have power, but convention set out strict parameters rarely crossed. Moreover, Sylvia was the appointed vice-regal head of state, not the elected legislative leader. She could read the speech from the throne, but she did not write it, dictate its contents, or give direction to the government. But Lefler and Hubich were also right: Saskatchewan lagged behind other jurisdictions since *The Saskatchewan Human Rights Code* did not specifically protect gay and lesbian people from discrimination on the basis of sexual orientation.

Lefler and Hubich were on the fringe of a much larger concerted movement to push both the provincial government and the federal government to make those changes—and in truth the government *was* listening. In the February 1993 Speech from the Throne, just two months after the fizzled Day Without Art protest, the intention was clear: "At this session, amendments to *The Saskatchewan Human Rights Code* will be introduced to prohibit discrimination on the basis of sexual orientation, family status or receipt of public assistance."[91] It was an important step in the right direction; however, if the University of Saskatchewan, Government House, and the provincial government breathed a sigh of relief assuming that they were finished with Lefler and his methods of protesting gay and lesbian rights, they were wrong.

9. THE HONOURABLE LEFT-HANDED GOVERNOR

If the run-up to Christmas 1992 was filled with problems, the New Year's Day levee was an excellent foil. It had become a major event in the lieutenant-governor's schedule, with more than 1,000 people attending it every year. Sylvia and the Government House staff thought that they should also host a levee in Saskatoon. After all, the Regina levee was always such a hit and major event. Planned for January 17, 1993, at one of Saskatoon's splashiest new hotels, the Saskatoon Inn, the Government House crew and Sylvia Fedoruk sat waiting for the expected crowds.

Trouble was the expected crowds didn't come. In a crushing disappointment, Sylvia and staff soon realized that people in Saskatoon had no idea what a levee was or why they should attend it. About 130 people showed up, many of whom were Sylvia's long-time friends, relations, and curling and basketball buddies. Where it took at least two hours in Regina to shake everyone's hand, in Saskatoon Sylvia was finished in no time. Too much food and too much space left the embarrassed staff with little to do but visit in the cavernous quiet.[92] At four o'clock, Sylvia went home to discover that her sewer at 49 Simpson Crescent had backed up because of tree roots growing through the pipe. A beleaguered city crew had to come on a cold January Sunday evening to roto-root the line, and Sylvia ended the disappointing day tucked into bed, nose resolutely buried in the sheets.[93]

Although the levee was a disappointment, Sylvia was the perfect person to shrug such a problem off and bounce right back into her role. It turns out that she took her long-practised private wit and fun, shared at Slobstick events, to thespian levels. In *The Mouse that Roared*, Regina's Globe Theatre celebrity-cast fundraiser play in the spring of 1993, based on a 1955 novel satirizing the Cold War, Sylvia brought lieutenant-governor gravitas and homespun charm to the role of housekeeper for the absent-minded professor. The Globe Theatre cast a cadre of Regina celebrities and politicians, from CBC's Costa Maragos to Chantal Devine, MIX-92 reporter Susan Butnik, CBC Radio's Peter Brown, and *Leader-Post* reporter Mike O'Brien. Director Susan Ferley cajoled the motley mix of masqueraders through the play, which garnered rave reviews and raised a cool $15,000 for the Globe Theatre. Fellow thespian Patrick Davitt—entertainment writer for the *Leader-Post*—called Sylvia "the delight of the show—personable, relaxed and jovial backstage, and a hit whenever she walked onstage." "If I could only sell what I know," opined Sylvia as the audience rocked with laughter at the double entendre of a housekeeper working in a house filled with nuclear secrets and Sylvia's alter ego as the lieutenant-governor privy to the private musings of premiers.[94] Practices and dress rehearsals and sold-out shows kept Sylvia busy through the spring, more than counterbalancing the sting of the failed Saskatoon levee.

A spring trip to the farthest edge of Canada to the annual Canadian medical physics conference at Mount Saint Vincent University in Halifax became an opportunity for another university to bestow an honorary title, Doctor of Humane Letters (*honoris causa*), on Sylvia at the spring convocation. Mount Saint Vincent has special criteria for the award: "We look to honour worthy recipients who have contributed to the betterment of society and humanity in any field, but in particular, improvement of the status of women, contribution to higher education, humanitarian and social service, involvement with and fostering of culture and the arts, or leadership in a field of endeavour."[95] Sylvia was a perfect fit. With now *four* honorary doctorates, she was recognized across Canada for her stature as a woman of substance and worth.

Sylvia's five-year term as lieutenant-governor was set to end September 7, 1993. But, with a federal election looming that fall, new appointments, by tradition, were halted and existing appointments extended. An appointment to the position is "not less than five years," with a subtext that meant a person was in it until the prime minister got around to appointing a replacement.[96] Sylvia, with no directions to the contrary, continued her public and political routines. The annual fall northern trip started in Stony Rapids, where Sylvia, as usual, was delighted to connect with youth, encourage them to stay in school, and hand out prestigious achievement and merit awards. A proposed trip to Wollaston Lake was abandoned; a meningitis outbreak was sweeping through the community, and Sylvia didn't want people to be congregating to see her and make the outbreak worse. Instead, she made an unscheduled stop in Black Lake, where both children and elders poured out to meet her. A taxi ride through the community went past the still-smouldering remains of the band office, which had burnt down just the night before. Denare Beach, Creighton, Cumberland House, La Ronge, and La Loche rounded out the trip. Students loved Sylvia for her "warm concern" and "genuine interest" in the north, her Mickey Mouse watch, and the stories about Charli.[97] In full circle, her final Government House Christmas card shows Sylvia once again posing with Charli, cosy in front of a warm fireplace.

9. THE HONOURABLE LEFT-HANDED GOVERNOR

If duty didn't call, Sylvia divided her down time equally between resting at home with Charli or spending time with her "Regina family," the Government House office staff and their children. "I think that, when she was in office, we were her family," Pat Langston mused. "Our kids were fairly young when Sylvia was in office. She got to know the kids well. Our kids were lucky to get to know her on the level that they did. She would have us over to Government House to eat Christmas dinner in the dining room—imagine that! Our kids gave her a Regina family while she was here. We were very important to her. We became more than co-workers. We kept those connections open to the end of her days. I loved her dearly. I treasure the time that we had together."[98]

Although Sylvia thoroughly enjoyed her busy, public role, her relentless self-drive (in sport or at work), on occasion, would crack her own spirit. The introvert needed to have a retreat, to be fiercely alone, to recover. Behind the public view of an impressive woman of substance, Sylvia hid a private problem. These dark times could last for two to three days and were self-medicated by strong drink. Evidence of these drunken retreats can be found in her archival files, particularly at times of stress as lieutenant-governor and, in her later years, as loneliness and age crept inexorably into her days. As recorded in day-timers filled with anticipated events, whole days or even two or three days in a row would be crossed out with a large X. These weren't unexpected sick days or illnesses. They were drinking binges. Comments coded with guilt ("misbehave" or "misbehave with Glenlivet") or self-recrimination ("stupid day" or "another stupid day"), followed by recovery coded with self-determination ("no more no more"), reveal a woman who fought, and sometimes lost, a private battle. The drinking brought physical injuries from falls, which had rolling effects, including broken bones and bruises, use of a wheelchair, or simply a modified schedule for recovery. The professional public image masked a private life with real pain.

Alcoholism is not a character flaw. As a younger woman, Sylvia was always willing to celebrate success, and there were many things in both sport and work to celebrate. An over-the-top, hail-fellow-well-met attitude served her well in international scientific circles as "one of the guys" and made some of her curling escapades more convivial. In later years and during her time in the public eye, Sylvia faced both internal and external anxieties. Alcohol was a way, on those rare occasions, to find release. It clearly did not get in the way of doing her job, though quiet stories of Sylvia lapsing into convivial public excess are not difficult to find in a small province. Our contemporary understanding of alcoholism as a disease and an addiction brings a more sympathetic perspective that Sylvia's generation lacked. In her world, an alcoholic binge was a matter to be hushed and hidden. Yet finding clear evidence of her alcoholic binges and the broken wholeness of her character raises a simple but powerful point: a person can struggle on occasion with something that he or she cannot overcome and still be astonishing. These two facts are not incompatible.

February 1994 saw Sylvia enter the legislative chamber to give her final Speech from the Throne to open the fourth session of the twenty-second legislature. She knew that her term was coming to an end. John (Jack) Wiebe, a farmer-politician from Herbert, had been selected as her successor, with his appointment set to begin on May 31. Sylvia seemed to share some skepticism of the appointment's political nature. She assiduously clipped and kept numerous newspaper articles that questioned the veracity of putting an obvious political appointee into a non-partisan position. The irony, of course, is that she had registered no such disdain when her old friend Ray Hnatyshyn accepted the federal vice-regal position as governor general even though he, too, had had a long political career. Sylvia took pride in the non-partisan nature of her own appointment and seems to have built an entrenched belief that all such appointments should be similarly non-political. Of course, this view somewhat wilfully and blindly ignores that there was a certain degree of cronyism and friendship involved in her own appointment via Hnatyshyn, though she was right, she had not been a political figure.

The Legislative Assembly chose to suspend normal activities on May 12 to give honour to Sylvia for her service. Government House brought in a second limousine for the day: one for Sylvia's four aunts and Merylyn Vann on hand for the celebratory day, a second for Sylvia. As had been the case throughout her career, she brought her family and friends along to view the world from the seat that she had worked so hard to win and had occupied with such grace.

Arriving at the legislature in the Government House landau, inspecting the troops, and accepting a fifteen-gun salute, Sylvia had a sense of coming full circle. She was escorted into the chamber and gave royal assent to a number of bills. Then the house took a recess to honour Sylvia. Speeches extolling her term of office rang through the room. The speaker said simply that Saskatchewan was

9. THE HONOURABLE LEFT-HANDED GOVERNOR

a better place because of "all the good things that you have done." Roy Romanow spoke of Sylvia's ability to combine the "dignity" of the lieutenant-governor's office with an "informal common touch," and her love of children, fishing, and the north gave "a very special human and personal dimension" to the vice-regal position. Rick Swenson, speaking for the opposition Conservatives, reiterated a simple message: despite stories to the contrary, Sylvia Fedoruk's life and career proved that a young person could, in fact, stay in Saskatchewan and build an accomplished, exemplary career. The speaker gave Sylvia a gift from the legislative members: a three-day stay for a wildlife expedition in the Cypress Hills, where she would enjoy early morning elk bugling, a moonlight coyote howl, and trout fishing. "I wish you good weather, good fishing, and no mosquitoes."[99]

Sylvia then spoke. After welcoming two groups of schoolchildren to the house, she freely admitted that during the speeches "a few odd tears dropped down." But then, she said, "I am of Slavic origin. We cry at funerals, weddings, christenings, everything." The position was not a job, she said, so much as a series of adventures. "I have thoroughly enjoyed being the Queen's representative in the province of Saskatchewan." Musing, Sylvia regaled the room with her three biggest learnings from the position: first, the position is more than ceremonial and is actually integral to the workings of the Saskatchewan government; second, she had a much higher appreciation for the hard work and long hours of all members of the Legislative Assembly, both inside and outside the chamber; and third, her travels north and south, east and west, across the province taught her about the "vitality and initiative" of Saskatchewan people. It's the people, she said, that are Saskatchewan's "most precious resource." Then Sylvia rose, departed from the chamber, and went back to the landau to get ready to host a farewell dinner at Government House.[100]

As Sylvia moved toward the end of her term, friends and relations took the opportunity to visit, for the first time or one last time, at Government House. Some arrived for the major government festivities, to be introduced in the legislature and watch Sylvia perform formal duties one last time, giving royal assent to bills. Others came for teas and evening dinners, soaking in the elegance of Government House and shaking hands with the provincial political elite. A few had more quiet, personal visits, including cousins Rod and Cathy Fedoruk and their children. An afternoon visit to

Government House included tours and photographs and time spent with both Sylvia and Irene White. One of the children, listening to Irene speak about the role, came to the same understanding as the young man at Weyburn a few years before: Sylvia Fedoruk served as the "left-handed governor" of Saskatchewan. "When I tried to correct her," Cathy wrote to Sylvia, "she was quite adamant that Mrs. White referred to you as the 'Lefthanded Governor.'"[101]

Living in the fishbowl of political life, despite fond memories and tears, Sylvia now looked forward to finally entering retirement. But the regret was palpable, nowhere more so than in her dayplanner. Her things were packed in Regina, moved to Saskatoon, and unloaded during a brutally rainy May that flooded her basement at Simpson Crescent yet again. Sylvia spent the next few weeks unpacking boxes while sorting out wet rugs, roofing, and electrical fixtures and trying to fix the recurrent problem of flooding. Her last official visit as lieutenant-governor was in Saskatoon, on the University of Saskatchewan campus at the Diefenbaker Centre, to attend and give brief remarks at the opening of an exhibit. Then her duties were finished. On May 31, the legislature reconvened, and aides-de-camp came to lower the flag outside her front door. Sylvia couldn't watch. In Regina, the new lieutenant-governor, Jack Wiebe, was sworn in. Her notes are sad: "And so the team of the 17th LG of Sask Sept 7-88 to May 31-94 comes to an end."[102] It was important, as per all of her most significant life milestones, that Sylvia considered her work as lieutenant-governor to be, indeed, a team effort.

There is no doubt, though, that Sylvia made an indelible mark not only on the Saskatchewan cultural landscape but specifically on the role and position of the lieutenant-governor. Her determination to visit schools, children, and the north created important paths for others to follow. The New Year's Day levee, expanded and honed, became an institution—though not, apparently, outside Regina. Under her guidance, Government House finally shook off its cobwebs of neglect, owned up to its refurbishment, and stepped firmly into the local and provincial tourism, public, and political scenes. Sylvia's willingness to attend an astonishing number of events per day put pressure on subsequent lieutenant-governors to keep up with her standards. As the pace quickened, office staff and responsibilities expanded, taking Government House from quaint side spectacle to a major and integral part of Saskatchewan political life.

9. THE HONOURABLE LEFT-HANDED GOVERNOR

Nonetheless, as sad as Sylvia was to leave the position, she could borrow some happiness from Charli, ecstatic that his all-too-frequent trips to the kennel, no matter now nice it was, suddenly stopped. Sylvia and Charli were able to return to Saskatoon in her car, with its specialized CHARLI licence plate, in time to plant her garden, reconnect with friends at the annual Slobstick golf tournament, and generally give up being the "left-handed governor" and get back to being just right-handed "Syl."

10. HURRICANE

FROM SPORTS TO WORK TO VOLUNTEERING TO NATIONAL and international science positions, to being chancellor and then lieutenant-governor, Sylvia Fedoruk was rewarded for her amazing accomplishments. Given the highest national and provincial honours, awarded honorary degrees, invited to give speeches and steal the show as a housekeeper in a local theatrical production, Sylvia was a media favourite. But in all lives there are storms, some of which come not from one's own making. Her storm came late in life, and it arrived as a punishing hurricane of social activism, art, and media that coalesced around and was directed specifically at Sylvia by graduate student Christopher Lefler at the University of Saskatchewan.

Ironically, Sylvia's accomplishments—scientist, chancellor, lieutenant-governor—appeared to draw his attention. Lefler saw Sylvia as symbolic of a society built upon silence and personal pain, reinforcing heteronormative cultural parameters that relegated homosexuality to a place of personal shame and deception. He used controversial artistic practices rooted in social activism to draw attention to catastrophic anguish over AIDS deaths in a contemporary Saskatchewan political cultural climate in which being gay was unwelcome.[1] His activism aimed to force a particular conversation, and his leverage point was Sylvia's connection to and obvious love for the University of Saskatchewan and the province. These connections were at the core of her personal brand of achievement and influence, volunteerism, cheerleading, and life work. Winding down from a successful run as lieutenant-governor, Sylvia enjoyed a relationship with her home province in which she was not only loved but also *beloved*.

As Lefler's actions unfolded, some Saskatchewan institutional and government leaders and media tried to mitigate and contain those actions by building a wall of protection and privacy around Sylvia. Their decisions and directions implicitly reinforced existing power dynamics via explicit choices about which and whose rights to uphold and defend (privacy rights, including issues of libel and decency, or artistic freedom and freedom of expression).[2] These are complex issues that some will find painful, but ultimately the following is a story of fierce loyalty.

Sylvia's first brush with Lefler, as described in the previous chapter, was as an invited dignitary for the Day Without Art protest at the University of Saskatchewan in December 1992. At the time, Christopher Lefler had just arrived at the university, the recipient of a $12,000 graduate student scholarship, with a proposed and accepted research program that aimed to confront issues of power, queer activism, and sexual politics. Lefler, an openly homosexual man, practised political activism using art as a medium. His work was dramatic and performative, designed to rock viewers back onto their heels or invite them to watch, step in, touch, smell, read. It was in the *experience* of Lefler's pieces that the *art* was performed. A more traditional artist-viewer relationship showcases the result of the artist's work, and the role of the audience is to offer appreciation or critique.

Lefler's art was different. It involved, invited, even demanded response. Audience was integral. Without the reaction of the audience, his art was incomplete. To ensure audience engagement, Lefler, who began his artistic career as an undergraduate at the University of Victoria, moved increasingly to craft art installations designed to elicit conversation, even fury.[3] Well centred within a larger North American artistic practice, his art was cutting-edge, controversial, and shocking for an essentially rural and small-town province such as Saskatchewan. From an artistic perspective, his work was articulate, well grounded, and theoretically rich. Lefler was initially welcomed and supported by the university via a graduate scholarship, an adviser, space to work, and collegiality.

On Valentine's Day 1993, two months after the thwarted Day Without Art protest, Lefler wrote to Fedoruk, sending the letter to Government House, Dewdney Avenue, Regina. Many letters

10. HURRICANE

arrive each week to the lieutenant-governor: invitations, announcements, commentaries, general correspondence, warm felicitations, letters from prisoners requesting pardons, letters from friends and acquaintances, raging missives from taxpayers and citizens angry about government decisions, and the odd letter from kooks. Delivered by Canada Post and opened by staff, the letters were sorted and answered as necessary. Some were read and given personal responses by Sylvia. Anything deemed suspicious or threatening was routinely passed over to the police.[4]

Lefler's letter[5] was neither suspicious nor threatening, but it was bold, full of pain and anger, and appears to have struck its intended reader like a hammer blow. Lefler's letter accused Sylvia of silence, of not using her position as lieutenant-governor to advocate for the rights of Saskatchewan's gay and lesbian community or defend those rights from politicians advocating an anti-homosexual agenda. "A group of hate mongers in this province Sylvia, have been persistent at describing homosexuals as intrinsically evil, and continue to misconstrue our demand for EQUAL rights into SPECIAL rights." Silence, he charged, is damning. "It is known that you, as the Queen's Representative can and could have over the past many years, voiced your outrage over . . . hateful comments. . . . But I suppose you made a choice not to. I and so many others however, have had to live with that decision. That denial. That contempt. That hate mongering. That violence." Lefler included along with the letter a pamphlet distributed by a Progressive Conservative MLA as proof of provincial political homophobia.

The letter went a step further, and that step unleashed the hurricane. Lefler's letter seemed to be driven by two fundamental and linked assumptions: the letter accused Sylvia of being a secret—"in the closet"—lesbian, and of not using her position to advocate for social reform. The letter asserted that Fedoruk's many accomplishments were achieved only by hiding her sexual orientation. But her orientation, according to Lefler, was actually "known . . . in the dark shadows and discreet whispers," a secret widely shared but blinkered, confined to knowledge shared privately rather than out in public space. The letter's confident assertion about Sylvia's private personal life could only have come via stories shared with Lefler by others on campus or in Saskatoon. He had no other ties to the province. Someone described Fedoruk as a known secret lesbian, providing Lefler with a story of group participation in a fiction that Sylvia was hiding in plain sight. The alleged open secret seemed to have been the starting point for Christopher Lefler's decision to focus his artistic practice on Sylvia Fedoruk.

Lefler's letter should be understood as a war cry of a younger homosexual generation against an older one. That cry forced a realization that in being reticent about homosexuality, in being silent, hiding, and not being seen or letting their voices be heard, the older generation of homosexuals were in fact part of the problem and not the solution. The younger generation, of which Lefler was a pivotal figure, invited the hidden voices of the past to come out into the open, to add their voices to the fight for equality, the fight for human rights, the fight to live homosexual lives in the open.

It's difficult to understand what Lefler meant this letter to do. Did he think that it would shock Sylvia into action? That she would, indeed, "come out" as a lesbian just because he sent her that letter? That Sylvia would become a public figure leading the work to address sexual-based inequality and stigma, which, in the early 1990s, still engulfed the province? It is ironic to recall that Lefler's *Masquerade* art protest at Day Without Art effectively subverted his own agenda. Sylvia had been scheduled to appear, which would have been viewed as support for the AIDS crisis and the homosexual community in general. His protest likely factored into her decision not to attend. Lefler's Valentine's Day letter also indicated a complete absence of knowledge of Sylvia Fedoruk's personality and public activism. Sylvia had never been a public advocate for social justice; at best, she was a supporter of the nuclear industry, women in science and sport, and better cancer research. She was not and never had been a social justice warrior or leader in any movement for change. If Lefler aimed to get her to lead a public conversation about the legal and moral morass of homosexuality in Saskatchewan in the midst of the AIDS crisis of the 1990s, then he missed the mark.

Even with its possibly misguided intention and outrageous language, the letter also clearly showed Christopher Lefler's pain. "So can you answer, Sylvia? Can you know my tears, can you feel my rage?" he asked. He also reached out. He assumed that Sylvia was an unacknowledged lesbian, bound by the perils and memories of a time period when it was illegal to be gay. "I wonder, Sylvia, how isolated you must be," Lefler wrote.

If Lefler was right and Sylvia was a gay woman, then indeed she would have had a difficult life. Pierre Elliott Trudeau had removed homosexuality from the criminal code only in 1969—almost twenty

10. HURRICANE

years after Sylvia had entered the working world as a professional. A member of the federal Science Council by 1972, followed by her appointment to the Atomic Energy Control Board in 1973, Sylvia, even if she had been a lesbian and wanted to come out, would scarcely have had the opportunity to do so. The federal government operated under the assumption that being homosexual could be a leverage point for blackmail; Sylvia, on the AECB, would have lost her position.[6] She resigned from the AECB only when she became lieutenant-governor—again a position in which open homosexuality might have struck her off the contender list. Lefler was also right to note that Saskatchewan lagged behind other jurisdictions in bringing homosexual and non-conforming relationships into human rights codes and amendments.

Lefler imagined Sylvia to be living a life of loneliness, isolation, and fear. His letter contained humanity alongside vitriol and pain. It was then, and is now, an uncomfortable letter to read. It was meant to be.

Neither Sylvia nor her staff knew quite what to do with it. Was the right path to ignore the letter, reply to it, or perhaps call in the police? There was no threat, nothing illegal in the words, though perhaps distasteful and possibly for Sylvia embarrassing and, to our current sensibilities, an invasion of her personal life.

Government House chose to pass the letter over to Bob Mitchell, then minister of justice and attorney general for the province under Premier Roy Romanow, to solicit professional advice. There is a connection between the office of the lieutenant-governor and the provincial government. The premier's office needed to know that the letter existed and had been sent to the sitting lieutenant-governor. What, Sylvia asked, should be done next?

Mitchell decided that the letter did merit a response. On March 19, Sylvia noted a meeting with the attorney general in her day-planner: "Mr. Mitchell re letter from the U of S grad student. He feels a response is necessary and will prepare for me."[7] That is a point worth repeating: the attorney general for Saskatchewan was given the letter, he deemed it of merit, and his office reputedly crafted the reply. It was not acceptable that the letter be quietly ignored; on the contrary, the top legal team in the province developed the response, according to Sylvia's notes.

On Government House stationery dated April 8, 1993, the letter was written, signed, and mailed. There is a sincerity in the reply but also a steely nerve. Thanking Lefler for his letter, the response crisply told him that he was out of line in two ways. First, the Office of Lieutenant-Governor was mainly a ceremonial role, with little ability to affect public policy. Second, the Office of the Attorney General adopted a personal tone, writing as if it were Sylvia speaking: "I think you have made cavalier and unwarranted assumptions about my own personal situations. Furthermore, you make these statements in quite cruel language, which is itself contrary to the respectful way in which you rightly argue that you should be treated as a gay man."[8] For a man requesting that the public act in a more civil and respectful way toward the homosexual community, the bitter and accusatory tone of the letter was indeed "contrary."

What neither Fedoruk nor Mitchell knew was that Lefler's artistic practice was based in part on collecting and exhibiting documentary evidence. As was common in the early 1990s, politically motivated artists working in areas related to power dynamics (race, class, gender, sexuality, institutional power, and so forth) would regularly keep or record correspondence or notes. It's a practice centred on making the invisible visible.[9] By crafting a reply to Lefler on behalf of the sitting lieutenant-governor, the attorney general's office unwittingly thrust Sylvia into an even more awkward and uncomfortable position. Lefler's true goal was to receive a letter in reply, a paper trail of correspondence. And the attorney general's office, not Sylvia (though she signed it), gave it to him.

Nothing further happened for many months, and no doubt Government House and the attorney general's office believed that their letter ended the correspondence. In the meantime, Lefler continued his artistic and scholarly work on power dynamics, art, and sexual politics. An articulate and thoughtful colleague and graduate student, he had developed deep friendships that moved beyond the university walls to Saskatoon's local arts community. Described as sweet, generous, and warm, Christopher spent time as a volunteer for various groups, hosted or attended dinner parties, and was both a popular guest and a great cook. One close friend was a single mom with a son, and Christopher taught him to ice skate, bringing the boy home on his shoulders from their sessions, both of them wreathed in smiles.[10] His scholarly and artistic practice might have been political and controversial, but as a person Lefler enjoyed a wide circle of warm friendships.

In the fall of 1993, he participated in an adjudicated, student-led art exhibition called *Staging Identities I* at the University of Saskatchewan. The students meant to explore how art intersected with their individual identities. Lefler, as he had expressly told supervisors and the art department, would create art designed to make the "invisible visible" and that he would specifically create art to address the practice of *outing*.[11]

Outing was, and remains, a highly controversial topic within the broader LGBTQ[12] community. Simply defined, it is the practice of publicizing someone else's sexual orientation or gender identity without that person's consent. It raises serious issues of privacy, libel, slander, and harm, let alone truth; few consider such practices ethical. A person who aims to "out" another usually chooses someone with social power or influence, such as a movie star, an athlete, or a politician. It is in such cases that the strongest arguments *for* the practice of outing are made. The argument is that, if society knows which prominent and influential people are gay and doing great jobs in their positions or leadership roles, then outing might help to confront social stereotypes and change the conversation in new ways. Lefler's letter to Sylvia made the same point: "What could you have said Sylvia, as a scientist in medical physics, as the most legally and media powered person in this province, and as a Lesbian?"[13]

The most extreme cases of outing target people who use their power to actively hurt the homosexual community. In this case, it becomes a weapon not of change but of retaliation, used when the person in power has made political or other decisions that hurt specific homosexual people or the larger homosexual community. But even in these possibly more acceptable cases, the practice is based on subversive and unexpected force and power, inverting the power dynamic from the politician or leader to the activist doing the outing. It therefore can be both a cruel and a crude political weapon. Outing has been known on occasion to cause both personal and professional harm to the individual outed or to cause few ripples at all.

Saskatchewan had been grappling with issues of privacy, debated and passed on the floor of the legislature and given royal assent by Sylvia Fedoruk herself. *The Freedom of Information and Protection of Privacy Act*, and *The Local Authority Freedom of Information and Protection of Privacy Act*, were two pieces of legislation introduced and passed under the Grant Devine government. Landmark acts, they sprang from an intent to promote freedom of information, "to make the government more open and allow people to play a more direct role in the government," and to "provide the public with the right to know the activities of [the] government as it touches their personal lives, while at the same time safeguarding the information that [the] government has on private citizens."[14] Sylvia spoke these words at the infamous prorogation speech of the Saskatchewan legislature in the evening of June 18, 1991. These acts, responding to public perception of government non-disclosure, aimed to make the government more accountable by creating freedom of information laws. Of course, there should be strictures on information, hence the concurrent definition of privacy rules. Recently in place, these laws had yet to be fully tested or understood in the Saskatchewan context. Moreover, the original privacy act did not explicitly protect sexual orientation.[15] The Roy Romanow government had just amended *The Saskatchewan Human Rights Code* in June 1993 to add sexual orientation, a move that should have done much to appease Lefler. But by then he had received the response letter from Government House.

Lefler's art installation for the *Staging Identities I* exhibit at the Gordon Snelgrove Gallery on campus on Monday, November 22, 1993, was deceptively simple and perhaps not immediately understandable as art. There was a chair, a black binder on a desk, and above the desk a poster image from the university's Day Without Art. Standing back, there was little to see—the desk looked like the typical desk of a student or even a professor or administrator. Stepping close, things were different. Inside the binder, should a person choose to open it, were the two letters: the one from Lefler to Fedoruk, and the Government House reply. Lefler's art was based on simple correspondence, but the artistic impact and power dynamic lay in the reader's response to reading a letter that called Sylvia a secret lesbian. Truth had no bearing; the suggestion bore all the power.

What ensued was a maelstrom that engulfed first the university, then the media, and then the provincial government in an all-out effort to erase the art exhibit, silence Lefler, and keep Sylvia's name out of the media. The energy expended to contain the impact of that art installation worked, in fact, as all energy does, to bring on an equal and opposite reaction. The university removed the binder; Lefler replaced it. It was removed again, and the gallery was temporarily closed.[16]

Behind the scenes, there was administrative chaos. Patrick Browne, then the vice-president academic, worked to correspond with the art department and Lefler. Iain Maclean, the university secretary, called Sylvia. Her Monday morning had been routine.

10. HURRICANE

There were Christmas cards and gifts to get organized. She spoke by phone with Dale Eisler, at the time a *Regina Leader-Post* reporter, to provide background information for a story. Her engagement diary hums with the contentment and busyness of a popular lieutenant-governor. By that afternoon, all contentment was swept away. Sylvia was on the phone with Maclean for hours. Her senior administrator, Irene White, put a call through to Liberal MP Ralph Goodale, who had just been elected in Regina-Wascana. A lieutenant-governor serves at the request and discretion of the prime minister, not a premier. As a result, it was critical to keep the local MP, and thereby Ottawa, up to date with all issues. Lefler's adjudicated art installation was perceived as the outing of a major public figure. The somewhat frantic efforts at containment by the University of Saskatchewan (removing the binder, interfering with an art exhibit) were a story that could explode in the media.[17]

All that week Christopher Lefler battled the university, trying to reset the exhibit, while the university repeatedly ordered him to refrain from any further public action. The university deemed the exhibit reprehensible, offensive, and "potentially libelous" and detailed its response in letters—the very medium that Lefler prized as part of his artistic practice. The university letters charge that Lefler's binder, desk, and chair installation "does not constitute art in any sense of the word." Lefler was warned that "failure to comply ... will result in your immediate suspension from the University and could lead to your expulsion." By Friday, the university acted. Lefler was suspended from campus and prohibited from entering university grounds or buildings during the period of his suspension. Campus police were informed.[18] Over the following week and weekend, the news finally broke beyond the insular campus community to the broader media. By Monday, December 6, CBC was calling Government House. Sylvia, supported by her staff, refused to grant an interview. She called Bob Mitchell, who told her to keep a low profile and go on with business as usual, attending scheduled engagements.[19] By December 8, the *Saskatoon Star-Phoenix* printed the gist of the story under the headline "Art Student Suspended, Banned for Exhibit." The report went on to say that the university found the work defamatory and libellous. The reporter added that "the work claimed a prominent Saskatchewan official is homosexual" without naming her.[20]

Sylvia's day-books hum with fear that the media would drop their discretion and reveal her identity. With few unmarried women within the provincial government, Sylvia noted in her day-book "more and more concerned. 'Could be maybe only two people.'"[21] It seemed to be a matter of time before she was publicly connected. But her fear was never realized in the print media. By what appears to have been tacit agreement, none of Saskatchewan's major daily newspapers, or their national counterparts carrying the story, ever published Sylvia's name in connection with the public controversy over Lefler's work, though the story itself made headlines. Instead, they simply followed the *Star-Phoenix*'s example by referring only to an unnamed "prominent Saskatchewan official."[22] Radio and television news directors did their part too. None granted Lefler a live interview, knowing that he would—and did—try to say Sylvia's name.

These apparently sympathetic (and probably legally prudent) measures by the media gave Sylvia media-sanctioned anonymity. Media managers regularly consider issues of libel and defamation, and the papers and broadcasters believed that they, like the university, had cause for concern. The popular lieutenant-governor was a media and public darling, and this story might have seemed to be the ultimate in betrayal. To expose Sylvia Fedoruk to the possible public backlash of a province still riven by homophobia, even through balanced, fact-based news reporting, was almost unthinkable. Lefler appeared to have no such compunction and spoke willingly to media, even to the point of seeking them out. Editing departments scrambled to slice and splice interviews to remove Sylvia Fedoruk by name, though the media stories continued to churn.

By December 8, Lefler's supervisor in the art department withdrew. The next day the university rescinded Lefler's scholarship funding, a move that Iain Maclean immediately reported to Sylvia.[23] The editor of the campus newspaper, *The Sheaf*, was called to the administration building and told not to print the story that it had written about the whole affair. The editor, in shock, complied.[24] Lefler and his art had been dealt with by the university in the most convincing and unflinching manner: Lefler stripped of funding and barred from campus pending a hearing regarding expulsion and the campus student newspaper told to shelve its story. As students moved into exams and the Christmas break, it's possible that many drew a quiet breath.

Did Sylvia request the measures taken by the university? It's impossible to know. Would she really have sued either the university or the media if they had reported her name in connection

10. HURRICANE

with Lefler's artistic installation? That's an improbable assumption. What is clear is that the university made an adamant and absolute choice. Forced to decide between protecting the artistic and scholastic freedom of expression of a graduate student and protecting the reputation, feelings, and privacy rights of Sylvia Fedoruk as previous student, employee, chancellor, and philanthropist, there was no debate. The university, and the media, threw their energy into protecting Sylvia.

That choice sent shock waves throughout many Saskatchewan circles. Although the media officially kept Sylvia's name from public view, the unofficial oral counterstory was on fire, blazing around supper tables, in classrooms and offices on campus, in newsrooms, on the streets, in quiet conversations, spreading outward. Containment was impossible. Some university students were appalled and questioned the heavy hand of administration. The arts community, both within and beyond the university, was outraged and split. Proper protocol had not been followed to remove the art installation, which, after all, had been adjudicated. Removal without discussion was tantamount to censorship. At what point, others wondered, was controversial art too controversial, and whose job was it to decide? Art students in classes at the time remember being told that Sylvia Fedoruk travelled around to small rural communities. She could be physically assaulted or otherwise hurt or embarrassed if people chose to shun her if they believed Lefler's story. That was the reason given for withholding her name.[25]

The province's gay and lesbian community was deeply divided. Some decried the practice of outing as akin to terrorism and reprehensible. The only time that such a practice could be acceptable is when the outed person is in a position of authority and uses that authority to persecute others.[26] Sylvia might have been the titular head of the province's government, but her real authority or leadership was limited. She certainly had never used her authority to persecute the province's gay and lesbian community; in fact, her aborted attempt to appear at the Day Without Art event on campus signalled her support for that community.

Others, though, wondered whether the issue had more to do with Lefler's stated homosexuality than his original art installation or attempt to out Sylvia. Perhaps, they suggested, the real issue was institutional homophobia. By the early 1990s, the university hosted a student-run club called Gays and Lesbians at the U of S (GLUS) and regularly ran stories in *The Sheaf* regarding minority and equal rights. These efforts signalled a large measure of progression since the university's handling of the Doug Wilson affair in 1975.[27] The university as an institution, in welcoming and supporting Lefler as a graduate student, also embraced his sexual orientation and political stance, since these were part and parcel of his art—until he directed that art toward Sylvia. Lefler lodged a formal complaint against the university to the Saskatchewan Human Rights Commission under the new provincial rules, citing its removal of his art installation as discrimination based on sexual orientation and infringement on his freedom of speech.[28]

The legal community was equally invested in the story. Was the original art installation, in fact, defamation of character or libel? Is it defamation of character to say that someone is a lesbian instead of a heterosexual? It would only be libel if the statement were untrue. What was the role of the new privacy law, which did not cover sexual orientation? Since privacy laws are rarely if ever strong enough to cover the privacy of public figures, could the new law, in fact, be invoked in this instance? Was Sylvia Fedoruk, as the appointed crown representative, a true public figure in the same way as an elected official? Those who advocated for women's and gender rights were also conflicted. Was Lefler invoking traditional patriarchy as a man effectively and deliberately invading a woman's privacy? Why not direct his ire at outing a male Saskatchewan corporate or elected government leader instead of a well-liked and respected but essentially vulnerable woman? Debate raged.

Instead of dissipating, the controversy grew throughout the winter, hitting national news, aided and abetted by Lefler, who shared his story. His work, from an artistic point of view, was not fully in action until and unless the media publicly connected his story with Sylvia Fedoruk. *The Sheaf*, which had started to cover the story in defiance of university administration, created a tag line for its February 17, 1994, issue: "Sired by a Hurricane, Dam'd by an Earthquake." The hurricane was Lefler and his activities and activism; the earthquake was the university and the Saskatchewan media working to dam and contain the response.[29]

On welfare, waiting for the university disciplinary hearing, Lefler continued to try to connect his work with Sylvia. The media move not to publish her name in effect created a wall of silence that thwarted his artistic practice and core point. In February, Lefler created a poster campaign both on the university campus (security did not escort him off the premises) and in targeted public spaces in

10. HURRICANE

Saskatoon such as Broadway Avenue and downtown. The posters again named Sylvia, but once again the press chose not to publish her identity while reporting the story. But Sylvia knew: her engagement diary notes a CBC Radio news brief about Lefler and the posters, followed by more media clippings of the affair. By the 21st, she had once again spoken with Bob Mitchell, deciding "no statement at present time."[30] Then again, what statement could Sylvia possibly make? An outright denial with proof of her heteronormativity would have nipped the whole story back in November. Many construed her public silence as an indication of the truth of Lefler's statement. Sylvia was backed into a corner, with no way out.

In today's social media age, the screen of privacy cast by the media around Sylvia would not exist. A picture of the original art installation shared online, or of the posters in February, would have connected Sylvia directly by both name and picture. The pre–cell phone technology of the early 1990s allowed the fiction; today the many sides of the story (institutional power, artistic censorship, the controversial and cruel practice of outing, privacy rights versus the right to free speech, the homosexual right to equality, and so forth) would be contested public discourse. Social media today, for most current issues both good and bad, lead and shape how institutions and other media respond, instead of the other way around.

The university closed Lefler's disciplinary hearing to the public, contrary to usual practice, again in an effort to protect Sylvia. It also delayed the date to May, after the bulk of students had left campus. Undaunted (or perhaps provoked) by these measures, Lefler engineered a major media story for his hearing. He sent out invitations, stating that "the University of Saskatchewan in conjunction with Christopher Lefler presents *The Wedding: Closet*." Arriving at the closed hearing down the halls of the new Department of Agriculture building, Lefler walked within a performance art installation, handcuffed inside a rolling metal "closet" as a homosexual "bride" going to a "wedding." If the university wanted the whole story kept quiet, Lefler brought it back into the public eye—and the media recorded his procession for the evening news.[31] The three-person disciplinary hearing board decided, in a two-to-one split, to expel Christopher Lefler.[32]

Meanwhile, Sylvia Fedoruk was counting down the days to the end of her term as lieutenant-governor. Although her five-year term had been extended because of the federal election, it was set to finish at the end of May. Her day-timer hints at the unexpectedness of the decision to bring in a new lieutenant-governor; it seems reasonable to conclude that the Lefler story prompted an unanticipated and hurried change. The end of her term could and should have slowed the story, at least from her perspective. After all, Sylvia would no longer be a public figure, the original argument for outing her. But Lefler put the story right back in the public spotlight.

While waiting on welfare for his disciplinary hearing, Lefler applied for, and won, a $9,500 Saskatchewan Arts Board (SAB) grant to pursue his artistic work. His project aimed to create a public art display using the voluminous university and other correspondence and media paper trail at the heart of the entire story, some 300 pages of correspondence. The grant marked a major shift in the direction of the story.

The SAB, a publicly funded entity established in 1948, is one of the oldest public arts funders in North America. It is governed by a provincially appointed board of directors, much the same as other Saskatchewan cultural, historical, and artistic programs. The board of directors works with the executive director, who in turn leads staff and an extensive program of services and grants. The SAB had developed a juried granting process using a large and revolving cadre of professionals to serve as artistic peers, each selected for expertise in a particular art form.[33] The juried, arm's-length granting board viewed Lefler's application in the spring of 1994 highly, whether despite or because of the controversy or simply because Lefler, at age thirty-one, was an articulate, leading-edge practitioner of and advocate for his work. His style of art, viewed within a North American context in which art had moved squarely into social commentary and political advocacy, was right on target.

Whereas Lefler celebrated the tacit support of the arts community via the award, the provincial legislature was incensed. Throughout May 1994, the legislature rocked with debate, and opposition leaders pressured Carol Carson, the minister responsible for the Saskatchewan Arts Board, about this particular grant. At first, she defended the board, citing the traditional, arm's-length process that deliberately kept political interference at bay. But the opposition was vocal, insistent, and knew that they had at least some public backing. How could the SAB defend granting Lefler so much money when the University of Saskatchewan had just *expelled* him for the same work? Possibly believing that backing the arts board decision would create a political nightmare, Carson capitulated. She formally requested that the SAB review its decision.

10. HURRICANE

Valerie Creighton, then the SAB executive director, defended the arm's-length and expert nature of the granting process, pointing out that Lefler was one of fourteen successful applicants out of a field of 200—no small feat to impress the judges by that measure. His work, as Lefler explained to the media, "explores what information is public and private and who makes that determination."[34] Creighton argued that "the controversy is irrelevant."[35] The implications of the artwork regarding defamation of character (as in Sylvia's character) were apparently not part of the jury's discussion. As before, no one—not the media, not anyone speaking in the legislature, and not the arts board—mentioned Sylvia by name. By May 24, Carson turned her back on both the SAB and the jury. She called the grant an abdication of the jury's and the board's responsibility: "I apologize to anybody who has been harmed in any way by the action of the Arts Board. It is a concern to us. Under the legislation I do not have the authority to overrule the Arts Board decision. I will say that I believe that they have abdicated their responsibility."[36]

Cast aside by its own minister and in the eye of the public storm, the SAB capitulated. The board of directors reviewed the grant, with Chair of the Board Wayne Schmaltz investigating whether Lefler's application had been submitted "under false pretences." Schmaltz suggested that the application didn't seem to match Lefler's public statements, as recorded in the media frenzy throughout the winter.[37] The SAB board of directors conducted a full review, including of Lefler's application (which contained the original two letters and some of the ensuing university correspondence), a meeting with the jury committee, interviews with Lefler and some of his supporters, and a review of "all of the news reports surrounding Lefler's expulsion from the university." Their finding was not that the application was given under false pretenses; rather, their finding was that the original two letters constituted a violation and invasion of privacy. It's important to note that the issue for the arts board was different from the issue for the university. The university cited libel, but the SAB cited violation of privacy leading to defamation of character, which would "hurt" Sylvia. On that basis, the Saskatchewan Arts Board, for the first and only time in its history, revoked an adjudicated and awarded grant.[38]

The media contacted Lefler. He refused to comment until the media began referring to the prominent individual by name. "It's the media's responsibility now to start telling the truth because I'm carrying the burden for everybody."[39] Other groups clearly agreed that

Lefler should not be the only one appalled by the decision to revoke the grant. The Saskatchewan Writers Guild came out strongly to defend the autonomy of arm's-length juried decisions and castigated the SAB for bowing to political interference.[40] The Saskatchewan Arts Alliance, an umbrella group representing more than fifty Saskatchewan arts groups, was equally appalled. It demanded an explanation of the SAB decision and President Dawn Martin argued that "an important role of artists is to challenge norms." Being challenging can mean that "artists work on the fringe of lawfulness" in order to shine light on areas of darkness and secrecy.[41] One of the SAB board members, George Glenn, resigned in protest over the Lefler affair.[42] In a scathing review of the political fallout, commentator Vern Clemence cut to the heart of the story: "Does it violate a law to say that someone is heterosexual?"[43] Wayne Schmaltz, chair of the arts board, did not escape unscathed. A producer with CBC Radio's performance department in Regina, Schmaltz was called into the offices of his managers that September and following the meeting resigned from the arts board by "mutual agreement." Later he also resigned from the CBC.[44] Meanwhile, Lefler filed another complaint to the Saskatchewan Human Rights Commission (SHRC), this time regarding the arts board decision to rescind his grant.[45]

By this time, Sylvia had moved beyond her public role as lieutenant-governor, returning home to Simpson Crescent in Saskatoon and picking up the threads of a private life. The move made her case stronger. As a private citizen no longer bound by the strictures of her former role, she was no longer a fair target for Lefler's artistic practice, if indeed she ever was.

In any case, Lefler's life had been thoroughly broken by the Saskatchewan response. Evicted from the university community, stripped of his arts grant, and hemmed in by a press unwilling to print Sylvia's name, Lefler eventually left the province. The shunned outsider to Sylvia as the protected insider, Lefler could only wait while his two Saskatchewan Human Rights cases wended their way through their machinations.

By the fall of 1994, there had been a bit of time to think and reflect on the whole story, and for some members of the legal community there was much to consider, and not all of it was easy. Future federal court judge Jim Russell, then a Saskatoon resident and sometime law professor at the university, waded into the controversy. Charging that Lefler had been ostracized by mainstream media and the provincial government, Russell penned an article entitled "A Gaze Blank and Pitiless as the Sun." It exposed "the pervasive pall of parochial conservatism and homophobic superstition" of Saskatchewan at the time.[46] Russell also did what no mainstream media outlet was willing to do: he named Sylvia Fedoruk. Published in the alternative media magazine *Fuse*, the article aimed directly at the Saskatchewan halls of power. Only alternative media such as *Fuse* or non-Saskatchewan-based university student newspapers were willing to publish Sylvia's name. It is of note that her records contain no consideration of suing any of them for libel, slander, or invasion of privacy.

In the *Fuse* article, Russell registered shock over the "range and severity" of the "punishments" meted out to Lefler, which Russell called "frightening." Although the university, the provincial government, and the arts board declared Lefler's work potentially libellous, none of them dared to say that his work was, in fact, unlawful. Russell also pointed out that the university and the arts board used different reasons for their actions. The university called the work potentially libellous, whereas the arts board cited breach of privacy. Russell scathingly called both suggestions "equally bogus" with no legal base.

In what amounted to a public legal opinion, Russell cast a serious legal eye on the whole case. When, he asked, did Lefler cause real or imagined harm to Fedoruk? Russell also took aim at public media, which he thought had abdicated their responsibility to investigate the issues with rigour, instead siding with the official line that publishing the letters was a morally reprehensible act. "The end result of their actions [the media, government, university, and arts board] has been to encourage the . . . view . . . [that] homosexual orientation remains a matter for personal shame that reflects badly upon public dignitaries who happen to be inclined that way. This, of course, is precisely Mr. Lefler's point."

In all of this, Russell charged, two of the Saskatchewan communities most affected had been the most silent: the academic community and the gay community. Both, he suggested, likely feared reprisal, in whatever form. The academic community appeared to be unwilling as a whole to make major waves on behalf of a student against its own administration. There was opposition, but it was muted. The power dynamic was clear. The gay community, possibly fearing retaliation or funding withdrawal for precarious non-profit initiatives, or other kinds of censure, was also mostly quiet. The media found an ample number of articulate spokespeople from

Saskatchewan's gay community to publicly condemn Lefler's practice of outing. Some saw the larger effect of his ongoing media spotlight as instigating further marginalization or reversal of any gain or support for Saskatchewan's homosexual community. Lefler's supporters melted away.[47]

Saskatchewan as a whole (the media, university, provincial government, and by extension many Saskatchewan people though not everyone) valued Sylvia Fedoruk, a Saskatchewan-born and accomplished woman of excellence, substance, and poise, over Christopher Lefler, a homosexual man from somewhere else who arrived in the province inclined to create art deliberately designed to incite controversy. The fact that his work aimed to foster a larger conversation and consider unpleasant truths was not considered justifiable. The one story was easy to celebrate, the other difficult.

By 1996, the Saskatchewan Human Rights Commission ruled in Lefler's favour against the university on the issue of freedom of expression. The commission found that the university did not have enough evidence to act the way that it did, that the letter did not constitute enough to take away Lefler's freedom of speech by removing his art installation. But the commission dismissed all other charges against the university and all charges against the Saskatchewan Arts Board.[48]

Lefler's story was finally at an end, and so, by extension, was Sylvia's unwitting role as the object of his controversial stance on homosexuality, outing, and art as a tool of political change. His artistic practice, at least in terms of public support, was also finished. Cast to the edges of oblivion, Lefler was never again the recipient of any artist grant in Canada. The door was shut.

In the end, what was the impact of Christopher Lefler's work on Sylvia Fedoruk's life history? The story revealed by Lefler's work entered Saskatchewan's oral history and was folded into Sylvia's identity as truth. When the subject of the controversy came up in social media as I was writing this book, a typical response was "Oh. I thought that [her sexuality as a lesbian] was a given fact."[49] Others were mystified about why it was ever controversial. Sylvia's sexual preference, whatever it might have been, does not matter in today's society. Such an attitude reflects current society's difference from the Saskatchewan of the early to mid-1990s.

For some, the question has been *what does the Lefler story add to Sylvia's story except sensationalism?* I find that question baffling. The Lefler-Fedoruk outing controversy reveals much about how

Saskatchewan operated at the time: the heartrending context of the AIDS crisis, artistic expression and its connection to political activism, censorship, the highly problematic practice of outing, political interference, the social and political climate of homophobia at the time, institutional power dynamics, media containment and muzzling, the fallout and crisis of rescinding a juried arts board grant, legal parameters and implications, a consideration of Saskatchewan insiders and Saskatchewan outsiders—all add social context and depth to Sylvia's story. Had Lefler aimed his art toward almost anyone else in Saskatchewan, Sylvia's story of accomplishment would have been the same, but our understanding of her impact and reach, and the lengths to which so many Saskatchewan institutions went to protect her image as scientist-athlete-leader (as if her image would somehow be tarnished were she a lesbian), would be missing—and that's important to understand her true place in the Saskatchewan story. There is much here for all to ponder and to consider how far we have come, or not, as the case may be.

The final question is *but was Sylvia a lesbian?* The answer, from a historian's perspective, is simple: there is little evidence, and most of it is circumstantial, to say so definitively. Sylvia made no public declaration of her sexuality at the time, nor did I find any in her public archival holdings. A few suggestive photographs or letters, if read in a particular way, might indicate evidence to someone already predisposed or trained to see a lesbian inside joke, mannerism, or relationship code. Sylvia did cohabit with another woman for twelve years, and their relationship was warm, close, and filled with love. That does not mean that the historical record reveals anything more. Friends described her tastes as appreciative of *camp*, a homosexual code word for anything over the top and theatrically ironic, such as Liberace, of whom Sylvia was an ardent fan. Circumstantial evidence viewed in a particular way does not become fact.

There has been excellent published academic research on Saskatchewan's gay and lesbian community, including work on a Saskatoon group covertly identified as the "on-campus lesbians," none of which names Sylvia Fedoruk.[50] The core truth remains: if she was a lesbian, then she was not public in that statement. If her sexual orientation was a fact that Sylvia wanted to share freely and discuss publicly alongside sport and scientific and social accomplishments, then she would have done so. Innuendo and hearsay, or even images and words in her archival record, cannot be distinguished from that which Christopher Lefler set in motion—it is impossible to tell the two apart. Moreover, and because of the storm set off by Lefler, it is equally impossible to publish a biography of Sylvia Fedoruk and not consider the issue of her sexual orientation. In the end, ambiguity holds.

It is worth considering, though, that Sylvia might have been a gay woman. Certainly, that thought puzzle opens a new understanding of her life of achievement. Sylvia was free to travel extensively for work, to build an astonishing career, and to spend a lifetime searching for better cancer treatment, excellence in sport and sport administration, audacity in leadership, and grace as both chancellor and lieutenant-governor. An excellent card shark, fisher, well able to down copious quantities of liquor on occasion, brusque, demanding, and commanding, Sylvia leavened these possibly more masculine traits with a nurturing warmth for friends and colleagues, deep intuition, compassion, driving wit, and fearless humour. She was, in the end, simply Syl, in all her complexity and mystery.

Christopher Lefler had reason and the right to create his art, to believe in his view of the role and purpose of outing, to give voice to grief from many personal losses because of AIDS, and to practise art as a vehicle for social advocacy, agitation, and change. Sylvia Fedoruk had reason and the right to cherish privacy. Lefler's art had *nothing to do with her*, she said. But that isn't quite true. Her archive is full of the Lefler story, and it mattered to her. The University of Saskatchewan, the public media, and the provincial government in turn made their own choices, always with the intention of protecting Sylvia. These actions, above all else, show just how much she meant to the province that she loved. It was when Sylvia was in her darkest personal space that so many in the province rose up as her champions. Her character and legacy cannot be separated from the deep respect and love that she garnered during the most difficult moments of her life.

Lefler's story is a part of Sylvia's story—and not a small one. His legacy left a decisive impact on our collective memory and public assumptions about Sylvia. In the end, though, the core truth of the story is not her sexual orientation or his artistic practice. The core truth is about the tenacity of loyalty even when the path is dark.[51]

11. SUNSET

DRIVING BACK TO SASKATOON IN THE SPRING OF 1994, HER dog Charli in the car, his name emblazoned on the personalized licence plate, plants crammed into the back seat and bags in the trunk, Sylvia Fedoruk undoubtedly went home with mixed feelings. The apex of her life, working for almost six years as the queen's representative and highest public servant in the province, was finished. Sylvia was torn between regret and elation. Turning into the driveway on Simpson Crescent, she laughed out loud to see the front door festooned with a massive dot matrix banner shouting "WELCOME HOME SYL!" from Garry and Merylyn Vann. It was indeed welcome for Sylvia to find her way back, slowly and gingerly, to the life of a private citizen. "First occasion since leaving office—bit strange—no aide de camp—nobody to drive me here—open car door—back to the real world—find my own parking space—pay the parking toll. However it is a good way to enter the next phase of my life."[1] Charli once again settled into the routine of life on Simpson Crescent, and the aura of having been such a popular lieutenant-governor set the tone for the sunset years of Sylvia's life. Sylvia remained popular. From invitations to give speeches and lectures or to golf in charity classics, she remained just beside the main glare of the public spotlight, with the freedom to decline invitations a bit more, rest a bit more, golf and fish and garden and barbecue and visit more. The toll of the pace of years criss-crossing the province, combined with occasionally less-than-robust health and the continuing saga of Christopher Lefler, left Sylvia grateful for some quiet stillness.

Artist Cyril Leeper with his two portraits of Sylvia Fedoruk, 1994. Top: Sylvia as chancellor. Bottom: Sylvia as lieutenant-governor.

That's not to say that Regina, Government House, or the provincial government forgot about Sylvia. Although it is standard protocol for the previous lieutenant-governor to remain quietly in the wings for one to two years to allow the public time to adjust to the new crown representative, on occasion there has been formal leniency toward this stricture. One such instance was the royal visit of Prince Edward to Saskatchewan in the summer of 1994. Sylvia remained an ardent royalist, perhaps even more so after her stint as lieutenant-governor. Government House issued a formal invitation to Sylvia to attend the Regina festivities, which included a gala performance at the Globe Theatre of *Dancing in Poppies* by Gail Bowen and Ron Marken, followed the next evening by a barbecue buffet in the ballroom at Government House. Sylvia enjoyed the bittersweet return to the place where she so recently held the vice-regal position.

11. SUNSET

One more honour awaited Sylvia. On October 6, she returned to Regina for the unveiling of her official portrait as lieutenant-governor by artist Cyril Leeper. It was held in the reading room of the legislative library, and Sylvia carried excitement into the room. Pulling the cord to reveal the portrait, she was delighted to hear the gasp of appreciation from the crowd. Leeper had painted Sylvia sitting straight in an antique chair, familiar blunt haircut, no glasses, with a long string of pearls and a flowing patterned skirt, setting off her Saskatchewan Order of Merit, Order of Canada, and Order of St. John medals. Her 1994 Christmas letter refers to the hall of lieutenant-governors' portraits as "Syl and the Guys."[2]

By 1995, Sylvia's garden was once again in full production. By late summer, Sylvia and Joyce McKee had re-established their kitchen connection and met regularly to can, pickle, and process beans, dill pickles and dill carrots, zucchini relish, canned tomatoes, chili or tomato sauce and salsa, yum yum pickles, zucchini marmalade, cucumber relish, squash marmalade, pickled sweet peppers, mustard pickles, and freezer jam from saskatoons. A favourite recipe book came from one of the ladies' groups at Calder, Saskatchewan, not far from Wroxton, where Sylvia had grown up. Her day-book even records the page numbers from the cookbook for which recipes she would use.

Most cooks have a standout recipe, the one for which they are known. For Sylvia, it was Syl's Dills, and she could be found making up to twenty-nine quarts in one day. "Have to go back for more dill at farmer's market," she would note in her day-planner. Clearly, cucumber crops went through a briny transformation under her hand. Pickles can be a finicky product with an uncertain outcome. Good cooks and canners might share tips and tricks, such as adding a small amount of alum or cream of tartar ("the tip of a steak knife") to each jar of pickled carrots or dills to keep them crisp. Everything from the kind of cucumber used to the quality of the water matters. Syl's Dills recipe was a secret that Sylvia reputedly shared with no one—but eventually the requests wore her down. She allowed publication of the recipe in a Saskatoon-based cookbook.

Sylvia either commissioned or was gifted an artist's rendering for her Syl's Dills, showing her face at the top of a dancing crunchy classic dilly treat. Sylvia promptly scanned the picture and kept it on her computer to be printed off onto labels and affixed to her prized gift jars of dills.

Syl's Dills logo, artist unknown.

SYL'S DILLS

An avid curler, Sylvia Fedoruk was inducted into the Canadian Curling Hall of Fame in 1986, and in the same year was voted YWCA Woman of the Year. She was appointed to the vice-regal position of Lieutenant Governor on September 7, 1988.

RECIPE: put two pieces of dill in quart sealer (if not available, I use one tsp of dried dill seed). Fill jars with cucumbers.

ADD:
1 ½ Tbsp sugar
1 ½ Tbsp pickling salt
¼ tsp alum
1 or 2 cloves of garlic
½ cup vinegar.

Fill with boiling water* and seal. Stand upside down for a couple of hours to make sure they are not leaking. If they leak, I just boil the liquid again and pour it over the cukes and add boiling water as needed. *Important to use Saskatoon water.*[3]

11. SUNSET

The recipe suits a single woman, able to make one jar or twenty-nine jars, depending on what she has on hand. It's not a mass recipe but an individualized map, making just the right amount every time. Sylvia's stricture to use Saskatoon water reminds gardeners and canners about the importance of *terroir* or sense of place. If Sylvia tried to follow this recipe in Regina or Yorkton, the results would not have been as good. There was something in the Saskatoon water, and particularly in the water that came into her house in Saskatoon's Greystone Heights area, that mattered. Sylvia would take Syl's Dills to parties and potlucks and to people's houses as gifts. Rumour has it that she even smuggled a jar over to Buckingham Palace to give to the queen—but that story seems to be a bit of a stretch. Nonetheless, if you invited Sylvia to your house for a meal, chances were high that she'd come through the door with a jar of Syl's Dills tucked under her left arm, her right outstretched to shake your hand.

An important component of Sylvia's post-vice-regal retirement career, aside from pickling and canning, was her appointment as a member of the Board of Governors of the University of Saskatchewan in 1996. The board is constituted by eleven people, including the university's chancellor, president, and president of the student's union, as well as two members elected by the university's senate and one member elected from the faculty association. The remaining five members are appointed by the lieutenant-governor. Sylvia was an automatic member of this board when she was chancellor; this time she was appointed. She joined the board alongside M.L. (Peggy) McKercher, serving as chancellor, Sylvia's good friend and teammate from the Huskiette basketball team. Sylvia's appointment came the same year as the Saskatchewan Human Rights Board decision against the university in the Christopher Lefler case, which cited the university as being in error for not upholding Lefler's right to freedom of expression. The appointment was a subtle but unmistakable reaffirmation of the university's close relationship with and support for Sylvia. As ever, she was entirely worthy of the appointment and an excellent and active board member until 2005.

Retirement isn't always easy, and life has a way of bringing unwelcome change. Sylvia had long since lost her mother and father to cancer, and the disease was once again stalking a close family member, her special younger cousin Merylyn Vann. Confidante, companion, friend, cousin, and near sister, Merylyn had helped to steer Sylvia through the mysteries of clothes shopping, the fun of helping to raise Merylyn's son, Michael, the dark media shadow of the outing controversy, and the

Merylyn, Michael, and Garry Vann c. 1980s.

give and take of family life for holidays and for every day. Merylyn had fought cancer valiantly for years, undergoing treatments even as Sylvia worked as chancellor and then as lieutenant-governor. As adamant as Sylvia herself about the role and importance of education, Merylyn had vaulted to the top of Saskatoon's educational heap as superintendent of the Department of School Services in the Saskatoon School Division. But the cancer, kept so long at the edges, finally flooded through. Nine years of ebb and flow, remission and resurgence, had burst the floodgates. By Christmas of 1996, Sylvia's day-planner notes, "Merylyn really slowing down." On New Year's Eve 1996, Sylvia visited the Vanns, and they all had a "tearful talk."[4] Sylvia returned home and crawled into her PJs shortly after five in the afternoon. She couldn't make merry and be out and about, ringing in the New Year, with such news on the horizon. Merylyn succumbed on January 22, 1997. Sylvia, along with Garry and Michael, were devastated. A bright light, such a fixture in all of their lives, was gone.

While Sylvia walked through the grieving process for Merylyn in 1997, the following year brought a special and unique honour, much treasured and celebrated. The minister of national defence invited Sylvia to be the sponsor for a new ship being added to the Canadian fleet, Coastal Defence Vessel K709. Sylvia flew to Halifax for the ship's christening. It took her two tries—"the bottle did not break on the first blow but I gave it another whack"—before the ship was christened and slid down the ramp and into the water,

11. SUNSET

where the HMCS *Saskatoon* floated majestically. Sylvia waved from shore as the ship chugged away. After vigorous test exercises, HMCS *Saskatoon* sailed through the Panama Canal and back up to the BC side into Canadian waters. Sylvia flew to Esquimalt for the commissioning ceremony, after which she climbed "on board my ship for a most enjoyable four-hour cruise."[5]

Although the Sylvia Fedoruk fonds hold such moments of public recognition and delight, the personal is clearly foremost. Cancer continued to stalk Sylvia's world. Close friend Joyce McKee also succumbed. As with Merylyn, what began as breast cancer spread throughout Joyce's body. Rallying with drugs, Joyce managed to live a few more years, including some much-needed lake time with good friend Vera Pezer at the cabin, before finally passing away in late December 1999. The one-two punch of Merylyn and Joyce left Sylvia much saddened and with a smaller circle of people with whom she felt most comfortable. An email out to friends far and near in 2000 noted how much she missed Joyce: "She and I made a good team in canning and freezing," she reminisced.

Living alone had its hazards. Sylvia learned this lesson to great dismay in the summer of 2000.

> I fell on June 30, bounced down a couple of steps badly bruising my back and driving my leg into the back door frame—end result a badly broken right ankle. It took me several hours to drag myself to the nearest phone and 911. By ambulance to Royal University Hospital where I had to wait 2.5 days before my name came up for orthopaedic surgery (I was on a morphine high by the time I got to the OR), stayed in hospital for a week, and am now using a wheel chair, walker and occasional crutches to get along quite well on my own.[6]

Sylvia's passionate independence and bravado in telling the story put a gloss on a summer of pain and bruising. Whatever caused her to fall, she paid dearly for it. Supported by a large cast of characters and crew, including neighbours who watered her grass, flowers, and plants, her favourite kennel for Charli, a housecleaning service, and even a lady who came to the house to cut her hair, Sylvia healed.[7]

Soon after the turn of the millennium, Charli, sporting much grey in his black moustache and beard, quietly passed away in 2001. The grass grew for almost a year over his resting place before Sylvia, healed from her summer fall in 2000, decided once again to add a dog to her domestic situation. As her 2001 Christmas letter notes, "I have acquired a new puppy. Charli (age 17 years 9 months) went to doggy heaven last January and it became quite a lonely house by the time the golf season was over—so much so, that I weakened and adopted a toy poodle-cockapoo cross on October 2. MaxC is a very energetic dog that will make Christmas a very chewy experience this year. Tough being a mother at the age of 74!"[8] Much like Charli, MaxC did not get his name on his own. He took on the C in honour of his role as the third dog and to carry forward a little remembrance of Charli. He grew and was rambunctious and busy and "aggressive," according to Sylvia, a huge contrast to both Tinker and particularly Charli, whose old age, deafness, and slowness seemed to suit Sylvia's retirement. MaxC was having none of that. Sylvia soon learned not to keep anything within his reach. In early 2002, he found a pair of her glasses and gnawed them to pieces, and he was a terror with Christmas decorations. MaxC was also a notorious barker, so much so that Sylvia resorted to buying an anti-barking collar that would shoot a mist of citronella spray every time he let loose. "It seems to be doing the trick but only time will tell whether we've solved the problem."[9]

Sylvia's cousin Michael Vann remembered the contrast between Charli and MaxC. "To go from low-key elder statesmen dogs like Tinker and Charli to Max, wow! He had energy like you wouldn't believe. He would just run in circles around the living room, fly across your lap, run around the room. Definitely a contrast from the docile low key to him. He was demanding and high energy."[10] If Tinker liked ice cream and Charli liked French fries, Sylvia soon discovered that MaxC's favourite snack was fruit, in enormous quantities. She would go to Costco every week and buy a tray of pre-sliced fruit, which she and MaxC would consume for breakfast every morning. With such a healthy diet, it's no wonder that he had more energy than the other two.

Hitting age seventy-five in 2002, Sylvia reflected in her Christmas letter that age "rocks you a bit when it seems like yesterday when I arrived here in Saskatoon to begin my studies at the University of Saskatchewan. A lot of water has flowed beneath our bridges since then and I've certainly had many an adventure during the last 56 years." "As for my golf game," she continued, "the scores are not the greatest but the golf courses are superb. It is always nice to remember that as I am golfing, it is much better to be looking down

11. SUNSET

on the grass rather than up!"[11] She kept busy, enjoying as much time outdoors as she could, golfing with friends in good weather at Riverside Country Club, a private golf and country club on the southern outskirts of Saskatoon, nestled against the river.

Sylvia remained active on the university's board of governors, and one particular campus project caught her eye. A set of memorial benches had been installed at a scenic point near the coulee next to the cancer clinic. The benches were in a prime location, used and enjoyed by walkers, hikers, and bikers looping their way around the campus. The problem was that these benches memorialized people whose backgrounds had nothing to do with the cancer clinic or cancer treatment advances in Saskatchewan. At the time, Gordon Barnhart (who had been the clerk of the legislature when Sylvia arrived in Regina as lieutenant-governor and had been among her confidants during the special warrants crisis) had returned to Saskatchewan and taken the position as secretary of the university. Barnhart recalled her chagrin at these benches. Sylvia personally financed their removal to the other side of the street near the law department building and paid for two new benches to be installed at the site, which she called "cobalt plaza." The benches paid credit to three of Saskatchewan's founding leaders for cobalt-60: Dr. Harold Johns, Dr. T.A. (Sandy) Watson, and Dr. C.C. Burkell. A memorial plaque, co-written and registered through the Historic Sites and Monuments Board of Canada, carried a simple version of the cobalt-60 story: "In 1951, Canadian scientists, here and in London, Ontario, opened a new front in the battle against cancer. Through a pioneering partnership, the two teams of physicists, physicians and engineers, working independently yet co-operatively, designed the Saskatoon and the Eldorado (London) cobalt teletherapy units. Both became prototypes for the first commercially available units, then called 'Cobalt Bombs,' which allowed gamma radiation to be focussed directly on cancerous cells. Decades of effective worldwide use have proven the dependability of these units."[12]

On the side of one bench, Sylvia had another plaque affixed: "The Hon. Sylvia Fedoruk, O.C., S.O.M., M.A., D.Sc., L.L.D., D.Hum.L., F.c.P.M., Member of Board of Governors and Member of the team that developed the Cobalt 60 Unit, donated these benches August, 2002."[13] With the stone benches and plaques, Sylvia created a small but lasting memorial to the role of the university in critical early cancer treatment and added her own perspective on the so-called cobalt race—it was a "pioneering partnership . . . working independently but co-operatively" and not a race at all. After all, she should have known—she was there.

In retirement, Sylvia took great enjoyment in reviving an old passion from her graduate student days: gambling. A far cry from playing for nuts and bolts and screws in the storage room beside the betatron down in the back basement of the physics department building, Sylvia still had a sharp eye and quick decision-making for cards. Visiting a casino with friends such as Irene Bell and Vera Pezer became more than a quick gambling escapade. Visits would morph into excursions, complete with Sunday brunch at Dakota Dunes Casino south of Saskatoon, a few hours of gambling, and maybe a coffee or snack before wending their way home. Or they'd do it the other way around: gamble for a few leisurely hours, then eat a hearty lunch. The pull to the casino was twofold. Sylvia enjoyed gambling, be it on the slot machines or, on occasion, at the blackjack table for a little extra spice. She also loved poker, had enjoyed playing it among friends all her life and in her later years, would watch poker games on television, and played poker on trips to Las Vegas. A lifelong learner, Sylvia as often as not would watch others play just to hone strategy and insight.[14] The second pull of a casino, though, was cheap or even free food or drinks. Sylvia could never resist a good bargain.

Even with his mischievousness and boundless enthusiasm—or perhaps because of them—MaxC was a "great pal," Sylvia declared, full of energy and very bright, though apparently untrainable. Soon after acquiring him, Sylvia took the puppy off to school to try to instill some discipline. By 2005, she decided to take him again to weekly obedience training in Saskatoon. "He is making progress but there is much more work to be done before I will be able to take him for walkies without use of a leash."[15] Family members hinted, though, that Sylvia was just as untrainable as MaxC. For all her set ways and demands on herself and others, she could not be strict with her dogs. The consistency required for good training just wasn't there. More often than not, the poor dogs would be bombarded with multiple commands, issued pleadingly, one after the other. Confused and unsure, and not particularly inclined to listen, MaxC tended to ignore Sylvia. Even the groomers had comments about his disposition and listening skills. They advised her not to let him have the run of the house. As usual, Sylvia nodded in agreement and determination, but once she and MaxC were home he asserted his role as the alpha of the household, and Sylvia, somewhat helplessly and with chagrin, complied.

Saturday mornings would find Sylvia visiting the Saskatoon farmers' market, a favourite weekly excursion. For years, including in 1988, when Ray Hnatyshyn courted Sylvia to become the next lieutenant-governor, she loved poking around, questing for fresh eggs, excellent baking, and the kind of garden produce that she didn't bother cultivating in her backyard plot at Simpson Crescent. In 2007, the Saskatoon Farmers' Market moved indoors, taking over space in the new River Landing development in the former Saskatoon Light and Power electrical garage near the river on 19th Street. Sylvia's weekly excursions shifted with great enjoyment of the new space, especially on soggy mornings.

Annual trips north to stay with friends in cabins beside La Ronge or McPhee Lake to do a little fishing and relaxing were spring and summer mainstays. Sylvia continued with these trips as long as possible, laughing in utter delight at the feel of a trout or snarly jackfish fighting hard at the other end of her fishing line. Long walks at McPhee with MaxC pulling her along, sniffing contentedly, gave her tranquility and rest, while an evening tipple of single-malt scotch by a roaring fire or on the deck gave her the sense that the world was gently presenting itself as it should. These quieter visits contrasted well with the annual hootenanny of the Slobstick, the all-ladies weekend that brought gales of laughter, piles of steak, and hours of contentment and competition out on the links.

As a lifelong researcher always on the slicing edge of technology, Sylvia was an early adopter of home computer technology, and she learned to use her computer with panache. She had no fear. Unlike so many others of her generation, she was familiar with computers from her medical physics work and would regularly prove her mastery. Sylvia switched from snail mail letters to email, carried on correspondence with friends near and far, and diligently searched eBay for esoteric and rare curling pins. She also printed stickers for her famous Syl's Dills. As soon as scanners for home use became available, Sylvia bought one and set about creating professional scans of her extensive personal photograph collection. It was a self-archiving exercise, documenting her life and major accomplishments from family portraits, varied sports careers, science accomplishments, fishing, friendship, and fun. A lifelong photographer, Sylvia became adept at photo manipulation. Cousin Michael, returning from a visit to Hawaii, brought his pictures to show Sylvia. One was almost perfect, a sunset off the beach and a girl wearing a big floppy hat. But just at the last second a bystander moved, and there was an elbow in the picture. Michael groaned, but Sylvia snatched it right out of his hand and marched over to her computer. In no time, the picture was scanned, cropped, manipulated, and fixed. There! Friends would enlist her help with scans and snaps, and Sylvia spent hours working on the Slobstick picture archive to create digital and video records. Adept with and fascinated by what computers could accomplish, soon Sylvia was not only scanning but also embellishing pictures with comments and side stories for posterity.

Recounting her curling pin sleuthing and escapades to a friend in 2002, Sylvia noted that she "was absolutely delighted the other day when I acquired a medal that had been won by a Nova Scotia team when they toured Scotland in 1909. My biggest search right now is to find a pin that was issued when the first Ladies World was held in 1979."[16] Sylvia also yearned to buy a 1927 original first Brier pin. She heard a rumour that Henri Bouchard had one for sale and launched polite inquiries: "I'll ask again: have you a 27 Brier Heart for sale? If so, I'm extremely interested and know that it would cost me good money if we came to an agreement." He replied, "je suis désolé," for he had just sold it to a collector in Quebec. Sylvia was quick to reply: "If you are fortunate to find another, remember me."[17]

One retirement project of which Sylvia was most proud was as patron of the Western Development Museum's *Winning the Prairie Gamble* exhibit. It was a $6 million campaign project, and she was instrumental on the steering committee and in tapping friends to donate funds. Sylvia also viewed it as an opportunity to collect, augment, and write her own family history for the *Family History Album*. Saskatchewan had been a major site of local history writing and publishing since the 1960s, producing thousands of much-thumbed community history books. Sylvia was a leading proponent of the new online *Family History Album*, "excited about having thousands of Saskatchewan stories available to people who surf on the net."[18] Her own contribution, "Fedoruk, Theodore and Annie (Romaniuk) & the Hon. Sylvia O. Fedoruk" (published anonymously, as per her hallmark modesty), is her voice in the exhibit.[19] Sylvia's Western Development Museum compilation offered an important road map and clues for this biography.

Although Sylvia took fewer long international trips after her retirement, she enjoyed shorter trips to the United States, including Las Vegas and California, to soak up the sun, golf, gamble, and go to professional league baseball games and cultural events. One trip was a major highlight: a visit to Hawaii to celebrate the wedding of Michael Vann in 2004. It was an intimate family affair, and Sylvia was delighted to be included. A beach wedding at sunset, followed by a garlic shrimp feast, seemed to be the ultimate in luxury and lavish personal celebration. Touring Oahu and Maui, Sylvia enjoyed the Polynesian Cultural Center and Pearl Harbor. Other trips that year were closer to home. Sylvia was a guest speaker at the 100th anniversary of the Ukrainian Orthodox Church near Donwell, the church in which her parents had been married and in which she had been baptized. Her sense of history, as well as connection to family and home near Donwell, Hamton, and Rhein, remained strong.

As Sylvia moved through the ease of retirement, her closest and richest relationship continued to be with the University of Saskatchewan. Active on the board of governors, she attended installation ceremonies, balls, President's Club functions, retirement parties, openings of new buildings such as the Physical Activity Complex and the Canadian Light Source synchrotron, as well as meetings and committee work, helping to set the direction for the university into its future. The two things she enjoyed most, she reported in her 2005 Christmas letter, were the board dinners held at the president's house on the bank of the South Saskatchewan River and her parking pass. That, as anyone who has tried to find good parking on campus knows, was worth its weight in diamonds, uranium, and gold. An additional perk was an invitation once again—and for the last time—to meet Queen Elizabeth II at a reception at the president's house at the University of Saskatchewan in 2005.

One of Sylvia's favourite gifts of retirement was ample free time to spend watching sports and cheering, particularly her favourite varsity sports right on campus. Woe betide the referees if Sylvia and her old sports friend Vera Pezer were at a game watching Huskie women's basketball or volleyball or men's football. "If she was in the stands," Vera noted, "you'd hear her. All the refs would know she was there. She called them on every close play, every questionable call."[20] Toward the end of her cheering life, the Huskies gave Sylvia a jersey emblazoned with her name and the number 1, as the number one fan of the Huskies.

Sylvia also gave generous support to students pursuing science or sport. During her time as lieutenant-governor, she set up the Fedoruk Family Foundation in 1991 and continued making donations to it through 1996. As a non-profit corporation, the foundation set up a number of scholarships and fellowships for University of Saskatchewan students, giving between $8,000 and $10,000 per year across a variety of recipients. In 2004, the foundation was dissolved, and funds were transferred to the University of Saskatchewan Fedoruk Family Fund with an initial bequest of over $200,000. By the end of Sylvia's life, the fund would support three bursaries: the Merylyn K. Vann Bursary for students with disabilities, the Sylvia Fedoruk Award in Women's Basketball for Huskie athletes, and the Sylvia Fedoruk Scholarship for women majoring in physics or engineering physics.[21]

The close and lengthy relationship with the University of Saskatchewan—as a student, as a lecturer and professor with the Department of Physics and the College of Medicine, as a physicist at the cancer clinic on campus, as a chancellor, financial supporter, and donor, as a rabid fan, and as a member of the board of governors—was crowned in 2006 with one more accolade. For a lifetime of achievement and service to her home university, Peter MacKinnon as president escorted Sylvia across the stage to present her to Chancellor Tom Molloy to receive the Doctor of Laws (*honoris causa*). The University of Saskatchewan, the last university to do so, awarded her the title of doctor.

In time, her engagement diary emptied. "Quiet day" or "Lonely day" or reminders to watch favourite TV shows, such as *Frasier* or *The Sopranos*, replaced the golf, travel, fishing, and U of S events. As independent as she loved to be, Sylvia had been surrounded by people and busy, engaged, and active for so long that, as her mobility became first impeded and then impaired, her world shrank. Time slowed down. Aging wasn't an easy process for Sylvia. Athletes tend to remember when their bodies took them with great ease wherever they wanted to go and to do whatever they wanted to do. As the years added numbers and the scale added pounds, Sylvia's body slowed down. With great reluctance and no small measure of grief, Sylvia slowed down as well. She fought back by regulating her blood pressure, eating lots of fruits and vegetables, and forcing herself to keep busy. But a nasty fall in September 2006 was a harbinger of what was to come, and her mobility and steadiness increasingly became an issue. By 2007, Sylvia started going three days per week for a ninety-minute physiotherapy and strength training fitness program. "Am pleased to report," she noted in her Christmas letter that year, "that I no longer do the Senior Shuffle nor do I need extra help in the 'sit to stand' exercise."[22]

11. SUNSET

University of Saskatchewan convocation, 2006, at which Sylvia was awarded a Doctor of Laws. Left to right: Vera Pezer, Garry Vann, Doreen Fairburn, Carol Walker, Sylvia, and Irene Bell.

No longer able to navigate her stairs, Sylvia was at last ready for her precious curling pin collection to become someone else's treasure. In about 2008, her friend Eileen Jewett of Alberta made a phone call to well-known Canadian curling pin collector Norman "Curly" Walz. Sylvia Fedoruk was ready to sell her collection. Would he be interested? Well, would he? Of course! Firing up his truck, Curly and his spouse, Marj Schell, travelled to 49 Simpson Crescent. There Sylvia sent them downstairs to her den. "It was a beautiful collection," Marj remembered, on display on every wall. "We carried every one of those frames upstairs," Marj noted with chagrin, and filled the truck. Sylvia, unsteady on her feet, watched as the precious pastime and much-loved collection trundled up the stairs, out the door, and into the waiting truck. The final count was over 6,000 pins, amassed in well over forty years of quiet contentment, gifts, trades, and the rush of discovery and negotiation. When Curly pulled away, Sylvia sat down in her living room, MaxC bounding around while her tears flowed.[23]

Limited mobility meant a scaling back in the garden, eventually leaving its caretaking to others. By extension, Sylvia lost her ability to can and pickle. No longer able to make her own Syl's Dills, she started sampling the offerings at the Saskatoon Farmers' Market. She'd bring home first this one, then that one, trying a different vendor each time. Finally, she found a lady whose recipe was the closest approximation to her own. Sylvia's cousin Garry Vann would be sent on the chase if Sylvia wasn't up to the trip, with specific instructions that it had to be this particular pickle, from that particular vendor. No other would please her taste buds.

In 2011, Sylvia's ongoing and warm relationship with the Western Development Museum (WDM) took another important step. The WDM received the original cobalt unit from the Saskatchewan Cancer Commission, which had been displayed (at Sylvia's insistence and support) in the ceiling of the cancer clinic. It was thought that the machine should be part of the WDM permanent collection as a unique and important artifact showcasing Saskatchewan's leadership in cancer innovation, technology development, and machining, instead of being visible only when someone was sick with cancer and going to the clinic. Sylvia worked with the museum, supplying technical papers and interviews, and was on hand for the opening of the exhibit, when over 300 people descended on the museum to celebrate Saskatchewan's leadership in cancer teletherapy.

As her lower legs and body became unsteady, so did her driving. Close friends recalled an ardent and determined driver whose time behind the wheel now resembled more of a low-speed game of demolition derby, gently bouncing off other vehicles with all-too-common regularity. They started to develop elaborate excuses for why they should drive and Sylvia ride: my car hasn't been used much and needs its carburetor blown out by an out-of-town trip; I've got to stop and pick up something that could spill, we'll use my car; I'm just *sure* it's my turn. Sylvia was stubborn, though, and relentlessly independent. By then, she had a van that gave her more room to get in and out and more room for groceries and MaxC should he be along for the ride. What were a few minor bumper scrapes and dents when Saskatchewan had such good provincial insurance?[24]

But despite regular workouts and physiotherapy, Sylvia's mobility continued to deteriorate—and that didn't sit well with the once-commanding athlete. Long-time friend Vera Pezer noted bluntly that "Syl hated getting old. She did not age well. It ran contrary to her high expectations of herself and did not suit her. For example, she proudly refused to use either a walker or a cane, despite increasing unsteadiness. She felt that was somehow beneath

11. SUNSET

Sylvia with MaxC, c. 2012.

her, not acceptable to admit needing help."[25] Another friend, basketball teammate Pat Lawson, said, "It bothered her a lot, to succumb to frailty. Nobody likes that, her least of all."[26] Sylvia's stubborn refusal to accommodate her changing circumstances would be, in a literal way, her downfall.

In September 2012, on a Saturday morning, Sylvia was at the Saskatoon Farmers' Market at the 19th Street location, happily browsing. She might have been loaded down with bags; she might have tripped over something in the aisle; she might have simply fallen, as she had before. This time, though, she fell hard. At age eighty-five and with bones more brittle than anyone expected, Sylvia shattered her pelvis and hip. She was rushed by ambulance to St. Paul's Hospital, where it soon became clear that, while her mind remained sharp, her body wasn't bouncing back from the shock. Friends and colleagues came to visit Sylvia, and the fall had transformed her from a no-nonsense practicalist to someone who needed a hug, a hand to hold, warmth to share. Mayor Don Atchison arrived with a huge surprise: a planned future Saskatoon road sign for Fedoruk Drive. A friend put it up on the wall for her to see. Recovery, yearned for by so many, wasn't to be. Years of working through typical seniors' cardiovascular concerns, fought with blood thinners and blood pressure medication, had taken their toll. The impact of the fall cascaded like dominoes throughout her body. Despite friends wondering if Sylvia wouldn't be more comfortable across the river, at her "own" Royal University Hospital, where she'd worked for so long and knew so many, the trip wasn't in the cards. On September 26, 2012, Sylvia Fedoruk quietly passed away.

The shock of her passing reverberated through Sylvia's small and close-knit circle. Her immediate family might have expected to be responsible for making funeral arrangements, but the Honourable Sylvia Olga Fedoruk, O.C., S.O.M., was a provincial treasure and past lieutenant-governor. The government of Saskatchewan's protocol office, quiet and efficient, stepped in. With the family's help and support to choose music and readings, the protocol office planned a state funeral in Saskatoon for October 5, 2012. As the news of Sylvia's death spread across the city and the province, flags dropped to half-mast, all except at one house: Sylvia's own. Her flag still flapped high in the late-September sunshine and cool breeze. It was a strange contrast. The reason? Sylvia's flagpole, remnant of her time as lieutenant-governor, was locked. It required a key to open the mechanism to send flags up and down the pole. It took two days of scouring the house before the key was found and Sylvia's own flag lowered. The kids at Greystone Heights school noticed. The flag had been an important part of classroom management. What was the weather doing? Kids and teachers would automatically look out the window to "the flag lady's" yard. If the flag was flapping wildly, then it was too windy for outdoor games, and alternative plans would be made. When it dropped to half-mast, they learned that their "flag lady" was Sylvia Fedoruk.[27]

At the news of her death, both provincial and national media hurried to publish heartfelt stories about Sylvia. It was difficult, the media soon realized, to encapsulate her life, exploits, and achievements in a single article. Sylvia's trailblazing work in medical physics and nuclear science, learning on the betatron, developing the cobalt-60, and then working on whole-body scanning with radioactive nuclides (a precursor to today's CT and PET scanning techniques) placed Sylvia at the forefront of some of today's most important cancer-fighting techniques. The number of lives that her work touched in Saskatchewan and around the world was uncountable, but a safe estimate would be millions. Then the media had to grapple with her history of sports achievement, from the record-setting first Canadian ladies' curling championship to varsity exploits, summer

11. SUNSET

ball, and Lobstick-level golf. All of those could then be crowned with the mention of her honours and awards, her election to the first female chancellorship of the University of Saskatchewan, and her hugely popular position as Saskatchewan's first female lieutenant-governor. The media had so many angles to consider.

Premier Brad Wall, who had met Sylvia on several occasions, reported that she was "very down to earth, someone who was as comfortable talking about curling as nuclear medicine." To commemorate Sylvia in a lasting way, Wall announced on October 4, 2012, that the much-lauded Canadian Centre for Nuclear Innovation at the University of Saskatchewan would be renamed the Sylvia Fedoruk Canadian Centre for Nuclear Innovation. "She was obviously Saskatchewan's most famous, most well-reputed nuclear scientist and this week when we're honouring her life, we think it's the perfect time to announce that we're naming it for her."[28] As Wall summed up, "she was the epitome of what is good about the province of Saskatchewan."[29]

Sylvia Fedoruk's state funeral was held at the Centennial Auditorium (now TCU Place) in downtown Saskatoon. Travelling by limo, cousin Michael Vann remembered that "the part that seemed so strange was they shut down the streets. You saw people saluting, officers saluting." He couldn't help but remember not the legendary figure that had such an impact on Saskatchewan but his very special "Auntie Syl."[30] The funeral was open to the public, and some 700 people were on hand to witness and mourn together. Piped in with bagpipes and an RCMP honour guard acting as pallbearers, her casket was draped in a Saskatchewan flag and topped with her three distinguished medals: the Order of Canada, the Saskatchewan Order of Merit, and the Order of St. John. Music came from the University of Saskatchewan's Amati Quartet and Greystone Singers along with Melfort's young Indigenous songster Kevin Arcand, interspersed throughout the ceremony.

Irene White, Sylvia's personal secretary as lieutenant-governor and close friend, opened with a reading of The Lord's Prayer. Words of remembrance by Lieutenant-Governor Vaughn Solomon Schofield and Premier Brad Wall set the tone of the proceedings. Wall summed up the sheer impossibility of her life: Sylvia must be "a character in a novel, or part of lore," he mused, since her life "couldn't possibly be true of one person." Three more speakers took the podium: the Honourable Dr. Grant Devine, Sylvia's first first minister and former premier of Saskatchewan; the Honourable

Roy Romanow, Sylvia's second first minister and former premier of Saskatchewan; and the Honourable Dr. Lynda Haverstock, former lieutenant-governor of Saskatchewan. Devine spoke of the difficulty in crystallizing the quality of Sylvia's accomplishments and her global impact as a role model and an icon. Romanow chose descriptive words emblematic of her character: *egalitarian, perseverance, principled, persuasive, sensitive, understanding*, with a *liberated transcendence*. Haverstock spoke of how Sylvia did not shatter a glass ceiling but exploded a cement ceiling to achieve her goals.

Dr. Vera Pezer, close friend to Sylvia and chancellor of the University of Saskatchewan, rose to deliver Psalm 23, The Lord Is My Shepherd. The University of Saskatchewan compiled a tribute video, including an extensive collection of photographs and Sylvia's last video interview. It offered a panoramic view of the many lives of Sylvia Fedoruk. The eulogy was delivered by Peter Mackinnon, past president of the University of Saskatchewan. He had been president when Sylvia sat as an appointed member of the board of governors. The two had worked closely on numerous committees, in which Sylvia's sharp wit, dry good humour, high standards, and firm expectations set a tone of excellence. From her earliest to her last days, he said, "there is not an ounce of humbug in the woman."[31]

Those in the audience heard Sylvia's character lauded, but her many close friends and relations knew not just the public icon but also a whole woman. Sylvia had had her share of pain and sorrow: losing so many of her closest family members and friends to cancer, the very disease that she had dedicated her life to beating back; a private person living in a political spotlight, unable to always control circumstances and sometimes caught in other people's public social activism agendas, or her occasional need to retreat fully to oblivion; a career academic who, despite tremendous successes, bore a weight of self-doubt from the lack of a Ph.D.; and a fiercely competitive athlete who took pride in accomplishment but was her own worst enemy and critic when things (a putt, a drive, a takeout, a layup, a block, a save) did not work out the way that she wanted. It was a case of a life being so nearly perfect that the stumbles or missteps, for Sylvia, would stand out.

Many went to the post-funeral meal for a chance to visit, cheer one another up, and regale each other with a few of their own stories about Sylvia—including those not quite as acceptable for public consumption. Perhaps someone recalled her worse-than-awful skills at skiing, of any kind. A Slobsticker might have told with laughter the

11. SUNSET

The Fedoruk headstone, Yorkton cemetery.

time that Sylvia missed her costume change one evening at Slobstick and came out with her babushka in place but not her pants. One of her fishing buddies might have recounted the time that Sylvia's wild cast caught her guide's cheek instead of arcing out gracefully into the water. A basketball friend might have remembered the "rampaging Amazon" whose scrambly style led to many bumps, lumps, and bruises or whose antics with the freshies included hiding fish in their beds. One of her International Atomic Energy Agency co-authors might have told tales from their near-illicit run across the communist border to eat in a restaurant behind the Iron Curtain or of Sylvia licking up spilled slivovitz off the only copy of their work. Someone might have brought up onions. A fellow graduate student could have told tales about secret poker games or using the cobalt-60 machine to radiate gophers out the window in between treating patients. Many hoisted a dram of single malt scotch to offer a proper toast and send-off. The post-funeral luncheon featured a few of Sylvia's closer personal friends, including Peggy McKercher and Pat Lawson, delivering a few anecdotes. A funeral is all about saying goodbye, and as part of that process stories offered the best way to remember all parts of Sylvia, from the role model to the renegade.

Sylvia Olga Fedoruk was laid to rest in the City of Yorkton cemetery, next to her mother, Annie, and her father, Theodore (Ted).

Nearby are buried aunts, uncles, and cousins, forming an extended family plot. Sylvia lies beneath beautiful large trees whose majesty lends protection and the whisper of wind through spring leaves, summer foliage, and fall snap and crackle. Protected by winter's snow blanket, she stays tucked away from storms.

In the years following the death of Sylvia Fedoruk, two major public sites were named in her honour. As she learned in her final weeks in the hospital, the City of Saskatoon named a major connecting road between Central Avenue and McOrmond Drive in the city's expanding northeast as Fedoruk Drive. It skirts the ecologically significant Northeast Swale. In the same area of the city is Sylvia Fedoruk School. Naming an elementary school in her honour was a fantastic way to showcase her close connection to schoolchildren and love of learning, two themes central to Sylvia's time as lieutenant-governor. At the official school opening in 2017, a number of Sylvia's friends and relations were on hand. The Sylvia Fedoruk school motto, Dream, Discover, Achieve, seems to be particularly apt as a way to crystallize her own life of dreaming, discovering, and achieving.

Sylvia Olga Fedoruk's lifetime of achievement in and legacy to Saskatchewan—with a thankful nod to Walkerville, Ontario—remains a fresh story that often instills pride in so many from Saskatchewan. It's a story of Saskatchewan Girl Makes Good, a winning combination of athletic excellence, academic scientific accomplishment, and a social climb from much-maligned Saskatchewan bohunk to glittering political leadership. With intelligence and wit, determination, some sarcasm and darkness, much warmth and grace, Sylvia was a whole woman who loved the province of her birth with a rare depth.

The final word goes to a young lady named Kieran, the granddaughter of Peggy McKercher, Sylvia's friend and teammate. When Kieran was ten years old, she interviewed Sylvia for a class project. Kieran's distillation of the essence of Sylvia is worth quoting for its simplicity:

> I think that Sylvia Fedoruk is a great person.
>
> I like her because she was trying to make a cure for cancer.
>
> She is very smart.

Sylvia Fedoruk is inspiring.

She is very kind.

She is a very athletic person.

I think that Sylvia is a very important person.

Sylvia Fedoruk did many wonderful things for our province.

She was working as a leader to help find a cure for cancer.

She is also in the Curling Hall of Fame.

Sylvia Fedoruk was also a former Lieutenant Governor of Saskatchewan.

All of these jobs show how big of a difference you can make even if you are from a province that isn't as famous as others.

My hero is Sylvia Fedoruk.[32]

AFTERWORD

THE SYLVIA FEDORUK FONDS AT THE UNIVERSITY OF Saskatchewan Archives are a proverbial gold mine for researchers working on Canadian medical history (particularly nuclear medicine), the Atomic Energy Control Board of Canada, the University of Saskatchewan between 1946 and the mid-2000s, Canadian women's curling history, Canadian women's ball history, the daily activities of a sitting university chancellor or provincial lieutenant-governor, European and South American travel in the 1950s and 1960s, and Saskatchewan fishing across the north, as well as Romaniuk and Fedoruk family histories.

The guide for the massive collection is a fifty-two-page overview. Such a document shortens and directs attention, allowing researchers to dive straight into areas of interest. That fonds overview is equivalent to a telephone directory, encyclopedia, and map. Measured and sorted and counted, the Sylvia Fedoruk fonds include almost thirteen metres spread over seventy-six boxes of records. Textual records (e.g., books, cookbooks, numerous letters and other correspondence, calendars and day-books, media clippings, papers and publications, greeting cards, Christmas letters, invitations and memorabilia, among other things) make up a large part of the collection. Sylvia had self-curated and arranged these textual files both in chronological order, starting in the 1940s and continuing to 2012, and by subject, including correspondence and memorabilia related to numerous activities, from her student days to her time as lieutenant-governor. Twenty-two boxes contain thousands of photographs, negatives, and slides, along with compact discs and VHS tapes.

There are also sixteen boxes containing physical artifacts and memorabilia. There are, among other things, framed photographs; numerous plaques, trophies, pins, and medals; framed and mounted degrees, certificates, and awards; newspaper clippings; posters; pennants and insignias; and name tags and flags, including her lieutenant-governor's flag. There are also beer and pop bottles, Ted Fedoruk's school bell, a taxidermy fish, her Huskies jersey, hats, a shawl, jewellery, carvings, pearls from her trip to Mikimoto Pearl Island in Japan, her Mickey Mouse and Goofy watches, and her laptop. Although some of the textual items in the collection are restricted for privacy reasons, the majority is available for viewing to the public. The fonds can be found at the University of Saskatchewan, Murray Library, in the Archives and Special Collections room on the third floor.

Several other physical items, such as academic robes, a silver tray presented to Sylvia by the government of Saskatchewan in recognition of her curling excellence, curling rock, broom, and sweater, as well as a few other small items, were transferred to the Western Development Museum. The museum also holds the transcript of an interview with Sylvia regarding the building of the cobalt-60 bomb, to go along with its exhibit. Other items are on loan and display at the Sylvia Fedoruk School in Saskatoon, and a few more are on display in a shadow box in the walls of Greystone Heights School in Saskatoon. Other items related to Sylvia can be found across Saskatchewan, from her portait in the legislature in Regina, to mementoes and artifacts at Government House, to the Sylvia Fedoruk Centre for Nuclear Innovation at the University of Saskatchewan and her chancellor portrait in the Peter Mackinnon building, to the Ukrainian museum on Main Street in Canora (and Canora's Sylvia Fedoruk Centre, where the Canora Curling Club operates). Her story touches and weaves through Saskatchewan's memory.

PHOTO CREDITS
(by page number)

SOURCE: SYLVIA FEDORUK FONDS, UNIVERSITY OF SASKATCHEWAN

- 11 MG435Fedoruk_BornDigitalMaterials_RomaniukScrapbook
- 14 MG435Fedoruk_BornDigitalMaterials_Alvina3Scrapbook
- 15 MG435Fedourk_BornDigitalMaterials_ScannedPhotos
- 21 MG435Fedoruk_BornDigitalMaterials_ScannedPhotos
- 28 MG435Fedoruk_Box40_4a_Photographs_Family
- 31 Photo by Merle Massie
- 34 MG435Fedoruk_BornDigitalMaterials_ScannedPhotos. *See also* MG435Fedoruk_Box34_IV_1f_Albums 1946-56
- 45 MG435Fedoruk_Box40_IV_4b_Photographs_1946-51
- 49 MG435Fedoruk_BornDigitalMaterials_ScannedPhotos
- 51 MG435_Fedoruk_Box47_IV_6a_Slides_007
- 54 MG435Fedoruk_BornDigitalMaterials_Alvina3Scrapbook
- 64 MG435Fedoruk_Box40_IV_4b_Photographs_1946-51
- 65 Photo by Merle Massie
- 76 MG435Fedoruk_Box34_IV_1f_Albums_1946-56
- 77 MG435Fedoruk_Box34_IV_1f_Albums_1946-56
- 85 MG435Fedoruk_Box34_IV_1f_Albums_1946-56
- 89 MG435Fedoruk_Box34_IV_1e_PhotoAlbum_1959-62_001
- 99 MG435Fedoruk_Box34_IV_1a_PhotoAlbum_1959-62_002
- 103 MG435Fedoruk_Box40_IV_4c_Photographs_"SOF Pictures" 1954-56
- 105 MG435Fedoruk_Box34_IV_1a_Albums_1959-62
- 108 MG435Fedoruk_Box34_IV_1a_Albums_1959-62
- 113 MG435Fedoruk_Box34_IV_1a_PhotoAlbum_1959-62_007
- 118 MG435Fedoruk_Box35_IV_1f_PhotoAlbum_1946-56_005
- 120 MG435Fedoruk_Box40_IV_4d_Curling, Hub, Pot of Gold 1960-65
- 121 MG435Fedoruk_Box47_IV_6a_Slides
- 131 MG435Fedoruk_Box41_IV_4g_1963-1974

PHOTO CREDITS

- 136 MG435Fedoruk_BornDigitalMaterials_ScannedPhotos. *See also* MG435Fedoruk_Box41_IV_4g_1963-1974
- 145 MG435Fedoruk_Box41_IV_4h_May 1973-April 1978
- 158 MG435Fedoruk_BornDigitalMaterials_ScannedPhotos
- 167 MG435Fedoruk_Box43_IV_4o_officialportraits. Courtesy of University of Saskatchewan.
- 195 MG435Fedoruk_Box43_IV_4o_Photographs_1988 Sept to April
- 196 MG435Fedoruk_Box43_IV_4o_Photographs_1988 Sept to April
- 199 MG435Fedoruk_Box43_IV_4o_officialportraits
- 223 Photo by Merle Massie
- 256 MG435Fedoruk_Box45_IV_4aa_1993-1994
- 258 MG435Fedoruk_BornDigitalMaterials_SylScannedPhotos
- 260 MG435Fedoruk_BornDigitalMaterials_SylScannedPhotos
- 271 MG435Fedoruk_Box47_IV_4gg_Photographs

OTHER SOURCES:

- 25 Southwestern Ontario digital archive (http://swoda.uwindsor.ca/content/206)
- 27 Regina, Government House Archives, Photograph collection, Sylvia Fedoruk files
- 47 St. Pietro Mohyla Institute 75th Anniversary Reunion booklet
- 62 University of Saskatchewan yearbook
- 171 Waskesiu Heritage Museum. *See also* Sylvia Fedoruk fonds, University of Saskatchewan, MG435Fedoruk_Box43_IV_4p_1988-89
- 186 Provincial Archives of Saskatchewan, 88-878-26
- 269 Garry Vann photo collection. Used with permission.
- 275 Photo by Merle Massie

NOTES

PREFACE

1. As related to me in 2018 by Patrick Hayes, University of Saskatchewan Archives and Special Collections, during one of my research visits.

1: BLIZZARDS AND FIREWORKS

1. The original church, built in 1903–04, was established the same year as the parish. On the southeast quarter of Section 20, Township 29, Range 3, west of the 2nd Meridian, the church still stands about two miles north of the Romaniuk farm. In the 1960s, this church was extensively renovated, inside and out, and the congregation purchased a house and a local school, moved them onto the site, and remodelled them to serve as the community hall. The bell tower, west of the front doors, still stands, its bell cheek by jowl with ropes, old chairs, and tools. The church and its graveyard filled with Romaniuk relations remain a magnet for this old Saskatchewan Ukrainian Orthodox community. See *Saskatchewan Ukrainian Historical Society, Saskatchewan Ukrainian Legacy: A Travel Guide to the Cultural and Historic Sites in the Ukrainian Bloc Settlement Communities* (Saskatoon: Saskatchewan Ukrainian Historical Society, 2006), 14.
2. See Bill Waiser, *Saskatchewan: A New History* (Markham, ON: Fitzhenry and Whiteside, 2005).
3. Ibid., 244–47.
4. "Fedoruk, Theodore, and Annie (Romaniuk) and the Hon. Sylvia O. Fedoruk," in *Winning the Prairie Gamble: Family History Album*, published online by the Western Development Museum, https://www.saskhistory.ca/fedoruk-theodore-and-annie-romaniuk-the-hon-sylvia-o-fedoruk/, April 15, 2001.

NOTES

5 Walter Liebrecht, "Looking Back: An Early History of Rhein," in *Rhein and District Golden Agers* (n.p.: self-published, n.d.), 26–28.
6 It was not until the 1929–34 government of J.T.M. Anderson that Minister of Highways Alan Carl Stewart laid out "for the first time a system of numbered highways that criss-crossed the settled portions of the province." C.S. Houston, "Stewart, Alan Carl," in *Saskatchewan Politicians, Past and Present*, ed. Brett Quiring (Regina: Canadian Plains Research Center, 2004), 218.
7 Ken Moroz, "Lysenko School: History of the Lysenko One Room Rural/Country School 1899–1959) Saskatchewan, Canada," April 16, 2005, www.lysenkoschool.blogspot.ca/2005/04/lysenko-rural-school-sd-494.html.
8 Theodore Onofrijchuk, *The History of R.M. of Sliding Hills No. 273 Mikado Sask and Their Centennial Park* (Yorkton, SK: The Enterprise, 1967), 45.
9 Years after it closed, Scotland School was relocated to the grounds of St. Vladimir and Olga Church north of Wroxton, where it is slowly crumbling.
10 Barry Broadfoot, *Ten Lost Years 1929–1939: Memories of Canadians Who Survived the Depression* (Don Mills, ON: PaperJacks, 1975), 239–40.
11 Onofrijchuk, *History of R.M. of Sliding Hills No. 273*, 47.
12 Several interviewees described Ted and Annie Fedoruk pushing Sylvia in both studies and sports.
13 This observation came from several sources but most distinctly from long-time friend Vera Pezer.
14 Sylvia Fedoruk, remarks to the Saskatchewan History and Folklore Society, September 24, 1988, Provincial Archives of Saskatchewan, 2007-294 Sylvia Fedoruk files, box 2, Speeches.
15 The marks that she earned that year were captured on the back of her grade nine certificate, signed on June 29, 1942, at Wroxton by Stephen Rajchuk, chairman of the local school board, and J. Bahrey, principal of Scotland School.
16 Waiser, *Saskatchewan*, 325–26.

2: WALKERVILLE WONDER

1 Information about Windsor is drawn from Larry L. Kulisek, "Windsor (Ont)," November 1, 2012, last edited March 4, 2015, in *The Canadian Encyclopedia*, www.thecanadianencyclopedia.ca/en/article/windsor-ont/.
2 Original data are from Voters Lists, Federal Elections, 1935–80, Ontario, Essex East, 1945, Library and Archives Canada (hereafter LAC), R1003-6-3-E (RG 113-B).
3 Windsor Architectural Conservation Advisory Committee, "The Village/Town of Ford City, Windsor, Ontario, Canada," 1996–97, https://www.citywindsor.ca/residents/historyofwindsor/Documents/Ford%20City%20Walking%20Tour.pdf.

NOTES

4   Sonia Sulaiman, "Walkerville Collegiate Institute Esto Perpetua . . . ," *Walkerville Times* 16 (2001), http://www.walkervilletimes.com/walker-high.html.
5   University of Saskatchewan Archives, Sylvia Fedoruk fonds, MG 435, box 23, Walkerville Collegiate, *The Blue and White* (yearbook), 15.
6   Voters Lists, Ontario, Essex East, 1945, LAC, R1003-6-3-E (RG 113-B).
7   *Chronicle of Canada* (Vancouver: Raincoast Books, 1990), 722.
8   University of Saskatchewan Archives, Sylvia Fedoruk fonds, MG 435, box 23, Walkerville Collegiate, *The Blue and White* (yearbook), 44.
9   For information about the Michigan-Ontario Ladies Fastball League, see Carly Adams, "Softball and the Female Community: Pauline Perron, Pro Ball Player, Outsider, 1926–1951," *Journal of Sport History* 33, no. 3 (2006): 323–43. The following paragraphs on women's ball draw heavily from this source.
10 For information on the All-American Girls Professional Baseball League, inducted into the National Baseball Hall of Fame in the United States in 1988, see the website of the league at www.aagpbl.org. Much of the information in this chapter is drawn from its public files. For more information on the Saskatchewan ladies who played in this league, see Paul Hack and David William Shury, *Wheat Province Diamonds: A Story of Saskatchewan Baseball* (Regina: Saskatchewan Sports Hall of Fame and Museum, 1997).
11 Adams, "Softball and the Female Community," 330.
12 Sylvia Fedoruk, videotaped interview with Roy Norris, c. 1994, University of Saskatchewan Archives, Sylvia Fedoruk fonds, MG 435, box 33.
13 Ibid.

3: RAMPAGING AMAZON

1   "Rally Highlights Welcome Program," *The Sheaf*, September 17, 1946, 1.
2   Sylvia Fedoruk, "Bursa Memories," excerpts from an address by Sylvia O. Fedoruk, Chancellor, University of Saskatchewan, on the occasion of the Mohyla Institute Seventieth Anniversary, November 8, 1986, in Mohyla Institute 75th Anniversary Reunion August 9–11, 1991, Saskatoon, Canada, 31, private collection of Merle Massie.
3   For more on the history of the St. Petro Mohyla Institute, see the Varsity View Community Association website at vvcasaskatoon.com. See also the booklets for the Mohyla Institute Sixtieth Anniversary Celebration, July 1–4, 1976, and the Mohyla Institute Seventy-Fifth Anniversary Reunion, August 9–11, 1991, private collection of Merle Massie. At this reunion, Sylvia attended as lieutenant-governor. She also gave an address at the seventieth anniversary, excerpts of which were included in the Seventy-Fifth Anniversary booklet.
4   "Women's Gym Notice," *The Sheaf*, September 28, 1946, 4.
5   "Track Meets Crowded by Re-Union Activities," *The Sheaf*, October 8, 1946, 4.
6   E.W. "Joe" Griffiths, "Looking Back at Some Real Champs—Sylvia Fedoruk," *The Western Producer*, April 4, 1963, 23.

NOTES

7   "Girls Prepare for Track Meet," *The Sheaf*, October 18, 1946, 4. Much of the information for this chapter came from reading *The Sheaf*. Copies are easily found online through the University of Saskatchewan Archives website. In the interest of easy reading, I've tried to limit the references.
8   "Varsity Track Teams Victorious," *The Sheaf*, October 22, 1946, 4. Betty Wilson later became Betty Wright, the wife of Saskatoon's long-time mayor Cliff Wright. Sylvia Fedoruk's sports connections led directly to municipal and later to higher-level political connections.
9   "Girl Cage Teams Already Training," *The Sheaf*, October 4, 1946, 4.
10 Ibid.
11 B.W. Currie, "The Physics Department, 1910–1976, University of Saskatchewan," 1976, University of Saskatchewan Archives, Department of Physics fonds, RG 2043.
12 D.V. Cormack, "The Saskatchewan Radon Plant, 1931–1962," *Physics in Canada* 41 (1985): 3–5. See also Stuart Houston and Bill Waiser, *Tommy's Team: The People behind the Douglas Years* (Markham, ON: Fifth House, 2010), 55–59.
13 Sylvia Fedoruk, speech at a tribute dinner to Harold Johns, June 1, 1999, Saskatoon, University of Saskatchewan Archives, Sylvia Fedoruk fonds, MG 435.II.4.h.ii.Dr. H.E. Johns (3), box 25, folder 8.
14 Martin W. Johns, *Bamboo Sprouts and Maple Buds, Being Memoirs of a Life Begun in West China in 1913 and Transplanted to Canada in 1925* (Hamilton, ON: self-published, 1992).
15 C. Stuart Houston and Merle Massie, *36 Steps on the Road to Medicare: How Saskatchewan Led the Way* (Montreal and Kingston: McGill-Queen's University Press, 2013), 122–23. As a professor in the wartime Radar School at the University of Alberta, Johns worked for the Commonwealth Air Training Plan during the war, training pilots in physics and math. Using a cast-off X-ray machine from Ottawa, he would X-ray aircraft casings to look for weaknesses. It was easy to lure him away from Edmonton: the university, in a decision that is sure to be astonishing, did not promote Johns to the rank of assistant professor. He was more than miffed.
16 First published as *The Physics of Radiation Therapy* in 1953, this textbook was republished as *The Physics of Radiology* in 1961 (Springfield, IL: Thomas) and went through a further two editions.
17 Harold Johns, "The Physicist in Cancer Treatment and Detection," *International Journal of Radiation Oncology, Biology, Physics* 7 (1981): 801–08.
18 "Betatron" (report), University of Saskatchewan Archives, Sylvia Fedoruk fonds, MG 435.II.4.h.i.1944–57, box 25, number 4.
19 "Atom Scientist to Visit Campus This Weekend," *The Sheaf*, December 13, 1946, 1.
20 Series of letters regarding the betatron and cobalt bomb, University of Saskatchewan Archives, Sylvia Fedoruk fonds, MG 435.II.4.h.i.1944–57, box 25, number 4.
21 Houston and Massie, *36 Steps on the Road to Medicare*, xix–xxi.

22 Shirley Nalevykin, "Huskiettes Tangle Monday with Household Science," *The Sheaf*, March 7, 1947, 4.
23 "Awards to Undergrads," *The Sheaf*, May 14, 1947, 10.
24 Sylvia's undergraduate degree was a Bachelor of Arts in Physics, not a Bachelor of Science.
25 See Effie Sinsmore, "The Sports Bag," *The Sheaf*, October 10, 1947, 6.
26 "Coeds Win in Track," *The Sheaf*, October 18, 1947, 6.
27 "Shorts in Sports," *The Sheaf*, November 25, 1947, 6.
28 Houston and Massie, *36 Steps on the Road to Medicare*, 118–36.
29 From the Canadian perspective, the betatron should be viewed as one of several new machines at the leading edge of atomic energy. In Montreal, Dr. J.S. Foster was leading a team working with one of Canada's first cyclotrons; Dr. W.J. Henderson of the National Research Council in Ottawa had developed a microtron; a synchrotron was being developed at Queen's University in Kingston; and a static accelerator was in use at Chalk River. J.E. Belliveau, "Canada's Miracle Machines," *Star-Weekly* [Toronto], February 4, 1950, clipping in University of Saskatchewan Archives, Physics Department fonds, physics scrapbook, RG 2043.
30 "Dr. H.E. Johns Outlines Betatron Research Program at Physics Club Supper Meeting," *The Sheaf* November 7, 1947, 3.
31 Muriel Snider, "25 Million Volts of Hope," *Saturday Night*, October 18, 1949, University of Saskatchewan Archives, Physics Department fonds, physics scrapbooks, RG 2043.
32 Physics researchers looking forward to its installation as a major part of their research program were L. Katz, R.N.H. Haslam, E.L. Harrington as department head, and Sylvia's mentor, H.E. Johns. *The Sheaf*, November 4, 1947, 2.
33 "Coeds to Play Sask League," *The Sheaf*, November 18, 1947, 6.
34 Hoop, "Fan Fare," *The Sheaf*, December 5, 1947, 7.
35 "Coed Pucksters Down Queen City Pats 2–0" and "Shorts in Sports," *The Sheaf*, December 12, 1947, 6.
36 "Shorts in Sports," *The Sheaf*, December 12, 1947, 6.
37 "Huskiettes Win at Regina over Weekend," *The Sheaf*, January 20, 1948, 5.
38 "Sports Weekend," *The Sheaf*, February 27, 1948, 1.
39 "Coed Sports Weekend Basketball," *The Sheaf*, February 24, 1948, 6; "Sports Weekend Success," *The Sheaf*, March 2, 1948, 6.
40 "W.A.B. Candidates," *The Sheaf*, March 2, 1948, 6.
41 "Voice of W.A.B.," *The Sheaf*, March 19, 1948, 1.
42 "Forefront Reached in Nuclear Research," *The Sheaf*, April 2, 1948, 4.
43 Sylvia Fedoruk to her parents, March 17, 1948, University of Saskatchewan Archives, Sylvia Fedoruk fonds, MG 435.II.3.d.ii.U of S—1946–49, box 24, number 3.
44 Most of the information about Sylvia's ball career was found by searching Google Newspaper Archives scanned pages of both the *Saskatoon Star-Phoenix* and the *Regina Leader-Post*. I read through the sports pages from 1946 to the end of 1955. See, for example, "Classy Ramblers

Down Regina Bombers Twice," *Star-Phoenix*, September 2, 1948, 17, and "Ramblers Bow to Calgary," September 4, 1948, 18.
45 Dale Eisler, editorial column, *Leader-Post*, September 8, 1988, A4.
46 See student enrolment statistics for the University of Saskatchewan at https://library.usask.ca/archives/campus-history/enrolment.php.
47 Determined to defend their Cecil Race intervarsity trophy, the team's veterans—Sylvia Fedoruk, Pat Lawson, Lydia Yaremchuk, Peggy Wilton, and Shirley and Jean Howes—looked forward to playing with their new teammates. Coach Ivan King, after coaching the Ramblers ball team in the summer and known for his relentless style and perfectionism, cast a keen eye on the hopefuls. "Female Hoopsters Begin Practices; Look Mighty Good," *The Sheaf*, October 1, 1948, 7.
48 "Huskiettes Look Good; Down Orphanettes 25–8," *The Sheaf*, November 16, 1948, 6.
49 "Huskiettes Winners in Campus Fixture," *The Sheaf*, December 7, 1948, 7.
50 "Physics Open House," *The Sheaf*, February 15, 1949, 3.
51 Snider, "25 Million Volts of Hope."
52 Quoted in Susan Swedberg-Kohil, "A Starring Role for an Achiever: Province Unanimously Applauds Appointment of Sylvia Fedoruk as Lieutenant Governor," in *History of Canora 1905–1990*, ed. Canora History Book Editorial Board (Canora, SK: Canora History Book Editorial Board, n.d.), 293–301.
53 Ibid.
54 Ibid. See also "Spirit of Youth Award Goes to Physicist Sylvia Fedoruk," *The Sheaf*, March 25, 1949, 1.
55 University of Saskatchewan Archives, Department of Physics fonds, RG 13 s10.3, Betatron Project minute book, 1947–51. The minute book tracked research meetings in the physics department, concentrating on research project requirements, funding sources, and personnel, particularly technicians and students. Sylvia was hired February 3, 1949, and continued until she finished her M.A. in 1951.
56 Snider, "25 Million Volts of Hope."
57 Ibid.
58 Sylvia Fedoruk, "The Growth of Nuclear Medicine," address at the 1989 Annual Conference of the Canadian Nuclear Association and the Canadian Nuclear Society, University of Saskatchewan Archives, Sylvia Fedoruk fonds, box 4.

4: COBALT BOMB

1 Eric Hutton, "The Atom Bomb that Saves Lives," *Maclean's*, February 15, 1952, 51.
2 Harold Johns, "The Physicist in Cancer Treatment and Detection," *International Journal of Radiation Oncology* 7, no. 6 (1981): 801–08.
3 The three packages were eventually destined for Johns in Saskatchewan, one for Dr. Ivan Smith in London, Ontario, and one for Dr. Gilbert Fletcher at the MD Anderson hospital in Houston, Texas.

NOTES

4   Canadian uranium produces a flux rate (volume of neutron production) high enough to energize cobalt-59. Cobalt, a common metal, would absorb an extra neutron (cobalt-60) through atomic bombardment. Cobalt-60 is also used to sterilize single-use medical equipment, from sutures to syringes, via radiation. See *Energize* [Cameco newsletter] fall 2017, https://www.camecofuel.com/uploads/downloads/Energize_Fall_2017.pdf.
5   Hutton, "The Atom Bomb that Saves Lives," 51.
6   Janet Mackenzie, "Saskatchewan's Cobalt-60 Beam Therapy Unit Inaugurates a New Era in Cancer Treatment," prepared for the Western Development Museum in Saskatoon, *Winning the Prairie Gamble*, 2002, copy in the Western Development Museum research archives.
7   Johns, "The Physicist in Cancer Treatment."
8   Hutton, "The Atom Bomb that Saves Lives," 49.
9   Ibid, 8.
10 "Halo Girls!," *The Sheaf*, September 23, 1949, 7. The 1949–50 Huskiette team, once again under the dominant hand of coach Ivan King, consisted of manager Ruth Noble and players Lydia Yaremchuk, Peggy Wilton, Pat Lawson, Ruth Reid, Cam Garnier, Syl Fedoruk, Jean Young, Gladys Campbell, Donna Pryor, and June Taylor.
11 "Win for Huskiettes but Scare from Royals: 30–24," *The Sheaf*, January 17, 1950, 6.
12 "Harlem Visitors Please," *Star-Phoenix*, July 12, 1949, 13.
13 Ibid.
14 See Paul Hack and David William Shury, *Wheat Province Diamonds: A Story of Saskatchewan Baseball* (Regina: Saskatchewan Sports Hall of Fame and Museum, 1987), 331.
15 www.attheplate.com/wcbl/remember.html, Emile Francis memories.
16 Sylvia Fedoruk, speech to Holiday Park Ladies Golf Club, University of Saskatchewan Archives, Sylvia Fedoruk fonds, MG 435, box 1.
17 Bill Ivens, "Saskatoon Machinist Played Big Part in Building First Cobalt Bomb Here," *Star-Phoenix*, October 2, 1952, 10.
18 Ibid.
19 According to the Registration Handbook 1950, the master's degree required taking "a minimum of a full academic year for a fully qualified resident student and in every case shall include the preparation of a suitable thesis." University of Saskatchewan, *Registration Handbook 1950*, University of Saskatchewan Archives.
20 As part of her training and good laboratory practice, Sylvia kept handwritten notebooks of her research work. These notebooks are part of the Sylvia Fedoruk fonds at the University of Saskatchewan Archives. Her original physics notebooks, her finished and bound thesis, and copies of many of her published articles, along with classic physics textbooks, were—thankfully—neatly organized. I spent days reading through them, taking photographs, and learning about her research, painstakingly teaching myself as I went along. It was frustrating, it was rewarding, and it helped me to understand the enormity of what Sylvia and the larger team led by Johns were trying to accomplish.

21 Dr. Allan Blair had passed away unexpectedly in 1948.
22 Sylvia Fedoruk, lab notebooks, "Depth Dose Measurements, Sylvia Fedoruk, 1951," University of Saskatchewan Archives, Sylvia Fedoruk fonds, MG 435, box 26.
23 Sylvia Olga Fedoruk, "Depth Dose" (M.A. thesis, University of Saskatchewan, 1951).
24 Ibid., "Acknowledgements," iv.
25 Harold Johns supervised or worked with a large number of graduate students. Their early 1950s work was specific to high-energy radiation, measurement, instrumentation, and development.
26 Sylvia Fedoruk, lab notebooks, Depth Dose 1950, University of Saskatchewan Archives, Sylvia Fedoruk fonds, MG 435, box 26.
27 Ibid.
28 "Fedoruk, Theodore, and Annie (Romaniuk) and The Hon. Sylvia O. Fedoruk," 2005, in the *Saskatchewan History Album*, https://www.saskhistory.ca/.
29 "U of Sask Teams Repeat: Fedoruk and Craddock Cop All Honours in Women's Golf," *The Sheaf*, October 24, 1950, 6.
30 "Large Turnout at B'Ball School," *The Sheaf*, October 7, 1950, 6; see also "King Running B'Ball School," *The Sheaf*, September 15, 1950, 2.
31 Sylvia Fedoruk, physics notebooks, note for March 2, 1951, University of Saskatchewan Archives, Sylvia Fedoruk fonds, MG 435, box 26.
32 Sylvia Fedoruk, physics notebooks, note for March 10, 1951, University of Saskatchewan Archives, Sylvia Fedoruk fonds, MG 435, box 26.
33 The experiment involved placing the irrigation chamber at A, which read 100 percent. Then Sylvia moved the chamber along a calibrated bench to B, recording the readings. She recorded that "if amplifier is not linear at high ionization rates it will not give high enough reading and graph will curl up for low values of x. NB. This experiment will work if inverse square law can be trusted!" Ibid., notes for March 14 and 15, 1951.
34 She changed the feedback point to the cathode, allowing for two feedback points: full and half.
35 Ibid., note for March 15, 1951.
36 In her notebook, Sylvia explained the theory behind her depth dose experiment setup: "Theoretical setup for zero area Experiment. If an ionization chamber is placed at a great distance from a small area treatment cone it sees effectively the primary radiation, or zero area radiation. Thus if different depth water cells are placed in positions indicated upon, the chamber will see a parallel beam of primary radiation as it passes through different depths of water. If have water cells of 0,2,4,6,8,10,12,14,16,18,20 cm of water able to get % depth dose for zero areas." Ibid., note for April 1, 1951.
37 "Radio-Active Cobalt Arrives Here for Deep Therapy Cancer Work," *Star-Phoenix*, July 30, 1951, 3.
38 Hutton, "The Atom Bomb that Saves Lives."
39 "Radio-Active Cobalt Arrives Here for Deep Therapy Cancer Work," *Star-Phoenix*, July 30, 1951, 3.
40 "Transferring Radioactive Cobalt," *Star-Phoenix*, August 18, 1951.

41 Hutton, "The Atom Bomb that Saves Lives," 53.
42 Ibid.
43 "Caps Eliminate Ramblers; Meet Clippers for the Title," *Star-Phoenix*, August 17, 1951, 15.
44 Sylvia Fedoruk's apartment locations are drawn from information in her files, cross-referenced with municipal or federal census records and Henderson's Directories.
45 Sylvia Fedoruk, Harold Johns, and T.A. Watson, "An Improved Clinical Dosimeter for the Measurement of Radiation." *Radiology* 62, no. 2 (1954): 177–82.
46 "Cobalt Unit for Cancer Installed," *Star-Phoenix*, October 23, 1951, 4.
47 H.E. Johns et al., "1,000 Curie Cobalt-60 Units for Radiation Therapy," *Nature* 168 (1951): 1035.
48 Hutton, "The Atom Bomb that Saves Lives," 52.
49 Ruth McLaren to Sylvia Fedoruk, February 21 1952, University of Saskatchewan Archives, Sylvia Fedoruk fonds, MG 435.j.viiii.1939–85.
50 Howard Hugill to Sylvia Fedoruk, February 25, 1952, University of Saskatchewan Archives, Sylvia Fedoruk fonds, MG 435.j.viiii.1939–85.

5: THE FRIENDLY ATOM

1 "Cobalt Unit Declared No Miracle Treatment" and "Standardization Sought by X-Ray Technicians," newspaper clippings, University of Saskatchewan Archives, Sylvia Fedoruk fonds, MG 435.h.i and MG 435.h.ii.
2 Ibid.
3 "Cobalt 60 Cancer Treatment, Used in Saskatoon, Increased Cure Rate," *Star-Phoenix*, January 19, 1952, 1. In this news story, claims about the "increased cure rate" come from Dr. I.A. Smith, who operated London's cobalt-60 machine.
4 The story of Sylvia radiating gophers was relayed to me by both Trevor Cradduck and Vera Pezer.
5 "Cancer Fellowship Awarded," *Enterprise* [Yorkton], n.d. 1952, in scrapbook newspaper clippings file, University of Saskatchewan Archives, Sylvia Fedoruk fonds, MG 435.2.d., box 18. See also "The John S. McEachern Memorial Fellowship Fund," same page.
6 Sylvia Fedoruk, "Tour of Radiological Centres. Report on Visit to American Radiological Centres by Sylvia Fedoruk. November and December 1952," University of Saskatchewan Archives, Sylvia Fedoruk fonds, MG 435.II.4.e, box 24, file 16.
7 Sylvia Fedoruk, "The Growth of Nuclear Medicine," remarks at the Annual Conference of the Canadian Nuclear Association and the Canadian Nuclear Society, Ottawa, June 1989, https://cns-snc.ca/media/history/fifty_years/fedoruk.html.
8 "Ramblers Even Series by Blanking Spartans," *Star-Phoenix*, August 5, 1952, 12.
9 Margaret Kesselering, "Teacher Made Physics Interesting So She Chose It for a Life Career," *Leader-Post*, February 13, 1952, 8.

10   Moulds remain a major part of cancer radiation from both the technician's perspective and the patient's perspective. Each mould is built to fit each patient in order to hold the head or other part to be radiated at a precise—and still—angle.
11   "Gil (Gilbert) Strumm, October 29, 1920–March 6, 2004," *Star-Phoenix*, March 9, 2004, D1.
12   University of Saskatchewan Archives, Sylvia Fedoruk fonds, MG 435. II.2.d.Scrapbooks 1951–56, box 18.
13   University of Saskatchewan Archives, Sylvia Fedoruk fonds, MG 435. IV.1.e.Regina Govins.
14   Obituary for Helene Sidaway (d. April 27, 2016), *Leader-Post*, April 30, 2016.
15   University of Saskatchewan Archives, Sylvia Fedoruk fonds, MG 435. IV.1.e.Regina Govins.
16   "Saskatoon Girls Declared Champs as Regina Defaults," *Star-Phoenix*, September 25, 1954, 19.
17   University of Saskatchewan Archives, Sylvia Fedoruk fonds, MG 435. II.2.d.Scrapbooks 1951–56, box 18.
18   "Saskatoon Girls Western Winners," *Star-Phoenix*, September 12, 1955, 16.
19   "Regina Cancer Clinic to Install Cobalt Unit," *Leader-Post*, April 3, 1956, 1; "Cost of Cobalt Unit $17,000," *Leader-Post*, April 4, 1956, 3.
20   Peter Dickof, speaking notes for Sylvia Fedoruk's retirement banquet, University of Saskatchewan Archives, Sylvia Fedoruk fonds, MG 435. II.2.j.iv.Retirement Binder.
21   Cam McKenzie, "Cam's Corner," *Star-Phoenix*, March 1, 1952, 19. See also Vera Pezer, *Stone Age: A Social History of Curling on the Prairies* (Calgary: Fifth House, 2003). McKenzie also talks about the Gradettes, a senior women's basketball team in Saskatoon sponsored jointly by the University of Saskatchewan and the U of S Alumni Association. It featured a mix of varsity students and graduates, including Peggy Wilton, Hazel Braithwaite, Pat Lawson, and Sylvia Fedoruk, with coach Ivan King. Sylvia wasn't ready to curl until she finished senior basketball. After the Gradettes, she would guard the basket for the Adilman Aces on winter weekends.
22   "One of Fedoruk's Careers Carved in Stone," *Star-Phoenix*, September 22, 1997, C4.
23   "Saskatoon Rink Sidelined," *Star-Phoenix*, February 20, 1958, 16.

6: PINPRICKS OF LIGHT
1   University of Saskatchewan Archives, Sylvia Fedoruk fonds, MG 435. II.2.j.vii.Notebook, 1959.
2   Cam McKenzie, "Cam's Corner," *Star-Phoenix*, February 2, 1960, 13.
3   See the January, February, and March 1960 issues of the *Saskatoon Star-Phoenix* to follow their play. This quotation comes from "Northern Crown for McKee," *Star-Phoenix*, February 12, 1960, 23.
4   "McKee Reaches Both Finals," *Star-Phoenix*, February 11, 1960, 18.
5   "McKee Wins Two Straight," *Star-Phoenix*, February 19, 1960, 19.

6   "McKee Rink Faces Alberta in Showdown," *Star-Phoenix*, March 17, 1960, 18.
7   "Saskatoon Girls Cart Off Western Title," *Star-Phoenix*, March 18, 1960, 19.
8   "Saskatchewan Quartet Wins Western Curling," *Daily Colonist* [Victoria], March 18, 1960, 10.
9   Sylvia kept a scrapbook of newspaper articles from 1959 to 1961. Few of the cuttings contain references to the newspaper or date. See University of Saskatchewan Archives, Sylvia Fedoruk fonds, MG 435.II.2.j.vii. Notebook, 1959.
10 Ibid.
11 An idea suggested by Sandy Watson.
12 Donald A. Fee and Sylvia O. Fedoruk, "Clinical Value of Liver Photoscanning," *New England Journal of Medicine* 262, no. 3 (1960): 123–25.
13 University of Saskatchewan Archives, Sylvia Fedoruk fonds, MG 435.II.2.j.vii.Notebook, 1959.
14 "McKee Loses First Game," *Star-Phoenix*, February 17, 1961, 17.
15 "McKee Rink Wins the Title Again," *Star-Phoenix*, February 18, 1961, 18.
16 The Kinsella article is among others in Sylvia's curling scrapbooks, in which Sylvia collected newspaper articles from across Canada. Dates and pages are not always available. While Kinsella played on gendered stereotypes, others used trite metaphors, such as these women were "switching kitchen brooms for curling brooms." Another noted that "there's probably no good reason why a lady can't slave over a hot stove and a cold rock too." University of Saskatchewan Archives, Sylvia Fedoruk fonds, MG 435.II.2.d.Scrapbook, 1960–61, box 18.
17 Ibid.
18 Ibid.
19 Ibid.
20 Ibid.
21 Ibid.
22 Vern DeGeer, "Buttons, Badges, Pins—1,675 of Them," *Gazette* [Montreal], March 1, 1967, University of Saskatchewan Archives, Sylvia Fedoruk fonds, MG 435.II.2.e.Clippings, 1964–94.
23 *Star-Phoenix*, January 24 and 25, 1962.
24 *Star-Phoenix*, February 5, 1962.
25 *Star-Phoenix*, February 9, 1962.
26 "McKee Rules Again," *Star-Phoenix*, February 15, 1962, 19.
27 Trevor Cradduck, interview with Merle Massie, October 4, 2018. I am grateful to Dr. Cradduck for helping me to understand how these machines work. Any remaining errors are my own.
28 Since Sylvia did not have a Ph.D. herself, she had to have one as a co-supervisor, usually Cormack.
29 Correspondence between Trevor Cradduck and Merle Massie, March 2019.

30 T.D. Cradduck and S.O. Fedoruk, "A Study of Collimators for Use in Radioisotope Scanning Techniques," *Journal of the Canadian Association of Radiologists* 13 (1962): 9–13, quotation on 9.
31 T.D. Cradduck, S.O. Fedoruk, and J.A. MacKay, "A 'Large Crystal' Scintillation Scanner," *Journal of Nuclear Medicine* 5 (1964): 27–39.
32 The information would be captured by two separate tracks of magnetic tape as well as by a dot scan. The team could then rerun the magnetic tape via an oscilloscope. On the oscilloscope screen, they could adjust the contrast or perform other enhancements to see differences after the scan was complete. From the oscilloscope screen, the team could take Polaroid camera photos, which could then be inserted into a scanner and viewed on a television screen, if required, using the contrast and brightness controls to add more depth.
33 Sylvia Fedoruk, untitled speech at a tribute dinner for Harold Johns, June 1, 1999, Saskatoon, University of Saskatchewan Archives, Sylvia Fedoruk fonds, MG 435.II.4.h.ii.Dr. H.E. Johns (3), box 25, folder 8.
34 Reid had constructed an innovative early brain scanner in the late 1950s.
35 "Camera Detects Cancer Cells," *Profess against Cancer: National Newsletter of the Canadian Cancer Society*, June 1964, University of Saskatchewan Archives, Sylvia Fedoruk fonds, MG 435.I.Clippings, 1965, box 1.
36 Trevor Cradduck, interview with Merle Massie, October 4, 2018.
37 University of Saskatchewan Archives, Sylvia Fedoruk fonds, MG 435.II.8.K.Athens, Brazil, 1964, folder 5.
38 Trevor Cradduck, as relayed to Merle Massie, October 4, 2018.
39 For more references to Sylvia's pin collection, see University of Saskatchewan Archives, Sylvia Fedoruk fonds, MG 435, boxes 1, 18, 28, 29, 34, 36.
40 University of Saskatchewan Archives, Sylvia Fedoruk fonds, MG 435.II.8.j.Travel Diary Harrogate Rome, 1965, box 31.
41 Ibid.
42 University of Saskatchewan Archives, Sylvia Fedoruk fonds, MG 435.II.8.j.Travel Diary, 1965, box 31, folder 4.
43 Craig Harris to Sylvia Fedoruk, n.d., University of Saskatchewan Archives, Sylvia Fedoruk fonds, MG 435.II.2.j.vi.Retirement Binder, 1986, box 23.
44 Theodore Fedoruk to Sylvia Fedoruk, November 24, 1966, University of Saskatchewan Archives, Sylvia Fedoruk fonds, MG 435.II.2.a.vi. Correspondence, 1966–77.
45 McKee won the Canadian ladies' curling championship with this team in 1969. Falk was later replaced by Sheila Rowan, and the team restructured with Pezer as skip. Pezer, Rowan, Morrison, and McKee won three back-to-back Canadian ladies' curling championships in 1971, 1972, and 1973.
46 DeGeer, "Buttons, Badges, Pins."
47 Years later, when submitting personal documentation to the Canadian government as part of the board screening process for the Atomic Energy Control Board, Sylvia had to admit that she had visited a

NOTES

communist-dominated area. University of Saskatchewan Archives, Sylvia Fedoruk fonds, MG 435.II.4.d.Atomic Energy Control Board, 1973–86, box 24.

48 Craig Harris to Sylvia Fedoruk, n.d., University of Saskatchewan Archives, Sylvia Fedoruk fonds, MG 435.II.2.j.ii.Retirement Binder, box 23, folder 9.

49 Ibid. See also AECB, box 24, folder 15.

50 "Scientist Invited to Conference," *Star-Phoenix*, March 22, 1968, clipping in University of Saskatchewan Archives, Sylvia Fedoruk fonds, MG 435.II.2.e.Clippings, 1964–94, box 21.

7: WE CALL THIS MEETING TO ORDER

1 Letters from Brenda Clark and Harold Johns to Sylvia Fedoruk, University of Saskatchewan Archives, Sylvia Fedoruk fonds, MG 435.II.2.j.ii.Retirement Binder, box 23, folder 9.

2 Elta Brown to Sylvia Fedoruk, University of Saskatchewan Archives, Sylvia Fedoruk fonds, MG 435.II.2.J.ii.Retirement Binder, box 23, folder 9.

3 Letters from Fred Wigmore and Elta Brown to Sylvia Fedoruk, University of Saskatchewan Archives, Sylvia Fedoruk fonds, MG 435.II.2.j.ii. Retirement Binder, box 23, folder 9.

4 Brenda Clark to Sylvia Fedoruk, University of Saskatchewan Archives, Sylvia Fedoruk fonds, MG 435.II.2.j.ii.Retirement Binder, box 33, folder 9.

5 "Incoming CLCA President Pleased with Calibre of Play," interview with Sylvia Fedoruk at the 1971 curling playdowns in Newfoundland, n.d., University of Saskatchewan Archives, Sylvia Fedoruk fonds, MG 435.I, 1971, box 1, folder 5.

6 "Some Outstanding Women," c. 1976, Saskatoon Public Library, Local History Room, clipping file on Sylvia Fedoruk. See also Victoria Lamb-Drover, "ParticipACTION: A Legacy in Motion" (Ph.D. diss., University of Saskatchewan, 2016).

7 Vera Pezer, interview with Merle Massie, January 2019.

8 As president, Sylvia was invited to become a director of the Sports Federation of Canada, a federal lobby group for amateur sport, in 1972 for a three-year term.

9 University of Saskatchewan Archives, Sylvia Fedoruk fonds, MG 435. II.8.Travel.h, Scotland Tour, Correspondence, Memorabilia, box 31. See also MG 435.IV.i and j, Scotland Albums.

10 Ibid.

11 *Soop* is the Scot's original word for "sweep."

12 For highlights of the Saskatoon reception of the Scottish team in 1967, and the calculations of the 1971 tour, see Saskatchewan Curling Association, Saskatchewan Curling: Heartland Tradition 1882–1990 (Regina: Saskatchewan Curling Association, 1991), 156–57.

13 For an overview of the relationship between Dominion Stores and the CLCA, see Vera Pezer, *The Stone Age: A Social History of Curling on the Prairies* (Calgary: Fifth House, 2003).

NOTES

14 Sylvia Fedoruk, untitled address to the Macdonald Lassie banquet, 1979, University of Saskatchewan Archives, Sylvia Fedoruk fonds, MG 435.I., 1979, box 1.
15 See University of Saskatchewan Archives, Sylvia Fedoruk fonds, MG 435.I.Correspondence, 1972, box 1.
16 Ingrid Jaffe, "New Cancer Treatment Facility Opened," *Star-Phoenix*, December 5, 1972, 3.
17 Ibid.
18 Peter Dickof, interview with Merle Massie, March 2016.
19 University of Saskatchewan Archives, Sylvia Fedoruk fonds, MG 435.I.Chronological, 1972, box 1.
20 Ibid., Grease River Lodge pamphlet and travel diary.
21 Ibid.
22 Ibid. A one-week stay at Grease River Lodge cost $425.
23 University of Saskatchewan Archives, Sylvia Fedoruk fonds, MG 435.I.Chronological, 1972, box 1, letter from Hap Cave.
24 The story of Tinker and the high rise was related by Irene Bell.
25 Michael Vann recounted many stories of gardening, travel with Tinker, and Sylvia's love of technology during interviews with Merle Massie for this biography.
26 University of Saskatchewan Archives, Sylvia Fedoruk fonds, MG 435.I. Chronological, 1974, box 1.
27 Michael Vann, interview with Merle Massie, November 30, 2018.
28 Ibid.
29 University of Saskatchewan Archives, Sylvia Fedoruk fonds, MG 435.I.Chronological, 1974, box 1.
30 Sylvia Fedoruk, "The Pin Box," *The Curler*, winter 1972, in University of Saskatchewan Archives, Sylvia Fedoruk fonds, MG 435.I.Chronological, 1972, box 1.
31 Jean Macpherson, "Happy Fellowship Remembered in Curling Badges," *Star-Phoenix*, October 12, 1974, in University of Saskatchewan Archives, Sylvia Fedoruk fonds, MG 435.I.Chronological, 1974, box 1.
32 Ibid.
33 Sylvia Fedoruk, "The Pin Box," clipping in University of Saskatchewan Archives, Sylvia Fedoruk fonds, MG 435.I.Chronological, 1972, box 1.
34 Norma Bicknell to Local Council of Women, Calgary, University of Saskatchewan Archives, Sylvia Fedoruk fonds, MG 435.II.4.Radiology.d, Atomic Energy Control Board, box 24, no. 15.
35 Quoted in Norma Greenaway, "Sylvia Fedoruk: A Range of Interests," *Star-Phoenix*, June 22, 1973, clipping in University of Saskatchewan Archives, Sylvia Fedoruk fonds, MG 435.I. Chronological, 1973, box 1.
36 This low-level radioactive waste site is now Canada's largest environmental cleanup project. The government is spending well over a billion dollars to contain and clean up the site. See Matt Flowers, "What You Need to Know about the Port Hope Area Radioactive Waste Cleanup," Waterkeeper.ca, November 9, 2016, http://www.waterkeeper.ca/blog/2016/11/8/what-you-need-to-know-about-the-port-hope-area-radioactive-waste-cleanup; and Philip Lee-Shanok, "$1.3B Cleanup

of Port Hope Finally Underway after Decades of Massive Planning," CBC.ca, April 1, 2018, https://www.cbc.ca/news/canada/toronto/port-hope-radioactive-waste-cleanup-finally-underway-1.4600654.

37 "Radioactive Leak from 3,000-Foot-Wide Ore Vein Found Reaching Up to 400 Homes in Elliot Lake," *Globe and Mail*, October 21, 1976.

38 "Nuclear Old Boys Love Secrecy," *Globe and Mail*, August 22, 1978; "Nuclear Power Insiders Accused of Leaving Public in the Dark," *Globe and Mail*, August 7, 1979.

39 Kirk Makin, "A-Plant Control Board Assailed for Bending to Hydro Pressure," *Globe and Mail*, August 9, 1979.

40 University of Saskatchewan Archives, Sylvia Fedoruk fonds, MG 435.I.Chronological, 1974, box 1.

41 "Fedoruk, Theodore, and Annie (Romaniuk) and The Hon. Sylvia O. Fedoruk," in *Winning the Prairie Gamble: History Album*, https://www.saskhistory.ca/fedoruk-theodore-and-annie-romaniuk-the-hon-sylvia-o-fedoruk/.

42 Ibid.

43 "Inquiry Hears Many Statistics," *Leader-Post*, April 26, 1977, 1; see also 3.

44 Florence Poorman, "Uranium Development," *Saskatchewan Indian* 7, no. 10 (1977): 19.

45 For a divergent view of the report, see Robin Hill, "Summary: Cluff Lake Board of Inquiry Local Hearings in Northern Sask: A Report on Some Discrepancies" (Saskatoon: Inter-Church Energy Committee, 1979). For the original documentation, see Cluff Lake Board of Inquiry series, including the final report, Provincial Archives of Saskatchewan, F 385-2.

46 Vera Pezer, interviews with Merle Massie, 2017, 2018.

47 Michael Vann, interview with Merle Massie, 2018.

48 Garry Vann, interview with Merle Massie, 2018.

49 Sylvia Fedoruk to Mr. A. Dagnone, September 8, 1976, University of Saskatchewan Archives, Sylvia Fedoruk faculty file, College of Medicine Dean's Office fonds, RG 2087.

50 University of Saskatchewan Archives, Sylvia Fedoruk fonds, MG 435.I.Chronological, 1977, box 1. See also MG 435.II.2.vi.Correspondence, 1966–77.

51 "Variety of Canadians Chosen to Meet Queen," *Star-Phoenix*, October 18, 1977, 3. See also University of Saskatchewan Archives, Sylvia Fedoruk fonds, MG 435, 1977, box 1.

52 "At Last, Sylvia Fedoruk May Get to Meet the Queen," *Star-Phoenix*, May 20, 1989, A9.

53 Michael Vann was with Sylvia in Yorkton when the queen came through. He remembered going to the street to wave, then wildly crossing town to another street to wave again. Michael Vann, interview with Merle Massie, 2018.

54 The speech can be found in University of Saskatchewan Archives, Sylvia Fedoruk fonds, MG 435.I.Chronological, 1980, box 1.

55 Ibid.

NOTES

56 See C.S. Houston and S.O. Fedoruk, "The Radiation Hazard in Hospitals: A Reappraisal," *Journal of the Canadian Association of Radiologists* 32, no. 2 (1981): 77–78; C.S. Houston and S.O. Fedoruk, "Saskatchewan's Role in Radiotherapy Research," *Canadian Medical Association Journal* 132 (1985): 854–64; Sylvia Fedoruk, "The Growth of Nuclear Medicine," in CAN/ABC *Proceedings Special Symposium on 50 Years of Nuclear Fission in Review*, Ottawa, vol. 1 (1989); and C.S. Houston and S.O. Fedoruk, "The History of Radiation Therapy in Saskatchewan," in *"A New Kind of Ray": The Radiological Sciences in Canada*, edited by John E. Aldrich and Brian C. Lentle (Vancouver: Canadian Association of Radiologists, 1995), 141–57.
57 Michael Vann, interview with Merle Massie, 2018.
58 See University of Saskatchewan Archives, Sylvia Fedoruk fonds, MG 435.I.Chronological, 1972–84.
59 University of Saskatchewan Archives, Sylvia Fedoruk fonds, MG 435.I. Chronological, 1982, box 1.
60 Bill Allan, "Cancer Clinic Workers Strike Limits Radiotherapy Treatment," *Leader-Post*, August 12, 1982, 3.
61 Bill Allan, "Cancer Clinic Workers Withdraw Services," *Leader-Post*, August 11, 1982, 1; Bill Allan, "Health Minister Proposes Conciliation to Settle Cancer Strike," *Leader-Post*, August 17, 1982, 1.
62 Michael Vann, interview with Merle Massie, November 30, 2018.
63 Ibid.
64 University of Saskatchewan Archives, Sylvia Fedoruk fonds, MG 435.I.Chronological, 1986, January–June, box 2.
65 Ibid.
66 University of Saskatchewan Archives, Sylvia Fedoruk fonds, MG 435, Saskatchewan Award of Merit, 1986, box 2.
67 Michael Vann, interview with Merle Massie, November 2018.
68 Letters, crafted with pomp and gravity or great humour and thanks, found their way to Saskatoon. Collected into a binder, the letters were presented to Sylvia at her retirement banquet, bringing wishes from everyone from the president of the AECB, J.H. Jennekins, to Premier Grant Devine, to Mayor of Saskatoon Cliff Wright, whose wife, Betty, had been a teammate back on the Huskiette basketball team. Colleagues from the illustrious Harold Johns and Sandy Watson all the way through to the technicians at the clinics sent in their good wishes and stories. See University of Saskatchewan Archives, Sylvia Fedoruk fonds, MG 435. II.2.j.vi.Retirement Binder, box 23.
69 Ibid.

8: MADAME CHANCELLOR

1 Memo to University Secretary's office, University of Saskatchewan Archives, Sylvia Fedoruk fonds, MG 435.I.Chronological, July–December 1986, box 2.
2 Donna Hoogeveen, a teacher from the Biggar district, was a graduate at fall convocation 1986. Her daughter Lesley recounted this story.

NOTES

3   Sylvia's unmarried status left a few odd holes in her invitation, which included a "partner," from the university's protocol office. Old friend and colleague Trevor Cradduck, Sylvia's one-time graduate student, was honoured to make the trek from London, Ontario, to witness her elevation and share in the special day.
4   Slobstick information is gleaned from several sources: the Sylvia Fedoruk fonds at the University of Saskatchewan Archives, which include references in her day-planners, invitations to the annual Slobstick, and an extensive video and photograph collection; Bob Florence, "Women's Annual Weekend a Club for Friends," *Star-Phoenix*, June 7, 2010; and interviews with Vera Pezer, Mona Finlayson, and Irene Bell.
5   "Slobstick XVII," sent from "Vera Blalock" (a.k.a. Vera Pezer) to the Slobstick crew, copy in University of Saskatchewan Archives, Sylvia Fedoruk fonds, MG 435.I.Chronological, March–June 1987, box 2.
6   Ibid.
7   Bob Florence, "Women's Annual Weekend a Club for Friends," *Star-Phoenix*, June 7, 2010.
8   The spelling mistake was clearly intentional. See "Slobstick XVII," University of Saskatchewan, Sylvia Fedoruk fonds, MG 435.I.Chronological, March–June 1987, box 2.
9   The Order of Merit is limited to twenty-four sitting members and is generally given only for the highest level of commonwealth service, such as premiers and prime ministers.
10 University of Saskatchewan Archives, Sylvia Fedoruk fonds, MG 435.I.Order of Canada, April 29, 1987, box 2, no. 12; Michael Vann, interview with Merle Massie, November 2018.
11 University of Saskatchewan Archives, Sylvia Fedoruk fonds, MG 435.II.4.d.Atomic Energy Control Board, 1973–86.
12 University of Saskatchewan Archives, Sylvia Fedoruk fonds, MG 435.I.Chronological, June–December 1987, box 2.
13 T. Dagnone to "Mrs. Fedoruk," University of Saskatchewan Archives, Sylvia Fedoruk fonds, MG 435.I.Chronological, June–December 1987, box 2, no. 11.
14 Correspondence between Saskatoon Library and Sylvia Fedoruk, University of Saskatchewan Archives, University Secretary fonds, RG 2009, 46-10, Chancellor's Correspondence, 1987–88.
15 University of Saskatchewan Archives, University Secretary fonds, RG 2009, Series 2, Records Relating to Joint Consultative Committee on Salary Matters, 1986–88.
16 Ibid.
17 "1988: Faculty Strike," *Events in the History of the University of Saskatchewan*, http://scaa.usask.ca/gallery/uofs_events/articles/1988.php.
18 Sylvia Fedoruk, speech, University of Saskatchewan Archives, Sylvia Fedoruk fonds, MG 435.I.Chronological, June 14–15, 1987, University of Windsor, box 2.

19 Sylvia Fedoruk, speech to Saskatchewan Women's Institutes on women in science, University of Saskatchewan Archives, Sylvia Fedoruk fonds, MG 435.I.Chronological, March–June 1987, box 2.
20 University of Saskatchewan Archives, Sylvia Fedoruk fonds, MG 435. II.2.h.iii.Day-Books, 1988
21 Correspondence, Order of St. John, University of Saskatchewan Archives, Sylvia Fedoruk fonds, MG 435.I.Chronological, September 26–October 15, 1988, box 3.
22 Sylvia equated her role as chancellor with being the "head cheerleader" in her speech to the University of Windsor in 1987. See University of Saskatchewan Archives, Sylvia Fedoruk fonds, MG 435.I.Chronological, June 14–15, 1987, University of Windsor, box 2.

9: THE HONOURABLE LEFT-HANDED GOVERNOR

1 Sylvia Fedoruk, remarks at Viscount School, May 3, 1989, Provincial Archives of Saskatchewan, 2007-294, Sylvia Fedoruk fonds, box 2, Speeches.
2 Sylvia revealed this anecdote at her final farewell speech in the legislature in May 1994, though she never revealed Hnatyshyn by name. That fact is only in her day-planner.
3 Provincial Archives of Saskatchewan, 2007-294, Sylvia Fedoruk fonds, box 2, Speeches, May 4, 1989.
4 University of Saskatchewan Archives, Sylvia Fedoruk fonds, MG 435. II.2.h.iii.Day-Books 1988–2000, July 1988.
5 Michael Vann, interview with Merle Massie, November 30, 2018.
6 Legislative Assembly of Saskatchewan, "Installation Ceremony for Her Honour Sylvia Olga Fedoruk O.C., S.O.M.," University of Saskatchewan Archives, Sylvia Fedoruk fonds, MG 435.I.Chronological, September 1988, box 3. The installation and farewell ceremonies for lieutenant-governors are legislative ceremonies, recorded in full in the Hansard record and usually printed as souvenirs.
7 Quoted in Marg Ommanney, "Fedoruk Wants to Focus on Children, Northerners," *Star-Phoenix*, September 6, 1988, A3.
8 For the formal installation service, see Legislative Assembly of Saskatchewan, "Installation Ceremony for Her Honour Sylvia Olga Fedoruk O.C., S.O.M.," University of Saskatchewan Archives, Presidential fonds, RG 2001, VI. Leo Kristjanson, 1988; see also University of Saskatchewan Archives, Sylvia Fedoruk fonds, MG 435.I. Chronological, September 1988, box 3. For media interviews following the ceremony, see Neil Scott, "Fedoruk Hopes to Set Good Example," *Leader-Post*, September 8, 1988, A3, and Dave Traynor, "Lieutenant Governor Sworn In: Fedoruk Focuses on Children," *Star-Phoenix*, September 8, 1988, A7.
9 Edward Willett, *Government House Regina Saskatchewan: An Illustrated History* (Regina: Government House Historical Society and Your Nickel's Worth Publishing, 2016), 12.

10 Will Chabun, "Never a Quiet Moment," *Leader-Post*, "Weekender," n.d., clipping in Government House Archives, Lieutenant-Governor's Scrapbooks, 1988.
11 See ibid. for historical information on Government House history and restoration.
12 Provincial Archives of Saskatchewan, 2007-294, Sylvia Fedoruk files, box 1, Marching Orders, September–December 1988.
13 "A Fitting Finish" (editorial), *Weyburn Review*, September 1988, in Government House Archives, Lieutenant-Governor's Scrapbooks, 1988.
14 For quotations, see "2000 at Jubilee Park Hear Lieut.-Governor," *Weyburn Review*, September 14, 1988, in Government House Archives, Lieutenant-Governor's Scrapbooks, 1988; see also Provincial Archives of Saskatchewan, 2007-294, Sylvia Fedoruk files, box 1, Marching Orders, September–December 1988.
15 Ned Powers, "Accolades Pour in at Arena Celebration," n.d., clipping in Government House Archives, Lieutenant-Governor's Scrapbooks, 1988; see also "Opening Features Sask. Talent," *Star-Phoenix*, September 10, 1988, clipping in ibid.
16 See University of Saskatchewan Archives, Sylvia Fedoruk files, MG 435.I.Chronological, September 1988, box 3.
17 Pat Langston, interview with Merle Massie, 2018.
18 Sylvia Fedoruk, remarks to the Provincial Council of Women, April 15, 1989, Provincial Archives of Saskatchewan, 2007-294, Sylvia Fedoruk fonds, box 2, Speeches.
19 Michael Vann, interview with Merle Massie, November 30, 2018.
20 We can track the increase in pace via the increase in office expenditures for travel and staff for the Office of the Lieutenant-Governor. Not all of the figures are available for Sylvia's time in office because of errors in reporting for the Office of the Provincial Secretary, which included expenses for the Office of the Lieutenant-Governor. Overall, though, expenses rose from about $160,000 per year to $235,000 per year in this time period. In 1988, the travel budget was $8,788. In 1989, Sylvia's first full year in office, the travel budget jumped to $31,148. Figures can be found in Public Accounts, Province of Saskatchewan, for the fiscal years 1988, 1989, 1990, 1991, 1992, 1993, and 1994.
21 University of Saskatchewan Archives, Sylvia Fedoruk fonds, MG 435. II.2.h.iii.Day-Books 1988–2000.
22 Multiple interviewees recounted Sylvia's horror of pantyhose.
23 Garry Vann and Carol Walker, interview with Merle Massie, November 2018.
24 See the Salaries Act, R.S.C. 1985, c. S-3, https://laws-lois.justice.gc.ca/eng/acts/S-3/page-1.html.
25 Sylvia's personal video of her office is found in University of Saskatchewan Archives, Sylvia Fedoruk fonds, MG 435, box 33, VHS, autumn 1987. I have drawn other details from interviews with Garry Vann, Pat Langston, and Irene White and from my own visit to Government House, where Carolyn Spiers graciously gave me a tour of its office side.

NOTES

26 The *Front Page Challenge* episode with Sylvia can be found online via the CBC Archives, https://www.cbc.ca/player/play/1180458051801. Merle Massie did the transcription.
27 Roy Romanow, interview with Merle Massie, November 2018. Sylvia pulled all of this off while part of her heart was no doubt in Saskatoon, where the men's Brier was taking place. But in between her legislative duties and tea with Mrs. Devine, she managed to sneak back to Saskatoon for at least a few of the last draws and the banquet.
28 In the twenty-first legislature, Sylvia prorogued the second session on March 8, 1989; opened the third session on March 8, 1989; prorogued the third session on March 19, 1990; opened the fourth session on March 19, 1990; and prorogued the fourth session on June 18, 1991. In the twenty-second legislature, she opened the first session on December 2, 1991; prorogued the first session on April 27, 1992; opened the second session on April 27, 1992; prorogued the second session on February 25, 1993; opened the third session on February 25, 1993; prorogued the third session on February 7, 1994; and opened the fourth session on February 7, 1994.
29 All of the Speeches from the Throne can be found in the Legislative Assembly of Saskatchewan, Assembly Records Calendar, Debates (Hansard). They are all scanned and online back to 1947. Saskatchewan, Legislative Assembly, Debates and Proceedings (Hansard), 21st Legislature, 3rd Session (March 8, 1989), http://docs.legassembly.sk.ca/legdocs/Legislative%20Assembly/Hansard/21L3S/890308Debates.pdf.
30 Andrew and Sarah's royal visit can be followed through Sylvia's day-books in the University of Saskatchewan Archives, MG 435.II.h.iii; Sylvia's chronological files, MG 435.I.Chronological, July 20–25, 1989, Royal Visit, box 5; Sylvia's photograph collection, MG 435.IV.4.r, box 43; Government House Archives, Lieutenant-Governor's Scrapbooks, 1989; Pat Langston, interview with Merle Massie, 2018; and Pat Langston photograph collection.
31 Saskatchewan, Legislative Assembly, Debates and Proceedings (Hansard), 21st Legislature, 3rd Session (August 25, 1989), http://docs.legassembly.sk.ca/legdocs/Legislative%20Assembly/Hansard/21L3S/89-08-25pm.pdf.
32 This story was relayed, with much laughter, by Pat Langston.
33 University of Saskatchewan Archives, Sylvia Fedoruk fonds, MG 435.II.2.h.iii.Day-Books 1988–2000, box 21, and iv.Day-Planners, 1984–94, box 23.
34 Saskatchewan, Legislative Assembly, Debates and Proceedings (Hansard), 21st Legislature, 3rd Session (March 19, 1990), http://docs.legassembly.sk.ca/legdocs/Legislative%20Assembly/Hansard/21L3S/90-03-19.pdf.
35 Saskatchewan, Legislative Assembly, Debates and Proceedings (Hansard), 21st Legislature, 4th Session (March 19, 1990), http://docs.legassembly.sk.ca/legdocs/Legislative%20Assembly/Hansard/21L4S/900319.pdf.
36 Ibid.
37 Ibid.

38 Correspondence between Trevor Cradduck and Merle Massie, February 2019.
39 Mark Wyatt, "Fedoruk Gave $200 to Federal PC Party," *Leader-Post*, October 5, 1990, clipping in Government House Archives, Lieutenant-Governor's Scrapbooks, 1990.
40 Ibid.
41 Ibid.
42 "Fedoruk No Partisan, Devine Maintains," *Leader-Post*, October 6, 1990, clipping in Government House Archives, Lieutenant-Governor's Scrapbooks, 1990.
43 Ibid.
44 Other clippings in the Government House Archives, Lieutenant-Governor's Scrapbooks, 1990, include Dave Traynor and Randy Burton, "Political Contribution 'Stupid Thing to Do,'" *Star-Phoenix*, October 6, 1990; "To Err Is Human," *Star-Phoenix*, October 11, 1990; and "Honor Demands Fedoruk Resign," *Star-Phoenix*, October 15, 1990.
45 University of Saskatchewan Archives, Sylvia Fedoruk fonds, MG 435. II.2.h.iv.Day-Planner 1984–94, box 22.
46 Saskatchewan, Legislative Assembly, Debates and Proceedings (Hansard), 21st Legislature, 4th Session (April 12, 1991), http://docs.legassembly.sk.ca/legdocs/Legislative%20Assembly/Hansard/21L4S/910412.pdf.
47 Ibid.
48 University of Saskatchewan Archives, Sylvia Fedoruk fonds, MG 435. II.l.c.i.Special Warrants, 1991, box 14, file 8. The folder contains numerous items of interest to political historians, showcasing Sylvia's intense scrutiny of the affairs of 1991. The following quotations are from this folder.
49 Saskatchewan, Legislative Assembly, Debates and Proceedings (Hansard), 21st Legislature, 4th Session (June 18, 1991), http://docs.legassembly.sk.ca/legdocs/Legislative%20Assembly/Hansard/21L4S/910618.pdf.
50 University of Saskatchewan Archives, Sylvia Fedoruk fonds, MG 435. II.l.c.i.Special Warrants, 1991, box 14, file 8.
51 Michael Jackson, *The Crown and Canadian Federalism* (Toronto: Dundurn Press, 2013), 154.
52 Ibid. See also Saskatchewan, Legislative Assembly, Debates and Proceedings (Hansard), 21st Legislature, 4th Session (June 18, 1991), http://docs.legassembly.sk.ca/legdocs/Legislative%20Assembly/Hansard/21L4S/910618e.pdf.
53 "Ending Session Was 'Right Thing' Devine Insists," *Globe and Mail*, June 22, 1991, A3.
54 Deputy Minister of Justice and Deputy Attorney General Brian Barrington-Foote to the Honourable Sylvia Fedoruk, June 26, 1991, University of Saskatchewan Archives, Sylvia Fedoruk fonds, MG 435. II.l.c.i.Special Warrants, 1991.
55 Legislative counsel and law clerk Merrilee Rasmussen issued two legal opinions on the use of special warrants, one in 1987 as a response to the situation that year, another in 1991. She was no longer special counsel when she issued the second opinion; she had, in fact, been let go by

the Devine administration, which thought that her opinions were biased by her political views. Nonetheless, these two documents, held in the Saskatchewan Legislative Library, were written in an accessible format and provide a thorough constitutional understanding of the issues. I am thankful that Rasmussen provided these important documents, which Michael Jackson used extensively in writing his book and which I used as I worked to understand the political situation of 1991 and the anger obvious in Sylvia's notes.

56 "Protestors Want Warrants Stopped," *Leader-Post*, June 17, 1991, clipping in Government House Archives, Lieutenant-Governor's Scrapbooks, 1991.

57 Deputy Minister of Justice and Deputy Attorney General Brian Barrington-Foote to the Honourable Sylvia Fedoruk, June 26, 1991, University of Saskatchewan Archives, Sylvia Fedoruk fonds, MG 435.II.l.c.i.Special Warrants, 1991.

58 Mark Wyatt, "NDP Says Warrants Illegal," *Leader-Post*, July 6, 1991; "Leaked Memo Has Spending Warning," *Star-Phoenix*, July 6, 1991, clippings in Government House Archives, Lieutenant-Governor's Scrapbooks, 1991.

59 University of Saskatchewan Archives, Sylvia Fedoruk fonds, MG 435.II.l.c.i.Special Warrants, 1991, box 14, file 8. Sylvia kept newspaper clippings, correspondence, legal opinions, and handwritten notes of conversations with Deputy Attorney General Brian Barrington-Foote, Premier Grant Devine, and others.

60 Gordon Barnhart, interview with Merle Massie, December 2018.

61 Provincial Archives of Saskatchewan, 2007-294, Sylvia Fedoruk files, box 2, Speeches, June 30, 1989 (handwritten and edited).

62 University of Saskatchewan Archives, Sylvia Fedoruk fonds, MG 435.II.l.c.i.Special Warrants, 1991, box 14, file 8.

63 University of Saskatchewan Archives, Sylvia Fedoruk fonds, MG 435.I, box 8, September 1991.

64 University of Saskatchewan Archives, Sylvia Fedoruk fonds, MG 435.II.l.c.i.Special Warrants, 1991, handwritten notes dated September 6 and 9.

65 David Robert, "Devine Prepares for Oct. 21 Election: New Democrats Ahead in Polls and Public in Snarly Mood for Change," *Globe and Mail*, September 21, 1991, A6.

66 Patrick Nagle, "Romanow Looks for War Cabinet," *Vancouver Sun*, October 23, 1991, A4; Robert, "Devine Prepares for Oct. 21st Election."

67 University of Saskatchewan Archives, Sylvia Fedoruk fonds, MG 435.II.2.h.iv.Day-Planners 1984-94, 1991, box 22.

68 Roy Romanow, interview with Merle Massie, November 20, 2018. The following quotations are from this interview.

69 Saskatchewan, Legislative Assembly, Debates and Proceedings (Hansard), 22nd Legislature, 1st Session (December 2, 1991), http://docs.legassembly.sk.ca/legdocs/Legislative%20Assembly/Hansard/22L1S/911202H.pdf.

70 Ibid.

NOTES

71 Roy Romanow, interview with Merle Massie, December 2018.
72 See Don Gass, "The Report of the Saskatchewan Financial Management Review Commission," 1992, submitted to the minister of finance.
73 The fraud investigation was summed up by *Globe and Mail* reporter Stevie Cameron as "financial irregularities and creative accounting practices." See "How the Gravy Train Went Off the Rails," *Globe and Mail*, February 6, 1993, D1.
74 Roy Romanow, interview with Merle Massie, December 2018.
75 Ibid.
76 Ibid.
77 Ibid.
78 Ibid.
79 Ibid. In an ironic turn, Sylvia would have had to sign at least a few special warrants in the spring of 1992 since the legislature was not recalled to sit until April 27, almost a month past its voted supply to the end of March.
80 Saskatchewan, Legislative Assembly, Debates and Proceedings (Hansard), 22nd Legislature, 2nd Session (April 27, 1992), http://docs.legassembly.sk.ca/legdocs/Legislative%20Assembly/Hansard/22L2S/920427.pdf.
81 Postcard from Sylvia Fedoruk to Irene Bell, Doreen Fairburn, and Hoppy the dog, in the collection of Doreen Fairburn. Also hand-notated copy of "Itinerary, Lieutenant-Governor of Saskatchewan, May 3–19, 1992," Doreen Fairburn files.
82 "Itinerary, Lieutenant-Governor of Saskatchewan, May 3–19, 1992," Doreen Fairburn files; handwritten notations of phone call to Pat Langston.
83 University of Saskatchewan Archives, Sylvia Fedoruk fonds, MG 435.I.Chronological, May 1992 (England), box 9.
84 Kenn Gardner Honeychurch, "Inside Out/Outside In (Sexual Diversity: A Comparative Case Study of Two Postsecondary Visual Arts Students)" (Ph.D. diss., University of British Columbia, 1996), 98–101.
85 As quoted in Peter Millard, "Human Rights and the PC Government," in *Devine Rule in Saskatchewan*, ed. Lesley Biggs and Mark Stobbe (Saskatoon: Fifth House Publishers, 1991), 33–48.
86 Bonnie Braden, "Protesters Say Gay, Lesbian Rights Need Protection," *Star-Phoenix*, December 2, 1992, A14.
87 Ibid. Lefler read the article that outlined Devine's opinion on homosexuality soon after arriving in Saskatchewan. It had a fundamental impact on Lefler's knowledge of how Saskatchewan politicians viewed homosexuality. See Honeychurch, "Inside Out/Outside In," 98.
88 Ibid., 99–101.
89 University of Saskatchewan Archives, Sylvia Fedoruk fonds, MG 435. II.2.h.iv.Day-Planners 1984–94, 1992.
90 Braden, "Protesters Say Gay, Lesbian Rights Need Protection."
91 Saskatchewan, Legislative Assembly, Debates and Proceedings (Hansard), 22nd Legislature, 3rd Session (February 25, 1993), http://docs.legassembly.sk.ca/legdocs/Legislative%20Assembly/Hansard/22L3S/930225H.pdf.

92 Eric Burt, "Many Missed Out on Fedoruk's Levee," *Saskatoon Sun*, January 24, 1993, 6.
93 University of Saskatchewan Archives, Sylvia Fedoruk fonds, MG 435. II.2.h.iv.Day-Planners 1984–94, 1993, box 22.
94 See Bernard Pilon, "Queen for a Play"; Bernard Pilon, "'Mouse' a Roaring Success for Globe," *Leader-Post*, May 8, 1993, D6; and Patrick Davitt, "Mouse Was a Roaring Good Time," clippings in Government House Archives, Lieutenant-Governor's Scrapbooks, May 1993.
95 "Doctor of Humane Letters, honoris causa (DHumL)," Mount Saint Vincent University, https://www.msvu.ca/en/home/aboutus/university-profile/senate/honorarydegrees.aspx.
96 "Doesn't Know," *Leader-Post*, August 27, 1993, clipping in Government House Archives, Lieutenant-Governor's Scrapbooks, 1993.
97 "Lieutenant Governor Tours North," *Northerner* [La Ronge], September 21, 1993, clipping in Government House Archives, Lieutenant-Governor's Scrapbooks, 1993.
98 Pat Langston, interview with Merle Massie, December 2018.
99 "Proceedings on the Occasion of the Farewell to Her Honour the Honourable Sylvia O. Fedoruk O.C., S.O.M., Lieutenant Governor of Saskatchewan," May 12, 1994, Legislative Building, Regina, in Government House Archives, Lieutenant-Governor's Scrapbooks, 1994.
100 Ibid.
101 Rod and Cathy Fedoruk to Sylvia Fedoruk, May 5, 1994, University of Saskatchewan Archives, Sylvia Fedoruk fonds, MG 435.I, March–May 1994 (1), box 11, folder 6.
102 University of Saskatchewan Archives, Sylvia Fedoruk fonds, MG 435. II.2.h.iii.Day-Book, May 31, 1994.

10: HURRICANE
1 The numbers of Canadians diagnosed with AIDS rose year over year throughout the 1980s and early 1990s. In 1992, 1,854 people were newly diagnosed; in 1993, 1,954 people were newly diagnosed; in 1994, 1,925 people were newly diagnosed. The cumulative number of Canadians living with HIV (the virus that leads to AIDS) was 32,995. See the History of Canadian AIDS Society website at https://www.cdnaids.ca/about-us/history/.
2 The story of Lefler and Fedoruk was then and is now found in newspapers, alternative media, radio and television (including an episode of the CTV show *W5* with Eric Malling), the Hansard record of legislative debate in Saskatchewan, law books, doctoral dissertations, and a video documentary. The story is also in people's memories—imperfect but conscious, with the power of insistence. In her day-planners and video collection, personal notes and correspondence, Sylvia acknowledged the impact of Lefler as a part of her own story, though at the time her public stance was one of denial.
3 Most of the information on Lefler, his art practices, and the events at both the University of Victoria and the University of Saskatchewan is drawn from Kenn Gardner Honeychurch, "Inside Out/Outside In (Sexual

Diversity: A Comparative Case Study of Two Post-Secondary Visual Arts Students)" (Ph.D. diss., University of British Columbia, 1996), https://open.library.ubc.ca/cIRcle/collections/ubctheses/831/items/1.0088798. Honeychurch used extensive interviews with Christopher Lefler to reconstruct and understand the trajectory and growth of Lefler as an artist. I believe that Saskatchewan would be well served by a thorough, book-length discussion of the events surrounding Lefler's time in Saskatchewan. This chapter, in truth, is a much-distilled and shortened version of what could and should be a more rigorous investigation.

4   Pat Langston, interview with Merle Massie, December 2018.
5   See Honeychurch, "Inside Out/Outside In," 103, where part of Lefler's letter is reprinted. The letter was not found in the Sylvia Fedoruk fonds at the University of Saskatchewan Archives or at Government House. It might still be within the University of Saskatchewan Archives, but none of the archivists was able to locate it. It is possible that the letter was never sent to the archives for historical safekeeping. Christopher Lefler kept copies of the letter, and it was shared with Honeychurch for his dissertation.
6   The Canadian government issued an apology and offered compensation in 2017 to federal employees who were victims of the "gay purge" between the 1950s and 1990s. See Jim Bronskill, "718 Victims of Canadian Government's Gay Purge Compensated in Settlement," Global News, July 13, 2019, https://globalnews.ca/news/5491739/gay-purge-victims-canada/.
7   University of Saskatchewan Archives, Sylvia Fedoruk fonds, MG 435. II.2.h.iii.Day-Books 1988–2000, March 19, 1993.
8   As quoted in Honeychurch, "Inside Out/Outside In," 104.
9   Joan Borsa, interview with Merle Massie, 2017.
10 Ibid.
11 Honeychurch, "Inside Out/Outside In," 104–05.
12 The acronym stands for lesbian, gay, bisexual, transgender, queer. We can trace the use of these terms over time. In 1993, the U of S campus club for gay and lesbian students was called GLUS: Gays and Lesbians at the U of S.
13 As recorded in Honeychurch, "Inside Out/Outside In," 103.
14 Saskatchewan, Legislative Assembly, Debates and Proceedings (Hansard), 21st Legislature, 4th Session (June 18, 1991), http://docs.legassembly.sk.ca/legdocs/Legislative%20Assembly/Hansard/21L4S/910618e.pdf.
15 In the original act, information that "relates to the race, creed, religion, colour, sex, family status or marital status, disability, age, nationality, ancestry or place of origin of the individual" was expressly protected, but sexual orientation was not. Sexual orientation was added, after sex, to this definition by royal assent July 6, 2001.
16 A detailed back-and-forth outline of the events of that November and December can be found in Honeychurch, "Inside Out/Outside In," 106–08.
17 Goodale wasn't available, but Government House spoke with his secretary to relay the gist of what was going on. See University of Saskatchewan

Archives, Sylvia Fedoruk fonds, MG 435.II.2.h.Day-Books 1988–2000, November 22, 1993.
18 See Honeychurch, "Inside Out/Outside In," 106–10.
19 University of Saskatchewan Archives, Sylvia Fedoruk fonds, MG 435.II.2.h.iii.Day-Books 1988–2000, December 6, 1993.
20 Duane Booth, "Art Student Suspended, Banned for Exhibit Deemed Defamatory," *Star-Phoenix*, December 8, 1993, A11.
21 University of Saskatchewan Archives, Sylvia Fedoruk fonds, MG 435.II.2.h.iii.Day-Books 1988–2000, December 7, 1993.
22 Booth, "Arts Student Suspended"; Duane Booth "Arts Student Awaits Discipline Ruling," *Star-Phoenix*, December 10, 1993, A5.
23 University of Saskatchewan Archives, Sylvia Fedoruk fonds, MG 435.II.2.h.iii.Day-Books 1988–2000, December 9, 1993.
24 T.M. Arsenault, "Point of View," *The Sheaf*, January 6, 1994, 6. Arsenault wrote that "the one thing that does frighten me is authority. . . . The point is these administrators frightened me. . . . They meant to scare me. . . . Administration should not be trying to frighten the student newspaper into printing what they want. That is abuse of power and that is something to be scared of."
25 As related to me by an art student at the time during a discussion of my book.
26 Terry Craig, "Outing Outrages Gays," *Star-Phoenix*, February 17, 1994, A3. See also Gens Hellquist, "Outing: The Injustice," *Perceptions*, March 1994, 6, and Peter Millard, "Outing: In a State of War," *Perceptions*, April 1994, 5.
27 For an overview of the story of Doug Wilson and the University of Saskatchewan, see Valerie J. Korinek, *Prairie Fairies: A History of Queer Communities and People in Western Canada, 1930–1985* (Toronto: University of Toronto Press, 2018).
28 Bonnie Braden, "Lefler Lodges Human Rights Complaint against University," *Star-Phoenix*, March 17, 1994, A12.
29 See "Sired by a Hurricane, Dam'd by an Earthquake," *The Sheaf*, February 17, 1994, 1.
30 University of Saskatchewan Archives, Sylvia Fedoruk fonds, MG 435.II.2.iv.Day-Planners 1984–94, February 21, 1994, box 22.
31 Lefler must have alerted the media, there in full force. Television and radio, as well as print, reported the story. Footage from the event appeared later on a *W5* episode with Eric Malling. A copy of that episode is in University of Saskatchewan Archives, Sylvia Fedoruk fonds, MG 435.III.3, "Eric Malling with Leffler [sic] Story," September 20, 1994, box 33.
32 Bonnie Braden, "University Student Stages Protest Prior to Hearing," *Star-Phoenix*, May 11, 1994, A7. Christopher Lefler's disciplinary hearing took place the same week that the provincial legislature honoured Sylvia Fedoruk for her service as lieutenant-governor. The three-person disciplinary board consisted of Dean of Education Murray Scharf, psychology professor Brian Chartier, and student Tiffany Paulsen. Paulsen later became a lawyer and served on Saskatoon City Council for sixteen years.

NOTES

33 See http://www.saskartsboard.com/menu/about/who-we-are.html for information on the SAB. I was awarded an Independent Artist grant from the SAB to work on this biography in 2018.
34 Mark Wyant, "Expelled Student's Grant Decried," *Star-Phoenix*, May 18, 1994, A12.
35 Ibid.
36 Saskatchewan, Legislative Assembly, Debates and Proceedings (Hansard), 22nd Legislature, 4th Session (May 24, 1994, evening session), http://docs.legassembly.sk.ca/legdocs/Legislative%20Assembly/Hansard/22L4S/940524e.pdf.
37 "Expelled Student's Art Grant under Review," *Star-Phoenix*, May 27, 1994, A15.
38 Dave Traynor, "Arts Board Rescinds Lefler's Grant," *Star-Phoenix*, June 14, 1994, A3.
39 Ibid.
40 "Writers Knock Carson Stand," *Star-Phoenix*, June 2, 1994, D1.
41 "Explain Lefler Grant Refusal, Artists Lobby Group Demands," *Star-Phoenix*, June 28, 1994, A5.
42 "Arts Board Member Resigns over Lefler Issue," *Star-Phoenix*, June 22, 1994, A3.
43 Verne Clemence, "Gay 'Outing' Not at Issue; Political Interference Is," *Star-Phoenix*, July 9, 1994, C8.
44 "Arts Board Head Quits after Potential Conflict," *Globe and Mail*, September 2, 1994, C2. I learned about Schmaltz subsequently resigning from the CBC via personal correspondence with a person who was also a CBC employee at the time.
45 The outcome of the SHRC complaints wouldn't occur until 1996, when the commission first tried to negotiate a settlement between Christopher Lefler and the university and then ruled against Lefler. That ruling was appealed and partially won when the SHRC decided that Lefler's right to free speech had been circumvented, though it dismissed the claim that Lefler had been discriminated against because of his sexual orientation. The commission dismissed all complaints regarding the Saskatchewan Arts Board.
46 Jim Russell, "A Gaze Blank and Pitiless as the Sun," *Fuse* 18, no. 2 (1994): 7–12. The following quotations from Russell are from this article.
47 Craig, "Outing Outrages Gays"; Hellquist, "Outing"; Millard, "Outing." The fallout and Saskatchewan's gay community's perceptions of the impact of Lefler's work were related to me by Valerie Korinek in personal correspondence.
48 Leslie Perreaux, "U of S Reluctant to Settle Student Artist's Complaint," *Star-Phoenix*, 12 October 1996, A3.
49 Social media comment to Merle Massie, fall 2017.
50 Korinek, *Prairie Fairies*, has provided important historical research and contemplation, including her own wrestling with the social conventions around being gay or lesbian on the Prairies. For her discussion of the "on-campus lesbians," see 103–04. One interviewee, speaking about this group, told Korinek that "everybody in town knows their little secret

NOTES

and yet they don't seem to want to acknowledge that in any way" (103). Korinek warned me during a personal visit that the Lefler story remains hugely controversial and could bring additional and possibly unwanted and unwarranted repercussions to me and this biography.

51 This chapter deliberately uses no images in homage to the Day Without Art movement and the continuing fight in Saskatchewan against AIDS.

11: SUNSET

1 Sylvia Fedoruk, handwritten speech to the Ronald McDonald House annual Canadian conference, University of Saskatchewan Archives, Sylvia Fedoruk fonds, MG 435.I.Mar–May 1994 (1), box 11, folder 6.
2 University of Saskatchewan Archives, Sylvia Fedoruk fonds, MG 435.II.2.c.ii.Christmas Letters 1994–2011, 1994 letter.
3 I found this recipe photographed from a published source on Pinterest. It is certainly Sylvia's own recipe judging from its contextual information. It's highly probable that the recipe was included in the annual Saskatoon Christmas recipe book, sent out for free from the *Star-Phoenix* and included with newspaper subscriptions. The editor of these books would request Saskatonians' best recipes, and many households kept copies for years in their recipe book collections.
4 University of Saskatchewan Archives, Sylvia Fedoruk fonds, MG 435.II.2.h.iii.Day-Books 1988–2000, 1996, box 21.
5 University of Saskatchewan Archives, Sylvia Fedoruk fonds, MG 435.II.2.c.ii.Christmas Letters 1994–2011, February 14, 1999 (for the 1998 year).
6 University of Saskatchewan archives, Sylvia Fedoruk fonds, MG 435.IV.5.19.CD-ROMS, 2000. The majority of these CD-ROMS are backups of Sylvia's hard drive of her computer, which included emails to friends. This quotation is from an email in July 2000 to an unrecognizable email alias.
7 Ibid., email to the same friend, July 28, 2000.
8 University of Saskatchewan Archives, Sylvia Fedoruk fonds, MG 435.II.2.c.ii.Christmas Letters 1994–2011, 2001 letter.
9 Ibid., 2003 letter.
10 Michael Vann, interview with Merle Massie, November 30, 2018.
11 University of Saskatchewan Archives, Sylvia Fedoruk fonds, MG 435.II.2.c.ii.Christmas Letters 1994–2011, 2002 letter.
12 Gordon Barnhart, interview with Merle Massie, December 3, 2018.
13 The listed degrees are Order of Canada, Saskatchewan Order of Merit, Master of Arts, Doctor of Science, Doctor of Laws, Doctor of Humane Letters, and Fellow of the Canadian College of Physicists in Medicine.
14 Michael Vann, interview with Merle Massie, November 30, 2018; Vera Pezer, interview with Merle Massie, 2017.
15 University of Saskatchewan Archives, Sylvia Fedoruk fonds, MG 435.II.2.c.ii.Christmas Letters 1994–2011, 2006 letter.
16 Sylvia Fedoruk to Mary Donald, c. 2002, University of Saskatchewan Archives, Sylvia Fedoruk fonds, MS 435.IV.4.S.CD-Roms, CD-R 115, box

NOTES

47. Sylvia had met Mary when Scottish women had travelled to western Canada for curling.
17 Correspondence between Sylvia Fedoruk and Henri Bouchard, University of Saskatchewan Archives, Sylvia Fedoruk fonds, MS 435.IV.4.S.CD-Roms, CD-R 120, Corrpinso2, box 47.
18 University of Saskatchewan Archives, Sylvia Fedoruk fonds, MG 435.II.2.c.ii.Christmas Letters 1994–2011, 2002 letter.
19 This online family history album repository has since been moved from the *Western Development Museum* site to www.saskhistory.ca. See https://www.saskhistory.ca/fedoruk-theodore-and-annie-romaniuk-the-hon-sylvia-o-fedoruk/.
20 Vera Pezer, interview with Merle Massie, 2017.
21 Susan Pederson, "Bettering the World through Life-Saving Research and Life-Changing Generosity," November 7, 2013, *University of Saskatchewan Donor News*, https://words.usask.ca/donornews/2013/11/07/bettering-the-world-through-life-saving-research-and-life-changing-generosity/. See also University of Saskatchewan Archives, Sylvia Fedoruk fonds, MG 435.II.2.b.ii.Fedoruk Family Foundation, 1991–2004. Trustees included Garry, Merylyn, and Michael Vann as well as Myrna Berwick as treasurer.
22 University of Saskatchewan Archives, Sylvia Fedoruk fonds, MG 435.II.2.c.ii.Christmas Letters 1994–2011, 2007 letter, box 16.
23 Curly Walz and Marj Schell, phone interview with Merle Massie, January 2019. See also University of Saskatchewan Archives, Sylvia Fedoruk fonds, MG 435.II.2.c.ii.Christmas Letters 1994–2011, 2008 letter, box 16.
24 Vera Pezer, interview with Merle Massie, 2016.
25 Ibid.
26 Quoted in Kevin Mitchell, "Fedoruk Left a Mark on Sports," *Star-Phoenix*, September 28, 2012, B1.
27 Story on a wall of Greystone Heights school, Saskatoon.
28 Quoted in Jane Caulfield, "U of S Nuclear Research Centre Renamed in Honour of Fedoruk," *Star-Phoenix*, October 4, 2012, A3; "Nuclear Centre Honours Fedoruk," *Leader-Post*, October 4, 2012, A3.
29 Quoted in Jennifer Graham, "Sylvia Fedoruk Dead: Former Saskatchewan Lieutenant-Governor, Medical Pioneer," *Huffington Post,* September 27, 2012; Mitchell, "Fedoruk Left a Mark on Sports"; "She Was at the Forefront of Canadian Medicine," *National Post*, October 3, 2012, B4; Jane Caulfield, "'A Leader in Every Respect,'" *Metro* [Saskatoon], September 28, 2012, 1.
30 Michael Vann, interview with Merle Massie, November 2018.
31 Stuart Houston's handwritten notations on the official state funeral service for Sylvia can be found in the University of Saskatchewan Archives, Sylvia Fedoruk faculty biography, Department of Medicine Dean's Office fonds, RG 2087.
32 From the tribute toast to Sylvia given by Pat Lawson and Peggy McKercher at the post-funeral gathering. From the files of Stuart Houston.

INDEX

A

Acme Machine and Electric Company, 66, 84, 117–18, 121
activism, 235–36, 238, 246, 252–54, 274
Adams, Carly, 31
Adams, Jack, 63
Advisory Committee on the Clinical Uses of Radioisotopes, 106
African American girls' softball team, 62
agricultural research station (Swift Current), 201
AIDS crisis, 224, 226, 235, 238, 253–54
alcohol/alcoholism, 24, 127, 129, 139, 143, 168, 170, 204, 229–30, 254, 275
All-American Girls Professional Baseball League, 30–31, 48, 89
Allan Blair Cancer Clinic (Regina), 87–88, 142, 159, 164, 187
Allis-Chalmers company, 44
Amati Quartet, 273
Amok Limited, 152–53
Anderson, J.T.M., 12
Anderson, Myrtle, 109, 114
Andre, Harvie, 185
Andrew, Prince, 200–201
Andrusco, Billy, 190
Appropriation Act, 212

Arcand, Kevin, 273
archives/artifacts, 2–4, 7, 169, 229, 253–54, 265–66
  diaries, 125–26, 138, 142–43, 182, 223, 243, 247, 260, 268
  interviews, 5–6
  memorabilia, 280
  oral stories, 5, 8, 252
art/art installations
  audience engagement in, 236
  and defamation of character, 246, 249
  freedom to express, 236, 252–53, 259
  and political advocacy, 248, 252
Atchison, Don, 271
Atomic Energy Commission, 41
Atomic Energy Control Act, 148
Atomic Energy Control Board of Canada (AECB), 8, 78, 150, 152, 155–56, 163, 168, 172, 184–85, 222, 279
  appointment of S. Fedoruk, 148–49, 153–54, 166, 178–79, 222, 239
  and betatron unit, 48, 55–56
Atomic Energy of Canada Limited (AECL), 148, 150
Auld, F.H., 77
Avery, Cheryl, 2

313

INDEX

B

Bailey's Funeral Home
(Yorkton), 155
Baldenstone, Jean, 110
Bannister, Mary, 114
barbecues, 168, 170, 206, 255
Barnhart, Gordon, 6,
194, 213–14, 263
Barrington-Foote, Brian,
209, 211, 215
baseball, 17, 30, 94, 100, 119–20, 267
ball playing, 1, 18, 21, 50, 92, 144
S. Fedoruk's skill at, 3, 69, 87–88
basketball, 36–37, 44, 46, 71,
87, 94–95, 157, 165, 227
S. Fedoruk's skill at, 3,
26, 61, 69, 88, 99
Bates, Lloyd, 65, 67, 74
Bayda, Justice E.D., 153, 185
Beechy Agricultural Fair, 166
Belding, Donna, 102, 105, 108–9
Bell, Irene, 6, 135–36, 144,
169, 201, 221, 264, 269
Bentley, T.J., 77, 93
Berlie, Elmer, 44
Berton, Pierre, 174, 197
Berwick, Myrna, 2, 6
betatron machine, 1, 38–39, 48, 62,
64, 69, 71, 83, 99, 158, 272
accelerators, 85–86, 93, 161
design of, 65, 79
as forerunner of cobalt-60
unit, 57
installation of, 50–51, 56, 66
program for, 39, 41–42, 44, 55
use in cancer treatment, 53,
55, 61, 80, 100, 141, 161
Bicknell, Norma, 149
Binner, Millie, 110
Blair, Dr. Allan, 38–39, 41, 55, 77
See also Allan Blair Cancer
Clinic (Regina)
Blair, Florence Mary, 77
Blakeney, Allan, 188, 217
The Blue and White
(yearbook), 27, 30
Board of Trade (Regina), 188
Bocking, D.H., 174

Borsa, Joan, 6
Bouchard, Henri, 266
Bowen, Gail, 256
Braithwaite, Hazel,
44–45, 63–64, 76
Braithwaite, Max, 174
Bridok School District, 13
The Brier, 110, 140, 146, 178
Bright, Addie, 114
Britton, Beth, 92
Bromnell, Dr. G., 86
Brown, Elta, 134–35
Brown, Peter, 227
Browne, Patrick, 242
Bruce Nuclear Power, 149–50
Brucer, Dr. Marshall, 86
Buckingham Palace, 139,
157, 221–22, 259
Burkell, Dr. C.C., 263
Butler Byers trophy (curling),
109
Butnik, Susan, 227

C

Caesium treatment unit
(Regina), 122
Cairns Field, 62–63, 88
Calgary Alexandras
baseball team, 48
Calgary Rose Bowl
(curling), 126, 128
campus lesbians, 253
See also lesbian
Canada Post commemorative
stamp, 178
Canada Winter Games, 136
Canadian Cancer Association, 55
Canadian Cancer Society, 38, 67, 85
Canadian CANDU (Canada
Deuterium Uranium)
nuclear power, 148–49
Canadian Club (Saskatoon), 183
Canadian Curling Hall of
Fame, 258, 277
The Canadian Encyclopedia, 174
Canadian Ladies Curling
Association (CLCA), 96,
137–38, 140, 163, 165

314

INDEX

Canadian Light Source synchrotron, 267
Canadian Nuclear Association, 86
Canadian Nuclear Society, 86
Canadian Society of Radiological Technicians, 83
cancer clinics, 101
  See also Saskatchewan cancer clinics
cancer diagnosis, 8, 107, 155
  scanning techniques for, 117, 122, 126, 178
cancer research, 41, 44, 57, 86, 116, 155, 238
cancer treatment, 8, 161, 178, 254, 263
  with betatron machine, 41–42, 44, 53, 55, 80, 86
  with cobalt-60, 57, 65–66, 83
  with radiotherapy/teletherapy, 37–38, 56, 60, 64, 67, 87, 94, 107, 222, 270
Canora Curling Club, 280
card playing, 72–74, 133, 254, 264
  See also gambling
Carson, Carol, 248–49
Carter, Pearl, 115
Cave, Hap & Slim, 142–43
CBC (Canadian Broadcasting Corporation), 227, 243, 247, 250
Cecil Race trophy (basketball), 37, 42, 46, 52, 61
censorship, of art, 245, 247, 253
Centennial Auditorium (now TCU Place), 158–59, 163, 165, 173, 273
Chalk River nuclear reactor plant, 29, 38–39, 57, 59–60, 64, 67, 141, 178
  and betatron program, 41–42, 53, 55
  and cobalt-60 machine, 74, 78, 84, 93, 148
Chamber of Commerce (Regina), 188
chancellorship at U of S, 77, 183, 193, 197, 259, 268, 274, 279
  role/duties of, 166, 168, 172–73, 175–76, 178–79, 190–91
  S. Fedoruk as incumbent, 157, 165–67, 171, 182, 184, 235, 245, 254, 256, 260, 273
Charles, Prince of Wales, 214
Charli (dog), 160–61, 181–82, 184, 223, 233, 255, 261–62
  at Government House, 194–95, 228–29
Chateau Laurier hotel (Ottawa), 156
Chaucer School, 15
Chauveau, Claude, 152
chemistry, 20, 34, 39, 42–43, 48, 99
children, as focus of L.-G., 186, 191, 196, 200, 204–5, 228, 231
Christie, Agatha, 139
Christie, "Bingo," 147
Christmas commemorations, 35, 135, 196, 204, 207
  cards/letters, 82, 159, 166, 228, 245, 252, 256–57, 262, 267–68
  concerts, 15–16, 21, 28
  gifts, 161, 194
Chromium 51, 123
cigarettes, 76, 120, 151–52, 155
City of Saskatoon Formation Committee, 136
Clark, Brenda, 122, 126
Clemence, Vern, 250
Cluff Lake Board of Inquiry, 153, 155, 185
CNR curling club, 96, 113
Coastal Defence Vessel K709, 260
cobalt-59, 38, 59, 64
cobalt-60, 82, 94, 263
  source/development of, 59–60, 62, 64, 69, 272
cobalt-60 isotope, 38, 84
cobalt-60 treatment head, 65, 74, 79–80, 84
cobalt-60 treatment room, 77, 88, 93
cobalt-60 unit/bomb, 1, 39, 81, 124, 141, 148, 158, 164, 263
  commemorative display of, 154–55, 172, 191, 270
  design/development of, 73–74, 78–79, 99, 118, 280

315

cobalt-60 unit/bomb, *continued*
  installation of, 83, 107, 116, 133
  preparation/testing of, 51, 56–57,
    61, 66, 68, 71, 88, 119
  for research, 93
  for therapeutic use, 66–67,
    73, 76–80, 82–85,
    93, 100, 161, 275
cobalt plaza benches, 263
Coben, Audrey, 144
Coben, Muriel, 48, 63, 74, 95,
  97–98, 102, 105, 108
Coben, Murray, 144
Coben, Shirley, 92
Cohen, Saul, 162
collimators, 116, 119, 121, 126
Collins, Mrs. E., 97
Community Development
  Bonds, 206
computerized tomography
  (CT) scan, 116, 272
Concerned Saskatchewan
  Citizens of Regina, 212
Consensus Saskatchewan, 205
Conservative Party of Canada, 207
constitutional crisis, 211,
  213–14, 216–17, 226
Convocation Hall, 76,
  78, 166, 224–25
Cooperative Commonwealth
  Federation (CCF) Party, 188
Copeland Scholarship, 55
Cormack, Doug, 67, 69,
  117, 122, 124
correspondence courses,
  provincial, 20–21, 25–26
Corrigan, Dr. K., 86
Cox, A.H., 69
Cradduck, Trevor, 6–7,
  117–24, 127–28, 206
Cranston, Toller, 190
Creighton, Valerie, 249
Crippen, Dot, 110
Cronkite, F.C., 77–78
The Cruel Sea, 174
The Curler newsletter, 147
curling, 46, 88, 111–12, 115,
  120, 144, 168, 227, 229
  as gendered issue, 97, 105
  as popular sport, 94–96
  S. Fedoruk's skill in, 1,
    100, 108, 273, 280
  tour to Scotland, 138, 146, 157
curling championships, 3,
  141, 168, 170, 266, 272
  bonspiels, 95, 102–4, 106,
    109, 112–14, 126,
    137–38, 140, 166
  playdowns, 98, 102–4, 106,
    109–10, 114–15, 128, 138
curling pins
  collection, as a hobby,
    113, 124, 127–28, 139,
    146–47, 265, 269
curling styles, 103, 105–6,
  111–12, 128, 138
Currie, B.W., 61, 70

D

Dagnone, Tony, 154
Dancing in Poppies, 256
Darlington power station, 149
Davis, Fred, 197
Davitt, Patrick, 227
Day Without Art, 224–26, 242, 245
  protest at, 225–26, 236, 238
depth dose measurements,
  67–69, 73, 79, 142
Detroit Red Wings, 63
Devine, Chantal, 186, 227
Devine, Grant, 159, 173, 204, 207,
  210–11, 215, 218, 220, 225, 273
  government of, 200, 205, 208–9,
    212–14, 216–17, 241
  and L-G appointment,
    182–83, 185–86
Diamond D ladies' curling, 106,
  110–11, 115, 128, 139
Diana, Princess of Wales, 214
Dickof, Peter, 6, 142
Diefenbaker, John, 183
Diefenbaker Centre (Saskatoon),
  161, 166, 232
discus throwing, 36, 44
Dominion of Canada scholarship, 29
Dominion Stores, 139–40

INDEX

Dominion Track and Field Championships, 81
Douglas, Tommy, 41–42, 64, 77, 111, 188
Douglas Point Generating Station, 150
Doug Wilson affair, 246
Duke University, 127

E

Eager, Evelyn, 174, 183
Eaton, Fredrik, Canadian High Commissioner, 222
Edward, Prince, Duke of Kent, 222, 256
Edward VIII, King, 21
Egnatoff, John, 165
Eisler, Dale, 213, 243
Eldorado Nuclear (formerly Eldorado Mining and Refining), 78–79, 143, 148–50, 153, 263
XI Congresso internazionale di radiologia, 122
Elizabeth, the Queen Mother, 21, 157
Elizabeth II, Queen (formerly Princess Elizabeth), 21, 78, 139, 156–57, 173, 185, 221–22, 267
Elliot Lake, radioactive leak in, 150
engineering, 30, 32, 34, 66, 124, 147, 177, 268
Epp, Ed, 67, 69–70, 85
Ernest J. Creed Memorial Medal, 29
Errington, Dr. R.F., 78

F

Fairburn, Doreen, 6, 169, 201, 221–22, 269
Falk, Jennifer, 128
Family History Album, 266
farming, 11, 20, 98
Fedoruk, Alexander, 11
Fedoruk, Annie (nee Romaniuk), 9, 12–14, 20, 35, 42, 98, 145, 155, 275
  as advocate for Sylvia's education, 26, 54, 130
  death of, 130
  marriage of, 10
  move to Windsor, 23–24
  return to Saskatchewan, 32, 43
  as school assistant, 15–18, 22
Fedoruk, Cathy, 231–32
Fedoruk, Martha (nee Boychuk), 11
Fedoruk, Michael, 11
Fedoruk, Rod, 231
Fedoruk, Stephen, 11
Fedoruk, Sylvia Olga
  accomplishments of, 1–3, 5–6, 163, 176, 178, 235, 265, 274
  athleticism of, 4, 17, 33–35, 37, 43, 45, 47, 53, 81, 95, 253, 274
  birth and christening of, 13
  character/personality of, 3, 5–6, 19, 27, 31, 45, 133–35, 150, 154, 163, 165, 274
  as Dame of Grace, 179
  death/state funeral of, 2, 272–76
  health/falls of, 226, 261–62, 268, 270–72
  intelligence of, 134–35, 149–50, 165, 178, 217, 276
  as leader in nuclear medicine, 155, 160, 277
  leadership in sport, 134
  in leadership roles, 1, 4, 27, 32, 82, 128, 130, 163, 178–79, 228, 253
  leadership style of, 163–64, 228–29, 254
  legacy/national recognition of, 80–82, 276
  mechanical mind of, 19, 21, 28, 30
  move to Windsor, 23–24, 81, 144
  as physicist, 61, 64, 67, 75–76, 81, 83, 85–87, 95, 101, 107, 133, 150, 178, 184, 253
  as professor/university lecturer, 93, 117, 149, 162, 178
  public/private persona of, 3–4, 133, 227, 229, 237, 250
  as researcher, 93–94, 100, 126, 178

317

Fedoruk, Sylvia Olga, *continued*
    retirements of, 138, 162–63,
        165–66, 179, 182, 232,
        259, 262, 264, 266–67
    as scholar, 19, 28, 32, 37,
        39–40, 57, 61–62
    speculated as being gay, 237,
        252–54
    as thespian, 227, 235
Fedoruk, Theodore (Ted),
    14, 35, 54, 275, 280
    death of, 155–56
    marriage/family life of,
        9–11, 20, 145
    move to Windsor, 23–24
    return to Saskatchewan, 32, 43
    as teacher, 11–13, 15–18,
        22, 43, 182
Fedoruk Family Foundation/
    Fund, 267–68
Fee, Dr. Donald, 107
feminism, 7, 177
    See also women
fencing, 36, 46
Ferguson Folstad Friggstad (3F), 162
Ferley, Susan, 227
financial crisis and austerity
    measures, provincial, 218–21
Finlayson, Mona, 6, 168–70
*I Congresso internacional de
    biologia e medicina nuclear*, 123
First International Conference
    on Medical Physics, 125
First Nations, 12, 153,
    156, 185, 192, 224
fishing, 74, 90, 142
    in the north, 48, 50, 68, 137,
        160, 178, 202, 265, 279
    as S. Fedoruk's pastime, 8,
        68, 143–44, 178, 202,
        215, 223, 231, 254, 268
fishing camps, 75, 137, 142–43
Fitton, Jean, 114
flood of 1974 (Saskatoon), 146
Ford Motor Company, 23–24
Forget, Amédée, Lieutenant-
    Governor, 189
Fortier, Ren, 147

Foster, Zola, 109
Fotheringham, Allan, 197
Fowke, V.C., 51
Frasier (TV program), 268
fraud investigation, 218, 222
*The Freedom of Information and
    Protection of Privacy Act*, 241
freedom of information laws, 242
freedom of speech/expression,
    236, 245–47, 252, 259
Front Page Challenge, 6, 197
Fuse magazine, 251

G

gambling, 264, 266
gamma rays, 60, 66, 116, 121
gardening, 10, 20, 98, 123, 145,
    153–54, 178, 192, 255
Gass, Don, 218
gas tax rebate program, 206
gay and lesbian/LGBTQ community,
    237, 240–41, 251, 253
    and equal rights, 245
    marginalization of, 252
    See also lesbian; S. Fedoruk,
        speculated as being gay
Gays and Lesbians at the
    U of S (GLUS), 245
gender
    and identity, 241
    and rights, 245–46
    and stereotypes, 40
General Electrics
    Corporation UK, 117
George, Dorothy (Dot), 48,
    75, 137, 143–44
George VI, King, 21, 157
Girls' Athletic President
    (at Walkerville), 27
Glenn, George, 250
Globe Theatre (Regina), 227, 256
golfing, 36, 88
    as S. Fedoruk's pastime, 1, 63,
        71, 90, 99, 135, 144, 223,
        255, 262–63, 266, 268, 273
    tournaments, 137, 168–69, 201–2

See also Lobstick golf tournament
Goodale, Ralph, 243
Gordon, Olive, 122, 128
Gordon Snelgrove Gallery, 242
Government House, 184, 187–88
   100th anniversary of, 208, 214–15
   aides-de-camp at, 203, 205, 224, 232
   Christmases at, 196, 204, 228–29
   closure as residence, 194
   as integral to political life, 232
   as museum and social home, 189
   New Year's Day levees, 204–5, 227–28, 232
   patronages of, 191
   protests outside, 212–13
   restoration of, 188–89, 232
   and royal visits, 201, 256
Governor General's Curling Club, 147
Governor General's Gold Medal, 55, 81
Gow, Jack, 106
Grand Challenge (curling), 95
Granite curling club, 96, 98, 109, 113
Grease River Lodge, 142, 144
Great Depression, 19, 23, 40
Green, Donald T., 78–79
Grey Cab Ramblers baseball team, 49, 62–63, 68, 74
Grey Goose Curling Club, 147
Grey Nuns hospital (Regina), 122
Greystone Heights School (Saskatoon), 145, 272, 280
Greystone Singers, 273
Griffiths, E.W. (Joe), 36
Gustin, Lyall, 162

H

Hagel, Glenn, 219
Hall, Emmett, 183
halothane, 107
Hamilton Tiger-Cats, 204
Hammersmith Hospital (London), 125
Hansen, Ina, 115
Hansen, Jennie, 7
Hanson, Stan, 173
Harelkin, John, 225
Harlem Queens ladies' softball team, 62, 68
Harper Hospital (Detroit), 86
Harrington, Dr. Ertle, 37–38, 41, 48, 73, 141
Harris, Craig, 127, 129
Harshaw Chemical Company (Cleveland), 117, 120
Haslam, R.N.H. (Newman), 39, 48, 61, 70
Haverstock, Dr. Lynda, 216, 274
Hayden, Michael, 174
Hayes, Patrick, 2
Hennigman, Mrs. Lou, 95
Herzberg, Dr. Gerhard, 39–40
Herzberg, Dr. Luise, 39–40
Hickley, Kathy, 109
Hilton Hotel (London), 221–22
Historic Architecture of Saskatchewan, 174
Historic Sites and Monuments Board of Canada, 188, 263
HMCS *Saskatoon*, 261
Hnatyshyn, Helen, 182
Hnatyshyn, Ramon (Ray), 182–83, 185, 213, 218, 230, 265
hockey, 44, 46, 53, 88, 95–96, 99, 123
Holiday Park golf course, 63–64
Holy Trinity Transfiguration Ukrainian Greek Orthodox Church, 155
home computer technology, 265
homophobia, 237, 244–45, 253
homosexuality, 224–25, 235, 238–39, 243, 245, 251–52
   and equal rights, 237, 247
honorary degrees, 176, 178, 206, 209, 228, 235, 268–69
Hotel Majestic (London), 125
Hotel Saskatchewan (Regina), 162, 187–88, 194
Houston, C. Stuart, 1–2, 4–5, 7, 79, 158
Houston, Mary, 7
Howe, Gordie, 63

INDEX

Hub City curling club, 96–97, 102–3, 106, 109–10, 113, 128
Hubich, Glenn, 225–26
Hudson's Bay Company, 143
Hugill, Howard R., 28, 81–82
human rights, 238–39
Hunt and Golf Club (Ottawa), 111
Hunter, Tommy, 172
Huskie men's basketball, 52, 71, 157
Huskie men's football, 192, 267
Huskiette women's basketball, 37, 42, 45–46, 50, 52, 61–62, 72, 87, 157, 259, 267
Huskiette women's hockey, 44–45, 47, 95
Huskiette women's volleyball, 53, 267
Hutton, Eric, 80

I

Indigenous community. *See* First Nations
International Atomic Energy Agency (IAEA), 101, 106, 120, 128–30, 140, 275
International Commission on Radiation Units and Measurements, 119
International Society of Nuclear Medicine, 94
iodine 131, 116
ionization chamber measurements, 69, 72, 76–77
Irwin, Fern, 115

J

Jackson, Michael, 183–84, 190
Janovsky, Martin, 190
Jardine, Tim, 7
javelin throwing, 36, 42–43, 50
Jeux Canada Games, 173, 178, 184
Jewett, Eileen, 269
John East Iron Works, 66
John Haig and Company, 139
Johns, Dr. Harold, 38, 99, 117, 119, 121, 124–25, 133, and betatron program, 39, 41, 44, 50, 53, 141
and cobalt-60 project, 51, 59–60, 64–66, 74, 78, 80, 82, 263
as research head, 48, 61, 70, 77, 84–85
as S. Fedoruk's mentor, 40, 57, 67, 73, 81, 86, 93, 158
Johns, Sybil, 40, 131, 133
John S. McEachern Memorial Fellowship Fund, 85
Johnson, Ben, 172
Johnson, Eldon, 111
Johnson, Frederick W., Lieutenant-Governor, 162, 194, 199, 212
Johnston, Maisie, 97
Jones, Henry, 111
Joss, Eileen, 137, 143–44

K

Kappy Kaplan Regina Bombers baseball team, 48
Karsh, Yousuf, 174
Karsh Canadians, 174
Katz, Leon, 39, 48, 61, 70, 141
Keighley, Bob, 137
Kennedy, Betty, 7, 197
Kensington Hotel (Edmonton), 157
Kindrachuk, Mike, 165
King, Gordon, 46
King, Ivan, 37, 44, 52, 71, 157
King George Hotel (Saskatoon), 47
King of Sweden's Curling Club, 147
Kinsella, Jack, 110–11
Klaudeman, Pauline, 103
Klondike, 174
Kodak Blue-Brand X-ray film, 107
Kornelson, Richard Otto, 69
Krasney School District No. 1121, 12
Kuhl, D.E., 127
Kulcheski, Dolores, 43, 54, 172, 182
Kulcheski, Mary, 42–43, 54, 145, 172

L

Langston, Pat, 6, 191, 222–23, 229
The Lassies, 140
Law, Bett, 138

Lawson, Patricia, 6, 43, 50, 87, 157, 271, 275
A League of Their Own, 30
Leeper, Cyril, 256–57
Lefler, Christopher, 4–5, 225
   art installation of, 243–45, 247, 252–53
   disciplinary hearing of, 247–48
   expulsion from U of S, 247–49
   and outing controversy, 226, 235–45, 248, 251–55, 259
   poster campaign of, 246–47
   as SAB grant awardee, 248–50
Legislative Assembly (Saskatchewan), 198, 200, 205, 208, 213, 230–31
lesbian, 225–26, 237–39, 241–42, 245, 246 252, 253
   See also Fedoruk, Sylvia Olga, speculated as being gay; gay and lesbian/LGBTQ community; sexual orientation
Lewis, Dr. W.B., 39
libel, 236, 249
Liberace, 158, 253
Liberal Party of Canada, 207, 243
Lindberg, Yvonne, 114
Lindy's fishing camp, 75
Lingenfelter, Dwain, 202, 210
Little Stinkers club, 52
liver scanning, 107, 116, 119
Lobstick Golf and Tennis Club Inc., 169
Lobstick golf tournament, 63, 137, 168, 213
The Local Authority Freedom of Information and Protection of Privacy Act, 241
Local Celebrities' Favourite Books display, 174
Local Council of Women (Calgary), 149
London Supremes baseball team, 30
lung cancer, 150–51
Lysenko School District No. 494, 12–13, 15

M

Macdonald, Sir John A., 187
Macdonald House, 222
Macdonald Tobacco Company, 139–40, 163
MacIntyre, W.J., 127
Mackay, C.A., 52, 70
MacKay, Johnny, 66, 68, 74, 78, 80, 117–18, 120, 122
Mackie, Rock, 6
MacKinnon, Peter, 268, 274
Maclean, Iain, 166, 242–43
Maclean's, 80–81, 83, 86
MacNevin, Barbara, 97–98, 102–3, 108, 110–11, 114–15
Macpherson, Jean, 146–47
Major, John, Prime Minister, 222
Major, Norma, 222
Mallard, J.R., 127
Manhattan Project, 117
Manitoba Bisonettes ladies' basketball team, 42–43
Maple Leaf Gardens, 111
Maragos, Costa, 227
Margaret, Princess, 21, 171
Marken, Ron, 256
Marshall, Larry, 104
Martin, Dawn, 250
Masquerade art installation, 225, 238
Massachusetts General Hospital (Boston), 86
Master Angler award, 137
Mauchel, Bob, 69
MaxC (dog), 262, 264–65, 269–71
Mayneord, W.V., 38, 60, 67, 70, 125
Mayo Clinic (Rochester), 55
McConkey, Pauline, 80
McFaull, Jack, 165
McFee, Rosa, 108, 114–15
McKee, Joyce, 74, 87, 95, 144
   as curler, 97–98, 103, 105–6, 108–15, 128, 138, 140, 168, 174
   friendship with S. Fedoruk, 94, 99, 101, 123–24, 126, 257, 261

INDEX

McKercher, M.L. (Peggy), 6, 157, 165, 259, 275–76
McLaren, Ruth, 28, 81
McMaster University, 38
McNaughton, A.G.L., 41, 56
media, 4, 40, 137, 183, 186, 216, 222, 235
   as alternative, 251
   containment of, 236, 244–46, 253
   and controversies, 226, 236, 241–49, 251–52, 259
   and Devine government, 209–10, 212
   newspapers, 6, 43, 74, 78, 104, 230, 244, 280
   and nuclear industry, 141, 150
   on S. Fedoruk's death, 272–73
   See also social media
medical electronic engineering, 117
medical histories, 2, 78–79, 158, 279
medical isotopes, 38, 84, 101
medical physics, 37, 40, 44, 52, 94, 101, 117, 124–25, 228
   as S. Fedoruk's area of expertise, 61, 86–87, 114, 131, 241, 265, 272
Medicare, 126
Meewasin Valley Authority (Saskatoon), 162
Merlylyn K. Vann Bursary, 268
Michigan-Ontario fastball league, 30–32
Miss Saigon, 222
Mitchell, Bob, 239–40, 243, 247
MIX-92, 227
Mohyla Institute/residence, 10–11, 35, 40, 48, 50, 62–63, 75, 133, 144
Molloy, Tom, 268
Monsarrat, Nicholas, 174
Montreal *Gazette,* 128
Moose Jaw Pixies basketball team, 72
Morgenroth, Norman, 40
Morrison, Dr. A.W., 78–79
Morrison, Lee, 128, 140, 168

Mott, F.D., 77
Mount Saint Vincent University, 228
The Mouse that Roared, 227
The Mousetrap, 139
Mulroney, Brian, Prime Minister, 181–83
Mulroney, Mila, 182
Munroe, John A., 174
Murray, Anne, 158
Museum of Science and Technology (Toronto), 155

N

Nalevykin, Shirley, 42
National Cancer Institute of Canada, 117
National Research Council, 70
   Division of Atomic Energy, 39
National Research Experimental (NRX) reactor, 59
Nature, 84, 86
Neo-watin paddlewheeler, 170–71
Nesbitt, Mrs. George (Violet), 95, 97
New Democratic Party, 188, 202, 207, 210–11, 213, 216
New England Journal of Medicine, 107
New York Rangers hockey team, 111
Nobel Prize for Chemistry, 39
non-confidence motion, 210–11
   See also Devine, Grant, government of
Normal School (Saskatoon), 11–12
North West Mounted Police, 215
Nuclear Chicago, 120
Nuclear Enterprises (Winnipeg), 121
nuclear fission, 29
nuclear fuel manufacturing, 148
nuclear industry, 148, 150, 166, 238
nuclear medicine, 39–40, 84, 129, 149, 158, 176, 273, 279
nuclear physics, 41, 52
nuclear research, 41, 149, 272
nuclear scanning techniques, 100
Nutana Collegiate, 35
Nutana curling club, 96, 109, 113

322

O

Oak Ridge Institute of Nuclear
    Studies (Tennessee), 86
O'Brien, Mike, 227
Office of Lieutenant-Governor
    of Saskatchewan, 162,
    166, 181, 194, 270
  and advocacy of minority
    rights, 237
  annual northern tour, 202-3,
    206, 215, 224, 228
  coat of arms, 204
  ending of S. Fedoruk's term,
    228, 231-32, 247-48, 250
  installation of, 184-87, 189, 199
  as non-partisan position,
    209-11, 213, 218, 226, 230
  role and duties of, 190, 197-98,
    200-201, 203, 211, 214,
    219-20, 232, 239-40, 259
  scandal of, 206-7
  S. Fedoruk's term as, 7,
    182-83, 235-36, 254, 256,
    258, 260, 263, 277, 279
  visit to Queen Elizabeth at
    Buckingham Palace, 222-23
  as held by a woman, 1, 3, 156,
    163, 184, 191-93, 221, 273
  See also Speech from the
    Throne (Saskatchewan)
Officer of the Order of
    Canada, 171, 179
Olympic Games, 140
one-room schoolhouses,
    11-12, 15-16, 19, 25-26,
    29, 32, 187, 204
onions, hatred of, 14, 35,
    98, 193, 208, 275
Onofrijchuk, Theodore, 16
Ontario Cancer Foundation, 78
Ontario Cancer Institute, 93
Ontario Hydro, 150
Ontario Institute of
    Radiotherapy, 38
Order of Canada, 172-73, 257, 273
Order of St. John (Most Venerable
    Order of the Hospital of St.
    John of Jerusalem), 179, 257,
    273
orders-in-council, 197-98,
    201, 215, 223
Orphanettes track and
    field squad, 37, 52
oscilloscope, 116
outing, as practice, 241,
    246-48, 252-54
  See also Fedoruk, Sylvia Olga,
    speculated as being gay
ovarian cancer, 130

P

Palliser Hotel (Calgary), 83
ParticipACTION movement, 136, 157
PC Canada Fund, 206
Pedenson, Gwen, 114
Pells, Audrey, 114
Pennington and Boyle, architects, 25
Perron, Pauline, 30
personal connections, 3-4, 82, 229
personal shopping services, 193, 221
Peters, P.H., 161
Petrie, W., 61
Pezer, Dr. Vera, 6-7, 120,
    128, 140, 154, 168, 170,
    261, 264, 267, 269, 274
Philip, Prince, Duke of
    Edinburgh, 78, 156-57, 173
photomultiplier tubes, 86, 116
physics and mathematics
    as science career areas,
    19-20, 28, 32, 34, 43,
    51, 57, 70-71, 82, 177
The Physics of Radiology, 38
physics research program,
    at U of S, 37-38
Pinder, Phyllis, 115
Pisipinook fishing camp, 75
Pittman, Agnes, 138
Point Lepreau power station, 149
political activism, 236, 252-53
Polynesian Cultural Center, 267
Poorman, Florence, 153
portraits, official, 256-57
positron emission tomography
    (PET) scan, 116, 272

INDEX

power dynamics, and human rights, 240–42, 251, 253
President's Scientific Advisory Committee, 141
Preston, Holly, 197
Prince Albert National Park, 63
Princess Margaret Hospital (Toronto), 93
Pringle, Bob, 207
privacy rights, 236, 242, 245, 247, 249, 251, 254
Progressive Conservative Party, 159, 200, 206, 210, 213, 216, 221, 231, 237
prorogation, 199, 205, 208–12, 216, 242
Provincial Council of Women, 191
public activism, 238

Q

Queen's Silver Jubilee Medal, 156
queer activism, 236

R

Raabel, Evelyn, 109
racism, towards First Nations, 224
radiation
    in cancer treatment, 55–56, 64, 263
    containing exposure from, 44, 51, 59, 66–67, 69, 77, 79–80, 141, 149, 152, 161, 164
    as high-energy, 83, 85–86
    output from cobalt-60, 76, 85
    transport and storage of, 148
    as used for scanning, 107, 116, 130
    as used for therapy, 38, 60, 70, 83, 85, 87, 93–94, 107, 130, 158–60
radiation physics, 93–94
radiation seeds, 77, 79
radioactive iodine, 87
radioactive nuclides, 272
radioactive ore, 150
radioactive rose Bengal dye, 107
radioactive tracer elements, 116–17

radioisotopes, 60, 123, 140, 148
Radiological Health Committee, 130
Radiological Society of North America Standardization Committee, 68
radiopharmaceuticals, 86, 116
radium, 38, 60, 70, 77
radon gas, 37, 150, 152
Rasmussen, Merrilee, 213
RCMP (Royal Canadian Mounted Police), 184–85, 201, 215, 218, 273
Red's fishing camp, 75, 143
Reed, Vera, 115
Reed-Curtis Scintiscanner, 107
Regina College Cougettes basketball team, 46
Regina Council of Women, 188
Regina Govins baseball team, 88–93
Regina Grey Nuns Hospital, 88
Regina Leader-Post, 89, 227, 243
Regina Lighting Company, 187
Regina Sports Hall of Fame, 91
Regina UCT Pats hockey team, 45
Regina Vocational Centre, 188
Reid, Dr. W.B., 121
Richards, Dr. Gordon, 38
Richardson, Ernie, 106
Rideau Hall, 172, 213
Riverside Country Club, 263
Robertson, Gordie, 104
Robinson, Svend, 225
Romaniuk, Anastasia, 42
Romaniuk, Dmetro, 10
Romaniuk, John (Ivan), 10, 54
Romaniuk, Oksana, 10
Romanow, Roy, 6–7, 186, 200, 216–20, 231, 239, 274
    government of, 218, 220, 242
Rowan, Sheila, 140, 168, 170
Royal, Joseph, 188
royal assent to bills, 198, 202, 210, 217, 223–24, 230–31, 241
Royal Caledonians of Scotland, 106
Royal Canadian Air Force (RCAF), 102, 113
Royal Canadian Legion, 188

Royal Marsden Hospital
  (London, UK), 38
Royal Montreal Curling Club, 147
Royal University Hospital
  (Saskatoon), 162, 261, 272
  See also Saskatchewan
    cancer clinics
royal visits, 21–22, 200–201,
  214, 256
rural crisis (1991)
  hospital closures, 219–20, 222
  outmigration, 205
Russell, Jim, 6, 250–51
Rutherford trophy (track
  and field), 37, 44

S

sales tax, harmonized, 216
Sapp, Allen, 172
Sarah, Duchess of York, 200–201
Saskatchewan Anglers
  Derby, 137, 162
*Saskatchewan: A Pictorial
  History*, 174
Saskatchewan Arts Alliance, 250
Saskatchewan Arts Board
  (SAB), 248–49, 252
  Independent Artist grant, 5, 248
Saskatchewan cancer clinics
  and chemotherapy, 130
  labour strike at, 159–61, 163
  plan/build of new clinic,
    161–64, 173, 178, 192
  at Saskatoon City
    Hospital, 55, 64, 87
  treatment equipment at,
    55, 66, 68, 107, 121,
    141, 154–55, 172
  at University Hospital, 66,
    83, 87, 94, 117, 130,
    154–55, 162, 166, 270
Saskatchewan Cancer Commission,
  38–39, 41, 53, 55–56, 67,
  76–77, 88, 135, 142, 159
  and cobalt-60 unit, 84, 154, 270
  as S. Fedoruk's employer,
    75, 82–83, 86, 93,
    130, 149, 178, 187

See also Saskatchewan
  cancer clinics
Saskatchewan Cancer
  Foundation, 161–63
Saskatchewan Centre of
  the Arts, 187
Saskatchewan Curling
  Association, 96
Saskatchewan Express, 190
Saskatchewan Financial Review
  Commission, 217–18
Saskatchewan Government
  Employees Union, 159
Saskatchewan Government
  Insurance (SGI), 88, 90
*Saskatchewan Government:
  Politics and Pragmatism*, 174
Saskatchewan Government
  Telephones, 48, 51, 88
Saskatchewan Healthcare
  Association, 159
Saskatchewan House, 188
*The Saskatchewan Human Rights
  Code*, 205, 225–26, 242
Saskatchewan Human Rights
  Commission (SHRC), 246
  and C. Lefler complaints,
    250, 252, 259
Saskatchewan Indian, 153
Saskatchewan Ladies' Curling
  Association, 97, 138
Saskatchewan Liberal Party, 216
Saskatchewan Order of Merit,
  162–63, 171–73, 179, 257, 273
Saskatchewan Pension Plan, 200
Saskatchewan Place arena, 190, 192
Saskatchewan Roughriders, 203–4
Saskatchewan Softball
  Association, 90
Saskatchewan Sports
  Hall of Fame, 91
Saskatchewan Wheat Pool, 22
Saskatchewan Women's
  Hockey League, 45
Saskatchewan Women's
  Institutes, 177
Saskatchewan Writers Guild, 250

INDEX

Saskatoon Aces basketball team, 87, 94
Saskatoon City Hospital, 71–72, 75
 See also Saskatchewan cancer clinics
Saskatoon Clippers baseball team, 63, 68, 87
Saskatoon Elkettes basketball team, 37, 46
Saskatoon Farmers' Market, 183, 265, 270–71
Saskatoon Gems baseball team, 63
Saskatoon Hub City Ramblers baseball team, 48, 75, 87–88, 90–94
Saskatoon Imperials baseball team, 170
Saskatoon Inn, 227
Saskatoon Ladies' Curling Association, 113
Saskatoon Light and Power, 265
Saskatoon Royals basketball team, 37, 45–46
Saskatoon Spartans baseball team, 63
Saskatoon Sports Hall of Fame, 174
Saskatoon Star-Phoenix, 73–74, 80, 102, 110, 146, 156, 213, 243–44
Saskatoon Symphony Orchestra, 66, 190
Saskatoon Vanguards baseball team, 90–91
Saskatoon YWCA Women of the Year awards, 162
Sauvé, Madame Jeanne, Governor General, 163, 184–85
Schacter, Sylvia, 138
Schell, Marj, 269
Schmaltz, Wayne, 249–50
Schofield, Vaughn Solomon, 273
Schurr, Benjamin J., 121
Science, 84, 86
Science Council of Canada, 140–41, 148, 156, 163, 239
scientific papers, published, 1, 84, 107, 141
scintillation camera, 117, 120–24, 126

scintillation crystals, 86, 116, 126–27
Scotland School, 16–17, 20, 22, 25
Second World War, 17, 23, 30, 40
Seeking a Balance: University of Saskatchewan 1907–1982, 174
sexual orientation, 226, 237–39, 241–42, 246, 252–54
 See also Fedoruk, Sylvia Olga, speculated as being gay; lesbian; outing, as practice
sexual politics, 236, 240
The Sheaf, 34, 36–37, 42–44, 46–47, 52, 244–45
Shenfield, L., 69
Shepherd, Marian, 40
Shore, Bob, 36
Sidaway, Helene, 90
Skaarsgard, Lloyd, 163
skiing, 135–36
Slobstickers, 169–70, 200, 265, 274
Slobstick golf tournament, 168–69, 171, 201–2, 227, 233, 266, 275
Smith, Dr. Ivan, 78
Smith, Kirkaldy and Dennison, 28
Smith, Ruth, 105
Smithsonian Institution, 155
Snowdon, Jean, 138
social activism, 235, 254, 274
social media, 6, 247, 252
sodium iodide crystals, 117
softball, 36, 43, 88, 90, 157
 See also baseball
The Sopranos (TV program), 268
South Bend White Sox, 48
special warrants, 209–14, 216–17, 220, 226, 263
Speech from the Throne (Saskatchewan), 198–200, 205–6, 208, 212, 217, 220–21, 230
Speech from the Throne (UK), 222
Spinks, J.W.T. (John), 37, 39–40
Spirit of Youth Award, 55
Staging Identities I art exhibition, 240, 242
Starrak, Vel, 110

326

State Opening of Parliament
(London), 222
Steps on the Road to Medicare, 1
St. John's Ambulance
Foundation, 179
St. Pat's Curling Club, 147
St. Paul's Hospital (Saskatoon),
271
Strand Palace Hotel (London), 122
strikes, labour
at cancer clinic, 159–61, 163
of U of S faculty, 175–76
Strumm, Gil, 48, 88–90
Summersgill, Bob, 73
Sutter, Chris, 162
Swenson, Rick, 231
Syl's Dills, 170, 193, 257, 265, 270
recipe, 258–59
Sylvia Fedoruk Award in
Women's Basketball, 268
Sylvia Fedoruk Canadian Centre for
Nuclear Innovation, 273, 280
The Sylvia Fedoruk Centre
(Canora), 280
Sylvia Fedoruk elementary school
(Saskatoon), 276, 280
Sylvia Fedoruk fonds, 169, 279
Sylvia Fedoruk Scholarship, 268

T

Tarnowetzki, Anastasia, 10
Taylor, Graham, 159
Teneyke, Trudy, 201
Tenth International Congress
of Radiology, 119
*36 Steps on the Road to
Medicare: How Saskatchewan
Led the Way*, 2
Thompson, Dorothy, 97, 104, 111
Thompson, Dr. W.P., 77
Thomson, J.S., 51
thyroid, 86–87
Tinker (dog), 144–46, 160–61, 262
Tofstead, Charrie, 37
Toronto Maple Leafs
hockey team, 111
tourism industry, 75, 122

track and field, 19, 26,
36–37, 44, 46, 50
Treaty Land Entitlement
Framework Agreement, 224
Tribute to Young Canadians Who
Have Achieved Excellence in
the Arts and Sciences, 156
Trudeau, Pierre Elliott, 238
Truscon Steel Company, 28
Tusa, Arnold, Speaker of the
House, 185–86, 208
Tynney, Phyllis, 162
typing skills, 21, 48

U

Ukrainian culture, 1, 7, 29,
35, 170, 184, 207, 221
Ukrainian Greek Orthodox
Church of Transfiguration, 9
Ukrainian museum (Canora), 280
Ukrainian Orthodox Church
(Donwell), 267
United Steel Workers of
America, 150
University Hospital (Saskatoon),
50, 65, 122, 154, 162, 166
See also Saskatchewan cancer
clinics
University of Alberta, 42, 50, 53
University of Bristol, 117
University of Chicago, 38
University of Manitoba, 50
University of Regina, 209
University of Saskatchewan, 1,
7, 38, 74, 141, 145, 168, 171,
224, 232, 267–69, 274
Archives and Special Collections,
2, 65, 101, 175, 182, 209, 280
Board of Directors, 259
Convocation Hall and
Administration building, 166
faculty strike at, 175–76
physics expertise at, 39–40,
44, 51, 57, 64, 67–68
S. Fedoruk as faculty,
149, 178–79, 279
S. Fedoruk as graduate student,
68, 70–71, 73, 77, 79, 86, 133

University of Saskatchewan, *continued*
  S. Fedoruk as undergraduate, 33–35, 41, 81–82, 93, 99, 107, 262
  and sports teams, 36, 42, 44, 46, 50, 61, 95, 113, 157
  Student Council, 46–47
  See also chancellorship at U of S; Lefler, Christopher, outing controversy
University of Toronto, 32, 34, 38, 41
  College of Engineering, 30
University of Victoria, 236
University of Western Ontario, 206
University of Windsor, 176, 178
uranium ore, 59, 267
  development of, 153, 156
  mining of, 148, 150, 152–53
U.S. Atomic Energy Commission, 129
U.S. Radiological Society, 72

V

Vancouver Kerrys baseball team, 92
Vanier, Georges, Governor General, 111
Vanier, Pauline, 111
Vann, Carol, 6
Vann, Garry, 2, 6, 163, 192–93, 207, 222, 255, 260, 269–70
Vann, Merylyn (nee Kulcheski), 19, 43, 54–55, 182–83, 202, 260–61
  as close family and friend, 163, 172, 191–93, 207, 222, 230, 255, 259
Vann, Michael, 6, 145–46, 154, 158, 160–61
  as close family and friend, 163, 183–84, 191, 207, 259–60, 262, 265–67, 273
Vanscoy Caps baseball team, 74, 87
veterinary medicine, 107
volleyball, 26, 47, 53, 71, 95, 99
volunteering/volunteerism, 8, 88, 130, 133, 178–79, 204, 235

W

Waiser, Bill, 7, 12, 22
Walker, Carol, 193, 269
Walker, Hiram, 24
Walkerville Collegiate Institute, 25–29, 32, 35, 37, 54, 81, 176
Wall, Brad, 273
Walz, Norman "Curly," 269
Ward-Heeler's Ball, 47
Waskesiu golf course, 63, 137, 169
water phantom, 56, 79, 85
Watson, Dr. T.A. (Sandy), 55, 67, 77–78, 84, 163, 263
The Wedding: Closet, 247
Western Development Museum (WDM), 266, 270, 280
Weyburn's 75th anniversary celebrations, 189–90
White, Irene, 184, 190, 192–93, 201–3, 212, 221–22, 232, 243, 273
whole-body rectilinear scanning, 117–21, 123–24, 126, 272
Why Shoot the Teacher?, 174
Wiebe, John (Jack), 230, 232
Wigmore, Fred, 135, 163
Wilson, Betty, 36, 50
Windsor Esquires female fastball team, 30, 32
Winning the Prairie Gamble, 266
Winnipeg Ramblers baseball team, 92
The Wit and Wisdom of John Diefenbaker, 174
women
  as ballplayers, 279
  as curlers, 96, 104–5, 112, 137, 139–40, 179, 279
  in politics, 7
  rights of, 246
  in science/non-traditional careers, 7, 40, 70, 141, 177–78
  status of/women's movement, 130, 141, 228
Women's Athletic Board, 46–47, 53
World AIDS Day, 224

World Health Organization
   (WHO), 107
World Softball Championships, 88
Worsley, Katharine, Duchess
   of Kent, 222
Wright, Betty, 157
Wright, Cliff, 157, 190

X
X-ray machines, 60, 71, 77, 83

Y
Yaremchuk, Lydia, 52
Yorkton Collegiate, 11
YWCA Woman of the Year 1986, 258

Z
Zero Energy Experimental Pile
   (ZEEP), 29, 32, 59–60, 79
Zuzak, Father, 155

ABOUT THE AUTHOR

MERLE MASSIE is a Saskatchewan historian and author, raised in Saskatchewan's forest fringe and trained at the University of Saskatchewan. She is co-author (with Stuart Houston) of *36 Steps on the Road to Medicare: How Saskatchewan Led the Way*, and her second book, *Forest Prairie Edge: Place History in Saskatchewan*, won a Saskatchewan Book Award in 2015. She now lives on the prairies, farming with her husband and writing Saskatchewan stories.

www.ingramcontent.com/pod-product-compliance
Lightning Source LLC
Chambersburg PA
CBHW030432300426
44112CB00009B/966